Praise for *From Reversal of Fortune to Economic Resurgence*

From Reversal of Fortune to Economic Resurgence is a masterpiece. The book proposes more explicit pathway to prosperity in Africa than any other book or scholarly journal article that I have ever read.

—**Adesoji Adelaja**, *John A. Hannah Distinguished Professor in Land Policy, Michigan State University.*

From Reversal of Fortune to Economic Resurgence – the book's title, poignant in its brevity – attests to the significant upheavals that some countries go through in their developmental journeys. The book is more than a diagnostic tool; it is a light of hope. The authors provide a model for all African states by proposing realistic leadership and institutional capacity-building measures. *From Reversal of Fortune to Economic Resurgence* shines brightest here. It is a forward-looking book for leaders, policymakers, and change-makers determined to shift the fate of their nations, rather than a recital of previous blunders.

—**Toyin Falola**, *University Distinguished Professor, Jacob and Sanger Mossiker Chair in the Humanities, The University of Texas at Austin.*

This is a seminal book – it is path-breaking in its analysis of Nigeria's development reversals from the 1960s and 1970s to the current period. Nigeria's decline is contrasted with that of Asian countries that made steady and dramatic progress in their economic growth, per capita income and industrialization. The authors take us on a journey of exploration of the deeper underlying causes of Nigeria's lack of performance – with insightful learning from Asia's experiences of technological learning, state capacity building and strategic leadership to help explain the many causes of Nigeria's lost opportunities to diversify and transform its economy. This is a must-read for African policymakers, students of economic development and international bodies that want to support Africa's efforts to transform its economy and society and meet its sustainable development goals.

—**Faizel Ismail**, *Director of the Nelson Mandela School of Public Governance, University of Cape Town.*

From Reversal of Fortune to Economic Resurgence is exceptional. It unpacks the poorly understood process of why African countries that showed great promise of development in the 1970s fell behind their Asian counterparts. It shows underdevelopment not as destiny but as reversible. It correctly connects leadership vision and industrialization. I highly recommend this book.

—Padmashree Gehl Sampath, *Chief Executive Officer, African Pharmaceutical Technology Foundation; Former Director, Global Access in Action, Harvard University; and Visiting Professor, University of Johannesburg.*

From Reversal of Fortune to
Economic Resurgence

From Reversal of Fortune to Economic Resurgence

Industrialization and Leadership in Asia's Prosperity and Nigeria's Regress

Banji Oyelaran-Oyeyinka and Oyebanke Abejirin

ANTHEM PRESS

Anthem Press
An imprint of Wimbledon Publishing Company
www.anthempress.com

This edition first published in UK and USA 2024
by ANTHEM PRESS
75–76 Blackfriars Road, London SE1 8HA, UK
or PO Box 9779, London SW19 7ZG, UK
and
244 Madison Ave #116, New York, NY 10016, USA
© 2024 Banji Oyelaran-Oyeyinka and Oyebanke Abejirin

British Library Cataloguing-in-Publication Data
A catalogue record for this book is available from the British Library.

Library of Congress Cataloging-in-Publication Data: 2024934494
A catalog record for this book has been requested.

ISBN-13: 978-1-83999-197-4 (Hbk)/ 978-1-83999-198-1 (Pbk)
ISBN-10: 1-83999-197-6 (Hbk)/ 1-83999-198-4 (Pbk)

Cover credit: Banji Oyelaran-Oyeyinka and Oyebanke Abejirin

This title is also available as an e-book.

CONTENTS

PREFACE

We embarked on writing this book to better understand the enduring quest for growth and development, especially in Africa. Clearly, economic growth or lack thereof does not explain all ills of society, but without it, life becomes very difficult for the majority. Besides, the main theme we are dealing with is how some countries advance and others get left behind in the development marathon. In this journey, much of Asia and China pursued and succeeded in their economic catch-up, that is in closing the gap between their economies, which we referred to as latecomers, in my book published in 2010.[1] African countries, on the other hand, have fallen far behind in large part due to several factors, including negative or relatively slower growth in the process of time, convergence of external shocks, conflicts and natural disasters. We assert quite clearly from the onset that catching up with more advanced societies starts with learning to acquire production technologies and building an industrial manufacturing capability base starting from the modernization of a country's agriculture. There is a broad agreement that an escape from underdevelopment requires explicit effort to transition from an agrarian to an industrial economy. This is made possible by the mastery of industrial technologies and building on this through learning/innovation. The long-run accumulation of technological and productive capabilities, an industrialization process that started in Western economies in the 1800s and which East Asia successfully emulated, explains the huge differences in living standards between rich and poor nations.

Why Africa fell behind and experienced development reversal has been discussed widely. Our position that puts knowledge and technological acquisition at the centre does not discount the role of other factors such as capital accumulation and human capital. It reinforces their relevance. We also see development as a long marathon process where several elements converge including institutional and organizational changes, national resources including capital stock. Apart from those supply-side factors such as investment in education that foster growth, how state's 'ideology' ensures distributive justice matters. A central factor that we analyse is resource dependence which has been a major obstacle to knowledge-driven structural transformation because it in turn impacts distributional issues. Resource rent-dependent countries promote institutions that encourage specialization in non-tradable sectors that ultimately undermine the industrial manufacturing sector. An important channel transmitting this is commodity exports which strengthen local currency thereby weakening the competitiveness of tradable especially manufacturing. Additionally, weak accountability to citizens and 'easy money' from oil revenue preclude the development of effective taxation administration means that oil-dependent countries have relatively low tax to GDP/capita.

In sum, the core elements of the sustainable development framework we are applying in this book essentially propose a roadmap for not just the transformation of the economy but society. Its core indicators include rising GDP per capita but are not limited to it. It includes increases in living standards reflected in standards of health and literacy.

We take our entry point from agriculture as this is where most countries take off. Worse still, the continent after 60 years of political independence still struggles with food and nutrition, the most basic rights of human beings. Africa is unable to feed itself. The region relies on imports and will remain so unless there is an urgent paradigmatic shift in the structures of African economies. Food imports cost Africa US$55 billion a year, but this could double to US$110 billion by 2030. Many African cities will double in size by 2050, increasing demand for food and other infrastructure and services.

The UN in a recent report estimates that around 735 million people are experiencing food insecurity globally, an increase of 122 million people since 2019. Seven, mostly fragile states – Somalia, Afghanistan, Burkina Faso, Haiti, Nigeria, South Sudan and Yemen – are now on the red alert of famine. This current condition means that African countries have experienced a development reversal rather than moving towards zero hunger by 2030. The world and more severely Africa are in fact worse off than we were in 2015.

It is why value added by agriculture to GDP offers an important indicator of progress, or a lack thereof, of the sector and more broadly of the economy. Agriculture value added as a share of GDP in Sub-Saharan African countries compared to that of the rest of the world in 2000 and comparatively in 2000 and 2022 as a percentage of GDP *is higher among Sub-Saharan African countries than in the rest of the world*. Nigeria's agricultural contribution to GDP has remained constant for 45 years at 22–25 per cent. In comparison, Tunisia stands at 10 per cent, Malaysia at 9.6 per cent, Thailand at 8.5 per cent, Netherlands at 1.6 per cent and UK at 0.6 per cent.

The same for proportion of employment in agriculture. For Nigeria, the percentage of agricultural employment in the population is 35 per cent. In contrast, South Korea stands at 5 per cent, Ethiopia at 65 per cent, Malaysia at 9.6 per cent, Thailand at 8.5 per cent, Netherlands at 2.3 per cent and UK at 0.7 per cent. History shows that no middle- or high-income countries in the world have more than 10 per cent of their population directly engaged in agriculture.

Countries that record significant positive change progressively record lower agriculture contribution to GDP. So, the high agriculture value-added recorded for Sub-Saharan African countries shows a lack of structural transformation and diversification into high-value, high- productivity products, which means Africa continues its reliance on non-processed agriculture. Poor countries record high agriculture as a proportion of GDP and as well a greater employment share. Rich countries have a greater contribution from manufacturing not agriculture. For example, while 70 per cent of global trade in agriculture is in semi-processed and processed products, Africa is largely absent in this market because the region remains an exporter of raw materials to Asia and the West.

African countries have essentially failed to exploit their vast agricultural resources, which is 65 per cent of all arable uncultivated land in the world. Neither have they benefited from the abundant minerals and considerable oil and gas deposits. Nigeria, which is the subject of study in the book, has experienced reversals, notable among which is income reversal. This has meant that poverty and inequality worsened over time. Nigeria sinks deeper into the mire of penury. The population of poor people in Nigeria exceeds the total population of South Africa, Namibia, Botswana, Lesotho, Mauritius and Eswatini combined.

We hereby welcome the reader to the fascinating journey that explores the intriguing realms of Asia and Africa. In this book, aptly titled *From Reversal of Fortune to Economic Resurgence*, we invite you to embark on a thought-provoking exploration that sheds light on the diverse pathways, histories and potential futures of these two distinct continents. As we delve into the pages of this book, we aim to uncover the decisions that have shaped the trajectories of Asia and Africa using Nigeria as the exemplar. Both continents boast rich cultural tapestries, ancient civilizations and breathtaking natural landscapes that have stood the test of time. However, despite sharing certain similarities, their paths have diverged, leading to different outcomes in terms of economic development, social progress and global influence.

Through systematic research and analysis, this book provides a comprehensive sector-level comparison between Asia and Nigeria, shedding light on the factors contributing to their contrasting fortunes. We will examine their historical contexts, geographical features and the unique challenges and opportunities that have shaped their respective narratives.

From the vibrant markets of Bangladesh and Vietnam in Southeast Asia to the vast savannahs of Africa, we will explore the intricate web of interactions between politics, governance, economics and the contrasting leadership. Our intention is not to merely highlight the disparities, but rather to inspire a deeper understanding and appreciation for the complexities inherent in the development trajectories of these two continents.

As we navigate through the pages, you will encounter a multitude of case studies and expert insights that paint a vivid picture of the challenges and triumphs faced by the diverse peoples of Asia and Nigeria. We deploy a unique sector comparative methodology using both objective data and case studies. The objective is to understand the causes of Africa's development reversal and hopefully learn how best to navigate a better future of shared prosperity for Africa.

We acknowledge the dynamic nature of both Asia and Africa. Our aim is not to provide a definitive assessment and a one-size-fits-all set of recommendations but to ignite a dialogue and foster a greater appreciation for the remarkable journeys these continents have undertaken.

We invite you, dear reader, to join us on this enlightening intellectual exploration as we try to unravel the mysteries and complexities that define the unique destinies of Asia and Africa. By the end of this book, we hope you will gain a fresh perspective, enriched knowledge and a renewed sense of curiosity about these extraordinary continents.

Banji Oyelaran-Oyeyinka and Oyebanke Abejirin
September 2023

Note

1 Oyelaran-Oyeyinka, B. and Gehl-Sampath, P. (2010), *Latecomer Development: Innovation and Knowledge for Economic Growth*, London: Routledge.

FOREWORD

By Toyin Falola

*University Distinguished Professor and Jacob and Sanger Mossiker Chair
in the Humanities, The University of Texas at Austin*

Nations have risen and collapsed throughout global history, typically impacted by a combination of internal and external influences. Few stories, however, enthrall and perplex researchers, policymakers and concerned global citizens as much as Nigeria's. In this competent and erudite book, readers are confronted with a rich and extensive knowledge of the compelling ideas on the possible transformation of one of the most important countries in the world.

Nigeria's journey from projected boom to relative stagnation is a tale that requires profound contemplation in a country endowed with massive natural resources, vibrant cultures and a promising economic trajectory. Professor Banji Oyelaran-Oyeyinka and Dr. Oyebanke Abejirin's *Reversal of Fortune* is a magisterial tome that addresses this mission not merely as an academic exercise but as a clarion appeal to redefine the African narrative. The book's title, poignant in its brevity, attests to the significant upheavals that some countries go through in their developmental journeys. With its vast agricultural capability and position as a major oil producer, Nigeria has historically been a beacon of hope on the African continent.

Nonetheless, the vicissitudes of time have seen the country's rising reliance on petroleum products and food imports. Such a situation asks, How did this reversal occur? What chain of events, decisions or missed chances resulted in this situation? These are some of the key questions that drive the data, the analyses and the recommendations.

The authors handle this problem with surgical precision, setting the stage in Part I by outlining the systematic deterioration of Nigeria's economic, social and political trajectories. Their in-depth examination of the country's historical and contemporary issues paints a picture of resource reliance ending in disregarding economic promise. The progressive decline in technical acquisition and stalled industrialization potential exposes a worrisome trend of squandered possibilities. The narrative's effectiveness comes from its critique and evidentiary method, bolstered by numerous graphs, charts and comparative studies. However, it is critical to recognize that Nigeria's story is not one of solitary misery. Part II contrasts Nigeria's experience with four Asian countries: Malaysia, Indonesia, Vietnam and Bangladesh. The disparity is startling. While these Asian countries have increased institutional capacity, expanded educational possibilities and improved economic performance, Nigeria has deviated from its developmental path. This comparative analysis sheds light on the critical role that leadership and state institutions play in catalysing innovation, establishing priorities and navigating globalization's difficulties and opportunities.

The notion of 'Dutch sickness' or resource reliance is a source of debate and interest in development economics. This notion is fully studied in *Reversal of Fortune*, revealing its institutional impact on African nations' long-term growth trajectory. While the major focus remains on Nigeria, the book's results apply to several other African countries and the rest of the developing globe. This detailed investigation dispels many myths about African invention by situating it in an economic, historical framework that spans both colonial and post-colonial periods. Part III of *Reversal of Fortune* approaches a climax, delving into the complexities of leadership and the laborious process of developing state capacities. Like any great academic work, the authors do not leave the readers despondent. Instead, they chart a path of optimism, supported by rigorous research and a vision for the future.

The route from the past to the present is seldom a straight line; instead, it is a series of zigzags interspersed by periods of clarity and uncertainty. As this book explains, leadership is one of the most important factors in this trajectory. It is impossible to overestimate the importance of visionary leadership in forging national destinies. It is the foundation upon which policies are developed, institutions are established and accountability and innovative cultures are fostered. The authors' central claim, supported by extensive data, is the critical necessity of leadership in preventing or minimizing the effects of large economic reversals. They argue persuasively that strong economies attain their success not through a sequence of coincidental circumstances but by implementing solid economic management practices. These methods are based on macroeconomic stability and growth paradigms that are robust, balanced, inclusive and opportunistic. A country's ability to protect its economy against significant downturns is at the heart of these policies.

This book, however, is more than just an analysis of what went wrong. Its brilliance is revealed by its solution-oriented attitude. *Reversal of Fortune* provides a blueprint for African countries to achieve quick, sustainable, balanced and inclusive growth by providing detailed information and evidence-based insights. The difficulty transitioning from reliance on natural resources to economic diversification is handled with refreshing pragmatism. The authors' proposal, presented rationally, convincingly and urgently, is for a reinvention of the state, the fostering of strong institutions and an emphasis on long-term economic diversification.

Furthermore, the writers' insights into African countries' technological and industrial issues are substantial. The book dives deeply into the historical processes that have shaped Africa's creative capacity. The authors emphasize that innovation is not solely the result of current restrictions. Instead, it is intricately related to a slew of interwoven elements that have shaped Africa's economic history, not just during colonial periods but also in the modern globalized globe. This illuminating viewpoint provides a new prism to observe and confront the continent's difficulties.

The broad popularity of the book's contents is another appealing quality. While it is an academic triumph, its significance extends beyond academia. This study will be invaluable to economic managers, policymakers and anybody serious about improving their economy. The book suggests a more concrete and actionable path to prosperity than many scholarly books on the subject. Professor Banji Oyelaran-Oyeyinka and Dr. Oyebanke Abejirin, the two brilliant authors, issue a rallying cry to all African nations: learn from history and design a course for a greater, wealthy future. They highlight the critical role of leadership and governance in nation-building and growth by highlighting the sharp disparity between Nigeria and its Asian peers. Malaysia, Indonesia, Vietnam and Bangladesh's stories, placed against Nigeria's, give a tapestry of lessons on how leadership may elevate or doom a nation.

The book's deconstruction of the so-called Dutch illness, or resource reliance, is one of its most important insights. By focussing on Nigeria's experience, the authors paint a comprehensive, multifaceted picture of how resource wealth might unknowingly contribute to a country's premature de-industrialization and the resulting institutional disintegration. This detailed understanding is critical, particularly when developing development agendas in resource-rich countries.

The book is more than a diagnostic tool; it is a light of hope. The authors provide a model for all African states by proposing realistic leadership and institutional capacity-building measures. *Reversal of Fortune* shines brightest here. It is a forward-looking book for leaders, policymakers and change-makers determined to shift the fate of their nations, not only a recital of previous blunders. The accolades that *Reversal of Fortune* has already received attest to its transforming power. The book has been praised by prominent economic development and policy design voices for its clarity, depth and actionable insights. As one reads through its pages, it becomes clear that this is not just another academic study but a guide for real-world change.

To conclude this foreword, it is appropriate to emphasize the book's essence, conveyed in its title. Fortunes can be turned around. The downward trend is not set in stone. The route to prosperity is within reach with competent leadership, effective policies and a nation's collective will. *Reversal of Fortune* reminds us that while history is important, it is up to us to influence the future. This book is recommended not only for anybody interested in Africa's rebirth and change but also as a necessary companion to realize a brighter, wealthy African continent.

INTRODUCTION: NIGERIA'S REVERSAL OF FORTUNE: INDUSTRIALIZATION SECTOR GROWTH AND LEADERSHIP FAILURE

Introduction

In 1960, the average GDP per capita worldwide was US$3,690, while it was US$1,320 in Africa; this is 35.8 per cent of global value. According to the World Bank's Economic Outlook database 1962 (first year for which global records were available), the most prosperous Asian states were with GNI per capita as follows: Malaysia ($300) and Philippines ($210). Thailand, Indonesia and South Korea had GNI per capita of US$100.

By 1990, the global per capita average had nearly doubled to US$7,170, yet Africa had only grown to US$1,458, 20.3 per cent of global average. In 2023, the figures are US$13,920 and US$2,273, respectively, meaning Africa's per capita GDP is a mere 16.3 per cent of the global average. Asia's average GDP per capita in 2023 is US$19,900, meaning that Africa's figure is 11.4 per cent that of Asia.

In the 1960s, most African countries were ahead of Asian countries in terms of income per capita, and leading development experts ranked Africa's growth potential ahead of East Asia's. The World Bank's chief economist at the time listed seven African countries that 'clearly have the potential to reach or surpass' a 7 per cent growth rate. According to the World Bank,[1] 'Africa's economic history since 1960 fits the classical definition of *tragedy*: potential unfulfilled, with disastrous consequences.' Contrary to expert predictions, African economies, including the seven identified by the World Bank Chief, suffered negative growths.

From the above, while most Asian and African countries were on the same levels of economic and industrial development in the 1950s to the early days of independence in the early 1960s, there had been a significant divergence in income starting in the late 1960s. The onset of the most recent developmental reversal coincided with the 1970's oil crisis and had persisted ever since. The large windfalls from the oil price rises first in 1970 and then in 1980 benefitted oil-producing countries such as Nigeria, Gabon and Angola, but prices of most tropical cash crops and minerals collapsed at the same time. When the oil prices crashed in the 1980s, the terms of trade declined in virtually all African countries. This setback continued until the mid-1990s when a new cycle of commodity price rises set in, which levelled off around 2015. Although the dominant pattern of specialization was in primary resource-intensive or land-extensive commodities, there were major shifts in the direction and composition of trade, two of which are worth highlighting. For example, in the export mix, the relative share of tropical cash crops, such as palm oil, rubber, sugar, cotton, coffee, tea, tobacco and cocoa, declined with the surge of highly valuable mineral resources such as gold, diamonds, copper, tin and, above all, crude oil.

We focus narrowly on Nigeria as the representative of Africa's most poignant reversal. Nigeria is the region's largest economy. Nigerians are known to be intelligent hard-working people; it has a dynamic youth population. The country has incredible cultural diversity. It has been for long periods the biggest exporter of crude oil and as well the largest movie (Nollywood) and music industry in Africa.

Nigeria is generally known as the 'Giant of Africa'. Its population is predicted to reach 400 million people by 2050, smaller only than India, China and the United States. Nigeria has all the potential to transform into a major global power, but thus far the giant remained crippled by several factors holding it back. The objective of this book is to examine Nigeria's arrested development by comparing it to its Asian comparators.

While there are several explanations for Africa's reversal, this book posits that one of the core causes of development reversal has been *Nigeria's loss of opportunity* to follow through with its industrialization efforts that were started in the 1970s and the lack of development of its agricultural base.

The country has experienced premature deindustrialization. Deindustrialization is a process of social and economic change caused by the removal or reduction of industrial capacity or activity in a country or region, especially of heavy industry or manufacturing industry.[2]

For example, about 50 years ago the increasing demand for and government policy of self-sufficiency in food production necessitated the call for establishment of a local fertilizer production industry. By the late 1960s and early 1970s, Nigeria established the first fertilizer firm in Nigeria, the Federal Superphosphate Fertilizer Company (FSFC) Limited, Kaduna. The company was a federal government project and produced among other products Single Super Phosphate fertilizer. The construction and installation of equipment started in 1974 and was completed in 1976 immediately after which production started. The factory stopped working decades ago.

Between 1985 and 1991, the textile sector in Nigeria recorded an annual growth of 67 per cent and, as of 1991, it employed about 25 per cent of workers in the manufacturing sector. At the time, 180 textile companies employed about one million people. The industry is now a shadow of itself, more details within the book.

As part of its strategic plan for pulp and paper production for domestic and export markets, the Nigerian government commissioned the Nigeria Paper Mill, Jebba, Kwara State, in 1969; Iwopin Pulp and Paper Company, Ogun State, in 1975; and Nigeria Newsprint Manufacturing Company in Oku-Iboku, Akwa Ibom, in 1986. The government's plan was for the three pulp and paper mills to provide tonnes of different papers in thousands every year and, of course, their performance was encouraging and promising. As of 1985, the Jebba mill, which was to be the largest in West Africa, was producing 65,000 tonnes of Kraft paper, liner and chipboards, sack Kraft and corrugated cartons per annum. *These plants have ceased to exist.*

These factories did not break even, not to talk of reinvesting their surplus cash and profit in the acquisition of technological capabilities and skills required to adapt, operate and maintain the imported technology in use. Within 10 years, 80 per cent of the trained technical staff of FSFC had left. The same fate befell Ajaokuta and Aladja Steel complexes, Nigeria's Aluminium Company, Aluminium Smelter Company of Nigeria and several state-owned projects. All are moribund.

The reasons include low plant availability due to prior poor technical preparation during the investment processes. Other factors include project and financial mismanagement, vested interest and weak bureaucratic capacity. These examples count among the thousands of White Elephants that litter the industrial wasteland in Nigeria.

The above summarizes the pattern and mechanics of industrial failure in Nigeria. Three points emerge. First, mastery of industrial-technological capability is a critical factor of success. Nations and firms accumulate this through continuous technological efforts over a long time. Second, it is also clear that technological knowledge is not easily absorbed, imitated or transferred contrary to conventional wisdom. No nation is willing to give another the science and technologies that made them rich. A nation must be deliberate and make explicit investment in acquiring the wide range of technical expertise required in all cycles of the project life. These include the capacity acquisition right from pre-feasibility, investment, operation and maintenance and so on. Third, specialized human capital does not consist only of theoretical knowledge; a nation must engage in learning by production, learning by

maintenance and learning to innovate by its own citizens. These are impera-
tives in the technology acquisition process.

The loss or lack of established industrial capabilities resulted from a perennial reliance on crude petroleum oil, which foreclosed its industrial progress.
The boom in trade in Nigeria in the two decades between 1995 and 2015
had its source in elevated oil prices. Consider the revenue of three African oil
producers in 2019 before the COVID-19-induced oil price collapse – Nigeria
(US$41 billion), Angola (US$32.3) and Libya (US$24.8). Oil prices expe-
rienced a major collapse from around US$60 to less than US$20 by April
2020. Every cycle of oil crisis therefore directly affects government revenue
and channels into public service delivery including health and education, the
fulcrum of human capital.

For this reason, income growth and fiscal health were tied inextricably
with oil revenues. Nigeria, despite being an oil-dependent country, failed
to master the art of refining its abundant crude petroleum after building
three major refineries in the last 50 years with a combined refining capacity of 450,000 barrels per day. The country with abundant crude and even
greater gas resources and a pool of scientists and engineers has become a
major importer of finished petroleum products. All of Nigeria's crude petroleum refineries are moribund due to a host of governance and management
challenges. Second, the country used to be a major exporter of agricultural
raw materials including oil palm, rubber, coconuts and still does sesame and
cashew among others. The challenge is that it has not only fallen behind in
traditional commodities exporter, but the country has also become a major
importer of food products because it is not adding value to its commodities.

The book systematically analyses how Nigeria has undergone a reversal
of fortune or a development reversal. While most African countries fit this
description, we will examine the case of Nigeria, the so-called *Giant of Africa*.
We analysed the phenomenon in all aspects of development, namely, social,
economic, political, industrial/technological, using available indicators. The
observed developmental reversal in economic and social outcomes almost
often triggers concomitant political outcomes, including social upheavals,
violent conflicts, street demonstrations, as we recently observed in Sri Lanka.

The COVID-19 pandemic triggered an unprecedented economic down-
turn leading to a decline of real GDP to an extent not seen in this century.
The health crisis led to massive financial and economic challenges. It affected
countries that derive their revenue from dependence on the export of commodities such as oil, minerals, and agricultural raw materials. Reduced global
demand led to the crash of oil and mineral prices; both events exacerbated
Africa's economic challenges and taxed the health system in the most severe
of ways. According to the African Development Bank, potential losses in

GDP are in the magnitude of US$173 and US$236 billion in 2021 and 2022, respectively. As these countries were recovering from the pandemic, along came the Russian–Ukraine war that exposed another deep dependency by African countries; the reliance on food especially grains imports estimated at US$45 billion in 2019.

There is a close correlation between the secular trends in trade with GDP growth. Over two decades between 1995 and 2014, several African economies grew and ranked among the fastest growing in the world, with annual growth rates of 5–10 per cent being no exception. The aggregate average annual GDP growth rates for sub-Saharan Africa (including South Africa) stood at an estimated 5 per cent since 1995.[3] Due to several structural and other factors, including faster population growth, total GDP growth and per capita growth rates post-1995 slowed and regressed to return to levels that were observed in the 1950s and 1960s. While most countries were affected, a few countries were worse off, especially commodity and oil-dependent countries. This was particularly so in the years 1985–95. These countries suffered further setbacks in the second half of the 2010s, when world commodity markets – especially the oil markets after 2014 – crashed and predictably growth rates fell back to very modest rates. The most recent and certainly most devastating is the synchronous impact of the COVID-19 pandemic, the financial meltdown and the extenuating Russia–Ukraine war, all between the years 2020 and 2022. The health crisis pushed an estimated 120 million people into extreme poverty and exacerbated the African economic conundrum. However, the recent pandemic and food security crises merely compounded and accelerated the simmering reversal that had set in much earlier.

Reversal and Progress: Asia and Africa in Regional Comparative Perspective

To better illustrate the secular trends in manufactured trade and growth, we examined two sectors, namely, manufacturing and agriculture; we draw data from the World Development Indicators database. We show the export share of both sectors for Asia and Africa in two parts, see Figure 0.1.[4]

From Part I of Figure 0.1, exports share of manufacturing in Asia grew faster and overtook that of agriculture right from the late 1960s, a typical manifestation of positive structural transformation. The gap between the two shares was marginal in the beginning of the study period. For instance, the shares of manufacturing and agriculture were 21.24 and 19.17 per cent respectively in 1962. The gap narrowed down to almost zero in 1964 but has been increasing since then. The shares of manufacturing and agriculture were 79.76 and 3.17 per cent respectively in 1995 and the gap narrowed down

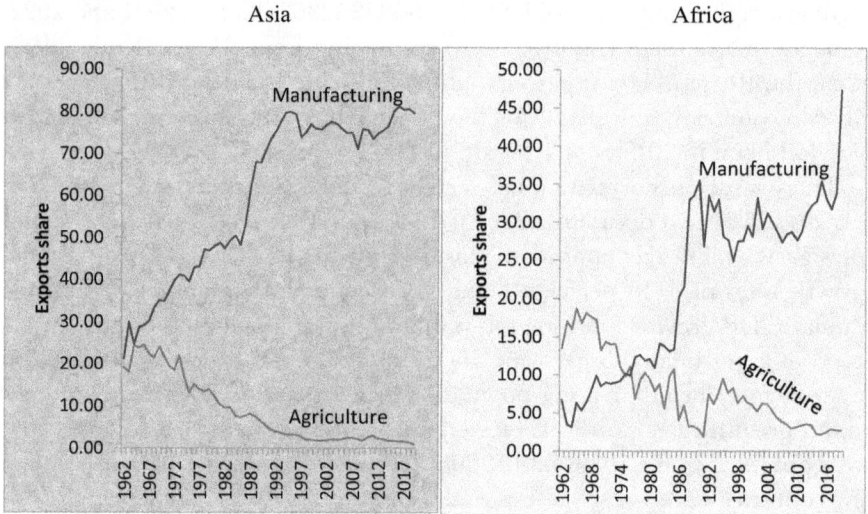

Figure 0.1. Exports shares of manufacturing and agriculture in Asia.

slightly but has been increasing since then. Noticeable is the fact that the share of agriculture has been continuously decreasing and share of manufacturing has been increasing. The findings suggest that Asian countries have been diversifying into manufacturing exports consistently leading to higher export share. The proportion of agriculture in overall export has been decreasing as a share of exports. The share of manufacturing exports reached 79.60 per cent while that of agriculture declined to 0.96 per cent.

From the second part of Figure 0.1 (Africa), until 1975, the share of agriculture export was higher than manufacturing. The situation changed with the share of agriculture declining while that of manufacturing increased for a time. An increase in the export share of manufacturing suggests that some of the countries in Africa did diversify into manufactures.

From a comparative perspective, while there was export diversification in both continents, the pace of diversification in Asia has been much faster with levels and complexities of products higher than in Africa and limited to a few countries such as South Africa and Morocco. What distinguishes the two regions is the pace of diversification represented by export share in manufacturing. For instance, the export share of manufacturing in Asia changed from 21.24 per cent in 1962 to 79.60 per cent in 2018 while in Africa it changed from 6.68 per cent to 47.27 per cent during the same period. From the findings, the pace of diversification in Africa has been far slower compared to Asia. Clearly, Africa's reversal of fortune is closely connected to its inability to achieve the level of diversification recorded in Asia. It may also be worth mentioning that within the African sample, South Africa and Morocco registered greater diversification than other countries on the continent.

Structure and Methodology

This book explores as its central question the wide divergence in income between Nigeria and four Asian countries namely Malaysia, Indonesia, Vietnam and Bangladesh. Additionally, these countries achieved a significant reduction in poverty and recorded equitable growth, especially after the 1970s. Nigerian citizens by contrast became poorer, and the country became more unequal over time. For example, Indonesia, Vietnam and Malaysia all had considerable natural resources and benefitted from the enormous oil windfall during the 1970s/1980s. These Asian countries have prospered while Nigeria faltered due in large part to the ways these nations managed their resource wealth. The policy and institutional differences that shaped the development evolution of these countries were critical to and ultimately defined the differences in outcomes.

While these four countries used oil income to build infrastructure and invested in productive assets, Nigeria's oil income was largely lost to official theft or wasted on White Elephant projects. According to a report from the Abandoned Projects Audit Commission President Goodluck Jonathan set up in 2011, it stated that 11,886 federal government projects were abandoned in the past 40 years, from 1971 to 2011, in Nigeria.[5] According to one commentator, 'Nigeria has become the world's junk-yard of abandoned and failed projects worth billions of naira.'[6] In stressing the economic implication of project abandonment to the society and the nation, the committee cited the case of Ajaokuta Steel Complex. This project commenced in 1979 with an estimated project cost of $650 million but remains uncompleted after spending over $5 billion.[7] During this period, the country spent about N2.1 trillion, an equivalent of $10.5 billion in importing steel into the country.[8]

Contrast the Nigerian story with South Korea, which began building a steel industry at about the same time as Nigeria. That country's steel sector became a major steel exporter creating about 65,000 jobs in the industry and now makes an estimated 60 billion dollars per annum in revenue,[9] and with this, reaping forward and backward linkages effect to the entire economy, hence, quickening its status as a major industrial power. The POSCO story is a sharp contrast to the Ajaokuta tragedy, unlike the monumental failure that it turned out to be, POSCO brings to life one of the world's great industrial success stories. While the industrial ascent of this project exemplifies the meteoric rise of South Korea's Pohang Iron and Steel Company and the incredible impact it has had on this small agrarian country, the Nigerian iron and steel story illustrates how to turn a blessing to a curse. In just about 25 years, POSCO became the largest steel company in the world and by its success transformed South Korea into the industrial age. The location of the Nigerian project became a sad and depressing site of a White Elephant.

What defined the striking outcomes is the choices made by the leaders of these countries: one was stuck on resource dependence while the other set of countries embarked on sectoral and economic diversification of their non-oil sectors starting with agriculture. Policies matter a lot. Indonesia initiated economic liberalization two decades earlier than Nigeria in 1967; while Nigeria did not initiate its economic liberalization until 1986 and subsequently reversed it.[10] We believe that this nexus of poor diversification cum excessive reliance on oil revenue income and the attending dysfunctional policy and institutional environment determined the fates of these countries. We take the view that history matters and that progress is path-dependent. Remote and immediate causes contributed to the structure of economies and the nature of engagement with global trade including colonial history and global rules such as the Multi-Fibre Agreement. The periodicity in this book starts from the period immediately around independence, that is, 1950–60 until the present. We take those institutions pre-independence and their aftermath signal and shape subsequent history. We will take our unit of analysis as the meso-level by examining in detail, sector growth and performance. We pair leading sectors in each country with the same sector in Nigeria and trace their evolutionary performance from post-independence till now. We trace where policies and performances divergence; we find this happened notably after the 1970s. We focus on this period because the oil super cycles and the oil bonanzas therefrom were pronounced in the post-1970s period.

A caveat. We recognize that cross-country comparisons are fraught with dangers of data, cultural contexts and interpretations. However, there is clearly broad evidence of a reversal of Africa's fortune and contrasting progress in Asian countries. This is well illustrated by sector performances. What has emerged from the analyses in the book is that Nigeria, a representative country for most oil-dependent African nations, need to wean itself of the pathology of natural resource dependence. Nigeria's industrialization, which took off with promise in the 1970s, was not sustained; and for the most part, poor leadership and bad governance undermined the process.

Notes

1 World Bank (1995), *Africa's Growth Tragedy: A Retrospective 1960-89*, by William Easterly and Ross Levine.
2 Dani Rodrik (2015), "Premature Deindustrialization," *Journal of Economic Growth*, 21: 1–33. B. Oyelaran-Oyeyinka (2016), *From Consumption to Production: The Whys and Ways out of Failed* Industrialization *in Nigeria*, Prestige Press.

3 African Development Bank (2015), *Growth, Poverty and Inequality Nexus: Overcoming Barriers to Sustainable Development*. AfDB: Abidjan. https://www.afdb.org/fileadmin/uploads/afdb/Documents/Publications/ADR15_UK.pdf; International Monetary Fund (2012). *Regional Economic Outlook: Sub-Saharan Africa – Maintaining Growth in an Uncertain World*. IMF: Washington DC; International Monetary Fund (2014). *Regional Economic Outlook: Sub-Saharan Africa – Staying the Course*. IMF: Washington DC..

4 We adopt the sector share of exports approach, which is a well-known proxy of exports diversification to estimate diversification in Asia and Africa. This is a measure of industrial manufacturing and technological capabilities. The selected Asian countries included in the analysis are Thailand, Vietnam, Malaysia, South Korea, China and India, while African countries are Algeria, Angola, Nigeria, Sudan, Botswana, Cote d'Ivoire, Ethiopia, Kenya, Mauritius, Morocco, Rwanda, Senegal, Tanzania, Uganda, Zambia, Congo, Dem. Rep. (DRC), Ghana, Mozambique, Libya, Egypt, United Arab Rep., South Africa and Tunisia.

5 O. C. Okereke (2017), "Causes of Failure and Abandonment of Projects and Project Deliverables in Africa." *PM World Journal*, 6(issue 1): 1. December 9, 2021 pmwj54 -Jan2017-Okereke-causes-of-project-failures-in-africa-featured-paper2.pdf (pmworldlibrary.net), accessed 9 December 2021.

6 M. E. Hanachor (2012), "Community Development Projects Abandonment in Nigeria: Causes and Effects." *Journal of Education and Practice*, 3(6): 33–36.

7 M. M. Andawei (2015), "Causes of Public Sector Project Abandonment in Nigeria: A Significance Index Analysis." *International Journal of Innovative Research and Advanced Studies (IJIRAS)*, 2(3): 70. Accessed on December 10, 2021, from Paper Title (use style: paper title) (ijiras.com).

8 I. Bunu (2011), "Presidential Project Assessment Committee Report." *The Punch Newspaper*. www.ccsenet.org/ibr *International Business Research*, 66(11): 2013159.

9 "Analysis: Ajaokuta: How Nigeria's Industrial Project Failed." https://www.premiumtimesng.com/news/headlines/253680-analysis-ajaokuta-nigerias-largest-industrial-project-failed.html, accessed December 25, 2021

10 Bevan, Collier et al., World Bank. accessed 4 August 2022. https://documents1.worldbank.org/curated/en/118981468775569456/pdf/multipage.pdf, accessed August 4, 2022.

Part I

Part I

Chapter 1

UNDERSTANDING DEVELOPMENT REVERSAL

'Technological change, then, accounted for sustained growth. It was not caused by economic growth, it caused it. It had no substitutes. Had there been no technological change, other forms of economic progress would eventually have ground to a halt.'
(Joel Mokyr, 1990: 148)

Introduction

Several different reasons explain the nature and processes of development and underdevelopment. This book posits that poor nations and in the specific cases of Africa are poor because of their technological backwardness. Paraphrasing the opening quote by Mokyr, because *there had been no technological change in large swathes of poorer countries – economic progress – may not have ground to a halt, it has neither been sustained enough to create wealth for the majority.* In other words, the central reason behind the wide and terrifyingly widening wealth gap between developed and developing countries is the gap in knowledge, especially scientific and technological knowledge. If natural resources alone were the basis of wealth, the Democratic Republic of Congo, Angola and Nigeria among others would not be too far down the prosperity ladder, yet they are among the poorest on earth.[1] Rich nations have a long history of *learning* and acquisition of knowledge, and using this knowledge to master nature and in transforming natural resources into high-value goods. Poor nations possess enormous natural resources but lag far behind in the technological knowledge necessary to transform their natural endowment into high-value goods. The cost of overcoming the knowledge gap built up over centuries is huge.

Worse, those countries blessed with oil and minerals are unable to add value to these precious gifts of nature, and on the contrary, oil for example has been associated with the phenomenon of 'resource curse'. In the face of acute shortages of vaccines, African countries have looked on helplessly while individuals in the Western nations received multiple booster vaccine shots. It was not about money. When these nations had money to buy vaccines, they were pushed to the end queue in the global supply chain. Vaccine nationalism ensured that as of July 2022, only 16 per cent of Africans on average had been vaccinated. While much of the developing world beg and complain about lack of global collaboration, a half dozen Western pharmaceutical companies dug into their arsenal of scientific and technological banks and came up with the mRNA vaccines. One of them is Pfizer. Pfizer which reported a 92 per cent operational growth in revenue to $81.3 billion for the full year 2021 compared with $41.7 billion for the full year 2020. On excluding the contributions of Comirnaty and Paxlovid, the revenue for the full year 2021 rose by 6 per cent operationally to $44.4 billion. Comirnaty is a COVID-19 vaccine jointly developed by Pfizer and BioNTech while Paxlovid is Pfizer's oral antiviral treatment.[2] While the crisis ravaged the world, a company with technological dominance in its sector reported a revenue almost three times the revenue from crude petroleum of Africa's largest exporter, Nigeria. The history of the company's agile response to the pandemic runs far deeper and goes farther back in history, 174 years ago. It was the development of deep-tank fermentation by Pfizer – which enabled the mass production of penicillin for use in World War II that laid the basis for much of what the company is today: a pharmaceutical juggernaut.[3] This story applies to all technologies from textiles, iron and steel, synthetic rubber to agriculture. The acquisition of knowledge, formation of skills and the evolution of large organization from aircrafts to shipbuilding is a marathon race, not a sprint. Successive forms build upon previous forms. As Isaac Newton, the famous English scientist, once said, 'If I have seen further, it is by standing on the shoulders of giants.' Of course, Newton was not literally standing on the shoulders of giants. Newton was explaining that his ideas did not come from him alone. Earlier works underpinned Newton's success in the discovery of the universe more than others did, and discoveries made by fellow scientists, either in his own time or earlier. Knowledge growth is cumulative; it has been growing exponentially over centuries.

Consider the story of one of the most widely used drugs in the world: Aspirin. While in its various forms it has been used to treat diseases, it was Dr Felix Hoffman, a German chemist at Friedrich Bayer and Co, who experimented with the chemical compounds (phenol group) and managed on 10 August 1897 to acetylate the phenol group and produce pure stable acetylsalicylic acid (ASA) for the first time.[1,2] In true fashion in which knowledge is built up, his work was supported and inspired by a number of other scientists including Arthur Eichengrün, Carl Duisberg and Wilhelm Siebel.[1,2,4] Dr Hoffman's discovery was the first time a drug had been made synthetically and was the birth of both aspirin and the pharmaceutical industry.[2] The new compound was named and registered Aspirin on 1 February 1899. The 'A' comes from acetyl and 'spir' from the first part of *Spirea ulmaria* (Meadowsweet), a botanical source of salicylic acid.[1] For most developing nations, catching up will become a Sisyphus challenge.

The rest of the chapter is organized as follows: The next section articulates the role of human capital in development followed by issues tying resource dependence and poor economic growth, economic diversification and institutions as determinants of progress and reversals. We conclude with a summing up of the chapter.

Human Capital Is the Key to Economic Growth

We have established that the source of wealth is technological change, and progress is advanced by the embodied human capital made of scientists, engineers and so on. For this reason, human capital is the largest component of global wealth, accounting for two-thirds of total wealth globally. While rich technologically advanced nations prioritize human capital, poor countries have developed a chronic affinity with natural capital which accounts for 9 per cent of wealth globally but makes up nearly half (47 per cent) of the wealth in low-income countries.[4] Unfortunately, developing African countries tend to mismanage their natural resources. The more successful Asian resource-rich countries have found the key to sustainable development using resource wealth to build their infrastructure and human capital.

Technological Capabilities of Earlier Industrializers Underpinned Successful Resource-Based Development

Historically, natural resources (NR) have played differential and deep-going roles in the rate and direction of economic growth of industrialized countries. One of the possible reasons for that was the conventional wisdom that a country's natural resources should naturally affect its economic growth positively. Several authors[5] put forward the notion that natural resources – notably coal as a source of energy – were among the primary drivers of the Industrial Revolution. Sachs and Warner (1995) published the first significant systematic study of economic problems associated with natural resources.[6] That study promoted the now widely held view known as the 'resource curse' hypothesis, although Richard Auty (1993) originally coined the phrase.[7]

The association of natural resources dependence with the resources curse is a relatively recent phenomenon, specifically after the 1950s (Aunty, 1993). This chapter specifically identifies resource dependence as a fundamental reason for poor industrialization and economic diversification of developing countries. Of the 15 least diversified countries in the world, 8 are in Africa.[8] In these countries, significant diversification appears to have taken place in Africa even among those with relatively higher income. At the current estimation, natural resources account for more than one-fifth of GDP in 5 of the 10 African countries with GDP per capita of more than $5,000. We show that oil dependence has a negative relationship with GDP. Historically, this has not always been the case as several countries, especially the most industrialized countries, prospered based on adding value to minerals and commodities for the most part of the nineteenth and twentieth centuries.

For example, the economic growth of the United States was, in part, made possible by resource-based industrialization in the twentieth century through the manufacturing of iron ore, coal, lead, nickel, zinc, antimony, copper and oil (Wright and Czelusta, 2007). However, this was because the United States had built a relatively strong industrial and technological base; it invested in research, innovation and technologies that enabled resource extraction and beneficiation. Strong state knowledge institutional structures such as engineering universities and the US Geological Survey supported this process; these provided the knowledge, skill and training in mining, minerals and metallurgy (Andersen, 2012). African countries, on the other hand, did not possess these capabilities in the pre- and post-colonial periods. Most still do not possess such capacity.

The European experiences including Scandinavia and Australia, among others, were not dissimilar; their experiences show that resource-based industrialization must be underpinned by strong legal, knowledge institutions and requisite technological capabilities. In the absence of these critical knowledge and pillars, perverse institutions that retard industrialization tend to develop and entrench. In the same manner, Sweden in the early phases of its development exported a boom of cereals and sawn wood and later, pulp, paper and iron ore from the mid-nineteenth century (Blomström and Kokko, 2007). The country embarked subsequently on diversification by the acquisition and adoption of technologies through learning, adaptation and subsequently innovation particularly by investing in dynamic domestic knowledge clusters. These comprised networks of private sector-led research institutes, universities, firms and public investment in industry-orientated skills formation.

In other words, unlike the low levels of scientific and technological human capital and weak knowledge systems with which poorer resource-dependent African countries started at independence, the experiences of more advanced resource-rich countries that had accumulated pertinent technology, skills and knowledge were different. The extant capabilities within these countries enabled the NR sector to lead the industrialization drive. By these, the technologies fostered backward and forward linkages of the natural resource sectors through new oil and mineral discovery, extraction and resource processing technologies and processes, as well as move the countries into new industries related to the resource sectors.

Australia is another country that invested heavily in human capital and engineering skills to harness its abundant natural resources such as bauxite, nickel, silver, copper and gold dating back to the 1960s. The investment consisted of training in engineering education and Research and Development (R&D) with mining accounting for 20 per cent of total R&D in 1995/1996 (Wright and Czelusta, 2007). Today, Australia is a world leader in mining software systems, home to global mining exploration ventures and an important global supplier of high-tech services and equipment to meet the demand for safer and cleaner mineral extraction and processing processes.

The country experiences reviewed above show that investment in domestic technological capabilities underlined the success of resource-based industrialization (downstream, upstream and horizontal). Investment in education and training especially engineering and vocational skills; strong public-private partnerships, and alignment of different policy tools, including industrial strategy ones, emerge as recurrent factors. Ultimately, these hinged on the countries' policy frameworks and institutional capabilities.

In an advanced economy with a strong industrial technological foundation, proceeds from hydrocarbons tend to flow into the productive sector of a country's economy to develop infrastructure that further supports critical sectors such as the design of manufacturing equipment, as well as R&D. All these investments in the long run strengthen the export base of developed nations and reduce their volume of imports leading to a favourable balance of trade. In Canada, for instance, the extractive industry (mining sector) contributed $109 billion or 5 per cent of Canada's total nominal GDP, and the industry's direct and indirect employment accounts for 719,000 jobs in 2019.

Unlike the experiences of the advanced industrial countries cited, today's mineral-rich African countries have not succeeded in industrializing. Studies including Auty and Evans (1994) provide evidence that mineral exports are negatively correlated with growth. While a slew of reasons given for the inability of countries to effectively transform natural resources to growth, namely, the Dutch disease, rent-seeking and conflicts, corruption and compromised political institutions, we stress that it is the lack of technological and industrial capabilities that leads to low economic diversification and unsuccessful structural transformation. For example, Africa's oil and gas sector makes only a small contribution to GDP despite generating most export earnings, as it is a highly technology and capital-intensive industry that employs few people. The materials and equipment used in the exploration and production are not produced in-country and therefore have limited horizontal interconnection to the domestic economy. There is minimal domestic manufacturing input in the oil sector, especially in oil product refining. The local content makes up about 5 per cent in goods and services. The same situation applies to Zambia's copper, for example.[9] The International Council on Mining and Metals (ICMM) estimated that domestic manufacturers supplied a very little share of Zambian mining inputs (ICCM, 2014). Domestic procurement was estimated to be around US$1.75 billion annually, of which 5 per cent (or US$87 million) represents locally manufactured goods (ICMM, 2014). The reasons for the weak systemic capacity include low horizontal integration of local suppliers, lack of competitiveness and relative technological capabilities to meet standards.

Economic growth experienced by several developing nations is tied to the income generated from rents and sales of resources in the international markets. However, exports of fossil fuels and minerals, even when it leads to annual growth in GDP, do not translate to improved human capital and manufacturing value added (MVA). Africa's industrial performance, measured in terms of industry value added (IVA) and MVA in GDP, has been lagging far behind comparator countries in Asia. MVA, which measures the degree of industrial processing, remains low in Africa, signifying the lack of industrial dynamism. This is consistent with the continent's reliance on exports of its abundant natural resources, especially mineral and agricultural resources, UNCTAD (2011). The phenomenon of the Dutch disease only in part explains poor industrial growth. This is because whenever there is a resource boom, the extra revenue accruing from the sale of natural resources (oil and minerals) triggers appreciation of the real exchange rate and subsequent contraction of the traded sector (Corden and Neary, 1982; Corden, 1984). This is, however, a short-term phenomenon but with impacts that are long term in nature; the most insidious being the displacement of policy focus from tradeable sectors, particularly industrial manufacturing, which requires long-term vision, planning and consistent investment.

Our basic proposition in this book is that natural resource abundance is not by itself a curse or a blessing. It is the nature of policies and the institutional context within which a country operates that determine the development trajectory and development outcome of NR assets. Country-specific factors influence the conversion of NR assets into opportunities or curse. These factors are broadly categorized into political stability, governance, quality of institution and economic policies. Natural resources are converted into opportunities by countries that have vision for long-term economic development while others see NR as an everlasting resource and remain solely dependent on these resources. Dominance of rent-seeking policies results into resource curse while use of NR as a means for development leads to resource blessings.

We have witnessed the uneven growth of GDP between Asia and Africa. Clearly, the state and institutional capabilities underlying the generation and diffusion of knowledge and how these underlying development dynamics affect industrial growth are central. In this chapter, we analyse the factors that separate countries that made rapid progress in 'catching up' and those that tend to be stagnating and 'falling behind'. In what follows, we interpret the theoretical literature on NR-dependence, implications for industrialization, economic diversification and what it all means for long-term development of African economies. Economic diversification, induced by structural transformation, is undergirded by industrial and technological capacity building resulting in a shift towards higher productivity sectors, higher skills employment and shrinking informal sector.

Is Natural Resource Curse or Blessing?

Are natural resources a 'curse' or a 'blessing'? The empirical evidence suggests that the trajectory of a country's development creates the resultant outcome: blessing or a curse. We have learnt from history that countries that make successful use of natural wealth by converting such into assets for their citizens do so by constructing a framework of sustainable macroeconomic policies, equitable governance system, intolerance of corruption and so on. For example, countries such as the United Arab Emirates, Norway, Singapore, and Malaysia among others, have turned their natural resources into blessings due to the obligatory focus on human resource development policies, expansion of physical and technological infrastructure. Subsequently, these countries went into a virtuous circle of economic growth which helped to raise the living standard of citizens.

On the other hand, some other countries, namely, DRC, Nigeria, Venezuela, Iran, Libya, among others, have witnessed their natural wealth turned into a resource curse due to lack of long-term vision of development, unequal distribution of income leading to social unrest, bad governance, presence of high levels of corruption and lost opportunity for industrialization. These countries have allowed an environment that fosters rent-seeking activities rather than creating institutional structures that turn their natural resources into assets. Dependence on oil exports tends to exacerbate inequality in society and increases the number of poor people. Examples confirming this assertion are Nigeria, DRC and Angola, where in recent decades the number of poor people has increased significantly.

There are two broad sets of explanatory variables, namely political factors focussing on the notion of resource curse (rentier state theories, rent-seeking, conflict, corruption, among others). The second set is economic variables (volatility of commodities cycles, Dutch disease and exchange rate fluctuations among others). What is becoming clear is that these factors do not point to some inevitability of bad outcomes resulting from resource abundance.[10]

The most prominent set of issues relates to resource boom, commodity super cycle and how these induce volatility and appreciation of the real exchange rate. Other notions include the connection between resource dependence and rent-seeking behaviour, the triggering of civil conflict, ethnic fractionalization particularly in the context of dysfunctional institutions and prevalence of corruption.[11] Finally, most critical for long development is that resource-rich developing economies tend to forgo industrialization and technological acquisition as well as experience the least diversification and structural transformation. This is an issue that is not often treated in the literature which we will take up more systematically in the next section.

Technological Capability Forms the Basis of Industrial and Economic Progress

Technological capability or technical competence is the ability of a firm to learn, master and execute its pertinent technical functions, including the ability to develop new products and processes; this is dependent on the accumulation of relevant technological knowledge and skills leading to higher levels of organizational efficiency (Patel and Pavitt, 1997). These types of competencies are closely aligned with the knowledge and skills or 'know-how' needed for successful performance (Craig, 2015). The concept of technical capability applies at the individual, firm, sector and national levels. At the individual level, it is traditionally measured by the knowledge and skill of an individual. Technological capability could be tacit or codified. Educational background and experience are used to measure technical competence. However, many unmeasurable characteristics of an individual also constitute competencies. In literature, these are regarded as behavioural competencies (Martone, 2003; Walsh and Linton, 2001). The characteristics such as sincerity, commitment and interpersonal skills come under behavioural competencies.

At the firm level, they go beyond individual competencies. Individual competencies are necessary but not sufficient to make up for the overall firm-level competencies. Firms need to provide opportunities for effective use of individual competencies. For instance, a firm needs to have in place an appropriate technological base so that individual competencies can be utilized for better performance of the firm. Institutional competencies also include individual competencies of the management team towards the goal and vision of the firm. Hence, it is necessary to distinguish between individual competencies of the workforce and the management team. Workforce competencies should be more related to the job while managerial competencies need to focus on managerial functions. For the assessment of technical competency, it may be useful to evaluate it at various levels such as workers, supervisors, managers and management team.

Individual and firm-level competencies alone cannot guarantee sectoral competencies. Like few competent individuals cannot make a firm technically competent. Similarly, few competent firms cannot represent a competent sector. For a sector to be competent, vertically and horizontally integrated firms need to be technically competent. Sectoral competencies necessitate competent backward-forward linkages. It may require a different kind of industrial structure such as the development of a sector-specific cluster for the sector to be more vibrant.

The development of national-level technical competencies is much more than simply individual and firm-level competencies. This is where the role of governments comes in. Individual competencies may be acquired by obtaining better education beyond the boundaries of a country. However, competencies based on tacit knowledge are dependent on socio-economic and inherent factors. These may not be derived from education. Technically competent firms may also be incorporated by a few individual, and minimal government support is needed in this endeavour. However, for the development of competencies at the sectoral and national level, government support is usually needed through education, training and subsidies for learning.

National technological capability is fostered in large part by soft and physical social infrastructure. Investment in roads, reliable and cost-efficient electricity supply and telecommunications among others underpin firm-level and national-level ICT. Among the social institutions, a good quality education system is central to the development of competencies. It is not only the educational system but also dynamic industrial development system needs to be in place to develop sector-specific competencies at the national level. The development of social infrastructure and industrial development systems is a long drawn process. Hence, the development of sectoral and national competencies is sometimes regarded as path-dependent (Patel and Pavitt, 1997). However, sectoral competencies might break path dependencies in case of paradigm shifts in technological progress. The emergence of new technologies may alter path dependencies. The development of social infrastructure and competencies is mutually reinforcing. The high competencies generate more wealth that in turn can be used to develop/improve social infrastructure.

The first group consists of the Newly Industrializing Economies that have successfully acquired advanced technologies, including high technologies. These countries have made the transition from copying and learning to the innovation phase. These are most notably Japan, Korea and China. China, Japan and South Korea combine to spend US$613 billion on R&D in 2018, taking three out of the top five global spots along with the United States (No. 1) and Germany (No. 4). The private sector plays the primary role, making up approximately 78 per cent of total R&D spending. China's total public and private science and technology expenditures in 2019 rose by 12.5 per cent over the previous year to US$322 billion, according to the National Bureau of Statistics.[12] Spending on basic research accounted for 6 per cent of the total; applied research, 11.3 per cent; and development, 82.7 per cent.

The second group includes middle-income economies, namely Thailand and Malaysia. They have had significant but varying levels of success in accumulating and adopting imported technologies. They have graduated from low to medium technology regimes shown in our schema. The third group consists of low-income economies in Asia, namely Indonesia, the Philippines, Thailand and Bangladesh, which are still at the level of mastering low technologies such as garments, leather and basic agro-industrial foods. In these countries, industrialization and diversification, especially the capability to transit into medium to high-technology regimes, two other strategies follow the well-known learning pathways.

First, these countries made sustained investment in human capital. This is the sum of the skills level of a country's entire workforce which includes managers and administrators; it is strongly related to the potential real income per capita of a country, and it is a function of the productivity of its labour. East Asian experience demonstrates that human capital is very important as a source of economic growth. The sources of competitive advantage in advanced technologies derive largely from superior education, training and skills developed through 'learning by using', 'learning by doing' and 'doing by innovation'. Diversification has been achieved through consistent and explicit technological learning in order to climb the industrial technological ladder from low-technology to high-technology regimes. This has been made possible by long-term investment in knowledge and skills upgrading required to master new technologies.

The analysis of Asian economies suggests an evolutionary transformation of export profile of China, Malaysia and South Korea from low-tech and natural resource-derived products to being predominantly based on manufactured products. The manufacturing activities in 1990 in China were limited to low-tech manufacturing such as articles of apparel and clothing accessories and so on in 1990 but shifted to high-tech such as electric machinery and appliances and telecommunications equipment from 2019. The technological competence of China in 1990 was relatively modest, but the country continually built better through sustained efforts that resulted in a high level of manufacturing capabilities, including exports of high-tech products in 2019. The technological capacity acquired resulted in the rapid diversification of the Chinese economy. In other words, both China and Malaysia have achieved horizontal and vertical diversification that achieved substantial agribusiness as well as manufacturing despite having a substantial endowment of natural resources.

The situations of South Korea and Malaysia are very similar. The two countries have made explicit efforts in developing their manufacturing capabilities despite Malaysia having a lot of natural resources. Consequently, both countries are highly competent technologically resulting in both product specialization and diversification. The case of India is somewhat different than other sample Asian countries. Its manufacturing activities were limited to non-metallic mineral manufactures and articles of apparel and clothing accessories in early 1990s but with sustained acquisition of manufacturing capability, it now produces and exports a wide range of medicines, pharmaceutical products and road vehicles. Its technological competence changed from low to medium in three decades. Although technological competence has improved, it falls in the low-level category of diversification. The case of Indonesia is very much to that of India, but its diversification level has been far more than that of India.

Evidently, the capability of a country to achieve specialization and diversification is directly associated with the technological capabilities of that country. We show trends followed by South Korea, Nigeria and China in Figure 1.1. From the figure, the share of Nigeria was highest (53.12 per cent), followed by South Korea (38.06 per cent) and China (8.82 per cent) in 1960. By 1967, Korea raced ahead and Nigeria's reversal had set in.

South Korea surpassed Nigeria in 1967 while China did the same in 1995. Although the share of GDP per capita in South Korea has been declining for the last two decades, its share is the highest (70.91 per cent) in 2020. The decline in the share of South Korea may be attributed to unprecedented growth in China. The GDP per capita growth may be higher in China compared to South Korea, but per capita income in the latter is much higher than the former. Finally, the income per capita share in South Korea, China and Nigeria is 70.91, 23.66 and 5.43 per cent in 2020. As is well known, the success of South Korea and China may be attributed to acquired advantages rather than natural ones. The development of the electronics sector in South Korea and a strong manufacturing base in China seems to have led to the increase in per capita income in these countries. In the forecast period, the shares are expected to follow the same pattern as that from 1960 to 2020.

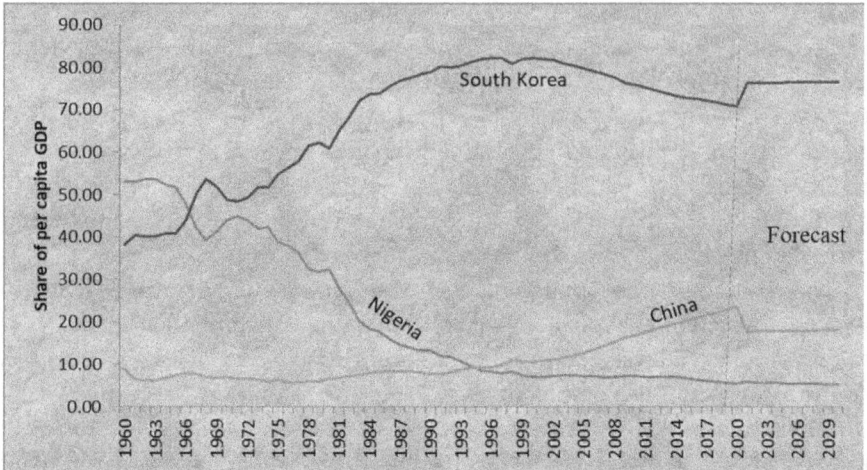

Figure 1.1. Trends in the share of GDP of South Korea, Nigeria and China. Source: Authors.

Natural Resource Dependence Undermines Industrialization and Innovation

A key finding resonating in the literature on resource abundance is the role of institutions in explaining resource blessing or curse. First, within strong institutional contexts, it is possible for policies to prevent the Dutch disease effect; however, this has been very rare in the experience of developing countries and hardly so in the African experience except for Botswana.

The conventional wisdom on resource abundance much earlier was that of a 'blessing' not a 'curse'. Several scholars attributed economic development of earlier industrial nations to their mineral and commodities abundance as the driver of economic development.[13] Latecomer countries that pursue technology-driven horizontal and vertical diversification especially at the low-income stage such as Malaysia and Vietnam have proved that *resource abundance*, as opposed to *resource dependence*, could supply the needed investment capital for latecomer economies to achieve sustainable growth.[14] In other words, the development outcome of a country possessing abundant natural resources including improvements in economic and human development is not as a result of the asset itself but rather on the rate and direction of technologies applied, the structure of knowledge institutions and the technological capabilities that a country explicitly invest in.

Economic development is driven largely by industrial manufacturing. The key requirement is technological learning, the driver for economic diversification and structural transformation. Countries that are locked into resource extraction and trade tend to record a decline in the traded sector once they begin to enjoy a resource trade boom. Studies show that higher resource revenue leads to the movement of labour from the traded (manufacturing at the core) to the non-traded sector. Given that manufacturing grows through learning by doing, there is a progressive diminishing of technological capital and, by implication, overall rate of industrialization. According to Esanov: 'The resource boom permanently lowers the rate of growth. One can show that non-resource GDP falls on impact after a resource discovery if the traded sector is capital-intensive.'[15]

An important reason why oil-producing countries experience technical lock-in is the difficulty of spillovers into other sectors due to the unique processing techniques and skills that underpin petroleum refining. Therefore, there is weak horizontal connection through the learning-by-doing process that occurs in the oil sector. This is echoed by the 'product space' framework whereby countries find it relatively easier to diversify by deploying capabilities acquired from other products they had specialized in, to master new sectors requiring the same skills and technical capabilities.[16]

Technological capability drives economic diversification

History shows us that nations accumulated wealth only from the accumulation of technological capacity that enables both horizontal and vertical diversification through learning to produce a more complex and wider set of innovation-driven products, goods and services. However, the negative externalities from resource boom almost always impact the traded sector (manufacturing), which is the engine of growth and the greater beneficiary from learning by doing and other positive externalities. Prolonged and non-mitigated influence of the extractive economy on non-resource export sectors impact the process of learning and competitiveness, which is a long-term process.

For example, the academic literature seems to suggest that resource boom impact and mineral dependence tend to manifest in negative outcomes largely in poor countries. The most poignant evidence is that these countries, after several decades of independence, remain dependent on multinational oil and mineral companies in both upstream and downstream activities. This is contrary to the experiences of the more developed economies and that of more advanced Asian economies that have achieved significant diversification; the latter over the last 40 years. In the early years of the twentieth century, the United States dominated the global trade and production of almost all major industrial minerals, surpassing nations with bigger mineral reserves due to its superior technical capacity.[17]

In regional comparative perspective with Africa, Asian countries like Malaysia, Korea and lately Vietnam have diversified significantly despite their significant deposits of natural resources. Malaysia's GDP and exports comprise significant manufacturing activities that drove the increase in GDP per capita. Over time, the share of low technology such as food and textiles in this country has reduced, while machinery accounts for a very significant share, and both machinery and other manufactures comprise a large majority of the added value originating from the manufacturing sector.

Malaysia, through deliberate policy actions, diversified its exports over the last five decades, while a country like Nigeria with very similar agricultural endowment did not diversify. Exports of manufactures by Malaysia reached 80 per cent of total exports by 2000, with the electronics sector accounting for a large share of the country's manufactured exports. Additionally, it succeeded with horizontal diversification of its rich agro-business sectors, namely, rubber, palm oil and petroleum industries that contributed to its dynamic industrial base.

Vietnam is endowed with other natural resources such as coal, phosphates, rare earth elements, bauxite, chromate, copper, gold, iron, manganese, silver, zinc, offshore oil and gas deposits, timber and hydropower. The contribution of natural resources to the economy diminished after 1980, and its contribution to GDP fell substantially. Subsequently, the country's focus shifted to manufacturing and services from agriculture and crude oil exports; it succeeded in diversifying economic activities rather than depending on natural resources. Thereafter, the percentage of GDP contribution of mineral and oil resources gradually reduced and is now relatively small as far as mineral, crude oil and natural resources are concerned. The GDP contribution of natural resources was highest (14.18 per cent) in 2008, while in case of crude oil, it was less than 10 per cent (8.98 per cent) in 2006.

Clearly, resource-rich economies may turn such assets into a curse by relying exclusively on these commodities as sources of export revenue, which exposes them to a regime of volatility and foreign exchange shocks. The blessing is lost when countries fail to develop autonomous capabilities for processing, such as oil refining, by which systemic learning is foregone. Investment in minerals-related knowledge seems a legitimate component of a forward-looking development programme.

In sum, the prevalence of resource curse is a peculiar feature of some but not all countries, especially developing countries that discovered minerals and oil resources in the absence of the pertinent technological and human capabilities to explore, extract and process them. Second, the phenomenon of resource curse, in terms of time frame, has become prominent only in the last 50 years which corresponds roughly to the period when most of these countries that bear the burden of a 'curse' attained independence. We suggest that a combination of a relatively strong knowledge system including universities and vocational education assets, legal and political institutions and the right technologies underpinned the resource blessing of the older nations.

Good Institutions Underpin Resource Blessing, Bad Institutions Foster Resource Curse

Institutions in Africa exhibit profound ineffectiveness in responding to development challenges.[18] The most telling recent examples have been the current and past outbreaks of pandemics, commodity price booms and bursts, locust invasions, among others. The devastating impacts of these profoundly damaging crises could not trigger short- and longer-term strategic solutions as there have been no institutions for responding to crises including production of medicines and vaccines. It is hard to find scientific organizations and institutions with comparable capacity as comparators outside the continent. When coupled with poorly functioning policy-making bureaucracies, Africa can be said to be characterized by a lack of both broad and specific competencies in their coordination functions. For the most part, we have a situation in which policy coordination is largely politically driven in the absence of strong market coordination.

A critical institutional gap is the lack of industrial and development finance structures dedicated to long-term industrial development. Poor financial commitment for meeting organizational goals results in disillusionment of scientists and policy researchers over time, leading to migration and brain drain. We also have here a lack of private sector trust in collaborations with public sector institutions; this has jeopardized the rise of a vibrant private sector since organizations that promote the growth of private sector firms are missing. Their inefficiencies give rise to the poor coordination of knowledge and economic production functions, leading to imbalances in the demand and supply for skills of the right kinds, quantity and quality mix at sectoral levels and over time.

Oil wealth tends to become a barrier to building and nurturing quality institutions that undergird industrial and scientific dynamism. Bureaucratic and political elites are entwined in corruption practices, patronage and granting of import licences and other privileges to friends and associates. Bad governance seems to be far more debilitating and explains in large part why oil bonanzas over several decades have undermined the performance of the Nigerian economy (Salai-Martin and Subramanian, 2013).

The race to occupy political office has meant that resource abundance engenders the appetite and propensity to vie for power; it is no secret that the path to high-level political office is strewn with all manner of financial voter inducement in low-income countries. Extractive economic regimes ensure that politicians have zero accountability to the electorate; the voters once bribed lose the right to 'democracy dividends'. Given the lack of accountability pressure, government business is not managed by competence and the beneficiaries are not those who build factories. In this way, natural resources abundance is a culprit in blocking the evolution of technological and institutional structures.[19]

Another reason why bad institutions undermine industrial growth is that natural resource windfall, rather than promoting traded sectors, pushes productive entrepreneurs into rent-seeking. Clearly, there are differences between countries with 'production-friendly institutions and others with rent grabbing-friendly institutions' (Mehlum et al., 2006a,b).

When resource-rich countries are blessed with requisite strong institutions such as Australia, Canada, the US, New Zealand, Iceland and Norway, and also Botswana (Acemoglu et al., 2003), wealth becomes a blessing. However, if institutions are dysfunctional, and the legal system is subject to the whims of the powerful, rent-seeking becomes far more profitable than manufacturing and other similar businesses requiring hard work. Evidently, weak institutions may explain the poor performance of oil-rich states such as Angola, Nigeria, Sudan and Venezuela, diamond-rich Sierra Leone, Liberia and Congo, and drug states Columbia and Afghanistan. These institutions are themselves products of long historical and colonial origins.

Natural Resource Dependence Harms Horizontal Diversification and Industrial Agriculture

An important historical difference between Asia and Africa is the achievement of the Green Revolution by the former followed closely by different levels of Industrial Revolution. Africa achieved neither. Agricultural productivity growth propelled by structural transformation depends in large part on the industrial manufacturing sector, especially its capital goods subsector, which could generate other productive inputs. The development of capabilities in industrial agriculture would determine productivity and ultimately long-term development performance of economies.

The significant difference in productivity undergirds the wide income per worker of farmers working in rural areas and those employing modern methods. What distinguishes the subsistence and modern industrialized agriculture is fundamentally in the productivity gaps, which transmits to, and is reflected in, differences in their living standards. This large and persistent difference in agricultural productivity gaps in 2020 is striking given that

Arthur Lewis (1954) pointed it out[20] in his 1954 *Manchester School* paper: Lewis summarized a part of his argument thus:

> *The main sources from which workers come as economic development proceeds are subsistence agriculture, casual labour, petty trade, [...] and the increase in population. In most but not all of these sectors, [...] the marginal productivity of labour is negligible.*

Development economists have stressed the pivotal role of manufacturing and clearly recognizing its inextricable link with agriculture. The lesson of history is that the development process is fundamentally linked to the reallocation of workers out of agriculture and into 'modern' economic activities.[21] When the transition, through structural transformation, does not occur, it leads to the misallocation of workers across agriculture and non-agriculture that explains in large part the international income and productivity differences. Oyelaran-Oyeyinka and Lal (2016) and Oyelaran-Oyeyinka (2020) made the point with empirical evidence that the reallocation of capital and labour to the most productive sectors through structural change fuels economic growth and significantly raises per capita income in low-income African and Asian countries.

The main sources of productivity growth are the adoption of advanced technologies and upgrading of endogenous skills of the workforce; both inputs are expected to result in higher productivity. According to a recent report by the OECD-FAO (2020: 25):

> Global agricultural production is projected to increase over the coming decade, in response to growing demand, albeit at a slower rate than observed over the previous decades. Most of the growth in production is projected to occur through productivity improvements, due to intensification and ongoing technological change leading to a further decline in real commodity prices, despite increasing constraints on expanding agricultural land in some regions.

According to an OECD-FAO (2016) projection, the top three exporters of rice by the year 2025 remain India, Thailand and Vietnam; these countries have been responsible for over 65 per cent of total exports. By 2025, Vietnam is expected to overtake India, making Vietnam the largest exporter. In this period, the export share of the top three exporters will drop to less than 60 per cent due to the emergence of Cambodia and Myanmar as major rice exporters.

Africa's Slow Transition from Subsistence to Industrial Agriculture

From the foregoing, there are two broad concepts of agriculture, namely, industrialized agriculture and subsistence agriculture. Industrial agriculture is underpinned by modern scientific and technological techniques designed to produce crops and livestock on a large scale and distributed based on modern supply chain logistics. One of the most important objectives of industrial agriculture is to increase crop yield, which is the amount of food that is produced for each unit of land.

Industrializing agriculture therefore involves the mastery of the applied sciences which encompass the full range of agro-industry including crop production horticulture, livestock, fisheries and forestry. The management dimension includes the art, science and business of producing crops and livestock for economic purposes. Central to raising yield is the application of a broad range of science and technologies such as crop breeding, production techniques, crop protection and economics among others. The investment in, and mastery of, the above technologies is what separates modern agriculture business from subsistence practices which characterize the life of the rural population.

Industrialized agriculture is therefore designed to realize economy of scale driven by mechanization – replacing animal and labour – leading to production of large quantities of food at lower costs. The adoption of industrialized agriculture involves the utilization of farm machines, investment in large irrigation systems and the use of chemical fertilizers, improved seed varieties and pesticides.

The agriculture sector accounts for a large percentage of employment and value added (VA) in developing countries. Usually, agriculture's share of employment is higher than its share of VA, meaning that VA per worker is higher in the non-agriculture sector than in agriculture. Also, as with most developing countries, measured VA per worker is ordinarily relatively lower in agriculture compared with other sectors of the economy such as manufacturing and services. In theory, based on simple two-sector models, the prediction is that VA per worker should be equal in agriculture and 'non-agriculture'.[22] However, VA per worker for most developing countries is four times higher in the non-agriculture than in the agriculture sector. In Sub-Saharan Africa, the difference is much larger; it could be as high as with a factor of 10.

These large agricultural productivity differences imply that African countries lag other regions by much wider gaps in agriculture than in non-agriculture (Vollrath 2009). In addition, the failure to modernize agriculture suggests that the problem of Africa's economic development is fundamentally connected to not just poor adoption of modern technological methods but also the dysfunction associated with 'misallocation' of workers across sectors, with too many workers in the less-productive agricultural sector.[23] There continues to be high contribution of the agricultural sector to GDP, which points to the poor diversification of most African economies. On average, in the region, agriculture contributes to 15 per cent of the total GDP, but this average masks the wide variations across the countries as we analyse in Figure 1.2.

Figure 1.2 shows the trend in agriculture VA as a share of GDP in Sub-Saharan African countries compared to that of the rest of the world, both in 2000 and 2019. The analysis shows that agriculture VA as a percentage of GDP is higher among Sub-Saharan African countries than in the rest of the world. The values in 2000 range from 2.79 per cent (Botswana) to 44.67 per cent (Ethiopia) in Sub-Saharan Africa and from 0.86 per cent (United Kingdom) to 21.61 per cent (India) in the developed countries. The high agriculture VA recorded for Sub-Saharan African countries shows a lack of diversification into high-value, high-productivity products, which means Africa continues its reliance on non-processed agriculture.

In 2019, Sub-Saharan African countries maintained higher values than the rest of the world, with values ranging from 1.89 per cent (South Africa) to 42.59 per cent (Chad) while values in the developed countries ranged from 0.61 per cent (United Kingdom) to 15.97 per cent (India). We plotted the values in 2000 against those of 2019. The chart shows that the share of agriculture VA in GDP declined for all the developed countries considered except Argentina in 2019 compared to that of 2000, whereas for some of the Sub-Saharan African countries such as Kenya, Mozambique, Mali and Chad the values of 2019 increased above the values in 2000.

The implications are myriad. First, the current structure of agriculture suggests that workers such as farmers in general, agricultural households

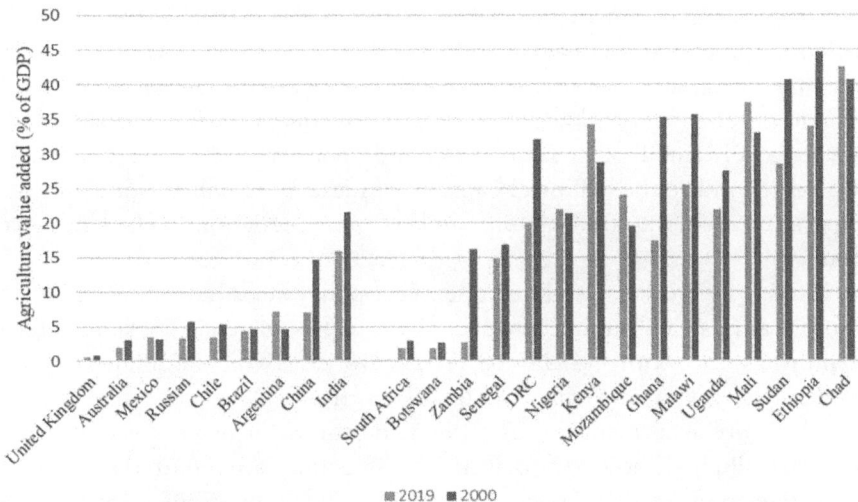

Figure 1.2. Agriculture value added (% of GDP) – 2000/2019. Source: World Development Indicators, World Bank (2020).

specifically, would continue to endure lower living standards compared with workers in manufacturing. Second, low productivity and limited value addition to agricultural commodities mean low GDP contribution of agriculture to the economy as well as limited sectoral employment opportunities for rural dwellers including women. Third, as the main source of income for Africa's rural population – estimated to represent 64 per cent of the total – low perpetuates mass poverty.

Fourth, Africa has and will continue to suffer from persistent and high incidences of undernourishment, far higher than other regions of the world, as it continues to import food staples estimated at around US$50 billion a year. Africa's rural farming population is made up of a predominantly high percentage of smallholder farmers (80 per cent) who cultivate low-yield staple food crops on small acreages of land and scarcely apply improved inputs (AGRA, 2014).

The situation of low productivity applies across the full value chain both at the farm level (low crop yield) and at the manufacturing processing level, which constitute a barrier to structural transformation that requires the rising productivity free up labour to move out of agriculture into manufacturing. In other words, the level of value addition and crop processing of agricultural commodities is low and post-harvest losses in Sub-Saharan Africa average 30 per cent of total production, meaning that the region loses over US$4 billion each year.[4]

For the foregoing reasons, the human capabilities and technological infrastructure to increase farm yields as well as MVA are extremely important, especially as global demand grows for high-value agricultural products including processed and packaged food increases relative to raw materials. VA processing activities in agro-processing create end-to-end, on and off farm jobs, raise incomes and, more broadly, the quality of life of rural dwellers, especially smallholder farmers. In addition, new techniques of production serve to raise the technical capacity of hitherto unskilled workers while integrating them into the virtuous circle of more modern and efficient value chains.

To improve workers' well-being, explicit policy steps have to be taken to improve Africa's agricultural productivity, which is currently ranked the lowest in the world, with US$335 of VA per worker. Achieving higher labour productivity and growth in yield to match that of Asia and other regions would require investments in education and training of farmers as industrialized agriculture is knowledge-driven. Urgent actions are required in the face of rapid technological and scientific advances and applications, as well as the challenges of climate change that equally threaten further negative effects on yield growth.

Summing Up

This chapter examines the direct and indirect impacts of oil dependence on African economies and specifically on the growth trajectory of the Nigerian. We attribute the reversal of fortune and development regress in part on its pathology of oil dependence.

We provide empirical evidence showing that continuous concentration on commodities exports is strongly related to relative economic instabilities and the undermining of the critical long-term learning required for technological capability acquisition. For Africa as a whole, the dependency figures are significant and troubling as commodity exports on average account for 80 per cent of total merchandise exports. In almost half of Africa's economies, commodity exports earn 90 per cent or more of merchandise export earnings. Nigeria experienced development reversal because the benefits of technical progress and value addition to its commodities were lost. The benefits of explicit industrialization were cumulatively lost over the last five decades while the opposite holds true for its comparator Asian countries.

To reverse the divergence, Nigeria needs to rely less on primary commodities and build capacity for value addition for its domestic market and to export processed commodities, as well as pay close attention to institutional capacity to diversify economies.

Notes

1 The top countries in 2022 with the highest GDP are United States: $20.89 trillion, China: $14.72 trillion, Japan: $5.06 trillion, Germany: $3.85 trillion, United Kingdom: $2.67 trillion, India: $2.66 trillion, France: $2.63 trillion, Italy: $1.89 trillion.

2 https://www.pharmaceutical-technology.com/news/pfizer-full-year-2021-revenues/, accessed July 3, 2022.

3 It was designated a National Historic Chemical Landmark by the American Chemical Society (ACS) in a special ceremony in Brooklyn, N.Y., on June 12, 2008. Source: https://www.eurekalert.org/news-releases/491868

4 https://www.worldbank.org/en/news/feature/2018/01/30/the-changing-wealth-of -nations-2018, accessed July 3, 2022.

5 Mikesell (1997), Kronenberg (2004).

6 Sachs and Warner (1995), "Natural Resource Abundance and Economic Growth." NBER Working Paper No. w5398, Available at SSRN: https://ssrn.com/abstract =225459

7 Sachs and Warner arrived at the conclusion that it was the effect of the 'Dutch disease' which had been studied by economists since the 1970s (McKinnon, 1976; Corden and Neary, 1982; Van Wijnbergen, 1984; Auty, 1994; Gylfason, 1999).

8 International Monetary Fund's Export Diversification Index (2020).

9 https://thenationonlineng.net/sanusis-critical-treatise-on-state-of-the-nation/, accessed July 28, 2021.

10 See Ross (1999) for an elaborate review of the factors on resource curse. (Echavarria, Vázquez Moreno, and Sherdek, 2016; James, 2019; Lederman and Maloney, 2007) among others have challenged the notion of resource curse.

11 Frederick van der Ploeg (2011). "Natural Resources: Curse or Blessing?" *Journal of Economic Literature*, 49(2): 366–420.

12 http://www.xinhuanet.com/english/2020-08/27/c_139322217.htm

13 Innis (1930, 1940, 2017) and Mackintosh (1923, 1935).

14 Viner (1952), Lewis (1955), Spengler (1960).

15 Akram Esanov (2012). "Economic Diversification: Dynamics, Determinants and Policy Implications." *Revenue Watch Institute*, 8: 1–26.

16 Hidalgo et al. (2007) and Hausmann and Hidalgo (2011)

17 The US share of world mineral production in 1913 was far in excess of its share of world reserves; mineral-rich countries like Brazil, Chile, Russia, Canada and Australia did much worse in developing new reserves and cheaper techniques (David and Wright, 1997).

18 Oyelaran-Oyeyinka and Gehl-Sampath (2010), *Latecomer Development.*

19 Acemoglu and Robinson (2006) made the point that growth of manufacturing can weaken the power of political elites.

20 Lewis (1955), Theory of Economic Growth.

21 Rosenstein-Rodan (1943), Lewis (1955), and Rostow (1960).

22 https://www.theigc.org/project/the-agricultural-productivity-gap-in-developing -countries/, accessed October 1, 2020.

23 https://www.theigc.org/project/the-agricultural-productivity-gap-in-developing -countries/, accessed October 3, 2020.

Chapter 2

MEASURING NIGERIA'S REVERSAL OF FORTUNE

Introduction

This chapter deploys different metrics of development to measure the reversal of fortune. Our basic assumption is that long-term development patterns of countries are driven by the rate of industrialization measured by increases in the share of manufacturing and share of manufacturing employment in GDP. A key feature of industrialized nations and those that achieved rapid growth in the last five decades is attainment of high rates of industrial growth. What sets these countries apart from laggard countries, especially in Africa, is the markedly higher rates of industrial development. In this chapter, we will use available indices of the industrial manufacturing sector of countries under examination in the book. We take the manufacturing sector as '*the main engine of fast growth*' (Kaldor, 1967: 48); this assertion is taken as causal as it characterizes not only the current most industrialized nations but also catching-up countries that have experienced rapid, sustained growth.[1]

The countries that made sustained efforts to acquire industrial technologies attained fast rates of economic growth while the other set of countries is poor and dependent on subsistent agriculture and natural resources. Industrialization became the main driver of economic development for the rich while resource dependence and weak technological base, among others, jeopardized the long-term growth of poor nations.

Our point of departure in measuring the divergence is the period after African countries attained political independence. It is after these countries gained independence that they can reasonably be expected to have the autonomy in deciding their own development agenda and in formulating supporting policies towards achieving development objectives.

We organize the rest of this chapter as follows. The next section articulates different dimensions of reversal, primarily technological, while country performance outcomes are measured using social, economic and health indicators. The final sections relate the reasons for the arrested development and the summing up.

Measuring Reversal

Economic reversal

We measure development of economies using comparative national income measures, the performance of the GDP. We track the trend in the GDP per capita and annual GDP growth for Nigeria compared to other countries from 1960 to 2020. Nigeria's reversal of fortune manifests in several dimensions, namely: economic, social, technological and industrial conditions. We examine the wide disparities in development metrics, particularly the levels and rates of growth of national incomes and Human Development Index (HDI). For example, among the countries we are examining in this book, the Republic of Korea (ROK) had the highest GDP/Capita in 2022 ($28,075), almost double that of the year 2000 ($15,414.29), two decades earlier. The figure increased by sevenfold in 40 years from 1980 ($3,679.11). On the contrary, the GDP/Capita for Nigeria $845 in 1980 declined to $290 20 years later and then rose to $2,424 in 2019.

Nigeria records a fall in GDP per capita between 2015 and 2020 from US$2,687 to US$2,097. This is a result of the cycles of crisis, recessions and instability in the country among many other internal political issues in the country. On the contrary, the GDP per capita figures show that South Korea had the highest GDP per capita of over US$30,000 in 2020. This implies a comparatively better standard of living for the people in South Korea. In general, while there was a broad increase in the values of the GDP per capita for all the countries from 1960 and 2020, Nigeria decelerated.

We next examined growth in GDP. Indonesia, India, Malaysia and Nigeria show a negative growth in 2020, only China experienced growth in 2020 among all the countries. Nigeria experienced the highest growth of 25 per cent in 1970, after this year there have been an oscillating increase and decrease in the growth level year after year from 4 per cent in 1980 to 8 per cent in 2010 and −1.8 per cent in 2020 showing decline in growth.

We measure quality of life using the UN's HDI; in 2019, Nigeria ranked 161st on the HDI. Clearly, without exception, minerals and oil producers in sub-Saharan Africa tend to have low HDIs, widespread inequality that is related closely to dependence on minerals and oil exports.

We are using sectoral patterns of change to study progress and regress. Structural change process is employed to study trends in sectoral performance using different indicators including industrial indicators, economic indicators, social inequality, health indicators and human development indicators. The annual sectoral data of Nigeria is compared with that of other countries including Vietnam, Malaysia, Indonesia, Korea, China, India and Turkey over the period 1960 to 2020.

Industrial indicators

We include several countries for comparison.[2] To analyse industrial progress and regress, we use the Productive Capacities Index (PCI) developed by UNCTAD as a proxy of industrialization. PCI has eight dimensions that encompass the contribution of natural resources as well as aspects based on acquired advantages. The results show a strong positive association between PCI and income levels of sample countries. Data for the analysis derive from WDI from 2000 to 2018.

To start, Nigeria's lack of industrial manufacturing dynamism is reflected in United Nations Conference on Trade and Development – UNCTAD's 2021 PCI. Nigeria ranked only 184th worldwide.[3] Comparatively, Mauritius (46th) and South Africa (74th) top in the continent. The PCI is a multidimensional index that measures productive capabilities of an economy. The dimensions of the index are human capital, natural capital, energy, transport, Information and Communication Technology (ICT), institutions, private sector and structural change. The human capital captures the education, skills and health conditions possessed by the population, the number of researchers and expenditure on research activities. Gender dimension is also included in the human capital variable while natural capital is based on the estimates of the availability of extractive and agricultural resources. Energy measures the availability, sustainability and efficiency of power sources, whereas transport measures the capability of a system network including roads, railways and air connectivity to take people or goods from one place to another.

ICT estimates the accessibility and integration of communication systems including fixed lines, phone users, internet accessibility and server security within the population. On the other hand, institutions measure political stability and efficiency through quality governance in terms of regulatory quality, effectiveness, success in fighting criminality, corruption and terrorism, and safeguard of freedom of expression. Private sector is defined by the ease of cross-border trade including import-export costs and support to businesses in terms of domestic credit and ease of starting and doing a business. The movement of labour and other productive resources from low-productivity to high-productivity economic activities, on the other hand, captures structural change. We extract PCI data from UNCTAD statistics database.

As mentioned earlier, PCI has eight dimensions that include contribution of natural resources as well as aspects based on acquired advantages. Hence, higher PCI value does not necessarily mean that the country has very developed industrial base. It might be due to the presence of large natural resources. For instance, the average PCI for China (34.61) during 2000 to 2018 is like that of Mauritius (34.48) during the same period. Therefore, it becomes imperative to analyse other indicators, and for this reason, we include MVA, employment share in the industry, growth of value added and export of high-tech products among others. Table 2.1 presents the indicators of industrialization along with PCI of all the sample countries.

These indicators of industrialization are consistent with that of the PCI. The average PCI in Nigeria is relatively low (20.54 per cent). This is consistent with other indicators of industrialization such as percentage value added to manufacturing (9.60 per cent), percentage employment in industry (11.48 per cent), annual growth of MVA (4.45 per cent) and percentage of medium and high-tech exports (38.35 per cent), which are also comparatively very low. Hence, PCI can be considered a reliable measure of industrialization. The MVA for China, for example, is 30.79 per cent, showing that Chinese industrial base is very strong, again consistent with its percentage contribution of value added to GDP. This is substantiated by PCI. The percentage of employment in manufacturing to the total, which is 26.53 per cent for China, compared with Nigeria and other African mineral producers, namely, Angola (8.11 per cent) and Botswana (19.39 per cent), is equally higher. The ROK has the highest PCI (41.94 per cent). The other indicators of industrialization for the country are as follows: Contribution of manufacturing to GDP (26.26 per cent), percentage employment in industry (26.01 per cent), annual growth of MVA (5.47 per cent) and percentage medium and high-tech exports (73.87 per cent).

All the countries that left Nigeria behind are manufacturing exporters while the country's main export products are crude petroleum oils and natural gas. The manufacturing sector is dominated by informal players that are mostly micro, small and medium enterprises. There is a thriving informal cross-border trade in light manufactured products and agricultural commodities within the ECOWAS region and with neighbouring countries in central Africa, but the value pales in comparison with Asian manufacturing powerhouses.

All indicators taken together, Nigeria has evidently suffered a reversal in the industrial capacity to produce, process and add value compared to its comparators (Figure 2.1). For example, Nigeria ranks 99th on UNIDO's Competitive Industrial Performance (CIP) index while South Africa ranked 52nd in 2020. The CIP Index measures industrial capacity on three metrics

Table 2.1. Industrialization and PCI.

Country	Average PCI	Percentage Contribution of MVA to GDP	Percentage Employment in Industry	Growth of MVA	Percentage Medium and High-tech Exports
Algeria	25.51	37.70	28.62	−0.08	2.18
Angola	20.27	4.55	8.11	6.56	9.04
Botswana	27.22	5.68	19.39	4.08	4.62
China	34.61	30.79	26.53	NA	56.71
DRC	18.87	16.88	8.74	1.12	NA
Cote d'Ivoire	21.74	13.59	11.85	4.07	30.35
Ghana	24.46	9.02	15.29	4.10	14.89
India	28.05	15.92	21.19	7.52	26.95
Kenya	22.95	10.47	6.98	3.15	20.31
Malaysia	32.81	25.39	29.09	5.04	66.14
Mauritius	34.48	15.29	30.39	1.84	7.84
Morocco	28.48	16.19	21.08	2.96	37.35
Mozambique	21.00	11.08	5.36	6.84	31.40
Nigeria	20.54	9.60	11.48	4.45	38.35
ROK	41.94	26.26	26.01	5.47	73.87
Rwanda	22.07	8.17	5.45	6.49	9.66
Senegal	23.90	18.12	12.73	3.26	19.01
South Africa	32.12	14.13	25.04	2.14	46.37
Sudan	21.21	6.72	14.37	4.66	NA
Thailand	31.25	28.71	21.37	3.87	60.99
Vietnam	28.51	16.79	20.19	9.16	33.04
Zambia	22.64	8.35	8.62	5.02	17.84

Source: Author's calculations.

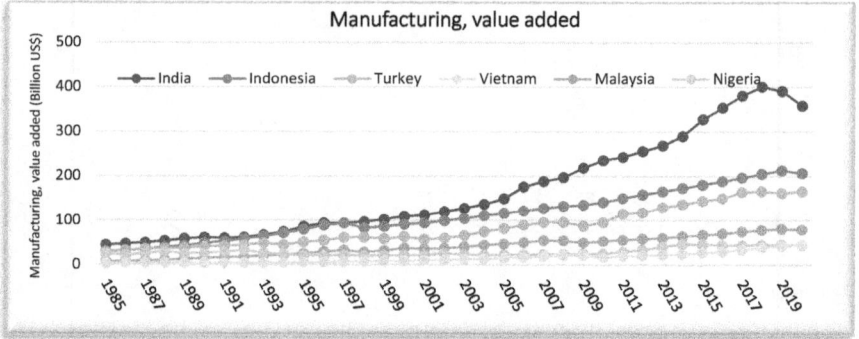

Figure 2.1. Manufacturing value added 1985–2019. Source: World Bank Indicators (2020).

namely: (i) the capacity to produce and export manufactured goods, (ii) technological deepening and upgrading and (iii) world impact. On average, industry in Africa generates merely US$700 of GDP per capita, less than a third of Latin America's output (US$2,500) and barely a fifth of East Asia's US$3,400. Nigeria's industry contribution to GDP is US$650, while manufacturing contribution is a mere 14.1 per cent, US$326.

Below is the evolution of MVA, showing Nigeria underperforms badly, it has basically stagnated.

Explaining Industrial Reversal

From our review in Chapter 1, export of fossil fuels and minerals, even when it leads to annual growth in GDP, does not translate to improved human capital while resource-dependent nations tend to do very little manufacturing value addition. Africa's industrial performance, measured in terms of IVA and MVA in GDP, has been lagging far behind comparator countries in Asia. MVA, which measures the degree of industrial processing, remains low in Africa, signifying the lack of industrial dynamism. This is consistent with the continent's reliance on export of its abundant natural resources, especially mineral and agricultural resources (UNCTAD, 2011). The phenomenon of Dutch disease only in part explains poor industrial growth. This is because whenever there is a resource boom, the extra revenue accruing from the sale of natural resources (oil and minerals) triggers appreciation of the real exchange rate and subsequent contraction of the traded sector (Corden and Neary, 1982; Corden, 1984). This is, however, a short-term phenomenon but with impacts that are long term in nature; the most insidious being the displacement of policy focus from tradeable sectors and, in particular, industrial manufacturing, which requires long-term vision, planning and consistent investment.

Not surprisingly, Nigeria ranks equally low on the Global Innovation Index at 118th with South Africa ranking the highest on the continent but only 58th worldwide.

Agriculture and manufacture share in GDP

We show the performance of the agriculture sector, industrial sector and manufacturing sector in terms of the contribution of each sector to GDP, see Appendices Figures A.1 and A.2. Agriculture shares in GDP for the comparator countries (China, Indonesia, South Korea and Vietnam) show a fall in values over the years from 1985 to 2020. Vietnam, for example, moved from 40 per cent agriculture share in GDP in 1985 to 15 per cent in 2020. This depicts a positive structural change and sectoral movement from agriculture to industry. On the other hand, the agriculture share in GDP for Nigeria remains consistently at the same level of 20 per cent to 25 per cent from 1985 to 2020. This implies that Nigeria remains an agrarian country and, consistent with this development, the level of value addition is low, limiting the share of off-farm processed agribusiness to GDP.

For industry share in GDP, China and Indonesia show higher shares over the years among the countries. The industrial share in GDP for South Korea has been at the same high level over the years. China and Indonesia show a slight decline in value from 2015 to 2020. Nigeria, on the other hand, shows a rise in value from 2015 to 2020. This explains that there is higher performance of the service sector in this period.

Figure 2.2 showsn irregular movement in the values of the manufacturing share in GDP across the countries. Indonesia had the highest value of 27 per

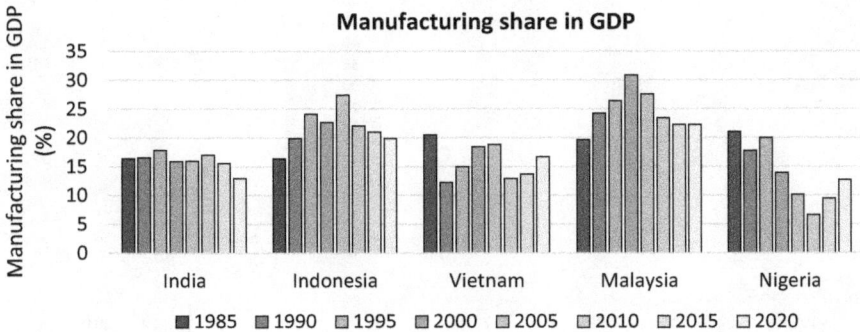

Figure 2.2. Percent manufacturing share in GDP. Source: World Bank Indicator (2021).

cent in 2005, Malaysia had the highest value of 31 per cent in 2000. Nigeria had its highest value of 21 per cent in 1985 and lowest value of 7 per cent in 2010, the value in 2020 is 13 per cent. In general, Nigeria shows poor performance in terms of manufacturing share in GDP. There has been a continuous rise in the MVA for all the countries over the year. India had the highest values of MVA from 1985 to 2020, while Vietnam and Nigeria are found at the bottom of the slope with values less than US$100 billion from 1985 to 2020. All the countries show irregular growth in MVA with a decline in 2020.

Social indicators and inequality

The distribution of income in a country is a measure of the level of development inequality in the country. The Gini index is used to measure the level of social inequality. Figure 2.3 shows the Gini index for Nigeria from 1985 to 2018 (chart on the left side) and its comparison with other countries (chart on the right side).

The chart on the left side is irregular downward sloping showing a decline and rise in the value of the Gini index. The index for Nigeria is within 35 to 53 which means there is high level of inequality in the country. Although the value of 2018 shows a decline in the level of inequality in the country. The comparison (right side chart) of the Gini index of Nigeria with other countries shows that Nigeria is one of the countries with high level of inequality. However, this inequality shows a decline in 2018.

Social and economic inequality matter for the economy. There is a strong relationship between inequality and slow growth, especially in poor countries.

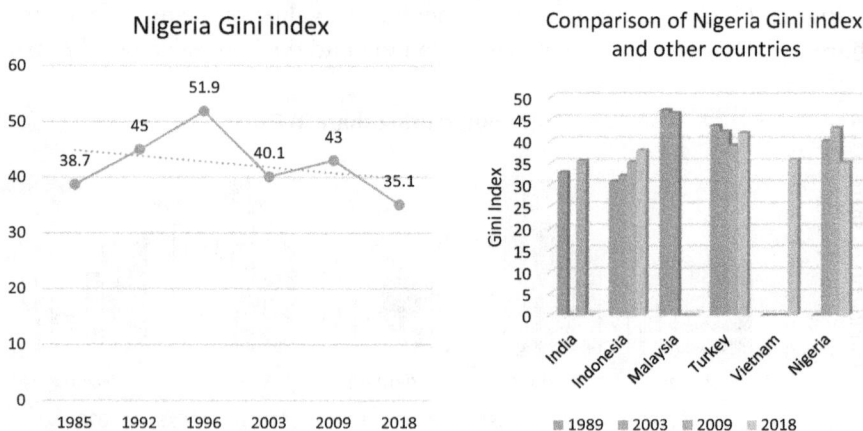

Figure 2.3. Gini index for Nigeria from 1985 to 2018 and its comparison with other countries. Source: World Bank estimate (2021).

Equally, there is a strong association between opportunity equality and human well-being reflected in better health and long life. Clearly, developing countries featuring high degrees of inequality tend to grow more slowly and will take a longer time to achieve desired development. What is described as destructive inequality has been shown to be growth-inhibiting – and growth is what relatively poor countries require the most. The effect of inequality on growth can be seen as a rough indicator of inequality of opportunity and limited social mobility in a particular setting, a phenomenon sometimes also referred to as 'destructive inequality'.

Health indicators

Income levels naturally determine spending on health and other social sectors. Countries with low and fluctuating income levels tend to experience constrained fiscal space and uncertainty in implementing developmental policies and plans. On the contrary, perspective planning and spending on the health sector could be possible with higher income levels. Consequently, the health sector is underserved, underfunded and, as such, underdeveloped in high rent-seeking economies. There have been several studies concentrating on rent-seeking and its impact on the health sector and human resource development; natural resource dependency inhibits human capital including education and life expectancy.[4] Clearly, the association of these health indicators with rent-seeking is broadly negative. The relationship of industrialization and development is well known. Industrialization, which enables countries to spend on the health and social sector, leads to better well-being outcomes for the people and human capital development.

We measure health and well-being using Global Hunger Index (GHI), health expenditure and the percentage of people undernourished (see Figure 2.4). The charts show that Nigeria's hunger index scores ranging from 28 to 32.5 (first chart). This places Nigeria's hunger level at 'serious'. Furthermore, Nigeria falls at number 103 among countries under hunger (second chart) indicating serious hunger. The third chart shows the percentage change in the GHI, Vietnam shows the highest decline in the hunger index with a percentage change of −48.3 per cent between 2000 and 2020. Nigeria also shows a reduction in the GHI with a percentage change of −28.4 per cent between 2000 and 2020. However, despite the decline, the country is still experiencing serious hunger.

Figure 2.4 showing the percentage of undernourished in the population shows that there has been a decline in the percentage of the population undernourished for the comparator countries (China, Vietnam, Indonesia and India between 2000 and 2020). Nigeria, on the other hand, shows

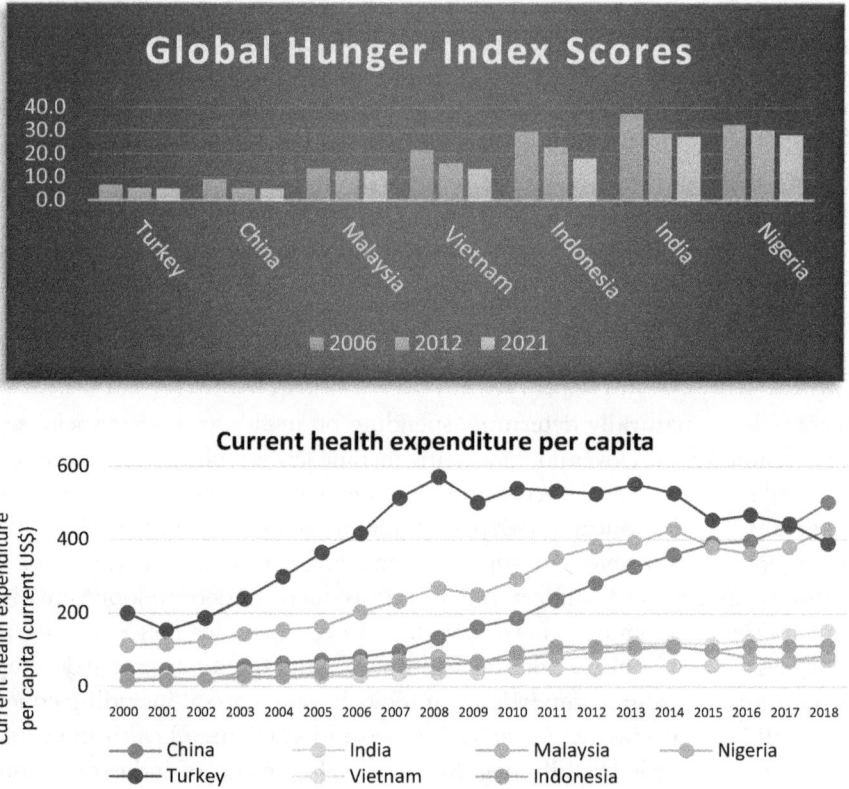

Figure 2.4. Health indicators. Source: World Bank estimate (2021).

increase in the percentage of the population undernourished from 8.8 per cent in 2013–2015 to 14.6 per cent in 2018–2020. In terms of per capita health expenditure, the second chart in figure 2.4 shows that over the years, the Nigerian government spent the lowest amount on the health sector compared to other countries, with per capita expenditure less than US$200 from year to year from 2000 to 2018.

Human development indicators

Figure 2.5 shows the human development indicators reflecting the overall level of development. The chart on the left side shows the HDI while the chart on the right shows the human capital index. Nigeria has the lowest HDI with values ranging from 0.4 to 0.5 over the years from 2003 to 2017. This implies that in terms of health (life expectancy at birth), knowledge and standard of living, Nigeria is still on average, and thus, a developing country.

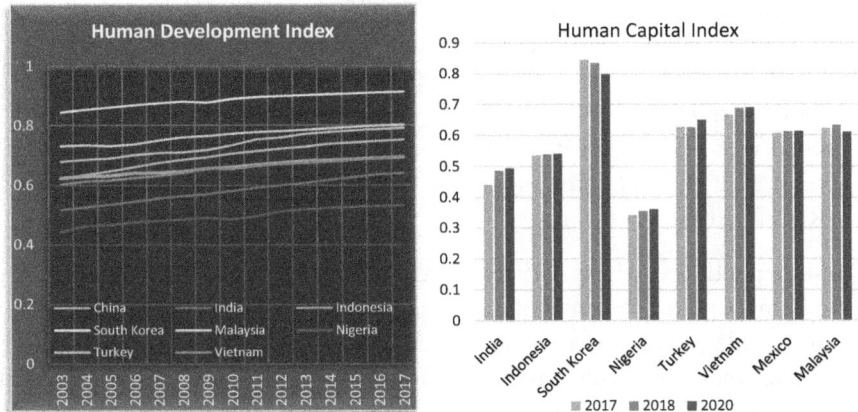

Figure 2.5. Human Development Indicators. Source: Human Development Index (UNDP); World Bank Health Nutrition and Population (2021).

South Korea, however, tops the chart with a HDI ranging from 0.84 to 0.92. Nigeria also has the least performance in terms of human capital development with a human per capita index of 0.34 to 0.36. Although there were slight increases in the values of Nigeria's HDI and HDI from 2003 to 2017, these increases are very minimal.

Around 60 per cent of youth are unemployed;[5] social and physical infrastructures are dysfunctional; and an unprecedented increase in crimes, insecurity and conflicts. This sad state of affairs has largely been blamed on the abuses of income generated from natural resources course.

In a 16-year period between 1980 and 1996, Nigeria's poverty level rose from 28 to 66 per cent. GDP per person in 1982 was US$860, it declined to US$280 by 1996. By 2020 this increased to 83 million Nigerians live in poverty while the projected poverty profile is estimated to increase to 90 million, or 45 per cent of the population, in 2022. Income reversal means that poverty and inequality have worsened over time. Nigeria sinks deeper into the mire of penury from the pillage of its common property. The population of poor people in Nigeria exceeds the total population of South Africa, Namibia, Botswana, Lesotho, Mauritius and Eswatini combined.

Explaining the Reversal

This book builds on earlier studies that came to the clear conclusion that industrialization processes stalled in most sub-Saharan African countries.[6]

> The countries that manage to pull out of poverty and get richer are those
> that can diversify away from agriculture and other traditional products.
> As labor and other resources move from agriculture into modern eco-
> nomic activities, overall productivity rises, and incomes expand. The
> speed with which this structural transformation takes place is the key
> factor that differentiates successful countries from unsuccessful ones.
> (Rodrik, 2014: 1)[7]

Post-independence when African governments initiated their autonomous
development plans, the onset of industrial plans began with the establishment
of large-scale public investments. These include iron and steel, aluminium,
cement and sugar factories all of which failed (Oyelaran-oyeyinka, 2016). Most
of the enterprises neither broke even nor made profit. Some never took off and
became 'White Elephants'. The idea of re-investing surplus cash/profit in the
acquisition of technological capabilities and skills required to adapt, operate
and maintain the imported technology in use did not arise. Technical management agreement was poorly prepared and did not include explicit clause
on technological capability acquisition. This was the case with the Nigeria's
Federal Superphosphate Fertilizer Company in Kaduna, Nigeria. While it
made provision for technical training for plant operation and maintenance,
within 10 years, 80 per cent of trained technical staff had left. The implementation monitoring process was poorly implemented. Knowing fully well
the state of power supply in Nigeria, no alternative was provided especially
during the performance guarantee test period. The soundness of the system
was therefore never established and the sources of the enormous technical
problems that manifested later could not be specifically located. Due to the
combination of these factors, plant availability and capacity utilization were
low right from the start. It would seem that poor preparation for the investment process planted the seed of future technical failures. The plant malfunc-
tioned badly, and the situation got worse with the departure of the Japanese
technical team. Eventually, the sulphuric acid plant was shut down, while the
rest operated poorly. The above more or less sums up the industrial ecosystem
in the country.

In sum, Nigeria embarked on an industrialization pathway, but the process
was arrested, and economic regress led to a reversal as the country underwent
an industrial crisis.

White Elephants and sunk costs

In Nigeria, the industrial landscape is littered with *White Elephants*. The term
'White Elephant' has its origins traced to East Asia where populations of

Asian elephants have lived closely with a human settlement for many centuries. Ancient kingdoms in East Asia regarded White Elephants as sacred animals and had (and still have in the case of kingdoms in Thailand and Myanmar) laws protecting the animals. Only the extremely wealthy individuals in a kingdom were able to own a White Elephant and, in most cases, only the monarch owned these animals. While ownership of a White Elephant commanded great respect in the kingdom, the owners of these animals had to incur great expenses to maintain the elephants that required huge amounts of forage. Therefore, in these, a gift of a White Elephant was usually seen as both a blessing and a curse; a blessing because a White Elephant was a sacred animal and a curse because maintenance cost was extremely expensive for an animal which had little (if any) practical use.

Take the case of ALSCON. ALSCON was once Nigeria's only aluminium steel plant. It is located in the city called Ikot Abasi. ALSCON was the community's second largest employer after the local council. ALSCON hired 1,800 direct natives while over 2,500 others worked for support services companies. Along with these jobs, the community also lost power supply after its closure in September 2014, since ALSCON had served as an electricity power source. In 1999, ALSCON satisfied Nigeria's aluminium needs of less than 20 per cent if its total production while generating US$324 million revenue from exporting the remaining 80 per cent aluminium products according to Nigeria's Bureau of Public Enterprises.

During the dictatorship of General Sani Abacha, the Nigerian government commissioned German provider of industrial services Ferrostaal AG and US company Reynolds International to build the aluminium smelter plant for US$3.2 billion. Though operations began in late 1998, they were halted in May 1999 due to insufficient working capital and gas supply. Ferrostaal maintained the plant in functional mode until operations restarted in 2006.

By 2003 when ALSCON was placed for sale, its asset base had depreciated by a third to US$1.03 billion, according to an audit report by PricewaterhouseCoopers. By 2012, ALSCON's value had plummeted by about 98 per cent to US$73 million. Since 2007, ALSCON's aluminium production under RUSAL never exceeded 11.4 per cent of its 193 metric tons installed capacity attained in 2012. In 2008, the smelter operated only operated at 4.97 per cent of capacity and RUSAL reported a loss of US$49.9 million, up from a $0.87 million loss the previous year. The 2012 income statement showed a loss of US$22.97 million. RUSAL's director, public/government relations, Tatyana Smirnova, attributed the huge losses to high production costs, despite alleged massive asset stripping by RUSAL.

A quote from lead director of Nigeria's Centre for Social Justice, a civil society group committed to promoting economic rights, sums up the conundrum.

'It's intriguing why the Nigerian government would invest US$3.2 billion of taxpayers' money to build ALSCON, only to be contented with a paltry 22.7% of a fair value of US$1.03 billion from a foreigner, against a 37.3% offer by an indigenous bidder.'

Summing Up

This chapter deploys several indicators to measure the phenomenon of development reversal and progress. The growth literature has shown that countries do experience dramatic reversals due to remote causes dating back to colonial experiences and more immediate causes such as we analysed for Nigeria in comparative perspective with Asian countries. Several African countries have experienced circular development changes due to external shocks including pandemics and oil and commodity price crashes. This book systematically analyses the developmental reversal experience of Nigeria since the post-independence period. We used several metrics of industrialization to demonstrate the notion that Nigeria's poor industrial progress has led to its poor social and economic growth.

Economic history shows that whereas countries move easily from the lowest levels of development to a next higher one, graduation into more advanced groups requires the mastery of more complex technological knowledge domain. We show that Nigeria's catch-up effort was derailed by several factors, including its damaging resource dependence and mismanagement of industrialization investments. Nigeria clearly underestimated the massive coordination efforts required to mitigate both market failure and government failure simultaneously. While the country developed an industrial policy and put in place development plans, it clearly failed to anticipate the scale effects, finance of the thresholds of scientists and engineers, and investment to close the huge deficit of domestic knowledge and physical infrastructure.

Notes

1 The Growth Report (2008).
2 Algeria, Angola, Botswana, China, Cote d'Ivoire, DRC, Ghana, India, Kenya, Malaysia, Mauritius, Morocco, Mozambique, Nigeria, Republic of Korea, Rwanda, Senegal, South Africa, Sudan, Thailand, Vietnam and Zambia.
3 https://unctad.org/system/files/official-document/aldc2020d2_en.pdf, p. 17.
4 Stijns (2006); Aljarallah (2020).
5 National Bureau of Statistics (2019), "Nigerian Gross Domestic Product Report." https://www.nigerianstat.gov.ng/
6 Wangwe (2014); Rodrik (2014); Newfarmer et al. (2019); UNIDO (2016); UNCTAD (2015).
7 https://drodrik.scholar.harvard.edu/files/dani-rodrik/files/globalization_structural _change_productivity_growth_with_africa_update.pdf

Chapter 3

EVOLUTION AND STRUCTURE OF THE NIGERIAN ECONOMY

Introduction

Forty years ago, Nigeria's income was six times that of China. In 2019, Chinese income became almost 3.45 times that of Nigeria. The widening disparities between the country and comparators including those we are studying in this book are truly shocking to say the least. There are other unsavoury evidences of development regress. Around 60 per cent of youth are unemployed; social and physical infrastructures are dysfunctional; and the country is in the throes of an unprecedented increase in crimes, insecurity and conflicts.

In a 16-year period between 1980 and 1996, Nigeria's poverty level rose from 28 to 66 per cent. By 2020, this increased to 83 million Nigerians living in poverty while the projected poverty profile is estimated to increase to 90 million, or 45 per cent of the population, in 2022. Nigeria has clearly experienced a development reversal and largely slipped into underdevelopment. Stagnation in income means that poverty and inequality worsened over time. Nigerians' daily sinks deeper into the mire of penury. The population of poor people in Nigeria exceeds the total population of South Africa, Namibia, Botswana, Lesotho, Mauritius and Eswatini combined. Nigeria has entered a development reversal.

The COVID-19 pandemic and its historic impact has combined with the widespread food inflation to slow economic progress including reversing gains on poverty reduction. The pandemic has been extremely disruptive in the long term as the fiscal space shrank with diminished development financing. Regardless of the sector's source of revenue, countries suffered huge gaps in income. Oil-dependent countries like Nigeria suffered a momentous price collapse, from US$61.5 in December 2019 to US$23.2 in March 2020. Overnight, the country's tax base shrank as domestic companies and sectors lost revenue; notably hard hit were the tourism and mineral and commodity sectors.

According to a recent World Bank report[1] following a 6.1 per cent year-on-year contraction in the second quarter of the pandemic year, 2020, Nigeria's economy contracted by 3.6 per cent in quarter three but subsequently expanded by 0.1 per cent in the last quarter of 2020. The economy moved out of recession faster than expected but growth remains sluggish.

The crash of oil prices transmitted its impact through economic growth, constrained fiscal space and through direct effects on prices and activity for both importers and exporters; indirect effects via trade and other commodity markets; monetary and fiscal policy responses; and investment uncertainty. Through these channels, oil prices can also have immediate repercussions. For example, in Nigeria, 'After rising throughout 2020, inflation accelerated from 15.7 per cent year-on-year in December to 17.3 per cent in February 2021 – its highest level since April 2017. The surge in food prices persisted as the pandemic and security problems continued to disrupt the food supply chain, while currency weaknesses and foreign exchange restrictions added upward pressure.'[2]

As an exporting economy with drastically reduced revenue, the country was forced by financial constraints to do a downward adjustment of both government spending and imports abruptly in the short term. Nigeria has relied on the trading and export of crude petroleum and agricultural raw materials for decades. With its abundance of natural resources, it is a key player in the West African subregion and Africa's largest oil exporter and natural gas reserve. This reliance on the easy path, or 'low-hanging fruit', has proved to be a non-optimal choice. As oil exports remained the mainstay of the economy, global oil price volatility continues to influence its growth trajectory. Nigeria's gross domestic product (GDP) grew at 7 per cent on the average between 2000 and 2014, a slump in oil price during the period 2014–2016 and consequent production shocks resulted in a GDP growth rate of 2.7 per cent in 2015 and the country's first recessionary contraction in 25 years (to the magnitude of 1.6 per cent) in 2016. Even though oil GDP growth stabilized in 2019, industrial performance was slowed by its weak energy sector. Overall, the COVID-19 global pandemic, the Russian–Ukraine war and climate change, especially the effects on agriculture, impinge on oil revenues, will raise government debt levels, slow domestic production and further dampen GDP growth rate.[3] We organize the rest of the chapter as follows: We sketch out the evolution of Nigeria's squandering of its oil wealth and how it has failed to achieve neither agricultural nor industrial revolution. The section that follows narrates the slow structural shift of the economy from agriculture to industry compared to selected Asian countries such as Malaysia. The final section provides a summing up.

Nigeria's production and export structure has remained less diversified relative to comparator countries with lesser natural and human resource endowments. Its export of petroleum and petroleum products, which account for about 90 per cent of total export volume, indicates the dominance of extractive sectors – usually characterized by low labour absorption rates and weak linkages with other sectors. The domestic market also suffers from spatial fragmentation with limited connective infrastructure.[4] Furthermore, gains from oil and gas exports tend to be eroded by exchange rate fluctuations, thereby limiting the competitiveness of other sectors of the economy.

History matters and progress is path-dependent

The squandering of the country's riches and lost time and opportunities will be difficult to recover. Consider the Nigerian oil and gas sector as an example of a colossal opportunity lost. The extant weak technological base is exerting incalculable damage. Nigeria has the second-largest oil reserves in Africa and yet is a net importer of Liquefied Petroleum Gas and myriad petroleum products. It has the ninth largest natural gas reserves and yet barely has enough gas to generate 5 MW of electricity. According to OPEC, the country exported US$27.73 billion worth of petroleum products in 2020, while the value of the country's petroleum imports in 2020 was US$71.285 billion. The country has an installed refining capacity of 445,000 barrels per day from four refineries that refined zero barrels of oil in 2020 because the refineries have broken down and are inoperable. In a country with the necessary metallic and chemical sector capabilities to produce, maintain and innovate, this situation will be unthinkable.

Again, while the country has massive gas reserves, its citizens have no access to electricity; Nigeria is among the top counties in the world with the highest number of portable generators. Dependence on imported fuel has put serious pressure on Nigeria's foreign exchange at the expense of other productive sectors of the economy. In the face of the Ukraine–Russia war, with oil prices soaring to 100 $/barrel, Nigeria cannot meet its OPEC quotas due to unprecedented crude oil theft and divestment from the upstream oil sector. Nigeria has proven gas reserves that can potentially provide a Gross Value Added of US$18.3 billion annually and 6.5 million full-time jobs to the domestic economy (PwC). Flared gas alone can power 5.3 GW of power through Modular IPPs and decentralized grids.

Due to a weak industrial base, Nigeria's oil and gas make only a small contribution to GDP, despite generating the bulk of export earnings, as it is a highly technology and capital-intensive industry that employs few people. We do not produce the materials and equipment used in the exploration and production domestically. There is minimal domestic manufacturing input in the oil sector, especially in the oil product refining. The local content makes up about 5 per cent in goods and services.

In sum, Nigeria's oil discovery and the dependence on this resource exerted a strong exclusionary effect on industrialization. It did so by displacing the tradeable sectors, especially industrial manufacturing, with the resultant outcome of arresting structural transformation of the economy over time. Second, dependence on crude oil led to the collapse of the agriculture sector, which successive governments have tried to restore. Nigeria in the 1950s/60s produced over 40 per cent of global oil palm; in 2022, it produced 2 per cent while Malaysia and Indonesia between them command over 80 per cent. Again, over the last 60 years, Nigeria lost massive opportunities to transform its agricultural sector, as did comparator countries in Asia such as India, Malaysia, Indonesia and Vietnam. By so doing, it lost time required for the long learning dynamics that are required for mastering technologies. The country has fallen far behind in competitiveness in key sectors compared with where it was as a strong global player in the 1950s/1960s.

The rising rate of open unemployment, widening inequality and deepening poverty levels all indicate the imperative to increase productivity and investment in Nigeria's non-oil sectors so as to foster inclusive growth. Countries that achieved optimal structural transformation did so by transitioning from low-productivity agricultural to high-productivity manufacturing activities.[5]

Even though Nigeria is the largest economy in Africa with a GDP of US$477.38 billion in current prices as of 2022 (IMF, 2024), its lower-middle income status (with per capita income of US$2,028.2) is indicative of its relatively low level of economic development among the wider comity of nations. While the Nigerian economy is endowed with both natural and human resources, it has remained a mono-economy, based on its specialization as a major crude oil producer and exporter. The oil sector contributed around 8.5 per cent to GDP in 2021 but 90 per cent of export revenue; it is the major source of foreign exchange earnings. Nigeria possesses a dual economic structure whereby a modernized economy exists side by side with the traditional sector. With respect to market size, recent estimates indicate that Nigeria is home to the largest number of citizens in Africa, with an estimated population size of over 220 million people (UNFPA, 2024).

Regional Social and Economic Disparities

The country has grown apart. Social, economic and regional inequalities are widening while poverty is far more prevalent in the Northern part of the country.

Number of people living in extreme poverty in Nigeria from 2016
to 2025
(in 1,000s)

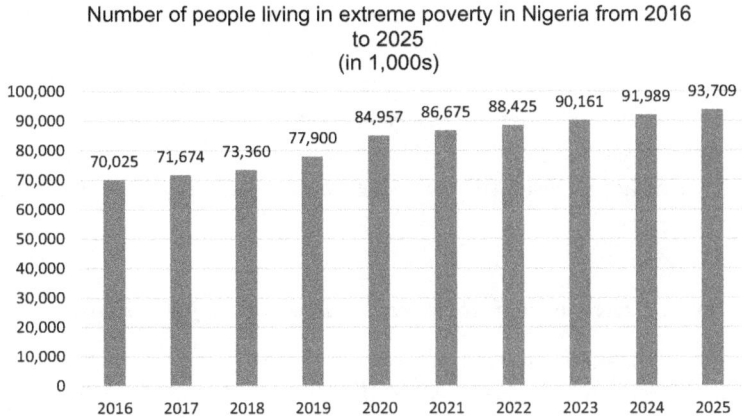

Figure 3.1a. Socio-economic outcomes of the reversal of fortune. Source: Authors plot WDI.

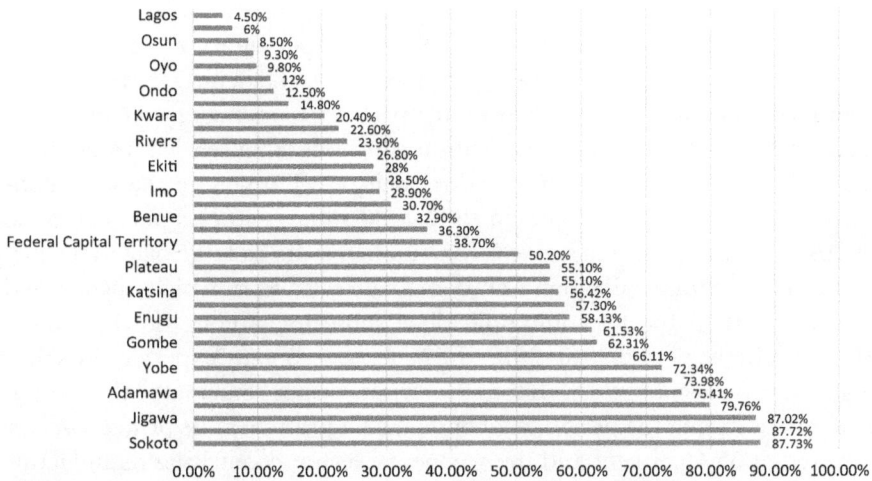

Figure 3.1b. Nigerian states – share of people in poverty (%) as of 2019. Source: Author's plot.

Nigeria achieved neither a Green nor an Industrial Revolution

Sequel to political independence in 1960, Nigeria evolved into an agrarian-based economy exporting agricultural produce such as palm oil, cocoa, groundnuts among others. Nonetheless, with the discovery of crude oil and the potential economic benefit inherent in the petroleum sector, Nigeria shifted its external trade focus to crude oil production. This led to a neglect of its agriculture sector, a paradox of a sort, a former cash crop exporter becoming a net food importer. Generally, the Nigerian economy remains vulnerable to shocks from the global primary commodity market. For instance, the economy booms whenever oil price surges and production remains unaffected; a case in point is the oil boom experience of the early 1970s. The economy is also adversely affected when oil prices and demand plunge. Recent examples include the recessionary episode, which occurred in 2016 following a global oil price crash that lowered the inflow of foreign exchange earnings and government finances.

Deindustrialization and slow structural transformation

The structure of Nigeria's economy for most of the past decades has remained largely skewed to the primary sector. The primary sector contributed most to nominal output when compared to the secondary and tertiary sectors in periods 1960–1970, 1971–1980, 1981–1990, 1991–2000 and 2001–2009. The output contribution of the secondary sector consistently declined on the average from 15.6 per cent during 1971–1980 to 5.7 per cent during the period 2001–2009. This trend suggests that Nigeria experienced a process of deindustrialization since the 1970s. In addition, the trend depicts that structural transformation of the economy from the primary to secondary sector is slow or nonexistent. By contrast, the sectoral contribution of services to nominal output has been on the rise for over three decades. The service sector contributed an average of 24.3 per cent in 1981–1990 and rose to 29.5 per cent in the 2000s. The rising trend in services contribution is due in large part to the privatization, commercialization and deregulation policies, which encouraged new entrants to the telecommunications subsector, among other factors.[6] However, in the period 2010–2018, the Nigerian economy experienced a dramatic structural change – such that the tertiary sector contributed the most to real output during the period, a whopping 52.5 per cent. The primary sector followed at 35.4 per cent and the secondary sector, comprising manufacturing and construction, constituted the least productive sector at 12.2 per cent.

We may also classify the Nigerian economy into the oil and non-oil sectors. This classification is relevant based on the heavy reliance of Nigeria on the crude oil sector. This fact may be attributed to the weak linkage of the oil sector to other sectors of the economy in terms of its low value addition.[7]

Structural Transformation and the Nigerian Economy

The concept of structural change differs across several spectrums. For instance, it could mean a shift in the share of GDP contributed by the agricultural sector to non-agricultural sectors such as industry and services. According to Kuznets (1966), there are structural change patterns that characterize a country's structural transformation. The patterns include (i) prioritizing the industrial sector over the agricultural sector, (ii) urbanization and (iii) increased employment generation by manufacturing industries. The United Nations Industrial Development Organization, UNIDO (2013) describes structural change as 'the ability of an economy to continuously generate new dynamic activities characterized by advanced productivity and increasing returns to scale'. For many fast-developing countries, manufacturing forms the core of such activities. Also, evidence from the growth experiences of emerging economies such as Brazil, India and China suggests that countries which possess the ability to develop their industrial base are characterized by increased productivity and sustained economic growth.

Structural transformation infers changes in productivity rates across sectors and the varying demand patterns, which could foretell the distribution of resources among sectors. For less developed countries such as those in parts of the Middle East, Latin America and sub-Saharan Africa, with an exception of South Africa, structural transformation to them refers to the latter. For instance, Nigeria experiences a switch in business cycles between booms and recession indicating that the problem is not commencing growth processes but its sustenance. Nigeria has not experienced a structural transformation type that involves the shift from a small-scale rural and urban self-employed and agriculture-based economy to a larger-scale, industrialized economy; such that has characterized the rapid growth of industrializing economies over the past decades. Although she has witnessed rapid GDP growth over the last 10 years particularly after rebasing its GDP in 2014 (except during the economic crisis of 2018 and the recent recession beginning from late 2015 caused by the fall in oil prices), Nigeria is rather a typical example of an economy experiencing growth without industrialization.[8]

Given the meso-level methodology applied in this book, we review the process of Nigeria's structural change that shows the trends in the country's sectoral performance. This analysis shows individual sector contribution to total output, that is, GDP. The relative productivity of the different sectors in comparator countries is used as a benchmark to describe the link between the level of industrialization, structural change and economic growth. We compare Nigeria with a few countries including Bangladesh, Indonesia, Malaysia and Vietnam. We use the annual sectoral data of these comparator countries over the period 1960 to 2021 (depending on data availability) against Nigerian data to illustrate the basic relationship between industrialization, structural change and economic growth.

Figure 3.2 presents the agricultural share in GDP across four countries.[9] The share of agriculture in GDP for Bangladesh, Indonesia and Malaysia shows a significant decline over the period. However, for Nigeria, the decline

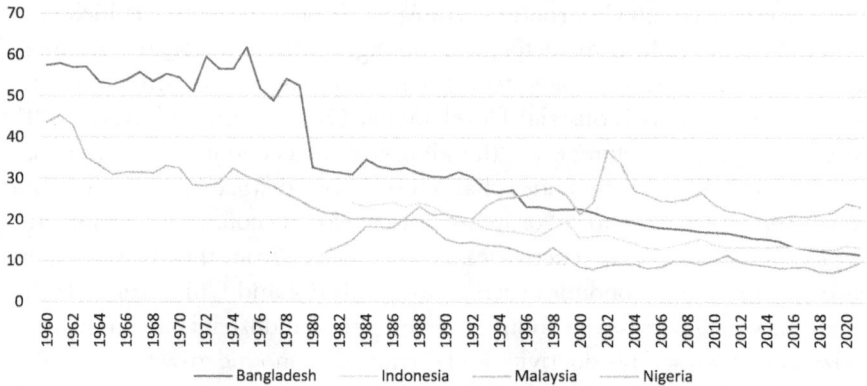

Figure 3.2. Agriculture, value added in Bangladesh, Indonesia, Malaysia and Nigeria (% of GDP). Source: World Development Indicators (WDI), The World Bank Group (2022).

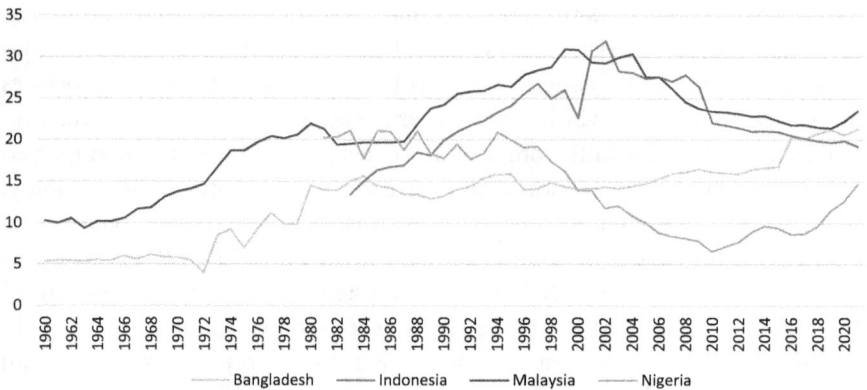

Figure 3.3. Manufacturing, value added in Bangladesh, Indonesia, Malaysia and Nigeria (% of GDP). Source: World Development Indicators (WDI), The World Bank Group (2022).

is less significant with its experience of a slight increase in 2018 which could be credited to the economic diversification programme implemented after the fall in oil prices that led to the economic recession in late 2015.

In Figure 3.3, which depicts manufacturing share in GDP across the four countries, between 1960 and 2021, we notice Malaysia and Indonesia share of manufacturing declining steadily about 2002 after periods of relative increase. All three countries have manufacturing as a percentage of GDP about 20 per cent in 2021, while Nigeria's is at 14.6 per cent. In contrast to the other three countries where manufacturing's contribution was stronger early on, Nigeria showed a volatile decline but began to rise in 2010.

Figure 3.4 shows contributions of services sector to GDP of the countries. The charts indicate an increase in the services sector share to GDP in all four countries, but a slight decrease in Nigeria in 2018. Overall, the economies were more service-orientated, having the service sector recording the greatest increase among other sectors considered, a phenomenon of premature deindustrialization of developing countries.

Furthermore, some studies suggest that structural changes can be measured using the GDP per capita (GDP per worker) indicator, which measures the productivity of a country with respect to its population (Herrendorf, Rogerson, and Valentinyi, 2013; Busse, Erdogan, and Mühlen, 2019). This coincides with one of the four drivers of structural change studied by van Neuss (2019) – changes in income, sectoral prices, input–output linkages as well as changes in comparative advantages via globalization and trade. In Figures 3.5 and 3.6, data on GDP per capita and GDP growth rate are juxtaposed in order to make observable any significant structural transformation leading to growth or the case of economic growth without structural transformation.

We consider GDP per capita for all five countries, including Vietnam, in Figure 3.5. With the exception of Malaysia, the four countries tend to have similar GDP per capita trends over the years. By 2021, Nigeria with US$2,085 is closest to Bangladesh, which has US$2,503. Malaysia's performance exceeds that of the other four countries, with GDP per capita rising over time and reaching US$11,371 in 2021.

In terms of annual GDP growth, we note volatility among all countries. However, Nigeria has longer periods of negative growth rates than the other countries under analysis.

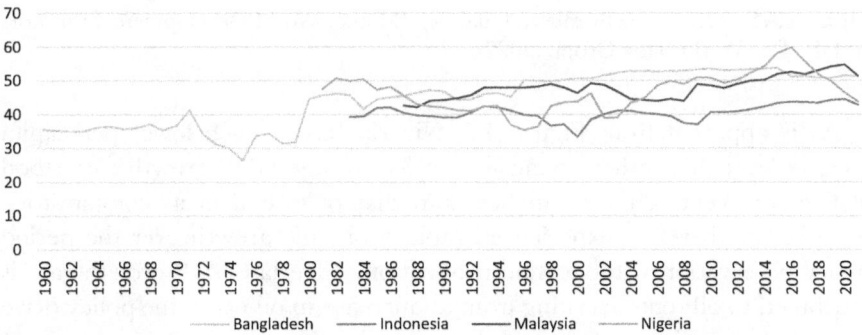

Figure 3.4. Services, value added in Bangladesh, Indonesia, Malaysia and Nigeria (% of GDP). Source: World Development Indicators (WDI), The World Bank Group (2022).

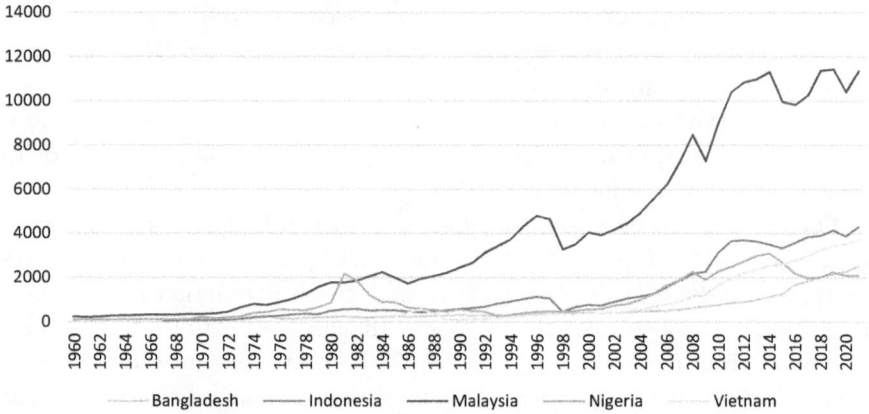

Figure 3.5. GDP per capita (current US$). Source: World Development Indicators (WDI), The World Bank Group (2022).

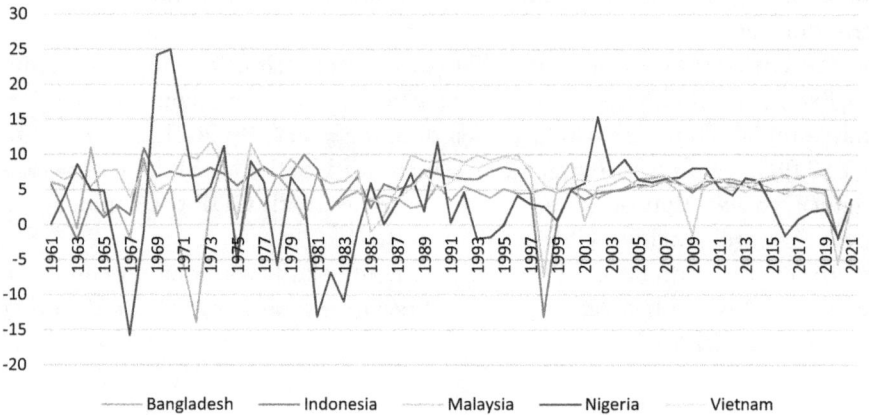

Figure 3.6. GDP growth rate (annual %). Source: World Development Indicators (WDI), The World Bank Group (2022).

As is apparent from Figure 3.5, Nigeria has a much lower per capita income level than other countries, yet its average GDP growth rate stood at 6.26 per cent, a record higher than that of several of its comparators. Nigeria has therefore experienced rapid economic growth over the period under observation without industrialization. Nigeria's GDP growth rate is attributed to oil rents accruing from an increase in oil price, the policy drive towards economic recovery and diversification in manufacturing and agricultural output. Also, the convergence hypothesis which states that there will be a convergence of a country's economic growth rate towards its steady state depending on its level of technology could also explain Nigeria's observed growth rates. On the other hand, China and other dynamic Asian nations experienced economic growth accompanied by industrialization.

We attribute poor industrial dynamism to the failure of successive governments to diversify the economy towards more complex products and services in the domestic and export basket. Nigeria has remained highly specialized in primary commodities. Economic diversification can be internal, in terms of the trend in manufacturing output as a percentage of GDP, and external in terms of exports diversification. Figure 3.7 illustrates a persistent decline in the trend of industry output as a percentage of GDP since 1981. Furthermore, using the IMF Theil Index (1962–2010) and UNCTAD export concentration index (1995–2018) to measure export diversification, there is evidence that over the period 1962–2010, Nigeria's exports have remained poorly diversified (see Figures 3.8a and 3.8b). The UNCTAD export concentration index presents some glimpse of hope as Nigeria's exports became only marginally better diversified. In this regard, the export concentration index was 0.85 in 1995 but by 2018 was better diversified at 0.79.

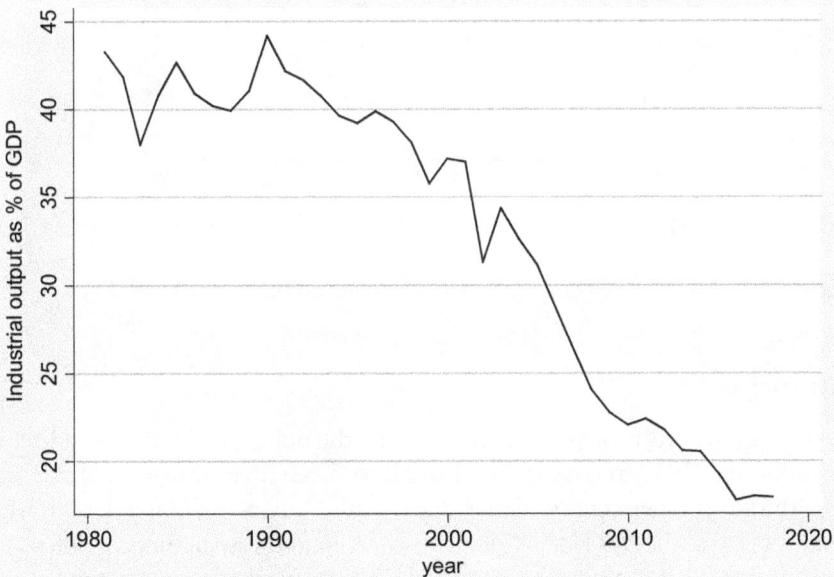

Figure 3.7. Industrial output as percentage of GDP (1981–2018). Source: Author's computation based on data from CBN statistical bulletin.

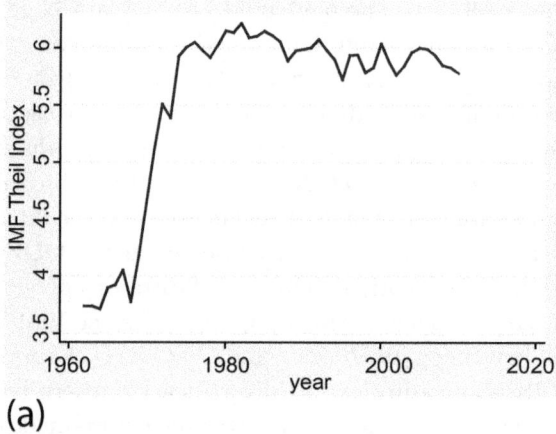

(a)

Figure 3.8a. IMF Theil Index. Source: IMF.

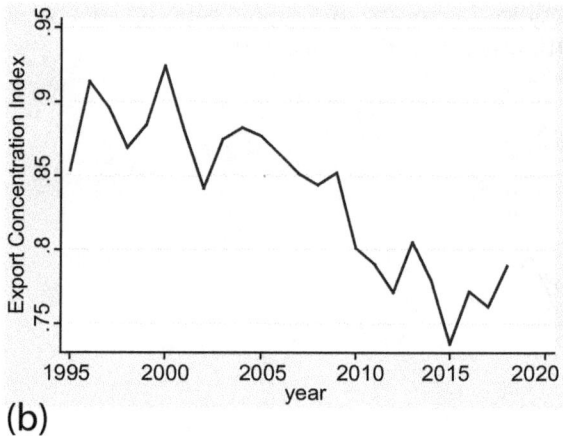

(b)

Figure 3.8b. UNCTAD export diversification index. Source: UNCTAD.

Summing Up

According to a study of 'growth miracles' by the published by the World Bank in 2008, only 13 countries in the world have been able to sustain an annual growth rate of 7 per cent or higher since 1950. Only two countries, both with small populations and highly idiosyncratic economic structures – Botswana and Oman – are among the group of 13 that have not grown because of industrialization.[10] Additionally, countries and regions that have de-industrialized or prematurely de-industrialized have experienced a slowdown in economic growth or, at worst, declining economic growth.

In this chapter, we sketched out Nigeria's poorly achieved structural transformation. The underlying reason is that the country did not sustain investment in learning and skills required to move from the lowest domain of artisanal and indigenous manufacturing to the domain of modern manufacturing. The necessary policies were put in place, the initial investments were made in capital stock such as oil refineries, aluminium and so on but all were moribund due to poor management and corruption. Several ingredients required to move from an agrarian to a modern industrial country did not materialize. On the contrary, the Asian comparators invested in higher knowledge domains, to master design and re-engineering of products and innovate. Nigeria did not make industrial progress sufficient to become competitive in manufacturing because it neglected its science and technology tertiary education. This domain is where individuals are equipped with technical and analytical skills; the country did not make the requisite public sector investments into building basic R&D capabilities for standards, metrology and other infrastructure.

Notes

1 https://openknowledge.worldbank.org/bitstream/handle/10986/35342/9781464817144.pdf?sequence=10&isAllowed=y, accessed 30 June 2021.
2 https://openknowledge.worldbank.org/bitstream/handle/10986/35342/9781464817144.pdf?sequence=10&isAllowed=y, p. 36, accessed 30 June 2021.
3 World Bank (2019, 2022).
4 World Bank Group (2018a, 2018b).
5 UNECA and AU (2013); Oyelaran-Oyeyinka and Ola-David (2017).
6 Asaolu et al. (2005).
7 Hirschman (1958); Baldwin (1966).
8 Oyelaran-Oyeyinka and Ola-David (2017).
9 Vietnam is excluded from the analysis as data wasn't available for it across the three sectors considered.
10 The Growth Report (2008).

Part II

Chapter 4

VIETNAM AND NIGERIA: DIVERGENT PATHS TO ECONOMIC DIVERSIFICATION

Introduction

Vietnam exported an estimated US$348 billion worth of goods around the globe in 2020, a tenfold increase when compared with Nigeria's exports in the same year. That dollar amount reflects a 97.1 per cent gain since 2016 and a 31.5 per cent increase from 2019 to 2020. In macroeconomic terms, Vietnam's total exported goods represent 30.3 per cent of its overall Gross Domestic Product (GDP) for 2020 – US$1.148 trillion valued in Purchasing Power Parity. Given Vietnam's population of 97.4 million people, its total US$348 billion in 2020 exports translates to roughly US$3,600 for every resident in the Southeast Asian nation.

In contrast, Nigeria's total exports of around US$34 billion represent less than 8 per cent of its GDP of US$432.3 billion. Nigeria's revenue basket remains constrained due to its export revenue concentration (dependence on oil and few primary commodities), trade concentration (dependence on a few trading partners – China and Europe) and high food imports (with most processed foods coming from outside the continent) necessitating the need and urgency for both economic and trade diversification as well as food self-sufficiency.

Contrasting the two, what is important is that although Vietnam's export revenue came largely from non-oil products such as phones and electronics goods that it shipped to the world, it also remains a major exporter of agribusiness. Agribusiness products such as footwear and textiles totalling over US$30 billion are exported out of the country. This not only equals Nigeria's total oil revenue but also far exceeds the less than US$3 billion revenue that Nigeria received from shipping out raw leather, cocoa powder, sesame, cashew and mainly raw agricultural commodities, which would be converted into finished products and re-exported to Nigeria.[1]

This chapter compares the contrasting economic performance of Nigeria and Vietnam, particularly focussing on the question of successful horizontal diversification and what that means for industrialization. It shows how the two countries are similar in several respects, especially in their initial conditions. Agrarian origins were the starting point for both Nigeria and Vietnam, and agriculture contributes around one-third to one-quarter to the economy. It shows that the key distinction remains that of value addition in a sector that is usually considered to be not key to industrialization. Vietnam's significant level of value addition through processing of its raw agricultural products into finished products is a key distinguishing factor when compared with Nigeria, which perennially ships out raw agricultural products.

In Vietnam, the exports of processed agriculture products expanded over time driven by rice, cashew, coffee, fisheries, vegetables and fruits. Over time, Vietnam continued to diversify its agricultural exports to higher-value crops, including vegetables and fruits, to the extent that the export value of vegetables and fruits has now surpassed export earnings from traditional commodities, such as crude oil, rice and black pepper. Progressively, Vietnam's oil exports declined despite rising oil prices. While oil prices are up by 26.3 per cent (y/y), a substantial decline in volumes caused oil export earnings to contract by 27 per cent in the first four months of 2018.[2]

This is in sharp relief when compared with an oil-dependent and agricultural raw materials exporter like Nigeria, where the structure of the Nigerian economy demonstrates a weak structural transformation and poor diversification over time. At independence in 1960, agriculture was the major source of the country's revenue. Between 1960 and 1969, it accounted for 50 per cent of the country's GDP and provided 64.5 per cent of export revenue. Smallholder farmers remain the mainstay of agriculture labour force while agriculture is still Nigeria's largest sector employer of labour. Crop production accounted for 90 per cent of Nigeria's agricultural output between 2012 and 2018. In 2020, export revenue from agriculture was only 2 per cent while Nigeria imported food products, and revenue from oil export was close to 80 per cent. This clearly is a regress. It symbolizes the structural rigidity of the Nigerian economy.

The negative impacts of commodity price volatility in Nigeria are not a theoretical discussion. For example, the COVID-19 pandemic transmitted significant hardship to both the oil and the non-oil export sector in Nigeria. The country was projected to lose over US$110.8 million to cocoa and cashew exports (US$90 million) in 2020. Agricultural exports like cocoa, sesame and cashew exports are predicted to suffer due to the pandemic that has locked down economies of nations across the globe.[3] A fall in cocoa exports of over US$100 million is attributed to declining prices resulting from falling demand in Europe. Sesame exports proved more resilient as it recorded a smaller decline in prices resulting from its more diversified export markets.

The term structural transformation infers changes in productivity rates across sectors and the varying demand patterns which could foretell the distribution of resources among sectors. For instance, Nigeria stemming from its dependence on oil tends to experience a switch in business cycles between booms and recessions indicating that the problem is not commencing growth processes but its sustenance. Nigeria has not experienced a type of structural transformation that leads to the shift from small-scale rural and urban self-employed and agriculture-based economy, to a larger-scale, industrialized economy; a shift that has characterized the rapid growth of industrializing economies over the decades. Although Nigeria has witnessed rapid GDP growth over more than a decade, particularly after rebasing its GDP in 2014 (except during the economic crisis of 2018 and the recent recession beginning in late 2015 caused by the fall in oil prices), it is rather a typical example of an economy experiencing growth without industrialization (Oyelaran-Oyeyinka and Ola-David, 2017).

Twenty years after the Vietnam War ended in 1975, Vietnam's economy was *one of the poorest in the world*. By the mid-1980s, per capita GDP was around US$200 and US$300. Subsequently, through a series of economic and political reforms, the country adopted what it termed a 'socialist-orientated market economy'. Up until the 1980s, Vietnamese industries depended on aid from Soviet Union. After 1985, the industrial weaknesses were recognized and more autonomy was introduced to enhance efficiency, which resulted in market-orientated economy called 'Doi-Moi'. In this strategy, indicative planning, that is, coordination of private and public investment and macroeconomic management system was implemented. In this industrial policy, the shift was majorly towards small industries and exports than heavy industries. Today, Vietnam is one of the high-performing actors of the emerging markets. Its economic growth of 6–7 per cent rivals China, and its exports are worth as much as the total value of its GDP. It manufactures anything from Nike sportswear to Samsung. China, Vietnam and India became the most dynamic traders among all Asian economies. The development of regional value chains in office and telecom equipment highly contributed to the pace of growth of economies such as Vietnam. Vietnamese exports of office and telecom equipment have grown considerably, accounting for 23 per cent of Vietnamese exports in 2018, up from 1 per cent in 2008.[4]

Notably, Vietnam has imitated successful Asian countries such as Republic of Korea (ROK) by pushing into relatively more complex product categories at its income level while also mastering horizontal diversification through processing agricultural commodities for export. It therefore expanded its export basket and a move into higher-value crops. Exports of processed agriculture products expanded, driven by rice, cashew, coffee and fisheries. Importantly. Vietnam continues to diversify its agricultural exports to higher-value crops, including vegetables and fruits, which surged 42 per cent in 2017 and 29 per cent in in the first four months of 2018. The export value of vegetables and fruits has now surpassed export earnings from traditional commodities, such as crude oil, rice and black pepper. Progressively, oil exports declined despite rising oil prices. While oil prices are up by 26.3 per cent (y/y), a substantial decline in volumes caused oil export earnings to contract by 27 per cent in the first four months of 2018.[5]

Unlike Vietnam, Thailand and Malaysia for example, raw materials remain the bulk of exports from African countries like Nigeria. In terms of destinations, a number of African countries have diversified their trade partners. China and India recently overtook the United States as Africa's largest bilateral trade partners.

The rest of the chapter is organized as follows: in the next two sections we present a performance of the leading sectors in Vietnam and how it has modernized and closely integrated with the international value chains and markets. Nigeria on the contrary has failed to attain the desirable horizontal integration. Next, we present case studies of how the cocoa and cashew subsectors performed in the two countries. The final two sections tease out the factors responsible for the divergent evolutions and sums up.

Sector Growth and Performance

Agricultural exports continued to expand with increasingly diversified underlying export basket and a move into higher-value crops. Exports of agriculture products also continued to expand driven by rice, cashew, coffee, fisheries, vegetables and fruits. Importantly, Vietnam continues to diversify its agricultural exports to higher-value crops, including vegetables and fruits, which surged 42 per cent in 2017 and 29 per cent in 2018. The export value of vegetables and fruits has now surpassed export earnings from traditional commodities, such as crude oil, rice and black pepper. Meanwhile, oil exports declined despite rising oil prices. Oil production and hence exports continue to be constrained by technical capacity constraints related to Vietnam's maturing oil fields. While oil prices are up by 26.3 per cent (y/y), a substantial decline in volumes caused oil export earnings to contract by 27 per cent in the first four months of 2018.[6]

Vietnam is endowed with several natural resources such as coal, phosphates, rare earth elements, bauxite, chromate, copper, gold, iron, manganese, silver, zinc, offshore oil and gas deposits, timber, hydropower. The natural resources diminished after 1980 and its contribution to GDP fell substantially. Subsequently, the country's focus shifted to manufacturing and services from agriculture and crude oil exports; it succeeded in diversifying economic activities rather than depending on natural resources. Subsequently, the percentage GDP contribution of mineral and oil resources gradually reduced and is now relatively small as far as mineral, crude oil and natural resources are concerned. The GDP contribution of natural resources was highest (14.18 per cent) in 2008, while in case of crude oil, it was less than 10 per cent (8.98 per cent in 2006).

Vietnam's agro-food sector is well integrated with international markets. Agro-food exports have increased eightfold since the early 2000s, and Vietnam is now one of the world's largest exporters of a wide range of agricultural commodities, including cashews, black pepper, coffee, cassava and rice. Two thirds of Vietnam's agro-food exports are delivered to foreign consumers without further processing. Agro-food imports have also increased significantly. The majority of agro-food imports form intermediate inputs into Vietnam's processing sectors.[7]

Since the mid-1980s, wide-ranging reforms have propelled the economy, including the agricultural sector; in the process there has been greater openness. The country's efforts in the direction of open markets have resulted in inclusive private sector participation in policymaking, greater private land use rights and a greater role for private firms in trade and investment. The government and market reforms resulted in rapid sustained growth in living standards and stable as well as inclusive economic growth. From a poor country that depended on handouts from the Soviet Union, Vietnam has transformed from one of the world's poorest nations to a lower-middle-income country.

Remarkably, unlike Nigeria, the agricultural sector in Vietnam has been relatively modernized experiencing dynamic significant structural transformation over the last five decades. The sector has undergone a movement shift away from staple foods to export commodities, in particular perennial crops such as rubber and cashew nuts, and to livestock production. Currently, crops dominate with rice accounting for around 25 per cent of the value of agricultural production. Agricultural production has more than tripled in volume terms since 1990. While the relative importance of agriculture in the economy has declined over time, agriculture remains an important sector, contributing 15 per cent to Vietnam's GDP and employing 40 per cent of the labour force.

Nigeria's Lack of Horizontal Diversification

In 1980, Vietnam's GDP per capita was around US$200 while Nigeria's was over US$800; it is US$2,097 by 2020, overtaken by Vietnam at GDP/ Capita of 2,785.72. Its growth was massive, from $106 in 1977 to US$652 in three years (1980), a growth of over 380 per cent. Figure 4.1 compares shares of GDP per capita growth in Nigeria and Vietnam. The figure shows that share of GDP per capita of Nigeria (74.63 per cent) was almost three times to that of Vietnam (25.37 per cent) in 1984. Data for Vietnam is not available before 1984. As mentioned earlier, GDP per capita has been declining in Nigeria while Vietnam has witnessed positive trend, and in 2019 the share of Vietnam surpassed that of Nigeria. Clearly, from the graph, the two countries have been going in the opposite direction with respect to per capita income growth; Nigeria experiencing a clear development reversal. The reason Vietnam has expanded its revenue base is because of its diversified exports and continuing industrial and technological capabilities that enabled it to move from simple agricultural processing to manufacturing machinery and integrated circuits among others.

The outcome of a robust economic growth and diversification is that Vietnam lifted 45 million out of penury between 2002 and 2018, with poverty rates declining sharply from over 70 per cent to below 6 per cent, the World Bank said. In 2018, 87 million Nigerians were classified as extremely poor, living on less than US$1.90 each day. In fact, Nigeria officially became the world's poverty capital that year. In 2019, when the COVID-19 pandemic was not an issue, Nigeria's economic growth rate stood at 2.21 per cent, lower

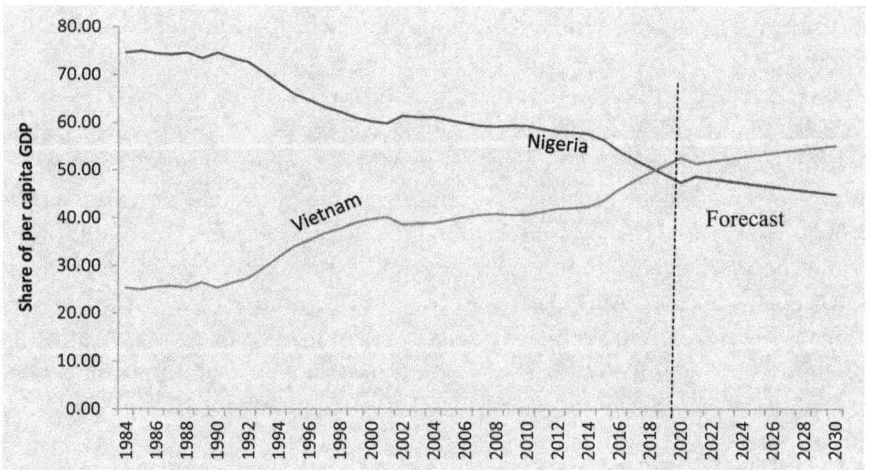

Figure 4.1. Trends in share of GDP: Nigeria and Vietnam. Source: Authors.

than the 2.6 per cent population growth rate. However, Vietnam averaged a 7 per cent growth rate – 6 per cent higher than 1 per cent population growth. When economic growth is higher than the population growth rate, the citizens are lifted out of poverty. In the fourth quarter of 2020, Nigeria's GDP growth stood at 0.11 per cent, while population growth was 2.6 per cent. This means that many Nigerians lived below the poverty line. The forecast values suggest that the share of Vietnam would reach 55.13 per cent while share of Nigeria is expected to further decline to 44.87 per cent in 2030.

Nigeria's structural change process can be observed by the trends in sectoral performance based on individual sector contribution to total output, that is, GDP. The relative productivity of the different sectors in comparator countries is also shown as a benchmark to describe the link between the level of industrialization, structural change and economic growth: China – a leading industrialization-centred economy, South Africa – an exception to the unsteady growth experience of sub-Saharan Africa and Mauritius – the only sub-Saharan African country that has achieved success in structural transformation, both in its economic structure and exports (Newman et al., 2016). The annual sectoral data of these comparator countries over the period 1990 to 2018 are used against Nigerian data to illustrate the basic relationship between industrialization, structural change and economic growth.

Figure 4.2 presents the agricultural share in GDP across the four countries using data of 1990, 2000, 2014 and 2018. The share of agriculture in GDP for China, Mauritius and South Africa shows a significant decline over the periods. However, for Nigeria, the decline is less significant with its experience of a slight increase in 2018 which could be credited to the economic

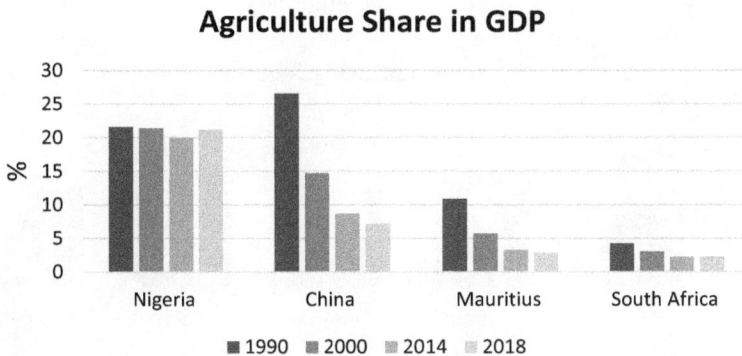

Figure 4.2. Agricultural sector contribution to GDP for Nigeria, China, Mauritius and South Africa (1990, 2000, 2014 and 2018). Source: World Development Indicators (WDI) (2019).

diversification programme implemented after the fall in oil prices that led to the economic recession in late 2015.

In Figure 4.2, which depicts the industry share in GDP across the four countries, using data from 1990, 2000, 2014 and 2018, China clearly has the highest percentage in its industry's contribution to GDP among the countries. For Nigeria, Mauritius and South Africa, the contribution of industry to GDP has been incoherent and more of a decline. The charts indicate an increase in the services sector share to GDP in all four countries, but a slight decrease in Nigeria and China in 2018. Overall, the economies were more service-orientated, having the service sector recording the greatest increase among other sectors considered, a phenomenon of premature deindustrialization of developing countries. Figure 4.3 shows the manufacturing sector contribution to GDP for India, Indonesia, Vietnam, Malaysia and Nigeria (1985, 1990, 1995, 2000, 2005, 2010, 2015 and 2020).

Agriculture remains the largest sector in Nigeria contributing an average of 24 per cent to the nation's GDP over the past seven years (2013 – 2019). In addition, the sector employs more than 36 per cent of the country's labour force, which ranks the sector the largest employer of labour in the country. A high level of the labour force in agriculture speaks to a lack of progress in modernizing the sector. Globally, the share of *Bulk Agricultural export is on the decrease* and increasingly accounting for a smaller share of the market; contrariwise, *the share of processed and semi-processed agricultural products has risen to 75 per cent of world share of agricultural exports by 2015.*[8] Horticultural exports accounted for around 12 per cent of global agricultural exports in 2014. Alarmingly, for the African region, not only has the proportion of bulk agricultural exports declined (from around 60 per cent to 42 per cent in 2014), the share of processed and semi-processed agricultural products rose only marginally to 35 per cent by 2015. This is both the challenge faced by and the opportunity

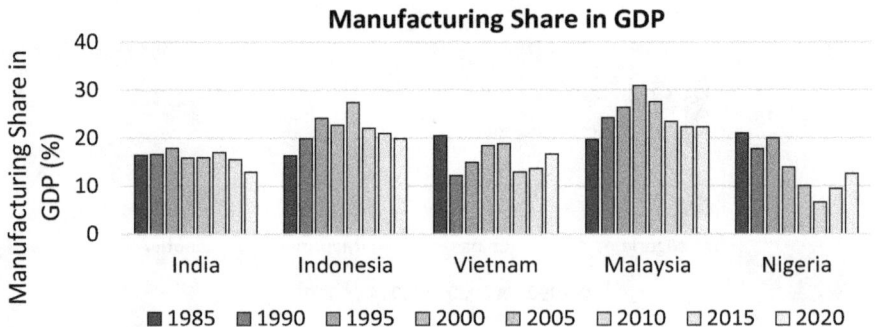

Figure 4.3. Contribution of the manufcaturing sector to overall country GDP. Source: World Development Indicators (WDI) (2021).

open to Nigeria. Nigeria must take advantage of this distinctive relative advantage in agricultural resources and landmass as well as the potential to supply not only raw agricultural goods for the local market but also a larger share of bulk and processed exports.

Paradoxically, while Nigeria has comparative advantage (and ranks top globally) in the production of a wide range of agricultural commodities, the country remains a major importer of food spending over 22 billion dollars, annually, on the importation of sugar, rice, wheat, tomato products, maize, dairy and other food items. For example, import bill figures showed fish to account for 1.9 per cent of total imports in 2018.[9] Also among Nigeria's top commodity imports are sugar, rice and palm oil with US$406 million, US$302 million and US$199 million worth imported annually, respectively.[10] Local production of such items must be prioritized to address the country's high import bill. Also, as the fifth largest exporting country of cocoa beans in the world, with a 5.3 per cent share of a global market that is worthUS $9.5 billion, it is imperative that Nigeria increased efficiency in production of such commodities, as well as processing.

An important factor behind the low aggregate productivity in Africa, Nigeria included, is low productivity in the agricultural sector. Despite significant amounts of farmland under cultivation, farming yields remain well below global averages. Growth in the agricultural sector has not kept pace with the needs of the country. This is fuelled by a convergence of factors such as weak urban/rural infrastructure resulting in considerable post-harvest losses, poor crop yields, comparatively low-level of mechanization, fertilizer use/capita and poor financing of agribusiness. Equally, Nigeria's population is growing faster than real economic growth: it is estimated to reach 410 million by 2050 and one billion by 2100. It has a young but increasingly illiterate population with around 60 per cent under 30 years old. The rising labour force of youth shall be characterized by low levels of human capital.

There are four broad sectors in Nigeria's agribusiness: crop production, fishing, livestock and forestry. Crop production is still largest accounting for about 87.6 per cent of the sector's total output. The others are livestock, fishing and forestry at 8.1 per cent, 3.2 per cent and 1.1 per cent, respectively. In four years (2016–2019), Nigeria's cumulative agricultural imports between 2016 and 2019 stood at ₦3.35 trillion, four times higher than the agricultural export of ₦803 billion within the same period.

The share of agriculture in Nigeria's total export earnings remains small compared to crude oil exports. For instance, in 2019, agriculture accounted for less than 2 per cent of total exports relative to crude oil (76.5 per cent). Nigeria's major agricultural imports include wheat, sugar, fish and milk, while the main agricultural exports include sesame seeds, cashew nuts, cocoa beans, ginger, frozen shrimp and cotton. Sesame, cashew nuts and cocoa account for more than half of the nation's agricultural exports, while wheat dominates agricultural imports. Agricultural export declined by about 11 per cent from ₦302.2 billion in 2018 to ₦269.8 billion in 2019. Nigeria's agricultural imports rose by 12.7 per cent from ₦851.6 billion to ₦959.5 billion during the same period, the highest value ever recorded in the country. Nigeria remains a net food importer – the agricultural trade deficit has widened with imports exceeding exports by ₦689.7 billion in 2019 compared to ₦549.3 billion in 2018.

Nigeria has 70.8 million hectares of agricultural land area with maize, cassava, guinea corn, yam beans, millet and rice being the major crops. Nigeria's rice production rose from 3.7 million metric tons in 2017 to 4.0 million metric tons in 2018. Despite this, only 57 per cent of the 6.7 million metric tons of rice consumed in Nigeria annually is locally produced leading to a deficit of about 3 million metric tons, which is either imported or smuggled into the country illegally. To stimulate local production, the government banned importation of rice in 2019.[11]

Sector Comparison: Cocoa and Cashew in Nigeria and Vietnam

We examine two commodities, namely cashew and cocoa, to show the loss revenue opportunities of export of raw materials. Cashew is a multi-billion-dollar industry, but the Nigerian cashew industry reaps only a small proportion of the overall value chain. The industry focusses on low-end raw nut production, losing substantial income to countries like India and Vietnam by not focussing on value-added products like the cashew kernel. Moreover, Nigeria receives the lowest international prices in Africa for its raw nuts due to concerns over production, processing and post-harvest handling. The few companies that have managed to carve a toehold in the US$1 billion cashew kernel market have a negligible market share and face extremely high competition.

The global market for cashews has grown tremendously, with world trade in raw cashew nuts more than doubling to 2.1 billion kilogrammes between 2000 and 2008. African countries, which produce more than half the world's supply, benefit little taken into consideration the overall value chain due to their lack of industrial processing capacity.[12] African producers – led by Côte d'Ivoire – accounted for almost two-thirds of the growth, but continent's farmers and exporters get only a fraction of the final retail price. Cashews thrive in the tropical climates of 20 Western and Eastern African nations, where about 90 per cent of the raw cashew nuts traded in the global market

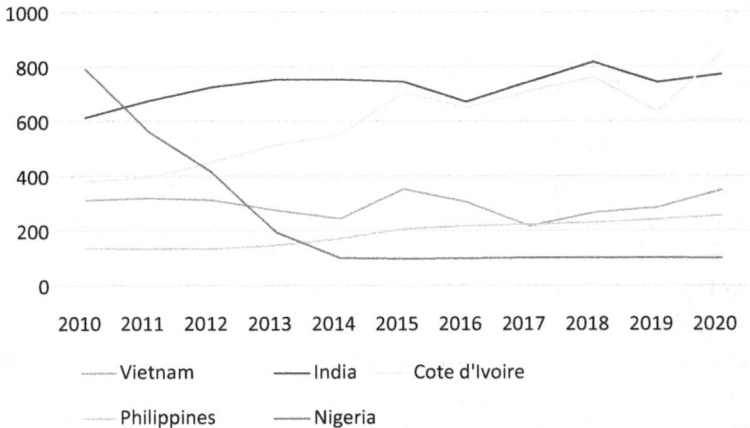

Figure 4.4. Cashew production in Five Select Countries.

are grown. Behind Côte d'Ivoire, the main producers are Tanzania, Nigeria, Benin, Guinea-Bissau, Mozambique and Ghana.See Figure 4.4 on cashew production in Cote d'Ivoire, Nigeria, India, Philippines and Vietnam.

Despite Africa's significant contribution to raw cashew production , less than 15 per cent of the continent's nuts are deshelled on African soil. The rest is exported mainly to Asia, where 85 per cent of the world's cashews are deshelled, which adds value to the commodity. Just two Asian nations – India and Vietnam – accounted for about 98 per cent of the world's raw cashew imports between 2014 and 2018. Even greater value is added in Europe and North America, where 60 per cent of traded kernels are roasted, salted, packaged and consumed as a snack or an ingredient in a drink, bar other product.

There is considerable cost to lack of, or limited processing of, commodities. According to UNCTAD, in 2018, the export price of cashew kernels from India to the European Union was about 3.5 times higher than what was paid to cashew farmers in Côte d'Ivoire – a 250 per cent difference in price. And after secondary processing in the EU, the price of the cashew kernels was about 2.5 times higher than when exported from India – and about 8.5 times more than when they left the farm in Côte d'Ivoire.

Value addition is a prerequisite for job creation, and higher wages for workers and subsequently an expanded revenue basket for the national and local economy. Diversification has benefits far beyond hedging against shocks; economic diversification is essential for economic development, especially in low-income and resource-dependent countries, as it can help fuel economic growth and poverty reduction.[10] Economic diversification also matters because, generally, it is accompanied by industrial upgrading due to technology diffusion and a movement towards higher productivity sectors and better paying jobs.

Cashew has tremendous potential as a 'cash crop' to generate foreign exchange and to create employment, especially for women, as well as curb desertification in the North and erosion in the South. The drought-resistant, environmentally-friendly cashew tree grows in the wild throughout Nigeria, leading to niche development opportunities in providing organic cashews with little additional financial burden to current production. There is a large and growing domestic and regional market for surplus kernels, as well as other cashew by-products. West Africa is now the major supplier of raw materials to the Indian processing powerhouses; cooperation between major exporting countries in West Africa could leverage improved prices. In addition, several USAID projects in Mozambique, Kenya, Tanzania, Ghana and Nigeria could be linked to create a significant critical mass of African organic cashews.

Vietnam cashew nuts

Vietnam has maintained its position as the world's largest producer and exporter of cashew nuts in 2020, exporting an estimated 450,000 tonnes of cashew kernels worth US$3.2 billion.[13] Vietnam has maintained its position as the world's largest producer and exporter of cashew nuts in 2020, exporting an estimated 450,000 tonnes of cashew kernels worth US$3.2 billion. Vietnam began to ship cashew kernels abroad in 1990 after the association was founded. The country exported 286 tonnes of cashew kernels for US$1.4 million that year. In 2004, the volume increased to 105,000 tonnes, worth approximately US$436 million. In 2006, Vietnam surpassed India for the first time as the world's top exporter of cashew kernels, with an export volume of 127,000 tonnes worth US$504 million. Since 2017, Vietnam has retained its position as the world's biggest hub for cashew processing and the largest exporter and importer of the product, accounting for over 50 per cent of the global processed cashew nuts. Although holding the title of 'the world's No 1 exporter', Vietnam has still mainly exported semi-processed cashew nuts, which are sold at an average price of US$10 per kilogramme, while finished products sold at supermarkets globally cost about US$30 per kilogramme.

According to the Food and Agriculture Organization of the United Nations, Vietnam in 2018 produced about 2.66 million tons of cashews, including their shells, a 23 per cent increase from the previous year. That was 3.4 times more than India, the world's second biggest producer, which grew roughly 790,000 tons, making Vietnam the undisputed leader. In 2018 Vietnam exported about 370,000 tons of the nuts, or 14 per cent of its total production. That also makes the country the world's top exporter by volume, according to the Vietnam Cashew Association.

Nigeria cocoa: a story of lost opportunities

Globally, Nigeria has lagged as with other commodities. Nigeria is the fourth largest producer of cocoa in the world, after Côte d'Ivoire, Indonesia and Ghana. It has a production volume of 245,000 tonnes of cocoa bean per annum, covering a 6.5 per cent share of global production. Although cocoa is the main agricultural export in Nigeria, cocoa production accounts for only 0.3 per cent of the agricultural GDP (Cadoni, 2013:). Cocoa is mainly exported as beans with limited processing activities within the country. Nonetheless, it is also exported as cocoa paste and cocoa butter to the Netherlands and Russia. Cocoa beans account for approximately 90 per cent of US$804 million worth of Nigerian cocoa exports, while cocoa butter and cocoa paste account for US$67 million and US$28 million, respectively. Cocoa production is projected to grow by 4 per cent per annum in coming years (NEPC, 2020). According to the Nigerian Export Promotion Council, the export markets for cocoa beans are Germany, Malaysia and the Netherlands, with untapped opportunities in Singapore and Turkey. The Netherlands is the largest export destination for Nigerian cocoa beans. It is also the largest export destination for Nigerian cocoa butter. It still offers an untapped potential of US$35.2 million for Nigerian cocoa beans. The Netherlands' imports of Nigerian cocoa beans and butter grew by 14 per cent on average per year during the period 2013–2017. Cocoa accounted for 20.8 per cent of all non-oil export in Nigeria in 2018. Nigeria earned US$338.17 million from cocoa and cocoa products in 2018 (NEPC, 2020). See Figure 4.5.

In Nigeria,[14] cocoa is primarily cultivated by small farmers, who account for over 80 per cent of production, typically on plots averaging 2.5 hectares (PWC, 2017). Unlike other major export crops, cocoa farming has traditionally been dominated by smallholder farmers. These farmers, as the main players in the cocoa value chain, experience structural poverty, poor organization and lack a significant voice in price setting, power dynamics and national decision-making processes. These issues are even more pronounced in the global value chain (Make Chocolate Fair (MCF), 2013). Smallholder cocoa farmers often endure low and unstable incomes, struggle to invest in their farms, cannot ensure proper working conditions for their workers, and sometimes resort to child labor. They possess the least bargaining power among the value chain participants, which make them vulnerable to poverty and targets for both local and international livelihood interventions. The

Comparing Cocoa Bean Production for Global Top 5 Producers *(in 1,000 metric tonnes)*

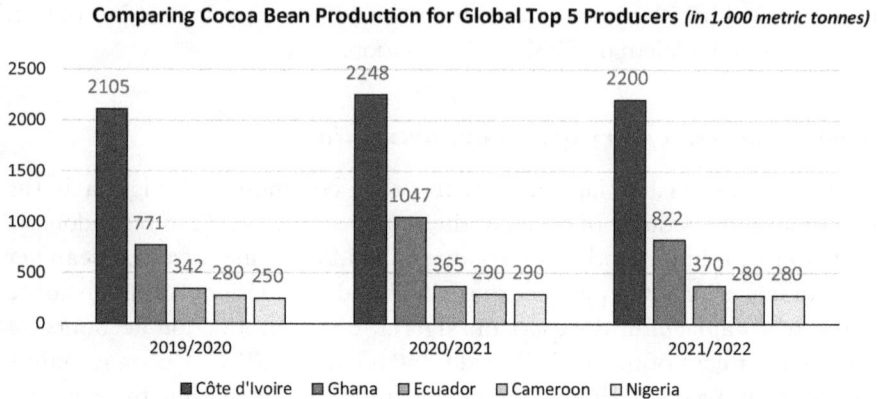

Figure 4.5. Comparing cocoa bean production for global top five producers (in 1,000 metric tonnes). Source: Author's plot from Statista.

plight of cocoa farmers in Nigeria is aptly described by Adesina (2013a: 3), the Minister of Agriculture under President Goodluck Jonathan.

> *The investment does not seem to [be] worth all the effort. Maintaining a cocoa farm – harvesting, fermenting, and drying – is difficult, manual labour. Conditions are rough. Many farmers live a life at or below the poverty line. Farmers have little bargaining power on price. As a result, young people are leaving cocoa for less labour-intensive jobs and better paying enterprises. What is left are ageing plantations and ageing farmers – many well over 50 years with an average life expectancy estimated at just 60. (Adesina, 2013: 3)*

Concerns regarding equity and price transmission are significant issues affecting the holding power and social conditions of the key players in this segment of the value chain. The relative inequality that spans the global cocoa value chain is highlighted by the Managing Director of Oluji Cocoa Products Limited:

> *The point here is that the wealth accruable lies somewhere beyond production volume. Some of us are really concerned because those who benefit more from cocoa are not the farmers or the regions that grow this commodity [...] The global cocoa trade is controlled from outside the borders of the growers. The major players have sold the idea that we are better off remaining as providers of raw materials feed their factories and should be contented with remaining on the fringes and the rent taking that goes with that as it were. While they are building industries around our cocoa and growing their economies, we remain in the same low end we have been occupying in the global value chain since 1910, when the first batch of cocoa was shipped out of Nigeria. (Ibirogba, 2018: 1)*

Historically, cocoa bean processing was primarily carried out in importing countries in Europe and North America due to the need for timely delivery and the short shelf life of semi-finished chocolate products. However, over the past two decades, the initial stages of cocoa bean processing have increasingly shifted to exporting countries. In Nigeria, the few companies that ventured into the cocoa processing industry have struggled to remain viable, with many going out of business. Currently, Nigeria has only four operational processing companies. In 2010, the country had eight functional cocoa processing companies, with one under construction and two non-functional (Adebayo et al., 2015: 143).

BOX 4.1 CASE STUDY: THE STORY OF MULTI-TREX

In 2018, Multi-Trex Integrated Foods PLC, which had the largest cocoa processing capacity in the country (65,000 tonnes of cocoa beans per annum), was taken over by the Asset Management Corporation of Nigeria (AMCON). Many cocoa processors, who invested billions of naira in response to the government's promotion of value addition across the cocoa value chain, have incurred huge losses as a result of the hostile business environment. The industry is currently estimated to be operating at 20 to 40 per cent of its full capacity. Cocoa processing factories in Nigeria operate at a very small scale compared to their West African and global counterparts.

Multi-Trex Integrated Foods PLC was incorporated in 1999 as a chocolate and confectionery manufacturing corporation. It produced cocoa liquor, cocoa cake mix, cocoa butter, cocoa powder and chocolate powder. It also produced cocoa-based consumer products for the local market. Multi-Trex has two factories with the combined installed processing capacity of 65,000 tonnes of cocoa per annum. It manufactured chocolate bars, drinks and other consumer products. The company was indebted to Skye bank (now Polaris Bank) for ₦8.5 billion in 2008. In 2011, when Multi-Trex defaulted AMCON bought the loan facility. In June 2015, Multi-Trex's factories were shut because it was neither able to pay back its debt nor access working capital to operate. In August 2017, both AMCON and Multi-Trex reached an amicable resolution, with the management of AMCON giving the company permission to carry out all necessary activities towards the eventual commencement of operation. Although it commenced operations in the last quarter of 2017, the company is still on the Nigerian Stock Exchange's caveat list. It appears to be distressed, having defaulted listing obligations, negative retained earnings and more. As Gayi and Tsowou (2016: 14) noted, this segment of the cocoa value chain is dominated by a few TNCs because cocoa processing is capital-intensive with high sunk costs (money that has been spent and cannot be recovered). It has experienced high horizontal market concentration with four big TNCs, namely Barry Callebaut, Cargill, ADM and Blommer Chocolate Company, controlling about 61 per cent of the market. These companies have consolidated their market share through mergers and acquisitions as they have sought to increase cost efficiency and attain greater economies of scale. High production costs have narrowed the margins for smaller companies making it difficult for those companies to survive. In 2017, Olam International acquired ADM with a Nigerian cocoa exporting subsidiary, leading it to become one of the top three players in the global cocoa processing industry. These big global brands have a competitive advantage with high research and development capacity and have continued to consolidate their hold in the industry (Manley, 2017; Terazono, 2014).

Manufacturing (industrial chocolate production) and distribution

Manufacturing activities include refining cocoa liquor and cocoa butter into smooth chocolate and cocoa beans for utilization in-house by manufacturers of chocolate products or by downstream confectioners, dairies and bakers. The main activities at this level in the value chain are the manufacture of chocolate confectionary, beverages and cosmetics. This is largely done by importing countries, but it is increasingly being done by exporting countries on a small scale. As part of the cocoa rebirth and cocoa transformation agenda, the Nigerian government has tried to promote local production and distribution of finished cocoa products such as chocolates, cocoa powder, cocoa biscuits and cocoa wine. Some companies have ventured into chocolate production in recent years. Some of these companies, such as Sunshine Chocolates, Loshes Chocolate, Kalabari Gecko Chocolates and Loom Chocolates, have been able to make modest inroads into the Nigerian domestic and export markets.

Divergent Development Paths: Vietnam Story of Successful Diversification

Development pathways are not just an outcome of sectors of specialization. They are a product of choices that determine the course of these sectors and

their performance. An important indicator of a country's economic performance is its unemployment rate. Vietnam's average unemployment rate was
2.37 per cent for 2020 up from 2.15 per cent one year earlier, according to
Trading Economics. Vietnam has imitated successful Asian countries such as
the ROK by pushing into relatively more complex product categories at its
income level while also mastering horizontal diversification through processing agricultural commodities for export. It expanded its export basket and a
move into higher-value crops.

So, what are Vietnam's Success Factors?
Governance's close correlation with economic diversification is demonstrated
by the World Bank's Worldwide Governance Indicators, which we will use
for our analysis in this chapter. In the case of Vietnam, the country succeeded in diversification from natural resource in part through building governance capacity. As rent-seeking from natural resources rises in Vietnam
during 1990–92, FDI inflow decreased. However, the net FDI inflow showed
increasing trend during 1994–1998 and 2015–2019. The overall FDI inflow
indicates a positive trend while rent-seeking on natural resources is declining. The control of corruption was an important factor. The rule of law is
another economic parameter depicting the creation of various laws and its
enforcement for transparent economic management and improvement of living standards of citizens. The data on control of corruption and rule of law
extracted from WDI online indicates the association between governance
and rent- seeking on natural resources. It shows that while corruption was
high in Vietnam during initial years, rent-seeking on natural resources also
was high. However, after 2005, various government policies promoted good
governance and subsequently institution of the rule of law became stronger
after 2016.

Concomitantly, the GINI index of Vietnam decreased as rent-seeking in
natural resources decreased after 2008; the GINI index shows improvement.
The association between natural resources and GINI index shows negative
trend indicating the country moving towards equality. Overall, Vietnam,
a country endowed with significant natural resources, has made successful
transition of turning natural wealth into assets. It has done so with reform of
macroeconomic policies, improved governance, building quality institutions,
reduction in corruption and paying due attention to human resource development among others. The country experienced major industrialization shifts
due to different policies promulgated over time. The various economic development initiatives were undertaken in the country through its five year plans.
The major shift in socio-economic development was achieved in Vietnam
after 1985 as the industrial weaknesses were recognized and reforms were

introduced in the system to enhance efficiency which resulted in market-ori-entated economy called 'Doi-Moi'.

Clustering and Agglomeration Policy

Apart from the policies, encouraging industry-led growth, cluster-based industrialization, infrastructure development and human capital formation were key success drivers in its export-led-growth strategy encouraged by the government since the beginning. Vietnam transited from the export of pri-mary products into the manufacture of industrial goods, which subsequently underpinned the growth and development miracle of other Asian countries before it. The exports of high-value products including technology and ICT could help it earn foreign exchange, which is utilized for the import of inputs, ensuring the production of quality products.

Vietnam's exports in 2019 were US$264.189 billion – 88 times Nigeria's non-oil export earnings in 2018 and 10 times Nigeria's oil export. A part of the reason is that Vietnam ranked 70th on the 2020 World Bank Doing Business, while Nigeria's ranking was 131st. The Asian country has a total installed electricity capacity of almost 48,000 megawatts. Still, with a dou-ble population, Nigeria has 12,500 installed generation capacity and 4,000–5,000 distribution capacity, with hydro as the main power source.

'Between 2002 and 2018, GDP per capita in Vietnam increased by 2.7 times, reaching over US$2,700 in 2019', the World Bank said in its 2019 report on Vietnam. Another strategy employed by Vietnam was access to education. School enrolment in Vietnam was 115 per cent in 2019, accord-ing to the World Bank, but 10.5 million children in Nigeria, especially in the north, are out of school, according to UNICEF, perpetuating poverty among the populace.

Through deliberate diversification strategy, Vietnam overcame oil dependence

The country is rich in natural resources such as coal, bauxite, petroleum and gas, hydropower, wood and so on. Out of these, the main mineral exports are coal and petroleum. The oil industry is state-owned by PetroVietnam, which runs under the Ministry of Industry and Trade. PetroVietnam started its production by investing in 1961, with exploration done by foreign oil companies.[15] It contributes in revenues to about a quarter of state budget. The country's oil production is carried out by PetroVietnam's upstream subsidiary, PetroVietnam Exploration and Production or through joint ventures in which the National Oil Company has at least 20 per cent equity interest.

PetroVietnam uses modern technology and advanced management methods for exploration activities. Its workforce is employed in large exploration and production activities and other downstream projects. It also provides high-quality oil and gas, especially drilling services. The downstream oil sector is run through two subsidiaries, namely, Petechim and PetroVietnam Oil Processing and Distribution Company. In 2006, Vietnamese government began to privatize the National Oil Company's non-oil-related business to raise capital for upstream and downstream projects and increase operational efficiency (ibid). The production and consumption of crude oil in Vietnam is depicted in Figure 4.6.

From the figure, crude oil production gradually increased and peaked in 2004. However, production started falling from 2005 as the production from major fields namely Bach Ho declined whereas small fields could not offset the decline. Between 2006 and 2010, 14 small fields were put into production, but output only increased slightly in 2009 and then continued to fall. During 2011–2015, 36 oil and gas fields started production, as a result it peaked in 2015 but continued to fall after that (ibid). Although Vietnam exports crude oil, it is a net importer of oil as well.

Exports of crude oil in Vietnam increased since early 1990s and reached peak in 2004, but subsequently experienced decline. The country's 60 per cent petroleum demand is utilized for the transportation sector.

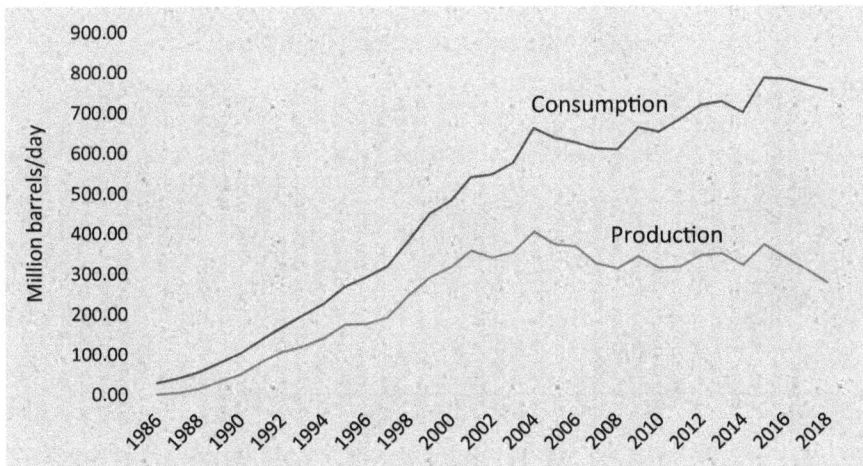

Figure 4.6. Production and consumption of crude oil. Source: International-US Energy Information Administration.

The Nigerian case

Since the implementation of the Structural Adjustment Programme in the 1980s, Nigeria has focused on liberalizing the trading environment, a strategy adopted to stimulate sustainable growth and development in the sectors of the economy. More recently, there have been far-reaching efforts to actively pursue diversification dealings through the adoption of various strategic policies. These policy changes have not succeeded in diversifying the Nigerian economy. Both oil and gas sector have continued their dominance in recent years. This may not be unconnected to the global decline in crude oil demand or COVID-19 pandemic. As the main export of the economy, the fall in global crude oil demand during 2015–2017 and 2019–2020 period may have resulted in lower export of oil and gas. Overall, the fluctuations in oil and gas signify how the policy environment, driven by several political, economic and social institutional variables, influences the diversification of the Nigerian economy.

The oil industry has remained the main source of Nigeria's export revenue for over 30 years now but has acted the central part, paradoxically, in determining the economic ruin of the country. The income generated from the oil trade accrued from 70 per cent to 90 per cent of Nigeria's overall external receipt from export business yearly (see Figure 4.7).[16]

According to OPEC, Nigeria spent US$264.57 billion importing petroleum products during the five-year period 2015 to 2020. The value of the country's petroleum imports in 2020 was US$71.285 billion, which indicated

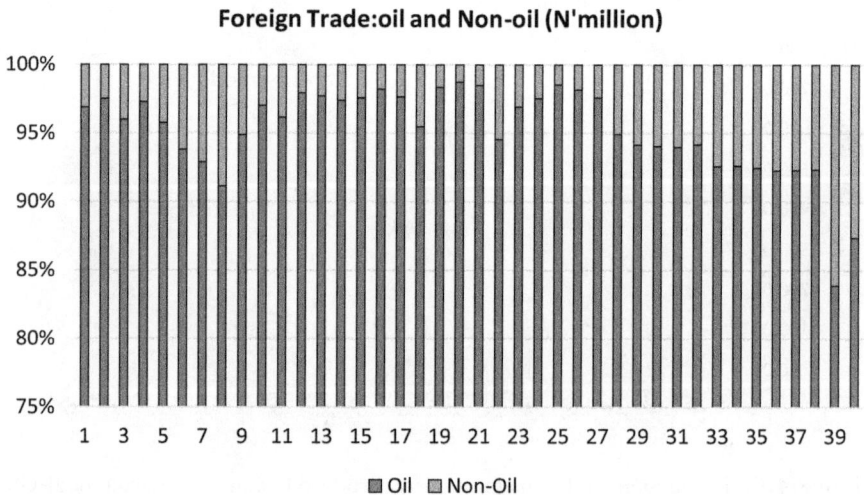

Figure 4.7. Nigeria's international trade for oil and non-oil. Sources: CBN Annual Statistical; Bulletin (2020).

that Nigeria's petroleum imports exceeded its exports by US$43.56 billion during the review period. These figures show that Nigeria's import of petroleum products consistently exceeded the nation's export for five years.

Table 4.1 shows that compared with major oil exporters, Nigeria is not an oil-abundant country but rather oil-dependent. Saudi Arabia exports almost five times what Nigeria exports. On a per capita basis, the value of Saudi Arabia's export per citizen is US$3,353 while that of Nigeria is US$122 due to its relatively large population. In volume terms for every 1000 citizens Saudi Arabia exports 325 barrels while that of Nigeria is 11 barrels.

Oil dependence results in huge export volatility, particularly for a country like Nigeria that suffers from revenue concentration and lack of diversification. For example, Nigeria was among the top oil-exporting countries that posted the severest declines in their international sales of crude oil that were led by Russia (down −40.2 per cent), Kuwait (down −39.2 per cent), Nigeria (down −38.7 per cent), Iraq (down −38.7 per cent) and Angola (down −35.4 per cent). For Nigeria with practically no other source of foreign exchange, this has resulted in a foreign exchange crisis that massively reduced the value of the local currency.

Table 4.1. Oil exporters: per capita export per BBL per day and USD/population.

Country	Crude Oil Export Value (billion USD) (% of Total Export)		Population (millions) (2020)	Oil Export/Per Capita (USD)	Oil Production BBL 1,000 People
Saudi Arabia	113.7	17.2	34.27	3353	325
Russia	72.6	11	146.2	49.6	73.2
Iraq	50.8	7.7	40.22	1263	120
United States	50.3	7.6	329.5	152.4	35.9
United Arab Emirates	47.9	7.2	9.89	6800	335
Canada	47.6	7.2	38.01	1250	101
Kuwait	28.3	4.3	4.271	6581	721
Nigeria	25.2	3.8	206.1	**122**	**10.75**
Kazakhstan	23.7	3.6	18.8	1220	88.7
Norway	22.7	3.4	5.4	4203	22.7
Angola	20.2	3.1	32.8	612	61.4
Brazil	19.6	3	212.5	93	12
United Kingdom	16.1	2.4	67.1	240	14.3
Oman	15.0	2.3	5.1	3000	217
Mexico	14.9	2.2	129	115.5	17.1

Source: Calculated from OPEC database.

Comparing Resource Endowment and Economic Performance

Vietnam is endowed with other natural resources such as coal, phosphates, rare earth elements, bauxite, chromate, copper, gold, iron, manganese, silver, zinc, offshore oil and gas deposits, timber, hydropower. The natural resources diminished after 1980 and its contribution to GDP fell substantially. Subsequently, the country's focus shifted to manufacturing and services from agriculture and crude oil exports. The value-added data for both manufacturing and services sectors refers to the net output of a sector after adding up all outputs and subtracting intermediate inputs. In the case of mineral and other resources, mineral rents are the difference between the value of production for a stock of minerals at world prices and their total costs of production. The minerals included in the calculation are tin, gold, lead, zinc, iron, copper, nickel, silver, bauxite and phosphate, while the oil rents are the difference between the value of crude oil production at regional prices and the total costs of production.

The percentage contribution of manufacturing and services to GDP rose, while its contribution to natural resources fell. Government policies undertaken in the 1980s shifted the focus of the country from natural resources to manufacturing and services sectors. This diversification policy resulted in a substantial contribution of both sectors to GDP. However, the contribution to GDP by the services sector has been much higher than that of the manufacturing sector. As far as growth of contributions during 1990–2019 is concerned, the services sector increased its share while the manufacturing sector growth was positive but did not witness the same magnitude as that of services. The CAGR of services and manufacturing sectors during this period has been 0.41 and −0.42 per cent, respectively. Vietnam is rich in natural and mineral resources but succeeded in diversifying economic activities rather than depending on natural resources. The percentage GDP contribution of mineral and oil resources has trended down while manufacturing rose. The GDP contribution of natural resources was highest (14.18 per cent) in 2008, while in case of crude oil, it was less than 10 per cent (8.98 per cent in 2006).

The Human Development Index (HDI) as measured by UNDP summarizes the average achievements in key human development. The parameters include health, education and the standard of living. The association between rent-seeking on natural resources and HDI is depicted in Figure 4.8. Reversal of Africa's fortune manifests in economic, social, technological and industrial conditions. The graph compares the reversal in living standards. Compared with comparator Asian countries, by analysing the disparities in development metrics particularly the levels and rates of growth of national incomes and HDI, the differences are stark, see Figure 4.8.

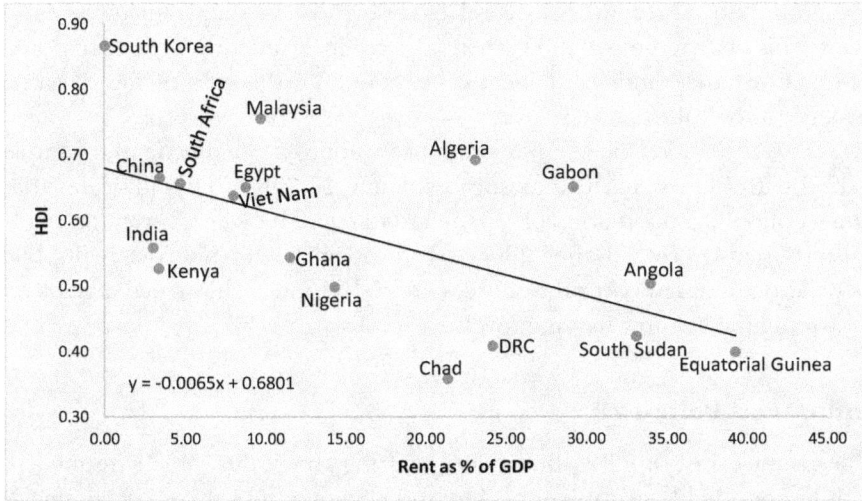

Figure 4.8. Association of HDI and resource rent. Source: HDI (UNDP); Rent (WDI).

We base the analysis on the figure on the average value (1996–2019) of rent on natural resources as a percentage of GDP and HDI. From the figure, HDI in South Korea, the most diversified in our sample, has the highest (0.87) with the lowest value of rent (0.03 per cent) while Chad has the lowest HDI and substantially higher resource rent (HDI 0.36 and rent 21.37 per cent). There is a negative association between the two suggesting they are inversely related to each other. The negative correlation between the two (−0.59) also indicates the same type of association.

As natural resources rent rises, the HDI does not increase, thereby indicating that the association between rent-seeking and HDI is inversely proportional. The figure also indicates that rent from natural resources was high (11.52 per cent) in 1990 while HDI was 0.48. In 2019, as the rent on natural resources declined to 3.37 per cent, HDI increased to 0.70.

The FDI inflow in a country depicts economic achievements and also its ability to promote competition in the domestic market. Hence the association between FDI inflow and resource rent are correlated. As resource rent increased in Vietnam during 1990–92, FDI inflow decreased. The net FDI inflow however recorded increasing trend during 1994–1998 and 2015–2019. The overall FDI inflow indicates a positive trend while rent from natural resources is declining. The control of corruption is another parameter to identify the extent of control of government in a country. The rule of law is an economic parameter depicting the creation of various laws and its enforcement for the betterment of citizens. Corruption, this was closely connected to rent from natural resources, was relatively high in Vietnam during its early years; this changed after 2005 when various government policies promoted good governance and subsequently institution of the rule of law became stronger after 2016.

The GINI index of Vietnam has been approx. 35 during the sample period with highest in 2010 at approximately 40 (39.3). This indicates that almost one-third population of Vietnam had equal income. As rent on natural resources decreased after 2008, GINI index showed improvement. The association between natural resources and GINI index shows negative trend indicating the country moving towards equality.

Industrial Policies

The country instituted its first reform during the 1980s which resulted in a shift from highly centralized command economy to a mixed economy. A comprehensive industrial policy was put in place which ensured consistency in industrial inputs and outputs, but the promotion of efficiency in the system was not focused. During this period, Vietnamese industries depended on aid from the Soviet Union. After 1985, the industrial weaknesses were recognized, and greater openness was introduced to enhance efficiency which resulted in market-orientated economy and was called 'Doi-Moi'. In this strategy, indicative planning, that is, coordination of private and public investment and macroeconomic management system, was implemented. In this industrial policy, the shift was majorly towards small industries and exports than heavy industries.

Many provincial/states-owned large enterprises had to be closed and some had to deal with retrenching employees and production as they faced losses due to government policies. As a result, overall industrial output fell by 3.3 per cent in 1989. Vietnam also had to face the challenge of limited funding from its exports and had to cut down on their imports due to the reason that their trade was earlier supported by Soviet aid. As this support was closed during the late 1980s, they had to cut imports sharply and emphasized policies towards the expansion of exports.[17] During 1990s, the current account deficit was compensated by large-scale petroleum and agriculture products exports. It was realized that these two strategies were not a long-term solution, and the focus should be shifted to expansion of manufacturing exports. But majority of state-owned industries were ill-equipped as they were oriented towards domestic market, and their product quality was not appropriate for international standards. Moreover, the Vietnamese domestic industry was not able to compete with China due to high tariff barriers.

During the early 1990s, the Vietnamese industry was primarily state-owned heavy industry with high production cost resulting in cost uncompetitive internationally. In mid-1990s, the embargo on Vietnam was lifted, and the country was able to attract FDI in its labour-intensive industries. In 1997, few foreign automobile companies were allowed to set up enterprises in the country; these firms were majorly assemblers of imported automobile parts. The enterprises were able to produce few thousand vehicles in a year. The FDI showed a hike from US$575 million in 1992 to US$2,041 million in 1994 (ibid). Most of the FDI was pushed into exports, particularly manufacturing exports.

After 2000, in order to expand the manufacturing base through export-oriented economy, many bilateral trade agreements were signed, such as the Vietnam–US trade agreement. The country joined the Asia-Pacific Economic Cooperation and WTO among others. During 2001–2005, GDP growth was about 7.5 per cent, while stabilization of the macro-economy was achieved as balance of economic parameters such as budget receipts and expenses, consumption and so on improved. The total investment capital also increased and major projects were undertaken. In this period, Enterprise Law 2005 was instituted that increased the participation of private ownership in the industry. So, with major industrial policy changes and complete removal of international trade barriers, manufacturing gained increasing competitiveness.

After 2005, the modern sectors, such as telecommunication and IT, were strengthened. In these sectors, the country involved private enterprises in Internet Service Provider business while the Internet exchanges were state-owned. FDI was also allowed in the telecom sector but with limited control. In order to further boost the economic development, two main types of economic zones have been established, near the land borders, coastal economic zones and border gate economic zones. More than 499 industrial parks were established by 2018 which several foreign-invested enterprises (7,745) and domestically invested (6,992) enterprises were established (Oh et al., 2020). Some of these high-tech enterprises support scientific and technology research and training focussing into building hi-tech industries, particularly, robotics, software industry, informatics and shipping. Also, supplementary industries were encouraged in these zones for better supply chain management. Consequently, Vietnam has become a major exporter of phones, textiles, electronic goods, computers and footwear.

The major objectives of Vietnam's five-year socio-economic development plan 2016–20 were to achieve GDP growth rate higher than the previous five years, accelerating the implementation of economic restructuring associated with growth model innovation, improving productivity, efficiency and competitiveness by strategic breakthroughs. These would be achieved through fully implementing market economy rules and international integration. In the current five-year plan, the government intends to restructure financial markets and enhance the stability of economic balances towards achieving trade surplus in order to regulate exchange rates according to market signals and increase foreign exchange reserves. Another milestone Vietnam wants to achieve is to accelerate and promote entrepreneurship support that encourages development of joint-stock enterprises providing robustness to small and medium-sized enterprises, and family businesses.

Summing Up

Vietnam is a Socialist Republic, located in Southeast Asia. The coastline of Vietnam covers more than 3,000 km long and the mainland area stretches to 331,690 square km. The country is administratively divided into 63 provinces and 5 municipalities. The terrain of Vietnam includes mountain and hills, delta and rivers. The country is rich in natural resources such as coal, bauxite, petroleum and gas, hydropower, wood and so on, out of which the main mineral exports are coal and petroleum. The oil industry is state-owned by PetroVietnam, which runs under the Ministry of Industry and Trade. Initially, the trade of Vietnam was based on crude oil exports. However, the crude oil exports peaked in 2004 and then gradually declined.

Subsequently, Vietnam shifted its focus from trade in natural resources to manufacturing and services sectors. This diversification resulted in substantial increase in the contribution to GDP of both the sectors. However, the contribution to GDP by the services sector has been much higher than that of the manufacturing sector. As far as growth of contributions during 1985–2019 is concerned, the services sector increased its share while the manufacturing sector has witnessed declining trend. The CAGR of services and manufacturing sectors during this period has been 0.41 and −0.42 per cent, respectively.

Various countries are endowed with natural resources. Vietnam is one of them that has made successful use of natural wealth into assets. It has done so by drawing on a strong macroeconomic performance, good governance, building quality institutions, reduction in corruption and due attention to human resource development.

The country has experienced dynamic industrialization due to activist industrial policies leading to strong growth and socio-economic development initiatives of its five-year plans. The major change in socio-economic development came after 1985 as the industrial weaknesses were recognized and greater openness was introduced in the system to enhance efficiency which resulted in market-orientated economy and called 'Doi-Moi'. Prior to this move the economy was a highly centralized command economy. After liberalization the strategy adopted a shift towards small industries support and growth and exports rather than heavy industries.

More than 499 industrial parks were established by 2018: housing several foreign-invested enterprises (7,745) and domestically invested (6,992) enterprises were established (Oh et al., 2020). Vietnam derives over 60 per cent of its GDP from industrial parks. The country's economic policies focused on diversification that enabled Vietnam to grow uninterruptedly for the last three decades. Despite its abundant natural resources, the country, unlike oil-dependent African countries, successfully diversified resulting in highly sustained growth. Consequently, Vietnam has become a major exporter of phones, textiles, electronic goods, computers and footwear.

Notes

1 Nigeria drags as Vietnam lifts 45 million citizens out of poverty – International Centre for Investigative Reporting (icirnigeria.org).
2 The World Bank (June 2018). Taking Stock: An Update on Vietnam's Recent Economic Developments. Retrieved from https://documents1.worldbank.org/curated/en/536421528929689515/pdf/127168-WP-TakingStockENG-PUBLIC.pdf on 23 June 2024.
3 Nigerian Export Promotion Council (2020), "Impact assessment of and Policy Responses to the Coronavirus Pandemic on Agricultural Exports." Retrieved fro mhttps://nepc.gov.ng/cms/wp-content/uploads/2020/04/Covid-19-impact-assessment.pdf on 22 June 2024
4 https://www.worldstopexports.com/vietnams-top-10-exports/
5 https://www.worldstopexports.com/vietnams-top-10-exports/
6 Source: The World Bank (June 2018). Taking Stock: An Update on Vietnam's Recent Economic Developments. Retrieved from https://documents1.worldbank.org/curated/en/536421528929689515/pdf/127168-WP-TakingStockENG-PUBLIC.pdf on 23 June 2024.
7 Viet Nam, "Agricultural Policy Monitoring and Evaluation 2020," OECD iLibrary (oecd-ilibrary.org), accessed November 9, 2021
8 Ibid., 2.
9 Daniel Workman (2019), "Nigeria's Top 10 Imports," *World's Top Exports*. http://www.worldstopexports.com/nigerias-top-10-imports/, accessed 4 November 2019.
10 Lawrence Pines (2019), "Nigeria Trade: What Are The Main Imports & Exports Of Africa's Most Populous Country?" *Commodity.com* https://commodity.com/nigeria/, accessed 4 November 2019.
11 https://www.fao.org/nigeria/fao-in-nigeria/nigeria-at-a-glance/en/
12 UNCTAD, https://unctad.org/news/cashing-cashews-africa-must-add-value-its-nuts, accessed November 5, 2021
13 https://en.vietnamplus.vn/vietnam-remains-worlds-largest-producer-exporter-of-cashew-nuts/191047.vnp, accessed November 9, 2021
14 This section draws heavily from Aiyede, E. R. (2021). Agricultural Commercialisation and the Political Economy of Cocoa and Rice Value Chains in Nigeria. *APRA Working Paper, 52*.
15 Trung, Viet and chat (2016).
16 Ibid. National Bureau of Statistic, "Nigerian Gross Domestic Product Report."
17 Perkins and Anh (2010).

Chapter 5

AN ASIAN GIANT OUTPACES THE GIANT OF AFRICA

Economic Diversification: Nigeria and Indonesia in a Comparative Context

Introduction

Indonesia is currently the largest producer of palm oil in the world; it supplies half of global demand. The country's oil palm plantations that have expanded over the years leveraged substantial economic growth and created notable downstream industries. At the beginning of the twenty-first century, the total area planted by palm oil was only 4 million hectares, but it expanded to more than 14 million hectares by 2020. The total planted area has grown more than 300 per cent in the last 10 years. Along with oil palm plantation expansion, crude palm oil (CPO), cooking oil and biofuel industries have continued to grow and are targeted not only at meeting the domestic market but also at fulfilling export needs. In 2021 by contrast, Nigeria's total plantation cultivation was just over 1 million hectares. Nigeria was the world leader of oil palm in the 1950s and 1960s producing 43 per cent of total global production. Nigeria was a significant exporter then, but currently, it produces a meagre 2 per cent of global output and has become a net importer of oil palm and products amounting to 3 million tonnes of fats and oils annually. The decline came with the discovery of crude petroleum in the 1970s. Most of the main crude petroleum oil producers are also oil palm and natural rubber producers. As with CPO, Nigeria has tumbled down the back of major global producers.

In 2021, Indonesia produced approximately 3.12 million metric tons of rubber and ranked as the world's second-largest producer of rubber and a part of the International Tripartite Rubber Council, together with Thailand and Malaysia. Indonesia, the second biggest exporter of natural rubber exports had a value of US$3 billion in 2020; it accounted for 26.2 per cent of worldwide sales.[1] Indonesia is the 26th largest exporting country and 31st largest importing country in the world; as at 2015, total export volume stood at US$161 billion while imports were at US$139 billion, which meant US$21.7 billion of positive trade balance. Top export destinations include the United States, China, Japan, Singapore and India while its import origin includes China, Singapore, Japan, South Korea and Thailand. Indonesia exports products that include coal briquettes, palm oil, petroleum, crude petroleum and rubber while its import products include refined petroleum, broadcasting equipments, vehicle parts, crude petroleum and telephones.

Nigeria on the other hand is a middle-income economy. It is an emerging market and mixed economy with leading growth sectors in financial, communication, manufacturing, entertainment and technology. It exports little in terms of manufacturing but rather, Nigeria is a major exporter of crude oil to countries around the world. Government's annual budget is usually estimated based on oil revenue projections which badly affect the economy when there is a fall in global oil prices.[2] Its major agricultural export products include frozen shrimps and prawns, sesame seed, cashew nuts, crude palm kernel and flour and meals of soybean. Other sources of exports are crude oil which amounts to 45.9 per cent, light manufactured goods 22.1 per cent, non-crude oil products 21.8 per cent, raw materials 5.85 per cent, solid minerals 0.3 per cent.[3] Notably, Nigeria has experienced slow economic growth since 2015. Growth slowed from 6.25 per cent in 2014 to 3.0 per cent at the end of 2015, with inflation increasing from 7.8 per cent to 9.0 per cent. This slow economic growth is partially attributed to fluctuating global oil prices, external shocks from the COVID-19 pandemic and in 2022 the Russian–Ukraine war. Structurally, the poor manufacturing export performance manifests in perennial balance of payment (BoP) crisis that has resulted in inadequate foreign exchange to fund requests for the country's imports.

We have evidence from other studies. In three-country pairs analysed by Henley (2015), Indonesia and Nigeria comparison reveals more apparent variation in economic performance relative to their similarities. Economic policies in Indonesia and Nigeria were disparate and reflected in the economic outcomes: sustained economic growth with poverty reduction in Indonesia and prolonged economic decline in Nigeria (Lewis, 2007; Henley, 2015). The common feature of Henley's and other earlier studies is that their comparative analysis has focused on the period between the 1960s to the late 1990s, during which the two countries were under military/authoritarian rule, and the analytical framework is centred on the explanation of the possible factors responsible for success in Indonesia and failure in Nigeria. However, Indonesia and Nigeria successfully transitioned to democratic rule in 1999 following the collapse of their authoritarian regimes in 1998. The analysis in the chapter goes beyond the democratic transition in the 1990s. Additionally, we focus on sectoral patterns and detailed case studies of commodities and exports to engage with the reversal thesis.

This chapter is organized as follows. First, we examine the macroeconomic conditions of the two countries followed by the sectoral sources of growth. The third part examines the nature and pattern of agricultural and industrial development from a comparative perspective. Chapter four interrogates the remote and more immediate reasons for the divergent development of Nigeria and Indonesia. Finally, we offer recommendations on how Nigeria can attain sustainable economic growth drawing lessons from the Indonesia case study.

Macroeconomic and Social Conditions

Indonesia is a sovereign country in East/Southeast Asia. The country is located in Southeastern Asia, an archipelago between the Indian Ocean and the Pacific Ocean with a total area of 1,904,569 sq km; total land area is 1,811,569 sq km; total water area is 93,000 sq km. The climatic condition of the country is tropical: hot, humid; more moderate in highlands, having its terrain mostly coastal lowlands; larger islands have interior mountains. Natural resources available in the country include petroleum, tin, natural gas, nickel, timber, bauxite, copper, fertile soils, coal, gold and silver. The population of the country is estimated to be 275,122,131.[4] Nigeria, on the other hand, is located in Western Africa, bordering the Gulf of Guinea, between Benin and Cameroon. The total area space is approximately 923,768 sq km and total land space is 910,768 sq km and total water space is 13,000 sq km.[5] The climatic condition of the country varies: equatorial in south, tropical in centre and arid in north. Natural resources available in the country include natural gas, petroleum, tin, iron ore, coal, limestone, niobium, lead, zinc, arable land.[6] Nigeria is the country with the largest population in Africa; significant population clusters are scattered throughout the country, with the highest density areas being in the south and southwest. The population of the country is estimated to be 219,463,862.[7]

Indonesia has a GDP of US$1 trillion and is ranked the 16th largest economy in the world, while Nigeria is ranked 32nd with US$397.3 billion. By GDP five-year average growth at 5 per cent, Indonesia ranked 31st in the world and Nigeria at 2 per cent ranked 132nd. Also, in GDP per capita, Indonesia with a GDP per capita of US$3.9k ranked 122nd in the world while Nigeria with a GDP per capita of $2k ranked 149th. Indonesia and Nigeria also have GDP per capita growth of 3.99 per cent and −0.67 per cent, respectively (see Table 5.1).[8] The two countries are similar in many respects, ranging from geography to economic, social and political challenges, but

Table 5.1. Gross domestic product and income for Indonesia and Nigeria.

Statistics	Indonesia	Nigeria
GDP	$1T	$397.3B
GDP growth, 1 year	5.2 per cent	1.9 per cent
GDP growth, 5-year average	5%	2 per cent
Population	264M	190.9M
GDP per capita	$3.9k	$2k
GDP per capita growth	3.99 per cent	−0.67 per cent
Purchasing Power Parity conversion factor	4238.11	110.03
Price level ratio of PPP conversion factor GDP to market exchange rate	0.3	0.34
GDP per capita, PPP adjusted	$13k	$6k
GNI, Atlas method	$1T	$384.8B
GNI per capita	$3.8k	$2k
GNI, PPP adjusted	$3.4T	$1.1T
GNI per capita, PPP adjusted	$13k	$5.7k

Source: Indonesia vs Nigeria Economic Indicator Comparison. Accessed on 29 July 2021, from https://georank.org/economy/indonesia/nigeria.

Indonesia has developed 'better' than Nigeria since the end of the 1960s.[9] The important role of crude oil in Indonesia and Nigeria has necessitated frequent comparisons between these two countries.[10] This chapter aims at a detailed comparative analysis of the political economy of Indonesia and Nigeria. We focus especially on the agricultural sector, specifically the oil palm sectors of the two countries.

In addition, structural and institutional factors are examined in explaining why Nigeria in particular has failed to achieve sustainable and equitable economic growth, despite its abundant natural resources compared to Indonesia which has been described as the powerhouse economy of Southeast Asia.

From 1950 to the late 1980s, Indonesian living standards rose to triple that of Nigeria. GNP per capita in 1987, on a Purchasing Power Parity (PPP) basis, was twice as high in Indonesia as in Nigeria (10.1 per cent and 5.0 per cent of the US value, respectively, per World Bank 1995). Even allowing for the fragility of this type of comparison, it is evident that over the period Indonesia moved from being a poorer country than Nigeria to being a substantially richer one. The incidence of poverty declined substantially in Indonesia and increased in Nigeria. There was also a weak trend towards greater equity in Indonesia. By the end of the period, Indonesia was by far the more equal society. These outcomes did not evolve in a steady progression: both economies experienced massive domestic and external shocks. The domestic shocks – war and hyperinflation – were country-specific, but the main external shocks

– the temporary oil windfalls – were common to both Nigeria and Indonesia. Although growth, equity and poverty outcomes diverged remarkably when viewed over the whole period, this is attributable to relatively brief periods after 1973 when external shocks were similar (well after the differing domestic shocks). Thus, the key question is why the performance of the two countries diverged during and after the oil shocks.

From Figures 5.1 and 5.2 Indonesia achieved a sustained reduction in infant mortality and significant improvement in life expectancy, especially after the 1980s. Nigeria made significant progress in reducing infant mortality from the 1960s through the mid-1980s. There has been a reversal since the pace was slowed in the decades that follow. The two countries are a study in contrasts; whereas life expectancy in Nigeria took the turn for the worse, that of Indonesia was one of sustained and continuous improvement over the years – from 48 years in the 1960s to 71 years in 2020. Nigeria achieved a marginal gain in life expectancy over the past six decades (see Figure 5.3). These have significant implication on population growth rates and in the annual stock of the population. From UN projections, the estimated population of Nigeria and Indonesia will be identical by 2038. Investment in human capital is an indispensable public policy priority if Nigeria is to use the growing population to stimulate sustainable economic growth.

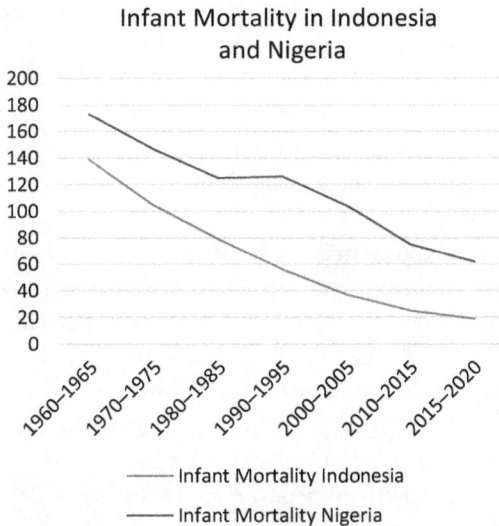

Figures 5.1. Comparing infant mortality rates in Indonesia and Nigeria between 1960 and 2020. Source: Authors from WDI.

Comparing Life Expectancy in
Indonesia and Nigeria
(1960–2020)

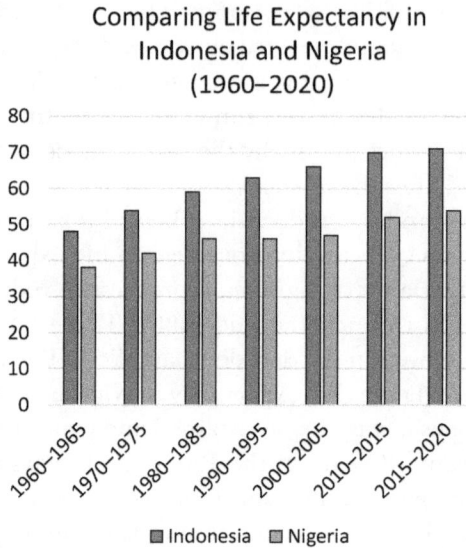

Figures 5.2. Comparing life expectancy in Indonesia and Nigeria from 1960 to 2020. Source: Authors from WDI.

Sector Sources of Growth

The lessons of this chapter throw up ever more compelling reasons for Nigeria to urgently move away from a monoculture oil-dependent economy to a diversified and high-quality exporter of processed and manufactured goods. Nigeria, Indonesia and Malaysia started with an economic model based on natural resources. We have shown in earlier chapters that these initial factor endowments tend to reach the limits of their economic contribution quickly. The chapter equally illustrates the importance of inclusive and diversified growth and further lay bare the unsustainability of natural resources dependence.

Agrarian agriculture practices prevent most of the poor who live in the rural sector, from benefiting from growth acceleration spillovers, including job creation and skills-enhancing effects. Export of agriculture raw materials is highly dependent on international prices; price volatility deriving from boom and busts transmits into similar cycles in the non-tradable economy. This undermines long-term high economic growth including job creation when the agricultural sector is modernized as well as poverty reduction in these high population growth environments. In addition, dependence on natural resources fails to foster the development of the human capital and skills that are the hallmark of every modern economy.

While Nigeria was famously known as a significant oil palm producer in the 1960s and 1970s, over the last four decades, Indonesia has left Nigeria

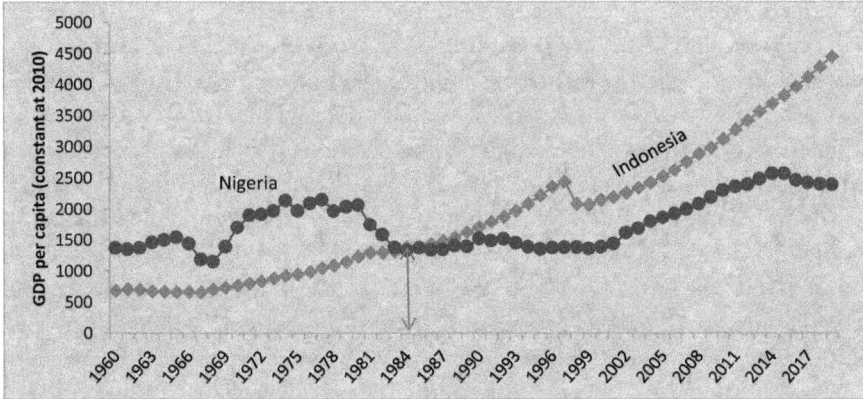

Figure 5.3. Indonesia and Nigeria's GDP per capita growth. Source: Author.

far behind to emerge as the global palm oil production giant. Malaysia and Indonesia between them account for around 85 to 90 per cent of total global palm oil production. Indonesia is the largest producer and exporter of palm oil worldwide. This chapter focusses on Indonesia and Nigeria both of which possess oil palm as a natural resource. One country succeeded while the other failed catastrophically. See Figure 5.3 showing clear reversals of development trajectories; the contrast with Nigeria, where growth stagnated in the 1970s and collapsed in the 1980s is dramatic.

Where they differ markedly is in terms of the nature and speed of sectoral diversification which underpins a country's transition from an agrarian society to an industrial nation. In the manner in which industrial diversification shielded countries from volatility, a country like Indonesia leveraged the concept of agricultural diversification to reduce risk to individual farmer's income as well as national and regional food supply risk. When a country relies on one or limited number of food crops, it faces direct risks from natural and market shocks as well as other hazards compared with a situation with a more diversified cropping system (Hedley, 1987). In situations of shocks to the economic system, agricultural diversification becomes an important response for attenuating the instability of rural income and therefore fostering rural economic growth and alleviating poverty.

The significance of this policy stance is manifested in agricultural development. The agricultural sector contributed to Indonesia's rapid economic growth and added to its sizeable public expenditure.[11] This promising growth potential attracted investments to Indonesia, mainly in the labour-intensive manufacturing sector. In contrast, Nigeria pursued investments in capital goods-led industrialization which failed disastrously at the expense of rural and agricultural development. Most of the industrial projects failed due to unstained investment and poor governance. It seems to lay the foundation for economic decline with the ripple effect of high poverty incidence and deterioration of living conditions that the country is witnessing currently.

There are two possible sets of explanations. First, the two countries adopted contrasting policies under similar political conditions of military rule. Indonesia focused on rural development and macroeconomic stability presumably because Indonesia had experience in managing social instability and economic crises in the past.[12] Nigeria by contrast invested heavily in industrialization setting up iron and steel plants, aluminium, fertilizer and other capital goods. In the process it neglected the agriculture sector not least because the country suddenly had access to easy income from crude petroleum export. But then the neglect of agriculture dates back to the colonial period.

> *More important than what the government did to support agriculture is how little it did. Only tiny amounts were allocated to primary production in the two development plans of the colonial period, which provided not much more than project lists. Only 6.5 percent was allocated to primary production in the 1946–56 plan and 11.9 percent in the 1955–60 plan. The development plans mark an important change in the role of the state in the economy.*[13]

The effect? 'The economy grew rapidly from 1960 to 1966, at about 5 per cent a year. Oil, public utilities, manufacturing, health, and education grew the most compared with other sectors, whereas agriculture was beginning to grind to a halt.'[14] The policy choice of industrial route, in hindsight, may not have been the most damaging but rather the way political institutions and corruption that developed around oil precipitated massive project failures.

The two countries deployed revenues from the oil boom to capital goods; the pattern of investment rates was not different in the two countries. We have seen that both recorded rapid industrial growth during the boom. While capital costs increased significantly in Nigeria, there was no commensurate output growth relative to capital accumulation. We will examine the reasons for the low growth later in the chapter, but one reason is that much of the monetary investment was not translated to capital accumulation. Due in large measure to poor project implementation and corruption, the country became a site of abandoned projects and inoperable industrial plants. Several examples abound in this book. For example, failure to manage its four crude oil refineries has turned the country into a net importer of petroleum products rather than an exporter. As we write this book, Zainab Ahmed, minister of finance, budget and national planning, says Nigeria spends on average 18 billion Naira (₦18.39 billion) or $40 million per day on oil subsidy. Subsidy or under-recovery is the shortfall for the underpriced sales of premium motor spirit (PMS), also known as petrol. The minister responded during an enquiry by the House of Representatives committee investigating petroleum products for subsidy regime from 2013 to 2022.[15]

This chapter shows that agribusiness is a critical sector for structural transformation and that a meaningful economic transformation may not be sustainable in the absence of a modernized industrial agriculture; this lack of agricultural modernization is what has left large swathes of African rural areas in poverty. This is illustrated by the contrasting experiences of the two comparator countries Nigeria and Indonesia.[16] While manufacturing export has helped to reduce poverty and fostered wealth creation, a country such as Indonesia, the biggest and one of the most important countries in the Asian region did so by horizontal diversification of agriculture. The country increased its per capita national income from US$200 (at constant 2,000 prices) in 1965 to more than US$1,000 in 2005 and was expected to reach US$4,200 by the end of 2020, and US$4,700 in 2022. In terms of capita GDP growth over the years 1965–1985, Indonesia ranked higher than any other Southeast Asian country apart from Singapore.

Sector Source of Growth: Oil Palm in Nigeria and Indonesia

Few Indonesian industrial sector has shown such robust growth as the domestic palm oil industry during the past 20 years. This growth is reflected by the country's rapidly rising production and export figures as well as by the growing quantity of its palm oil estate area. Driven by increased global demand and higher yields, palm oil cultivation has been expanded significantly by Indonesian farmers and conglomerates (at the expense of the environment and at the expense of production figures of other agricultural products such as cocoa or coffee because farmers switched to palm oil plantation due to the promising perspectives). The largest proportion of Indonesia's palm oil output is exported. The most important export destination countries are China, India, Pakistan, Malaysia and the Netherlands. Although the numbers are very insignificant, Indonesia also imports some palm oil, primarily from India.

Within the span of only a few decades, Indonesia has become the world's foremost producer of CPO, overtaking Malaysia in 2007.[17] With a production of 23.9 Mt in 2011, Indonesia accounts for 49.7 per cent of world production followed by Malaysia (37.8 per cent), Thailand (3.2 per cent), Nigeria (1.8 per cent) and Colombia (1.7 per cent) (see Figure 5.4). A third of Indonesian production is consumed domestically – roughly 7.82 Mt in 2012, mainly due to growing demand from urban areas – with the rest being exported. Demand for CPO is driven by many major importing countries, with India ranking first (7.8 Mt), representing 47 per cent of Indonesia's CPO exports, followed

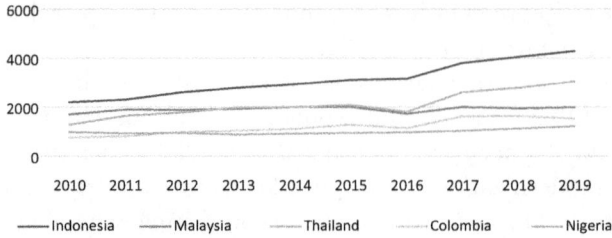

Figure 5.4. CPO production by top producers (2020–2019).

by China (6.3 Mt; although it mainly imports other palm oil products), the European Union (5.2 Mt) and Bangladesh (1 Mt), representing 10 per cent of all Indonesian exports.

Several factors explain the economic success of the Indonesian palm oil industry: investments in agro-industrial assets, governmental support and increasing global demand. These translate into high prices. However, palm oil production also presents its challenges. Intensive palm oil production requires initial investments that individual farmers can rarely afford. As a result, much of the Indonesian CPO market is dominated by large firms that in turn capture much of the benefits.

Factors explaining divergence with Nigeria[18]

As early as the 1960s in West Africa, the Ivory Coast had on the one hand planted 60,000 hectares from 1961–71 and planned to cover another 10,000 hectares from 1972–76, thereby increasing its relative importance as a producer by 1980. In Nigeria, on the other hand, not much progress was anticipated in output as the country was hardly reaching, by 1980, the pre-civil war, 1966 level. The Nigerian Government plans for planting and replanting did not achieve the expected and sufficient progress. Nothing seems to have changed even now in 2022. Rather than deploy its relatively good research results from R&D systems, its production systems have relied on outputs from wild groves, which in Nigeria accounts for over 90 per cent of total production. This source has continued to decline due to ageing trees and increasing difficulties in finding the necessary labour to ensure maximum exploitation of the groves. Predictably, Nigeria is now a net importer of palm oil since the 1980s. On the contrary, Southeast Asia has increased its total share of world output on account of more extensive plantings and higher yields, while the share of the traditional African producers has declined. Nigeria's strategy of relying on age-old traditional methods rather than adopting an industrial agriculture pathway has cost the country dearly: regrettable lost opportunities.

Research and Development: The success of Indonesia's oil palm has drawn on strong research and development work that led to progressively high yields over time. The country has steadily increased its replanting programme, and replanting adopted better suited varieties developed from hybrid research and cloning. The availability of land in Indonesia, coupled with years of high seed sales, record energy prices, and high vegetable oil prices are factors that resulted in Indonesia continuing to lead the world in palm oil production. Its leadership will likely continue for years to come.

In 2021, Nigeria's oil palm research was allocated ₦2.441 billion (US$5 million), its biggest funding in 10 years although notoriously budget is usually indicative and may not be fully disbursed. The Nigeria Institute for Oil Palm Research centre, located in Benin, Edo State, is the government's central research body for oil palm, coconuts, date palm, raffia and other palms.

In the 1950s and 1960s, Nigeria was considered the leader in the world's palm oil market. The production of palm oil went beyond domestic consumption, and the excess was exported. However, in the past decades, the country has become an importer of palm oil. In the early 1960s, Nigeria's palm oil production accounted for 43 per cent of the world production. However, Nigeria is currently struggling with less than 2 per cent of global output, according to data from United States Department of Agriculture. Nigeria was the top importer of Malaysia palm oil in the Sub-Saharan Africa region with 287,000 metric tons.

The Quality Seed Factor: The long-run extraordinary performance of the oil palm sector has also been a result of a steady supply of high-quality seeds, seedlings and young palms from specialized breeders and nursery operations that constitute a key pillar of the industry. The availability of quality hybrid seeds is essential for establishing plantations and replanting. Only the highest quality seeds are selected for use. The country has evolved a successful system of selection and certification that throw up high-quality seed characteristics.[19]

Coordination of palm oil areas and by holdings

The country has managed the ownership coordination through a mix of government holdings, private companies and smallholders: 45 per cent of total palm area is owned by private companies, followed closely at 43 per cent by smallholders, and the government comprising the remaining 12 per cent.[20] Smallholders are frequently part of partnership schemes with private companies. The coordination role provided by state institutions ensured that while being essentially a plantation crop, the oil palm industry has evolved in a way that successfully adapted to accommodate smallholders. This successful integration of this set of actors has been important for poverty alleviation in Indonesia, positively affecting millions. It led to significant improvement in living standards, including income, education and health levels that are attributed to the economic development benefits of oil palm cultivation.

Another important characteristic of this commodity is that it is a relatively low-priced oil that is used in a wide variety of products including foods and cosmetics. Global demand for palm oil has soared in the last three decades, driven by massive demand in food, consumer products and more recently as the raw material for biofuel. The continuing and insatiable demand by India and China fuels Indonesia and Malaysia's supplies and there remain prospects of increasing demand for edible vegetable oils. Dietary changes in the United States and the changing perception of consumers in relation to wellness have induced food manufacturers to find alternatives to trans-fat, partially hydrogenated oils, which contribute to heart disease and other medical problems.[21] In addition to being cost-competitive relative to other vegetable oils, palm oil is semi-solid at room temperature, making it ideal for baking and food production. Additionally, palm production is being promoted as a sustainable energy alternative around the globe, especially in European countries. Through the use of subsidies for biofuels, European governments have promoted the demand for palm oil in Europe.

Oil palm is the most productive vegetable oil crop, yielding more oil per hectare than any other major oilseed commodity. For example, the oil yield on a per unit area basis from properly maintained oil palms is significantly greater than oil yields from commercially grown rapeseed and soy. In terms of energy balance, it takes less sunlight to produce a unit of oil. However, on the basis of oil yield per man-day it is not as competitive because of the labour-intensive plantation management and harvesting of the fruit. This is less an issue in areas of Indonesia where labour is more readily available. Given the current situation, these characteristics appear to favour oil palm as a renewable energy source for the near future, until cellulosic technologies advance to an operation level. In addition, this activity raises several broader issues: primary forest protection, biodiversity conservation, climate change, poverty alleviation and energy production. This highlights the need for research into palm oil from the socio-economic and agronomic points of view.

Explaining Divergent Sectoral and Economic Diversification

This chapter shows that leadership, institutions and governance at micro and macroeconomic levels shape the divergent paths of these two countries. While the two countries share remarkable similarities, management of different sets of political economy forces and factors have accounted for the wide and widening developmental disparities between the level of economic development of Nigeria and Indonesia. We examine in outline form, the political and economic strategies that have helped Indonesia, the world's fourth biggest country to become and remain an economic powerhouse (an Asian Tiger) and what essentially Nigeria, Africa's biggest and the world's seventh biggest country, could learn from Southeastern Asian nation.

The key factors include the intertwined dimensions of relative levels of transparency, sectoral and economic diversification, targeted infrastructural development, and good governance, strong scientific and political institutions. Clearly, Nigeria has demonstrated a frustratingly low level of performance in the aforementioned variables. This is unlike Indonesia which has, comparatively, utilized a relatively more transparent system and progressive political economy strategies to enhance development, better management of its diversification agenda, leading to a more diversified economy that thrives not just on oil, but equally agribusiness, the service sector and Information Communication Technology.

Based on export-orientated industrialization since 1993, more than 50 per cent of Indonesia's exports consisted of manufactured goods; in a sharp contrast, in Nigeria, oil has remained predominantly the most important source of foreign exchange, while industrial exports are insignificant. What is however notable is the timing of the boom in the Indonesian industrial exports compared with that of the growth of its GDP. Rapid income growth was triggered in 1967 and grew sustainably until 1982, less than 5 per cent of Indonesia's exports began in 1983 and was a complete decade later in 1993. In other words, Indonesia's economic take-off had set in way before – by a full 15 years – it emerged as a dynamic industrial exporter. This means there was a clearly another source of GDP growth that preceded manufacturing export (see Figure 5.5).

The explanation lies in the innovations made to the agricultural sector, particularly in food-crop agriculture. Between 1968 and 1985 areal yields of rice, the staple food, rose by almost 80 per cent while total rice production grew almost three times faster than population growth. In 1974, Indonesia was a large rice importer in the world; by 1984, it was self-sufficient. The key factors responsible for the boom in food production were innovations applied to a largely subsistence agriculture base and the consistent application of new technological inputs.

These include higher per hectare use of artificial fertilizer in food-crop farming which increased by a factor of 10 in the years 1968 and 1985. The attainment and impact of this Green Revolution were dramatic in raising on-farm incomes, and as well, the prosperity and health of the rural economy.

On the contrary, in Nigeria, neither the initial agricultural nor the subsequent industrial stage of this transformation took place. While there are

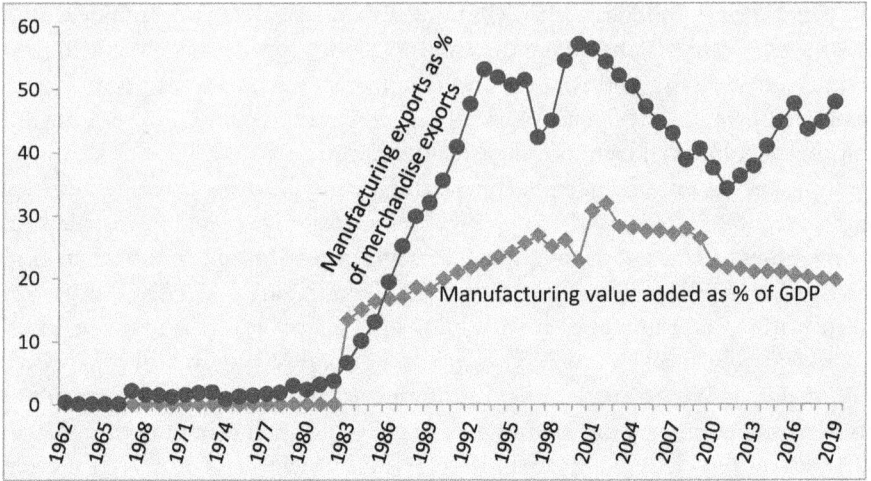

Figure 5.5. Indonesia agro-industrialization 1962–2019. Source: Authors.

major ecological differences with Asia, these differences should not be reasons for inaction. There have been significant breakthroughs in maize and cassava breeding, as far back as in the 1970s some of them achieved on Nigerian soil at the International Institute of Tropical Agriculture in Ibadan. However, in Nigeria as with several other countries in the region, the slow pace of modernization and lack of investment in innovations including in agricultural extension services prevented the potential of new varieties from being realized (Holmén, 2005).

Clearly relying on economic growth through easy exports of natural raw materials will not be enough to create the base for accumulating national wealth. Sub-Saharan Africa especially will have to address the persistent issue of food imports in the face of land and resource abundance. The old pattern of prospering solely through commodity trade has been shown to be a sub-optimal strategy compared with specialization in processed agriculture.

Sectoral growth and innovation

Indonesia like Malaysia has developed considerable processing capabilities off-farm including key product segments such as the fractionated palm oil product segment of the CPO. This is an important input into the food and beverage industry. The presence of vitamin A gives this product segment edge over the other segments making its utilization in edible products more desirable. Its extensive use in the food industry is expected to drive the market demand. Additionally, there is also significant demand for CPO from cosmetics and pharmaceuticals end-use industries as it is a crucial ingredient to produce many products from these industries.

Oil palm will continue to be important in other sectors apart from food and beverages which globally dominated the market with a revenue share of more than 65 per cent in 2021. Changing urban demand patterns in emerging and developing countries, its high share is attributable to increasing usage of the product end-use applications of the industry and increasing product portfolios that demand palm oil as a raw material. The rise in the global population has also affected the global product growth boosting the product demand in the international market. Yet stark differences are observed between Indonesia and Nigeria's production volumes and ability to respond to the global demand (see Figure 5.6).

With a scanty difference between their revenue share following the food and beverage end-use segments are personal care and cosmetics and biofuel and energy end-use segments. These are growing segments and are expected to attain prompt growth in the coming years as the advancement of technologies will occur.

Sectoral level governance

In 2009, the Government of Indonesia (GoI) introduced a mandatory standard called Indonesian Sustainable Palm Oil (ISPO). ISPO aimed, in a stepwise approach, to reach ambition levels of international certification schemes like RSPO. However, ISPO is not yet recognized on international

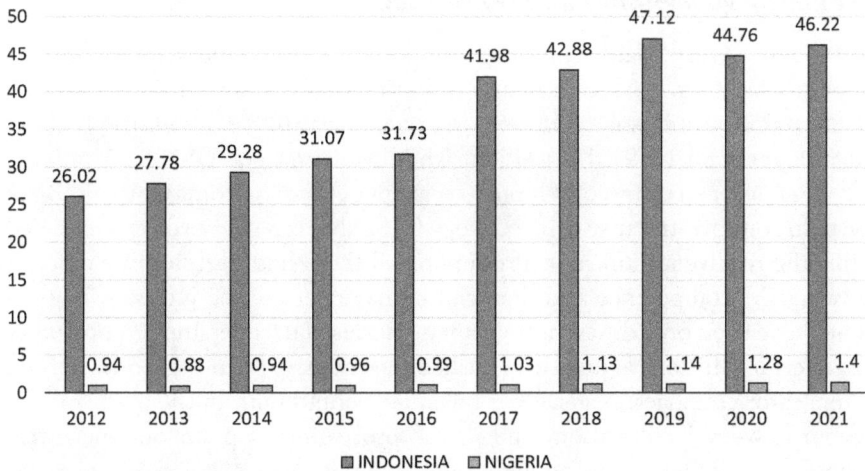

Figure 5.6. Production volume of palm oil in Indonesia and Nigeria from 2012 to 2021 (in million metric tons). Source: Authors.

CPO markets in a comparable way, as the level of ambition is still lower (see section on *Sector Sources of Growth*). Nevertheless, the ISPO scheme promotes sustainable palm oil production as follows. Under ISPO a set of seven principles (see below) have been defined which are further specified by corresponding criteria for different aspects of oil palm production. They basically refer to prescribing actions that are expected by the stakeholders in the oil palm value chain. During the introduction of ISPO, the Indonesian Ministry of Agriculture established an appraisal commission as an authoritative body in order to assess the compliance of stakeholders in the oil palm value chain with ISPO standards. The goal of the GoI had been that by 2014 all oil palm companies would be certified under ISPO, which however was not the case. In particular, the aim of the ISPO scheme is to define standards for the establishment and sustainability management of oil palm plantations including transportation, processing and marketing. These standards are formulated by principles and criteria and are meant to be legal guidelines for sustainable oil palm production. ISPO includes the following principles: (1) Licencing system and plantation management, (2) technical guidelines for oil palm cultivation and processing, (3) environmental monitoring, (4) labour standards, (5) social responsibility, (6) empowerment of local communities and (7) sustainable business improvement. In 2015, ISPO was revised and became mandatory for palm oil companies and voluntary for smallholder farmers (Ernah et al., 2016). Due to a lack of monitoring, however, the credibility of the ISPO standards is generally regarded as low (Brandi et al., 2013).[22]

Economic governance and institutions

In 1965, the World Bank[23] invested around US$2 billion into over 45 projects in Southeast Asia, Africa and parts of Latin America to support the growth of the palm oil industry. Indonesia received US$618.8 million, the highest; Nigeria received US$451.5 million, while Malaysia got US$383.5 million. Nigeria remained the second-largest recipient of funding from the World Bank for palm oil investments with six projects. Sadly, only one project succeeded while the rest went bankrupt. Presumably, if there had been a more efficient governance, competence and financial management of the industry, Nigeria could have been on a different trajectory of industrial leadership. Opportunity loss at critical historical junctures pushed the country down the ladder behind comparator countries. Nigeria has fallen far behind both in the on-farm ecosystem (low-level cultivation) and in the processing of palm oil where real economic value lies; from potential global export leader, Nigeria is now the sixth-highest palm oil-exporting country in Africa. The country imported about 350 and 400 million MT of palm oil in 2019 and 2020, respectively.

The government of Nigeria in November 2015 launched a programme called the Anchor Borrowers Programme (ABP) to provide farm inputs in kind and cash to smallholder farmers to boost agricultural production and for the country to reverse its negative BoP on food. Farmers included under this programme are those cultivating cereals, cotton, roots and tubers, sugarcane, tree crops (cocoa, rubber, oil palm, etc.) legumes, tomato and livestock. The loans are disbursed through any of the deposit money banks, development finance institutions and microfinance banks, all of which the programme recognizes as participating financial institutions. According to the guidelines of the programme, upon harvest, benefiting farmers are expected to repay their loans with harvested produce, which must cover the loan principal and interest, to an 'anchor' who pays the cash equivalent to the farmer's account. As with many such programmes, more is heard but seems not much impact on the targeted sectors. We are unaware of any impact assessment of the ABP despite the huge sums announced by the Central Bank of Nigeria.

At the broader political level, Nigeria has experienced chaotic governance with cycles of coups and countercoups while Indonesia projected a more stable political order, which contributed to economic development. This may partly account, for example, for the substantial foreign aid and investment partnership received by Indonesia compared to Nigeria in the former's journey to a developmental state. Hence, while Nigeria remains a fragile, close-to-failing state, the two Asian nations made the successful transition to an economic and social giant in the 1990s. It is not only that. In contrast to Nigeria's institutional lacuna featuring weakly performing, corrupt and divided institutions, Indonesia/Malaysia managed to transform that problem and became a more capable state in the area of policy formulation, execution and economic development generally. In other words, Nigeria was and continues to be held back by the politics of distribution, a feral political economy in which officeholders corner a substantial chunk of national revenue.

An important issue with oil dependency is ethnic fractionalization and the resulting conflicts over distribution and 'sharing' of resources. There is a strong connection of resource dependence and rent-seeking behaviour; the triggering of civil conflict, ethnic fractionalization particularly in the context of dysfunctional institutions and the prevalence of corruption.[24] The academic literature shows that growth that depends on increasing resource abundance could trigger conflicts in countries combining weak institutions and corrupt elite structure. When countries' development trajectory and output structure depend on oil and other minerals alone, the propensity to violent conflict intensifies (Collier et al., 2003).

Nigeria has additionally experienced unusual spate of violent conflicts and terrorism. Befuddling is the reality of a country that brought peace to Liberia and Sierra Leone but is unable for the most part to provide basic security to its citizens. Natural resource wealth has elicited violence driven by group inter-ests and competing interests. In conflict-rife environments, three main factors put the environment in an unstable situation (World Bank, 2011). First, the lack of trust between elites and the mistrust of the state by citizens due to eth-nicity and disillusionment that attends widespread poverty and inequality in poor countries. Second, the difficulty of respecting contracts and agreements since institutional change can increase the risks of violence in the short term; this is due to political backlash from the groups that lost power or economic benefits; and finally, institutional transformation can be quickly derailed from external security threats or economic shocks that derail progress. In short, fractionalization and conflict both violent and non-violent thus lead to over-dissipation of resource rents.

In Indonesia, the Javanese group asserted itself as a dominant ethnic group providing a measure of political continuity in Indonesia while Nigeria continues to be buffeted by an unresolved nationalities' question and deadly competition over the distribution of national resources viewed as a zero-sum game. While Indonesia, because of its relative stability, enjoyed political lon-gevity among office holders, there has been a rapid flux of Nigerian office holders resulting in the frequent interruption of well-laid-out policies with every government seeking to start afresh rather than continue the policies of its predecessors. Crucially, Indonesia subsequently outpaced Nigeria not just in growth (contrast Indonesia's impressive GDP growth at 7 per cent annu-ally to Nigeria's 3 per cent between 1970 and 1990) but in the alleviation of poverty with Nigeria descending recently to the world's poverty capital while Indonesia reduced the proportion of citizens living below the poverty line from roughly 60 per cent in the 1970s to less than 30 per cent by the begin-ning of the 1990s.

A final factor is that Indonesia has done much better than Nigeria in managing its population growth while Nigeria's continuously increasing population threatens to become a Malthusian nightmare and a demographic disaster.

Transparency in the economic development of Indonesia and Nigeria

Countries around the world spend an estimated US$9.4 trillion a year on procurement – 15 per cent of global GDP. Indeed, United Nation figures estimate that public procurement can account for 15–30 per cent of GDP for many countries. However, according to the United Nations Office on Drugs and Crime and the Organization for Economic Co-operation and

Development (OECD), 10–25 per cent of the value of public contracts is lost to corruption. This means that corruption, such as fraud, waste and abuse by government contractors, costs up to US$2.35 trillion globally on an annual basis.[25] According to Transparency International, in its July 2018 report, on recommendations for open contracting, 'procurement is one of government's most economically significant activities, but it also poses one of the greatest public sector corruption risks.'[26] One of the main reasons this corruption can flourish is that countries lack transparency when it comes to work being done by government contractors operating on an hourly basis. In virtually every country, government contractors work on an 'honour system' where there are no procedures in place to verify invoices for the hours worked by these contractors. This occurs in both developed and emerging countries. In fact, transparency International's Corruption Perceptions Index 2017[27] found high corruption in more than two-thirds of nations. One of the index's five recommendations is that civil society and governments should promote laws that focus on access to information. This access helps enhance transparency and accountability while reducing opportunities for corruption.

In addition, transparency is an essential strategy to prevent fraud. In a report by the International Monetary Fund in 2016, it was explained that

> *although transparency is a general prerequisite for the proper functioning of the market, it is also a core component of an effective anti-corruption policy. Transparency plays a critical role in ensuring the efficient allocation of resources by allowing the market to evaluate and impose discipline on government policy, and by increasing the political risk of unsustainable policies. In addition to these important functions, transparency can play a key role in preventing corruption and promoting good governance.*[28]

Thus, it can be deduced that productivity, transparency and effective accountability are intrinsically connected. Empirical evidence has shown that a lack of transparency and integrity can affect a country's productivity and economic growth.[29]

Indonesia's economy has expanded strongly over recent decades, notwithstanding the sharp economic contraction that occurred during the 1997–1998 Asian financial crisis. This strong pace of growth has seen Indonesia become an increasingly important part of the global economy. It is now the fourth largest economy in East Asia[30] – after China, Japan and South Korea – and the 15th largest economy in the world on a PPP basis. Indonesia has been described as the powerhouse economy of Asia. Indonesia's economy is now roughly the size of Brazil's and is half again larger than the economy of South Korea. The Indonesian economy has shown considerable resilience.[31]

Table 5.2. Corruption Perceptions Index for Indonesia and Nigeria.

Rank	Country	2020	2019	2018	2017	2016	2015	2014	2013	2012
149	Nigeria	**25**	26	27	27	28	26	27	25	27
102	Indonesia	**37**	40	38	37	37	36	34	32	32

Source: Transparency International: Corruption Perception Index. Table accessed on July 29th, 2021, from https://www.transparency.org/en/cpi/2020/table/cze.

Weathering the global economic uncertainty relatively well, it achieved annual growth rates averaging around 5 per cent over the past five years. The country continues to be an attractive investment destination, with its abundant natural resources and well-educated young population. Along the line of transparency, recent reform measures have put greater emphasis on improving regulatory efficiency, enhancing regional competitiveness and creating a more vibrant private sector through decentralization. Public finances have been relatively well managed, and debt has been kept under control at under 35 per cent of gross domestic product.[32] In the aftermath of the 1997 Asian Financial Crisis, the government took custody of a significant portion of private sector assets through the acquisition of nonperforming bank loans and corporate assets through the debt restructuring process and the companies in custody were sold for privatization several years later. Since 1999 the economy has recovered, and growth has accelerated to over 4–6 per cent in recent years.[33]

The Corruption Perceptions Index,[34] Transparency International's flagship research product, is the leading global indicator of public sector corruption. The index offers an annual snapshot of the relative degree of corruption by ranking countries and territories from all over the globe. According to the 2020 estimation, Indonesia ranked and scored 102/180 as shown in Table 5.2 and 37/100, respectively, while Nigeria ranked and scored 149/180 and 25/100, respectively.[35]

Differences in economic management and differential economic growth

The Indonesian economy has recorded strong growth over the past few decades, and in recent years the firm pace of economic expansion has been accompanied by reduced output volatility and relatively stable inflation. Indonesia's economic performance has been shaped by government policy, the country's endowment of natural resources and its young and growing labour force. Alongside the industrialization of its economy, Indonesia's trade openness has increased over the past half century. Undoubtedly, there is a lot Nigeria can learn from the management techniques applied by Indonesia in its race to the status of a developmental state and economic player on the world stage. Notwithstanding the sharp economic contraction that occurred during the 1997–1998 Asian financial crisis, Indonesia's economy has expanded strongly over recent decades. This owes greatly to the considerable change in the structure of the Indonesian economy. Historically, the economy has been heavily weighted towards the agricultural sector, reflecting both its stage of economic development and government policies in the 1950s and 1960s to promote agricultural self-sufficiency. A gradual process of industrialization and urbanization began in the late 1960s and accelerated in the 1980s as falling oil prices saw the Indonesian government focus on diversifying away from oil exports and towards manufactured exports.[36]

In addition, another strategy which aided the economic growth of Indonesia is a prudent financial macroeconomic policy which is one of the reasons why the country was resilient to the global financial crisis of 2008–2009. Both public and private debt dropped sharply (as a percentage of GDP), international reserves developed rapidly, and inflation was kept under control.[37] Another key element that accounts for Indonesia's recent economic growth is domestic consumption. In line with rising per capita GDP and low borrowing costs, Indonesia's private consumption is robust. It accounted for 56 per cent of the country's economic activity in 2011, and future projections indicate that it is to grow further.[38] Obviously, the Indonesian experience provides a toolkit from which Nigeria can borrow from and take-home lessons in the areas of macroeconomic policies and sound management of public finances.

Public finance mismanagement

Again, poor management of public finance is evident in revenue-to-GDP ratio. The ability of a government to collect tax – to fund public goods and services in developing countries – is a measure of governance capacity. Taxation provides the largest share of government revenues in almost all countries and is relatively predictable and sustainable, in contrast with non-tax revenue sources such as official development assistance and royalties. In most European countries, it is between 30 and 50 per cent. In 2019, the Asia-Pacific (24) average tax-to-GDP ratio was 21.0 per cent below the OECD and LAC averages (33.8 per cent and 22.9 per cent, respectively) and higher than the Africa (30) average (16.6 per cent, 2018 figure). Tax-to-GDP ratios in the 24 Asian and Pacific economies ranged from 10.3 per cent in Bhutan to 48.2 per cent in Nauru.

'Nigeria, unfortunately, has the distinction of having about the lowest revenue-to-GDP ratio in the world', the standard rule of thumb is that for the government to provide the basic services and law and order, it needs between 15 to 20 percent of GDP as being revenue, and this will be both at the federal and state levels combined. In Nigeria, it was eight percent in 2019. In 2020, in the middle of the COVID-19 crisis and with the fall in oil prices, that went down to about between five and six percent.[39]

Structural factors are a key determinant of tax-to-GDP ratios across economies. These include the importance of agriculture in the economy, openness to trade and the size of the informal economy. Agriculture, for example, is a challenging sector to tax: most people in the agriculture sector in developing economies are on low incomes and many are not registered for tax purposes.[40] In addition, agriculture benefits from numerous tax exemptions. For example, Malaysia allows an agriculture allowance to be deducted from profits of eligible businesses; and goods and services related to the agriculture sector are exempt from import duty and excise duty.

Summing Up

The comparison of Nigeria and Indonesia in this chapter offers dramatic evidence of developmental reversal driven in the main by contrasting policy choices at critical junctures of the nation's histories. We used the case of oil palm in the two countries to illustrate the divergences in approach and concomitant performance. Over the space of five decades, the oil palm sector that was Nigeria's main export commodity declined as with other commodities replaced by crude oil export. Clearly, Indonesia recorded success in industrialization and economic development. More than 70 per cent of the Indonesian economy was formerly dependent on agriculture, it has been reduced to only 40 per cent due to economic diversification.[41] Nigeria needs to also reduce its dependence on the oil sector and pay more attention to the non-oil sectors. Nigeria can learn from Indonesia's determination to improve its agricultural sector, especially the palm oil seedling.

The loss of competitiveness in commodity export was compounded by the lack of evolution into processing and value addition and in acquiring capabilities for economic diversification. Sectoral and structural transformation translated to a higher standard of living for Indonesians arising from a GDP double that of Nigeria. Indonesia equally achieved a relatively more equal society through equitable growth.

There were seven distinct areas of policy divergence: First, Indonesia was deliberate in targeting agriculture as a means of poverty reduction. Second, it gave higher priorities to a commodity in which it had a significant comparative advantage using its vast landmass to outpace Nigeria which does not have a shortage of land itself. Third, Nigeria relied on natural forces to grow the oil palm while Indonesia applied science to increase yield per unit of land. Fourth, Indonesia made an explicit effort and moved away from import-substituting industrialization while Nigeria remained stuck in import substitution. Fifth, while both have considerable natural resources, Nigeria lags far behind in manufactured exports. Sixth, Indonesia has been better at managing public finance and corruption, relatively. Seventh and more central to this book, Nigeria has lost the opportunity to develop industrial capacity over the last five decades due to its pathology of resource dependence and short-term easy income policy. We have shown the outcome of these policy stances using a number of metrics of economic performance of the two countries; it is clear why and when they began to diverge.

What do we recommend? Clearly, the Nigerian government should make greater effort and implement policies for the diversification of the economy. For over 25 years, successive Nigerian governments' effort to industrialize the economy has been a failure. This lack of success in industrializing the agriculture sector has in the main led to the country's desired economic growth. In turn, these policies will help contribute to sustaining economic growth of the country. Additionally, the country and its policymakers need to focus on policies which foster more rapid and targeted infrastructural investment towards industrial development and sustained economic growth.

At the sectoral level, Nigeria needs more explicit investment in growth and transformation strategy for agribusiness. The key objectives are: first, to raise the productivity of on-farm activities (primary agriculture) as a way to generate competitiveness in the downstream (off-farm) areas. Second, facilitation of more effective coordinative structures across the agricultural value chains. This will include for oil palm, for example, assisting smallholders to cluster and eliminate atomistic spot markets and replace with organization fostering effective vertical integrations. Third, creating incentives to expand manufacturing processing of higher-value farm products from CPO. This recommendation applies to other crops treated in other chapters. Processing generates automatic backward and forward linkages in ways that feed productive value chain development approaches that establish strong links with primary agriculture.

Fourth, strengthen organizations and institutional structures that upgrade and foster access to knowledge, skills and quality certification. Agribusinesses in Nigeria's oil palm sector have been short on skills due to a lack of continuous learning and a lack of public investment in R&D and manufacturing processing infrastructure. While some private sector organizations have thrived including on-farm and off-farm processing, much of the skills remain locked in these organizations. Growth of off-farm agribusiness, especially small and medium private enterprises, depends on public sector support as the cases of Indonesia and Malaysia oil palm industry demonstrate. This is largely absent in Nigeria.

Notes

1 "Indonesia Natural Rubber Exports Value" (2020), Statista, accessed June 26, 2022
2 The World Facts Book. July 26, 2021, https://www.cia.gov/the-world-factbook/coun-tries/indonesia/. July 2021 est, accessed 26 July 2021.
3 NBS 2017, Cited in Muhammad Fuad Othman and Ismail Bello (September 2019), "Indonesia-Nigeria Foreign Economic Relations: A Partnership for Economic Development." *Journal of Economic Cooperation and Development*. Accessed from https://www.researchgate.net/publication/336140912
4 The World Facts Book. July 26, 2021, https://www.cia.gov/the-world-factbook/coun-tries/indonesia/. July 2021 est, accessed 26 July 2021.
5 The World Facts Book. https://www.cia.gov/the-world-factbook/countries/nigeria/, accessed July 26, 2021.
6 Ibid.
7 Ibid., July 2021 est.
8 July 26, 2021, https://georank.org/economy/indonesia/nigeria, accessed 26 July 2021.
9 Ahmad Helmy Fuady (2015), "Aid and Policy Preferences in Oil-Rich Countries: Comparing Indonesia and Nigeria." Accessed from https://doi.org/10.1080/01436597.2015.1041490
10 Ibid.
11 Afriyanti et. al. (2023); Thorbecke (1998).
12 The adoption of prudent macroeconomic policies was due to the experience of hyper-inflation and mass poverty that paved the way for Suharto's emergence as president in the first place. The economic stabilization programs were mainly targeted at control-ling inflation, ensuring food security and getting relief from the debt burden.
13 https://documents1.worldbank.org/curated/en/118981468775569456/pdf/multi-page.pdf, p. 35, accessed July 27, 2022.
14 Ibid., 44.
15 https://punchng.com/fg-spends-n18-397bn-on-petrol-subsidy-daily-minister/, accessed August 19, 2022.
16 This Indonesian case study draws on D. Henley (2012), "The Agrarian Roots of Industrial Growth: Rural Development in South-East Asia and Sub-Saharan Africa." *Development Policy Review*, 30(51): 525–47.
17 This section compiled from, Baudoin et al. (2017), Oilworld (2011), Jacquemard (2012), Wahid et al. (2004), Kehati et al. (2006), Levang (1997), Sevin and Levang (1989).
18 Compiled from USAID, Commodities Intelligence Report. https://ipad.fas.usda.gov/highlights/2007/12/indonesia_palmoil/

19 A germinated seed is cultured in the pre-nursery for 3 months, then moved to a nursery to develop for an additional 9 to 10 months. After this initial phase from germination to plant establishment of one year, the plants are culled for the best characteristics and then planted in the field. After 30 to 36 months in the field, the young palms begin to produce the first harvestable fruit bunches. The first bunches are small and weigh only 2 to 3 kg, and the individual fruitlets comprising the bunch are small in size. Peak harvest (or palm productivity) occurs from years 8 to 15.

20 Indonesia Bureau of Statistics (BPS, 2006).

21 https://ipad.fas.usda.gov/highlights/2007/12/indonesia_palmoil/, accessed June 23, 2022.

22 https://www.oeko.de/fileadmin/oekodoc/BioMacht-palm-oil-report.pdf, accessed June 25, 2022.

23 World Bank, oil palm, Indonesia, Nigeria, support, 1965 - Search (bing.com), accessed, June 27, 2022.

24 van der Ploeg, *Journal of Economic Literature*, 2366–420.

25 Alex Konanykhin (2018), "How Transparency can Help the Global Economy to Grow." July 27, 2021, https://www.weforum.org/agenda/2018/10/how-transparency-can-help-grow-the-global-economy/, accessed 27 July 2021.

26 July 27, 2021, https://www.transparency.org/whatwedo/publication/recommendations_on_open_contracting_for_open_government_partnership_national, accessed 27 July 2021.

27 July 27, 2021, https://www.transparency.org/news/feature/corruption_perceptions_index_2017, accessed 27 July 2021.

28 IMF Staff Discussion Note (May 2016), "Corruption: Costs and Mitigating Strategies." July 27, 2021, https://www.imf.org/external/pubs/ft/sdn/2016/sdn1605.pdf, accessed 27 July 2021.

29 Americas Business Dialogue (2018), "Action for Growth: Policy Recommendations and Plan of Action 2018-2021 for Growth in the Americas." https://americasbd.org/en/2018-report/

30 Stephen Elias and Clare None (2011), "The Growth and Development of the Indonesian Economy." July 27, 2021, https://www.rba.gov.au/publications/bulletin/2011/dec/pdf/bu-1211-4.pdf, accessed 27 July 2021.

31 Anthony B. Kim (2020), "Indonesia: An Asian Powerhouse Growing Fast." July 27, 2021, https://www.dailysignal.com/2020/07/09/indonesia-an-asian-powerhouse-growing-fast/, accessed 27 July 2021.

32 Ibid.

33 Ibid.

34 Transparency International. "Corruption Perception Index." July 27, 2021, https://www.transparency.org/en/countries/indonesia, accessed 27 July 2021.

35 Transparency International. "Corruption Perception Index." July 27, 2021, https://www.transparency.org/en/countries/nigeria, accessed 27 July 2021.

36 M. S. Goeltom (2007), "Economic and Fiscal Reforms: The Experience of Indonesia, 1980–1996," in *Essays in Macroeconomic Policy: The Indonesian Experience* (Jakarta: PT GramediaPustaka), 489–506.

37 https://www.indonesia-investments.com/culture/economy/general-economic-outline/item251.

38 Ibid.

39 https://www.thecable.ng/nigerias-revenue-to-gdp-ratio-lowest-in-the-world-says -world-bank

40 https://www.oecd-ilibrary.org/sites/cb712500-en/index.html?itemId=/content/ component/cb712500-en

41 Othman and Bello, "Indonesia-Nigeria Foreign Economic Relations."

Chapter 6

DIVERSIFICATION SUCCESS AND FAILURE: MALAYSIA AND NIGERIA

Introduction

Nigeria exported US$33.5 billion worth of goods in 2020. The biggest export is crude oil, a commodity that represents three-quarters (75.4 per cent) of its total exported goods by value. With a population of 206 million people, the total export value translates to roughly US$160 for every person. Compare a country like Malaysia. In 1990, Malaysia's export was US$32.8 billion. Nigeria is at where Malaysia's export capability was 30 years ago. That country with a population of 33 million people, exported goods worth US$234 billion in 2020, translates to roughly US$7,100 for every resident. In other words, Malaysia progressed; it did so through a strong *Vertical Diversification* from its modest agricultural base (rubber and oil palm) by investing explicitly in high-tech sectors capabilities, especially electronics. It did not neglect its agricultural sector but rather through *horizontal diversification* industrialized its agricultural sector. Malaysia's biggest export products by value in 2020 were electronic integrated circuits, refined petroleum oils, palm oil, vulcanized rubber clothing or accessories and solar power diodes or semiconductors. Petroleum oil contribution to Malaysia's export declined over time.

On the other hand, Nigeria's pathology of oil dependence became entrenched over time. Nigeria's oil exports in 2019 were 94.1 per cent of total exports, where oil rents amounted to 9 per cent of GDP. The poorly diversified structure of the Nigerian economy reveals the constrained export revenue of the country. The oil and gas sector makes only a small contribution to GDP despite generating most of the export earnings. By nature, the oil and gas sector is a high-technology and capital-intensive industry relative to agribusiness and other low/medium manufacturing sectors (textiles, garments, leather processing, consumer goods, etc.), and employs relatively few people. The oil sector is an enclave, geographically delimited. According to OPEC, Nigeria spent US$264.57 billion importing petroleum products during the five-year period from 2015 to 2020, which means that Nigeria's petroleum products imports exceeded its exports by US$43.56 billion during the period.

More pointedly, due to two sets of factors, namely technological knowledge and overall educational attainment, there has been a wide and growing gap between the two regions.[1] In the export of what was Africa's comparative advantage,[2] much ground has now been lost to Asia in the export of traditional African agricultural products like palm oil, coffee and cocoa.[3] Specifically, Nigeria and Malaysia were practically at the same income per capita. However, there has been a significant divergence in income per capita figures of the two countries over time (see Figure 6.1). Except for 1981, Malaysia consistently had a higher income per capita than Nigeria.

This chapter provides a comparative analysis of Nigeria and Malaysia to emphasize the imperative for economic diversification, strategic investment in key resources and enabling institutions in fostering economic growth and development. In the sections that follow, we analyse the evolution of the macroeconomic conditions as well as structural changes. We use examples of the two countries' rubber and oil palm industries to conduct detailed case studies and to tease out key factors of success and failure. The final section sums up our findings.

At independence, close to 50 years ago when colonialism ended or was at its last phase for African countries, Africa and Asia were largely rural peasantries with low living standards. Since then, the two regions have

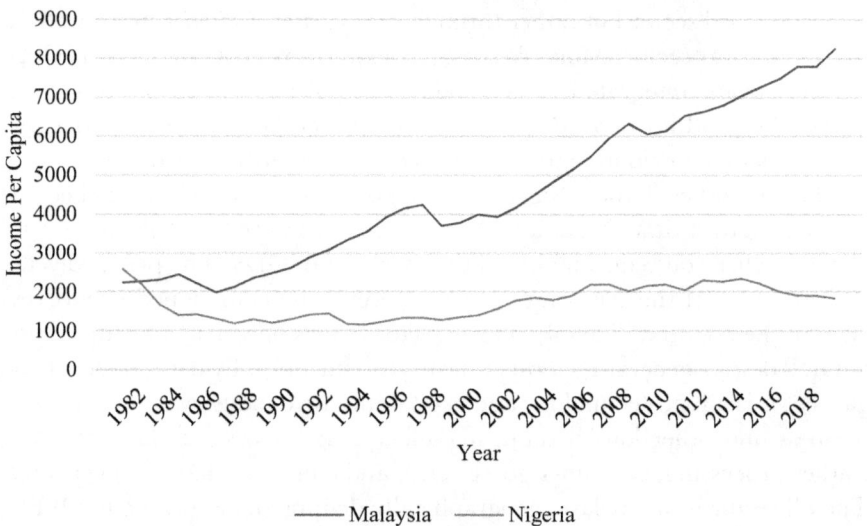

Figure 6.1. Income per capita ($US) for Nigeria and Malaysia, 1980–2020. Source: Calculated by authors, WDI.

experienced a sustained divergence in paths and processes of development. On the one hand, one region has advanced into export-oriented manufacturing industries with a strong base of technological capabilities while the other has remained largely agrarian with low technological capabilities across most sectors. Concomitantly, while one region has raised the standard of living of its people, a large swathe of Africa has experienced regress.

Malaysia's Economic Context

Malaysia typifies an economy that though endowed with abundant natural resources has been successful in diversifying its economy over its five decades of post-independence growth and development. Since the country gained its independence from England in 1957, the economy has diversified beyond agriculture and primary commodities. The economy shifted from being one dominated by tin, agriculture and exports of agricultural commodities to an economy that is more industrialized. Its manufactured exports now constitute a sizeable share of total exports and GDP while agriculture's share of GDP dropped over time. Agriculture's share of GDP dropped from about 44 per cent in 1960 to about 23 per cent in 1980, 8.6 per cent in 2,000 and 10 per cent in 2021. Manufacturing on the other hand increased from 10 per cent in 1960 to 22 per cent in 1980, 31 per cent in 2000 and 24 per cent in 2021. Interestingly, services have been a major contributor to GDP, rising from 43 per cent in 1987 to 46 per cent in 2000 and 52 per cent in 2021 (see Figure 6.2).

Malaysia's growth record has not been a uniform one as the country has experienced volatile growth in its economic history. Over the course of its post-independence years, it has experienced periods of slow and fast growth.

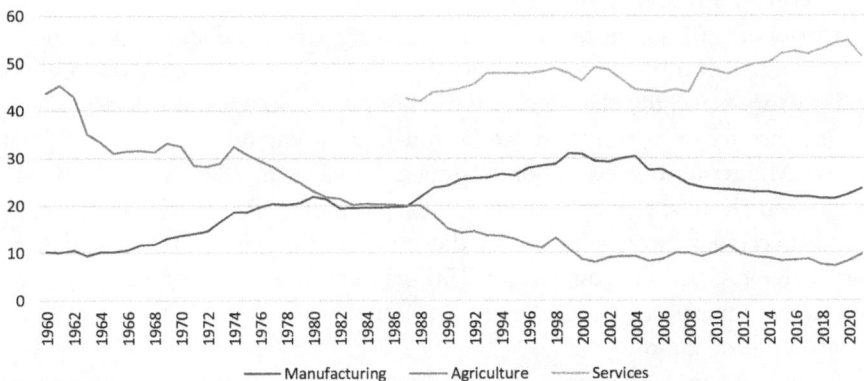

Figure 6.2. Malaysia manufacturing, agriculture and services, value added (% of GDP). Source: Author's calculations, The World Bank Group (2022).

In the late 1970s, public investment played a more active role in the economy to support affirmative action policies. Economic growth of the 1980s was high relative to the 1970s. This growth was engineered by the drive for industrialization, introduction of pro-growth policies and a push for heavy industries that began in the second half of the 1980s. During the 1990s, growth averaged more than 8 per cent per annum up until the verge of the financial crisis where there were more liberalization, greater foreign direct investment (FDI) inflows and an expanded role for private investment.

From 1991, export diversification become intensified and at a fast pace as the export of goods and services grew at 17 per cent per annum. The trade intensity ratio, which was about 86.9 per cent of GDP in 1970, increased to about 228.9 per cent by 2000. Malaysia's export structure has witnessed dramatic change from the export of tin, rubber and palm oil, which dominated its export in the 1950s and 1960s to exports of manufactured goods such as electronics and electrical products. Imports of intermediate goods were on the increase due to investment in manufactured export. The basis for this export-led growth in the manufacturing sector is due to the industrial policy approach adopted by the Malaysian government, which supported exporters by providing tax holidays and creating export processing zones. The government also used tariffs, import restrictions and government procurement of locally produced goods to promote exports and protect domestic manufacturers.

Economic growth has been accompanied by the greater importance of trade to the Malaysian economy and the growth of the manufacturing sector from the 1980s until date. FDI played a central role in the diversification of the economy while growth of the manufactured exports has contributed much to the diversification of Malaysia's exports. Generally, Malaysia has kept its economy relatively open.

In essence, Malaysia has achieved a strong *Vertical Diversification* from its modest agricultural base (rubber and oil palm) by investing explicitly in high-tech sectors especially electronics. It did not neglect its agricultural sector but rather through investment in R&D and human capital, industrialized the sector. Malaysia's biggest export products by value in 2020 were electronic integrated circuits, refined petroleum oils, palm oil, vulcanized rubber clothing or accessories and solar power diodes or semiconductors. In aggregate, those major exports accounted for 37.6 per cent of overall export sales from Malaysia. That percentage suggests a relatively concentrated range of high-value exported goods.

In contrast to Malaysia which developed a strong manufacturing export capability, subsistence agriculture still dominates Nigeria's rural economy although services have grown faster becoming a stronger contributor to GDP than manufacturing. Agriculture's value-added share of GDP rose from 12 per cent in 1981 to 25 per cent in 2001 and was 23 per cent in 2021. Manufacturing, on the other hand, fell from 20 per cent in 1981 to 14 per cent in 2001 and was 15 per cent in 2021. Notably, services' contribution hovers around 40 per cent, falling from 48 per cent in 1981 to 44 per cent in both 2001 and 2021 (see Figure 6.3).

Nigeria is a leading producer of cash crops such as cashew; but as with cocoa and oil palm, it exports raw cashew mostly. This is one of its notable failures, the lack of horizontal diversification into processed good which fetch higher revenues. For example, one tonne of raw cashew fetches US$1,200 while processed cashew nuts sell internationally for US$10,000. Nigeria as with most African producers exports most of its in-shell cashew nuts in raw form. David Pilling of *Financial Times* describes the unequal trade relations of the twenty-first century thus: 'For centuries, the world's most advanced economies used African slaves to pick their cotton and harvest their sugar in places such as the US and the Caribbean. Slavery has been banned. The West would now prefer to leave these workers where they are to produce what the world needs. The power relations remain essentially unchanged.'[4]

The poorly diversified export structure of the Nigerian economy is revealed in the far lower export revenue of the country. Nigeria is placed among world-leading export nations that sell oil seeds rather than refined oil products and is a major competitor delivering crude oil rather than refined petroleum products and cocoa beans rather than chocolate to international markets.

Next, we take a closer look at Nigeria and Malaysia's rubber and palm oil sectors in terms of: (1) performance measured by production and export over

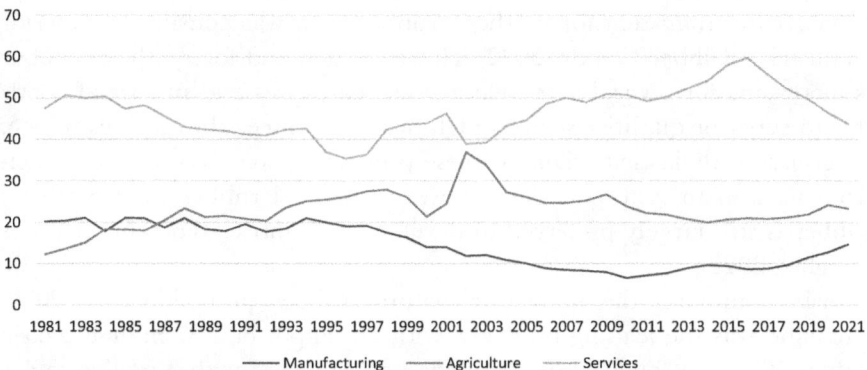

Figure 6.3. Nigeria's manufacturing, agriculture and services, value added (% of GDP). Source: The World Bank Group (2022).

time and (2) Manufacturing Value Added mainly successful in Malaysia and (3) success or failure factors.

Rubber and Rubber Products

Rubber is a natural resource and raw material whose durability, elasticity, heat and abrasion resistance puts it in high demand for essential products in sectors such as transportation, communication, construction, industrial, medical and packaging. The largest uses were first for tyres, then non-tyre automotive, footwear, industrial and finally other uses (Fortune Business Insights, 2022). The demand in the automotive industry for tyres is huge given qualities of being abrasion tear resistance and flexibility. Non-tyre automotive applications include the production of adhesives, floor mats, gaskets, crap tubes, hoses, among others.

Rubber has traditionally been used in footwear production as it provides durability, traction and comfort given it is lightweight and offers protection against chemicals, electricity and water. Rubber combined with different chemicals and polymers are used in the making of pacemakers, respirators, surgical supplies and feeding nipples. It is also used in the making of mouldings, roofing and sealants in constructions, as well as air brake diaphragms, conveyors, elevator belts and other material handling equipment.[5]

According to Statista, the global market size was around US$39.7 billion in 2020 and is expected to reach US$68.4 billion by the end of 2026, growing at a CAGR of 8.0 per cent.[6] Another market research estimates it at US$40.77 billion in 2019, with a projection of US$51.21 billion in 2027, with a CAGR of 5.3 per cent.[7] Rubber is available for use in both natural and synthetic forms. Traditionally, demand for natural rubber has always been greater than that for synthetic rubber, as it was considered superior (Industrial Rubber Goods, 2022). However, demand for synthetic rubber is increasing for several uses such as footwear, tyres and industrial goods due to superior qualities such as high heat resistance, abrasion resistance, toughness and elasticity. Due to these properties, some consumers switch from natural to synthetic uses. However, natural rubber over synthetic rubber is still largely preferred in developing countries (Fortune Business Insights, 2022).

Asia dominates the market in natural rubber production. In 2020, Thailand was the leading producer, with an output of 4.37 million metric tonnes. This was followed by Indonesia and Malaysia with 3 million and 1 million metric tonnes, respectively. According to a report by Ivory Coast's Association of Natural Rubber Professionals (APROMAC), Ivory Coast, producing 900,000 tonnes was the fourth largest producer, while Nigeria with 200,000 tonnes was the 12th largest global producer, and the second in Africa.[8]

The Malaysian and Nigerian rubber and rubber products industry overview

The British colonists introduced rubber to Malaysia after its introduction to Singapore in 1877. Malaysia had an ideal soil, climate and plenty of land suitable to produce natural rubber. Production increased in the 1890s after there was a huge demand for rubber. Tin and rubber were for many years Malaysia's primary exports. By the 1930s, Malaysia was producing up to half of the global rubber production and 'was the world's largest producer and exporter of natural rubber for much of the 20th century'.[9] Europeans then owned most of the plantations. A significant number of the plantations were turned over to Malaysians after independence in 1957, and some were converted to palm oil plantations.

Traditionally, smallholders contributed a significant amount of rubber produced. Reports from the rubber board note that those with less than 40 hectares (99 acres) contribute 95 per cent of Malaysian's production.[10]

The sector has not been without its challenges. Among them are competition and declining productivity which forced many farmers to abandon rubber production; by some estimate, up to 300,000 hectares of the 1.4 million hectares of rubber planted were abandoned between 1999 and 2003, in some cases in favour of oil palm production, which was viewed to be more lucrative. Malaysia has become one of the largest importers of rubber, with rubber manufacturers having to import rubber. By 2015, Malaysia became the sixth largest producer and exporter of rubber, being overtaken by Thailand, followed by Indonesia, Vietnam, China and India.[11]

Like Malaysia, Nigeria has favourable weather conditions and vast arable land conducive to produce rubber. Estimates show that about 18 million hectares of land, mainly located in the rain forest area of the country, are suited for cultivating natural rubber in Nigeria (Okwu, Eguavoen and Okore, 2015). Currently, natural rubber is produced in both the Northern and Southern parts of the country. Rubber-producing states include Abia, Akwa Ibom, Anambra, Bayelsa, Benue, Cross River, Delta, Ebonyi, Edo, Ekiti, Kogi, Kwara, Ogun, Ondo, Osun, Oyo, Kaduna and Taraba. Nigeria does not produce synthetic rubber. The country's failure to diversify beyond oil has however also impacted the rubber industry. Rubber was historically a key agricultural export commodity. In the 1960s and early 1970s, it was the fourth most valuable agricultural export commodity, following cocoa, groundnuts and palm kernels.[12] It however suffered a decline, given the emergence of petroleum as a main source of revenue.

In Nigeria, the land area under cultivation increased between 1965 and 1980 but has been declining since then. In 1965, 36,084 estates were producing rubber and a total of 243,479 hectares (ha) was under cultivation. In 1980, 53,000 estates cultivated 248,800 ha. This dropped to 50,000 estates cultivating 200,000 ha by 2000. At least 75 per cent of the estates are small holdings. While there was an increase in the total number of estates cultivating rubber over the period, either the size of cultivated land or productivity per estate declined, given the drop in land area cultivated.

The Malaysian and Nigerian rubber and rubber products industry historical sector performance

In this section, we compare the performance of the Malaysian and Nigerian rubber and rubber products industry along three criteria – production of natural rubber, area of natural rubber harvested and yields from 1961 to 2018.

Area of natural rubber harvested (Ha)

The area of natural rubber harvested reflects the area from which rubber was gathered and is measured in hectares. It excludes areas from which crops were planted but were not harvested due to crop failure, crop damage, among others. From 1961 to 2018, area harvested in Nigeria was approximately 73,000 Ha to 360,000 Ha while area harvested in Malaysia ranges from approximately 1.0 million Ha to 1.9 million Ha. Comparing the trends in the two countries as seen in Figure 6.4, we find that Nigeria has not harvested up to half of the areas of rubber harvested in Malaysia over the years.

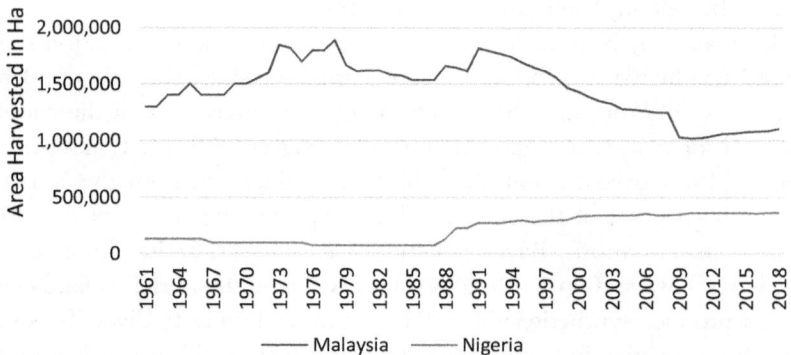

Figure 6.4. Trends on area of natural rubber harvested in Malaysia versus Nigeria (1961–2018). Source: Food and Agriculture Organization (FAO) (2022).

Notably, the area harvested in Malaysia shows a steady decline from the 1990s until 2017. However, there was a slight increase in the area harvested in 2018. The area harvested in Nigeria on the other hand is seen to increase consistently from 1988 to 2018. The area harvested in Nigeria between 2000 and 2018 was four times that harvested between the 1960s and 1990s.

Yields of natural rubber (tonne/Ha)

Rubber yields refer to harvested production per unit of harvested area for crop products. Rubber yields in Malaysia range from 0.52 to 1.03 tonnes/ Ha and 0.32 to 0.85 tonnes/Ha in Nigeria between 1961 and 2018. The yield recorded in both countries fluctuates over the years. In Malaysia, the least values were recorded in the 1990s while the highest yields were recorded in the 1970s and 1980s.

In Nigeria, the highest values were recorded in the 1960s and 1980s. However, a fall in yield values was recorded in the 1990s. From 2000 to 2018, yield remains steadily low at less than 0.5 tonnes/Ha. Comparing the trend in natural rubber yields between Malaysia and Nigeria as seen in Figure 6.5, we find that Malaysia performs better than Nigeria.

Natural rubber production (Tonnes)

The rubber production data measures the actual harvested production from the field and excludes harvesting losses and those not harvested. It captures quantities both consumed and used by the producers and those sold. We find that in Malaysia, the production output of natural rubber ranges

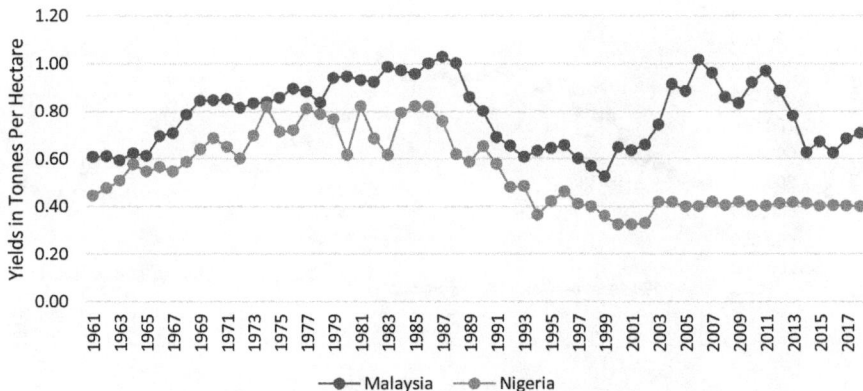

Figure 6.5. Trends in yields of natural rubber in Malaysia versus Nigeria (1961– 2018). Source: Food and Agriculture Organization (FAO) (2022).

from approximately 669,000 to 1.7 million tonnes from 1961 to 2018, with the greatest outputs between the 1960s and the 1980s. Production fell in the 1990s, and this fall is still noticeable between 2000 and 2018. This might be because of the possibility of shift in focus of the priority value chain in Malaysia. For Nigeria, the reverse was the case as we can see higher production levels from the 1990s to 2018, although, there was a slight fall in production values between 1999 and 2002.

Comparing the production trends in Malaysia and Nigeria in Figure 6.6, Malaysia performs far better than Nigeria. While the lowest production value in Malaysia was 669,000 tonnes, the highest value of natural rubber produced in Nigeria was 155,000 tonnes. This shows that Nigeria has not been able to harness the full potential of natural rubber, if done; Nigeria could be a net exporter of rubber.

Nigeria and Malaysia's rubber and rubber products – manufacturing value addition

Malaysia has been successful in diversifying from the production of rubber to being a major play in the industrial rubber sector. Malaysia continues to thrive in the rubber manufacturing market. The strong industrial rubber sector became a major beneficiary of the pandemic as the Malaysian rubber products sector which witnesses the total exports exceeded RM40 billion for the first time with an export revenue of US$10.96 billion in 2020, increased by 75.6 per cent as compared to the exports in 2019. The strong performance in exports was contributed by the latex goods sub-sector which posted a year-on-year growth of 95.3 per cent in 2020. The latex goods sector comprises mainly medical devices such as gloves and catheters. The sector made up 90

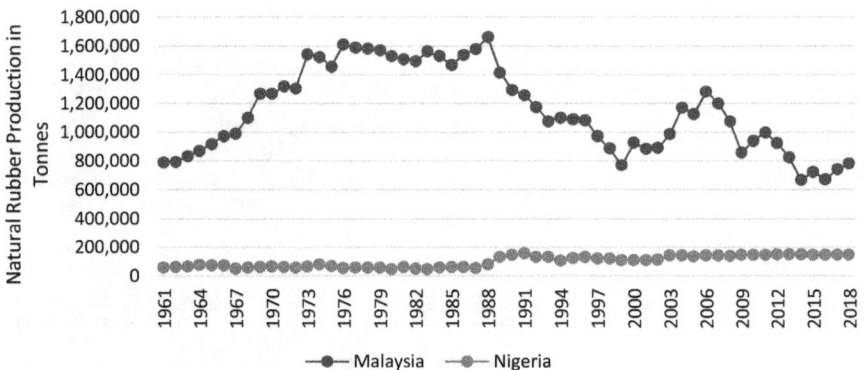

Figure 6.6. Trends in natural rubber production in Malaysia versus Nigeria (1961–2018). Source: Food and Agriculture Organization (FAO) (2022).

per cent of the total rubber products exports in 2020, increased from 81 per cent recorded in 2019. The increase resulted from high demand from the medical and health sectors worldwide, in the effort to curb the spread of the COVID-19 pandemic. Rubber gloves alone made up 86 per cent of the country's rubber products exports. Globally, Malaysia has been supplying more than 60 per cent of the world's demand for rubber gloves, and the Malaysian Rubber Council estimates the share to expand to 68 per cent in 2020.

BOX 6.1 SUCCESS IN RUBBER PRODUCTION MANUFACTURING AMONG MALAYSIAN COMPANIES

Top Glove and Kossan were the largest and second-largest glove makers as at 2018. Their R&D activities have been characterized by entrepreneurial astuteness to pursue niche advantages. In advancing from the initial to higher stages of innovative activities, TopGlove and Kossan showed similar trajectories. Both firms initially acquired basic knowledge and technology from the Malaysia Rubber Board (MRB). At the intermediate stage, they gained public assistance in the provision of technologies of practical use (Kawano, 2017). However, at the highest upgrading stage, Top Glove and Kossan relied on their own efforts to develop human resources and in-house R&D and to formulate business strategies to secure niche markets in the developing countries or low-income countries not targeted by multinational pharmaceutical companies. In these markets, Top Glove and Kossan operated as original design manufacturers and original brand manufacturers. However, they remained in the OEM business to keep cordial relationships with foreign pharmaceutical customers. This is because they understood that glove manufacturing is a niche industry tied to natural resources susceptible to price fluctuations on the one hand and subject to market control by foreign pharmaceutical companies on the other. Top Glove and Kossan departed from the 'catching up' strategy central to the East Asian development model; their business strategies combined catching up and reaching down to create original development styles. Their development paths indicate alternative ways of acquiring and creating the technological and managerial capacity to innovate (Kawano, 2017).The founders of Top Glove and Kossan were strong leaders who charted their firms' development trajectory amidst growing complexity and turbulence in the business environment. They had exceptional foresight, determination and a sense of independence. Without much government assistance or the legacy of big family businesses, the two Chinese Malaysians with higher education and some business experience searched for knowledge, strategies and solutions that allowed their firms not only to survive but to expand and progress.

Generally speaking, large foreign firms that have abundant financial resources and an assured access to the global market are more competitive than local firms in the development of final products. However, in the case of the rubber glove, it was local entrepreneurs of Chinese descent who successfully developed and marketed high-quality gloves using the basic technologies developed by the public research institutes.

Source: Culled from Kawano (2018).

BOX 6.2 DISENABLING ENVIRONMENT LEADING TO EXIT OF RUBBER MANUFACTURING COMPANIES

Two companies Michelin and Dunlop producing tyres in Nigeria decided to exit the country. Dunlop had a factory in Ikeja in Lagos state where it produced car and truck tyres and contributed about 15 per cent to national tyre consumption.

The Nigerian enabling environment for businesses can be difficult. Businesses face challenges such as the lack of a reliable public power supply and inconsistent government tariff policies. Local manufacturers also face stiff competition from imported products.

Source: Oji (2019); Editors (2007); Staff (2017).

Nigeria and Malaysia's rubber and rubber products – success or failure factors

Malaysia's natural rubber production (upstream production) seems to be declining, and there are socio-economic and political factors for this continuing decline. However, rubber manufacturing (downstream sector) is thriving. In Nigeria on the other hand, natural rubber production and rubber manufacturing are both declining. We find various factors that have contributed to these trends in both countries.

First, public sector intervention is critical in providing favourable policies and setting up enabling institutions, investment in R&D, the dissemination of technological knowledge to local firms and encouraging basic techno-logical learning and adaption, particularly in the upstream that is, natural rubber production. In Malaysia, the government set up institutions like the Rubber Research Institute of Malaya and the Lembaga Getah Malaysia (LGM), which were critical to enabling the growth of the sector. RRIM, later renamed the MRB, has over time focussed on improving methods of cultiva-tion, pest control, processing and developing high-yield clones. RRIM also established a laboratory and a library for recording data, archiving research papers, disseminating new knowledge, providing advice and training courses to smallholders and planters. LGM on the other hand carried out R&D and provided technical support to glove manufacturers in resolving prob-lems that emerged in glove manufacturing. Malaysian Rubber Research and Development Board (MRRDB) was set up for the purpose of public–private R&D cooperation.

Government policies also influenced the sector positively and, at other times, negatively. The Federal Land Development Authority's (FELDA) land resettlement programme, which helped Malay people become independent farmers, also contributed to improving the sector, as many in the FELDA programme were engaged in natural rubber production and received tech-nical assistance from RRIM. Tax-free breaks and pioneer status were also provided for companies interested in going into glove manufacturing. Young scientists of diverse ethnic backgrounds were sent to study in the United Kingdom and the United States of America. These scientists returned to RRIM with cutting-edge knowledge and later some joined the private sector and contributed to its growth. The government's poverty alleviation scheme, REP, also brought a significant number of people to work on the rubber plantations.[13]

Second, innovation also greatly encouraged the success in the tapping of rubber and production of rubber products. In Malaysia, rubber research institutions supported innovation that inspired the industry, leading to:

(1) the introduction of spiral and modern tapping systems which reduce damages to the rubber tree and allows renewal of tapping panels.
(2) Modern breeding techniques that led to the development of superior clones.
(3) the adoption of agronomic practices which led to the optimization of inputs to maximize outputs and yields; and
(4) the modernization of processing techniques and standardization of rub-ber grades, beginning with sheet rubber as well as the Green Book grades to crumb rubber processing methods. This Technically Specified Rubber matched the ease of processing and presentation of synthetic rubber.[14]

Third, strong linkages between the public and private sector led to great success of the industry. The public sector working to provide an enabling market and responding to the needs of the private sector is key. In Malaysia, the MRRDB was established for the purpose of public–private R&D cooperation. Private sector firms in Malaysia benefit immensely from the R&D, knowledge sharing and favourable policies of the public sector institutions. Again, commercial estates in Malaysia served as 'experimental farms' up till the 1970s. They acted as platforms to adopt and refine new ideas and methods. In later years, the switch by estates in Malaysia to the production of other crops, particularly oil palm, led to a break between the science sector and the commercial firms that served as test beds.[15]

Moreover, a vibrant and entrepreneurial private sector contributes to developing innovative and specialized rubber products and exploring niche international markets in the downstream market.[16] In Malaysia, Chinese–Malaysian firms including Top Glove and Kossan have led the way in technological innovation and are leading firms in the rubber glove industry of the medical examination glove market. In Nigeria on the other hand, the lack of an enabling environment frustrated many private sector firms and led to their exit from the business. There is therefore a lack of dynamism and companies to develop products even when international markets demand for it.

The role of skilled manpower in the sector was critical. Proper tapping of rubber requires specific techniques while manufacturing of rubber products needs trained rubber technologists. In Nigeria, inexperienced tappers end up using techniques which are harmful to the rubber trees. In Malaysia, RRIM and its successor PRIM have been responsible for the training of technical personnel within the Malaysian Rubber Industry. RRIM was also responsible largely for the birth of the Malayan Chapter of the Institution of Rubber Industry in 1960. This emphasis on having trained personnel to employ new technologies significantly helped Malaysia in key parts of the downstream sector, particularly latex gloves.[17]

Again, preparedness and dynamism are key success factors. Malaysian firms have been able to thrive during periods of crisis, based on their initial preparedness and dynamism. In the late 1980s, there was a significant demand for latex gloves, especially disposable examination gloves, stemming from the HIV/AIDS epidemic in the late 1980s. Specifically, US import of gloves rose from by almost 500 per cent from 3.9 billion pieces in 1989 to 25.29 billion in 1998. A further boost in the usage of medical examination gloves and condoms came with the outbreaks of SARS, the avian influenza and COVID-19. Malaysian firms have been able to increase their demand and exports during these periods. By 2017, Malaysia's rubber glove industry had 63 per cent of the world's medical examination glove market.[18] On the other hand, the Nigerian rubber industry has not been able to respond to changes in the international market, even in cases where it would have led to a boost in the sector.

In both countries, we find that socio-economic factors are key determinants in the competitiveness, advancement, or failure of the industry. On the one hand, the poverty alleviation scheme, REP, in Malaysia brought people to the rubber plantations yet, socio-economic factors including the opportunity cost of land, ageing population, the urban shift and higher career expectations undermined the economic progress of the rubber industry. The urban pull saw young Malaysians moving to the urban areas and leaving cultivation in the hands of the older generation.[19] Indeed, low returns on rubber caused Malaysian planters to switch to oil palm during the 1980s and 1990s. Indonesia and Thailand continued to plant rubber as it was still profitable for them. This led to the two countries overtaking Malaysia in the early 1990s.

Although Malaysia's downstream sector developed as an auxiliary to the upstream sector to add value to exports as well as act as a buffer against low price of rubber, the downstream sector has overtaken the upstream sector. Today, upstream is no longer able to match the needs of downstream and Malaysia imports from neighbouring companies to meet this need. Synthetic rubber meets a big part of the need, with Malaysia using almost as much synthetic as natural rubber.[20] Again, Malaysia has a lot of experience in natural rubber. It now has at least three synthetic rubber plants but most of the synthetic rubber knowledge 'resides offshore and is transferred via technical service provided by suppliers and importers. For Malaysia to stay ahead of the curve in nitrile glove production, and in the production of tyres, GRG and IRG (which use more SR than NR)' it must gain the necessary technology and expertise. But how?[21]

There are many factors that have contributed to the failure of rubber in Nigeria; prominent among them has been a lack of institutional support and prioritization by the government. There are also instances of discontinued programmes even when they were initially set up. Indeed, the potential benefits of encouraging the growth of natural rubber and the production of natural rubber products have not been appreciated or harnessed. For example, the government established the *Anchor Borrower's Programme* in 2015 to support farmers and boost production. Thus far, the ABP has supported over 4.8 million smallholder farmers to produce 23 agricultural commodities. These include cocoa, cotton, cassava, rice, oil palm, tomato and livestock (Mojeed, 2022). Rubber was however not included among the products for the ABP.

Rubber's inherent functions, such as its long gestation period of five to seven years, have served as a deterrent not only to investors and smallholder farmers but also for the government's ABP. According to Mr Peter Igbinosun, president of the Natural Rubber Producers, Processors and Marketers Association of Nigeria (NARPPMAN), an association with 10,102 registered members, 'They said because rubber has a very long gestation period, therefore they have no funds to appropriate except for rice and other immediate economic crops that yield early enough' (Amuge, 2021). Mr Igbinosun made an appeal to the government to include rubber as one of the country's cash crops, given its economic values and enormous by-products. The COVID-19 pandemic, for example, showed the importance of rubber and its by-products. A well-developed rubber industry could have attenuated the scarcity of many medical and surgical products, boosted manufacturing, and created jobs. Table 6.1 summarizes the key policies and initiatives that affected the rubber sector.

Unfavourable land tenure system and institutional rigidities have also led to difficulties in accessing land for cultivation. Moreover, many farmers lack funding, modern infrastructure tools and incentives needed to boost production. Continuous appeal for funds from the government as noted by the president of NARPPMAN have gone ignored. The decline in Nigeria rubber also resulted from aged rubber trees and insufficient replanting by local farmers.[22] The credit system is poorly developed, and development loans and grants needed to expand rubber plantations across the country are scarce.

Poor agricultural practices and insufficient knowledge about how to develop the sector have also contributed to its demise. The industry has suffered from untrained, inexperienced and exploitative tappers who employ damaging tapping techniques such as slaughter tapping, therefore diminishing the number of surviving rubber trips. Farmers and stakeholders need to be trained and retrained on technical methods including plantation establishment, nursery production, pest control measures, maintenance and marketing.

Essential partnerships and practices which could also ensure the sustainability of the sector are lacking. The first as we earlier noted are effective and established partnerships between the government and the farmers. Another is partnerships between the farmers and academic and research institutions which could be a source of cutting-edge information and knowledge to enhance proper skills and agricultural practices to boost production. Partnerships between farmers and industry, for example, the automotive, medical and footwear industries, would also be beneficial. Finally, youth-inclusive programmes that expose potential young farmers to the benefits and practices of the rubber production are needed to ensure the long-term sustainability of the sector.

Despite the many challenges, NARPPMAN is seeking to expand the current rubber hectarage of 200,000 held by industrial plantations and smallholder farmers by planting an additional 160,000 hectares in 24 states over the next 10 years. They envision this would create 640,000 direct and 160,000 indirect jobs.

Table 6.1. Summary of government policies and initiatives in agriculture that affect rubber production.

No	Implementation Year	Policy/Intervention
1	FAO 1965–1968 policy document	Prepared by FAO and aimed to increase production of rubber from about 67,000 metric tonnes in 1965 to a production target of 120,000 metric tonnes by 1973/1974 and reaching 220,000 metric tonnes by 1979/1980. In order to accomplish the aforementioned targets, a master plan for rubber plantation development was drawn up to cultivate 221,829 ha in the then Mid-Western Region (Edo and Delta States), 57,242 ha in the Western Region (Ondo, Ogun & Osun States) and 81,109 ha in the Eastern Region (Abia, Akwa Ibom, Cross River, Rivers and Imo states).
2	National Research Institute; 17 April 1972	Establishment of Rubber Research Institute of Nigeria (RRIN) by the Federal government by the merging of two research institutes.
3	April 1977	Establishment of the Nigerian Rubber Board, a Marketing Board. This and other Commodity Boards were discontinued in 1986 with the introduction of the Structural Adjustment Programme (SAP) leading to a more liberalized marketing arrangement.
4	1986	The introduction of SAP and devaluation of the local currency. One objective of SAP was to restructure and diversify the economic productive base and reduce the dependence on the oil sector. SAP had a positive impact on rubber production particularly from 1988 to 1996 which saw a 60 per cent increase compared to the 1980–1987 production period.
5	1995	Introduction of the National Accelerated Industrial Crops Production Programme. It made some funds available for the multiplication of planting materials (budded stumps in the case of rubber) which were then distributed at subsidized prices.
6	1998	Intervention by the Petroleum (Special) Trust Fund (PTF). Allisee and Company submitted a report on the resuscitation of the rubber industry to PTF which were to finance the project on behalf of the federal government. PTF was scrapped when Nigeria returned to democratic rule and action was not taken on the Allisee & Co report.
7	2000	Establishment of the Nigerian Rubber Consultative Study Group. This was made up of resource persons from the Rubber Research Institute of Nigeria (RRIN), the National Tree Crops Development Unit of the Department of Agriculture in Benin City and the National Rubber Association of Nigeria. The Study Group was mandated by their organizations to review the state of the rubber industry in Nigeria and make recommendations to government on how the declining production of natural rubber could be redressed to make Nigeria self-sufficient in natural rubber production and utilization and capture a sizeable portion of the world market.
8	Presidential initiative on rubber	Support was to last for 10 years, but it was discontinued after one year.

Source: Charles (2020); Okwu, Eguavoen, and Okore (2015).

Oil palm and oil palm products

Palm oil has been used widely in different societies. It is a form of edible vegetable oil obtained from the flesh of the fruit of the oil palm tree. The harvesting of oil palm tree is usually distributed over the entire year. However, its fruit bearing is in response to rainfall patterns. In most parts of Central and West Africa that experience two rainfall seasons, there are two peak harvesting periods for oil palm. On the other hand, southern hemisphere tropical monsoon regions like Southeast Asia, Malawi and Zambia usually have a single peak harvesting season corresponding to their singular long rainy season.[23]

Palm oil became a highly sought-after commodity by British traders, the oil being used as industrial lubricant for the machines of Britain's ongoing Industrial Revolution, as well as forming the basis for various brands of soap such as Palmolive. By 1870, palm oil constituted the primary export of some West African countries such as Ghana and Nigeria. By the 1880s, cocoa had become more highly sought-after, leading to the decline of the palm oil industry and trade within these countries.

Oil palm is a perennial crop with a life span of over 25 years. It has a particularly low land footprint compared to many annual oilseed crops. Specifically, it has a global annual production of 81 million tonnes of oil from about 19 million hectares while soybean and rapeseed, being the second and third largest vegetable oil crops, collectively yield 84 million tonnes of oil while occupying over 163 million hectares of increasingly scarce arable land.[24]

The two oils have varying fatty acid compositions, are extracted by different mechanical processes, are used for different industrial uses and go through different supply chains after extraction. Palm oil has a relatively high saturated fat content, with a melting point of about 35°C, making it more suitable for edible uses.[25] About 80 per cent of palm oil produced is utilized for human consumption including as cooking oil, food oil, margarine, specialist fats and basic vegetable fat.[26] An estimated three billion people utilize palm oil in their regular diet, and it is commonly used as cooking oil for many foods made in Africa and Asia. Palm kernel oil is less dense, with a melting point of about 24°C and is used for more purposes that are non-edible. Palm kernel oil is a major ingredient in different kinds of detergents, soaps and cosmetics. Collectively, palm oil and palm kernel oil constitute ingredients found in at least half of the products found in a typical supermarket.[27]

Another significant usage of the oil palm crop is for livestock meals. Palm oil and palm kernel oil can be used as butterfat substitutes in milk replacers for young animals when replacing mother's milk.[28] Palm kernel meal, which is a pulpy mass that is left over after oil has been extracted from palm kernel seeds, is often dried and processed and used as feedstock for cattle.[29] It's high cost and high availability make it a choice input for feed ingredients, which include maize and soybean in freshwater fish, livestock feeds, poultry boiler and swine.[30] Palm kernel meal is packed with carbohydrates, fat, minerals and proteins.[31] In 2019, an estimated 7.6 metric tonnes of palm kernel meal were exported, with 98 per cent coming from Indonesia and Malaysia. The European Union, New Zealand and Japan respectively are the biggest importers of this feed, where it is used for different feed formulations, particularly for ruminants such as cattle. In 2019, they collectively accounted for 75 per cent of global imports.[32] Table 6.2 sums up some of the uses of oil palm.

The global oil palm industry in terms of annual production was worth est. US$60 billion and employed 6 million people directly and an additional 11 million indirectly, as of 2019.[33] From 2019 to 2020, global production of palm oils was over 81.1 Mt, with 8.8 Mt being palm kernel oil and 72.3 Mt from palm oil. Several sources estimate that there will be a continued increase in

Table 6.2. Oil palm products and uses.

Uses	Product	Properties
Food Products	Margarine Palm oil for food Salad dressings Mayonnaise	Very rich in Vitamins A and E
Health Products	Supplement in Vit. A deficient children	Vitamin A
	Anti-ageing	Vitamin E
	Anti-cancer	Antioxidant
Industrial Products	Soaps	Better foaming Perfume retention abilities
	Candles	Burns longer Drips and smokeless compared to wax paraffin candles
	Cosmetics	Moisturizing
	Toothpaste	Softener
	Fertilizers	Biomass
	Animal feed	Protein-rich meal
	Power generation	
	Energy	

Latest Development	Replacement of petrol and
	    diesel in automotive
	    industry.
	Has been tested in Malaysia.
		Palm-based methyl esters are
		    green fuel. It doesn't
		pollute the environment.
		No carbon.

Source: Compiled by authors.

Table 6.3. Major centres of global oil palm cultivation in 2020.

Rank	Country	Palm Oil Production	
		Mt	%
1	Indonesia	42.5	58.8
2	Malaysia	18.5	25.6
3	Thailand	2.8	3.9
4	Colombia	1.5	2.1
5	Nigeria	1.0	1.4

Source: Goggin and Murphy (2018).

global demand for palm oil and by 2050, demand will be between 93 and 156 Mt.[34] Indonesia, Malaysia, Thailand, Colombia and Nigeria were the main cultivators in 2020 as seen in Table 6.3.

Malaysian and Nigerian oil palm and oil palm products industry – an overview

Generally, it is agreed that the oil palm has its origins in West Africa's tropical rain forest region. The belt runs through the southern latitudes of Nigeria, as well as Cameroon, Côte d'Ivoire, Ghana, Liberia, Sierra Leone, Togo and into the equatorial region of the Congo and Angola. Palm kernels began to be exported in 1832, with British West Africa accounting for 157,000 tonnes by 1911. At the time, Nigeria accounted for 75 per cent of these exports (FAO). By 1920, oil palm was cultivated on 100 hectares in Nigeria,[35] growing exponentially to 20,000, 320,000, 3.38 million and 4.2 million by 1930, 1970, 2003 and 2008, respectively. The rapid and sustained growth can be attributed to strong and consistent institutional support and incentives to a wide array of actors including firms and research organizations.[36]

Africa, led by Nigeria and Zaire (Democratic Republic of Congo), was the global leader in the production and export of palm oil for the first half of the twentieth century. Malaysia and Indonesia surpassed Africa in total oil palm production by 1966. In 1983 for example, Malaysia produced over 3 million tonnes of palm oil while Africa's production was 1.3 million tonnes.[37]

While oil palm is indigenous to Nigeria, the industry is structurally complex consisting of a significant number of unplanned plantations. Of the country's estimated 2.5 million hectares of oil palm, estates and the smallholder system, which is characterized by unarticulated but important plantings by different individuals, cultivate only about 214,000 hectares. The rest of the plantation is under the semi-wild grove system. The production output both in terms of fresh fruit bunches and palm oil is not readily estimated before disposal in sales and consumption. Despite these lapses in exact statistics, the estimates of oil palm production in 2007 in the country were about 900,000 metric tonnes of palm oil and 400,000 metric tonnes of palm kernels annually. Output from this industry has not been stagnant but has grown steadily overtime; however, it has not kept pace with domestic and global demands.[38]

Nigeria consists of different agro-ecological environments, which in 1987 was grouped into five farming system zones – North-West, North-East, North Central, South-West and South-East. However, the oil palm groove in Nigeria is spread through the South-West and South-East zones and marginally across the North Central zone. The following challenges characterize virtually all oil palm states in Nigeria:[39]

(1) sterile and unproductive palms due to the use of adulterated and unimproved planting materials; (2) lack of input supplies, and supplies such as fertilizers being very expensive where available;

(3) use of traditional methods of processing fruits which often led to a loss in oil yield;

(4) very weak extension and advisory services; and

(5) poor infrastructure such as road networks.[40]

Unlike Nigeria, palm oil is not native to Malaysia and was first introduced to the country (then Malaya) as an ornamental plant in 1870. Its use as a crop was developed in 1917 when the first commercial plantation was established. English landowners mostly operated the plantations and the plantations were highly consolidated as opposed to Nigeria's plantations which were not as organized (see Table 6.4).[41]

Different studies identify specific phases in the development of the palm oil industry in Malaysia: (1) the experimental phase spanning the late 1800s/ early 1900 to 1916; (2) the plantation development phase from 1917 commencing with the first commercial plantation established at Tennamaram Estate in Batang Berjuntai, Selangor till about 1960; (3) the expansion phase from

Table 6.4. Comparing the oil palm industry in Nigeria and Malaysia.

	Malaysia	*Nigeria*
Firms (Holding)	Highly consolidated Category I, II, III	Not organized. Mostly small scale (60 per cent wild grove) small, medium and large
Nature of Actors	Estates	Small in size
Total Harvested	5,189,344 Ha (as at 2018)	3,724,802 Ha (as at 2018)
Nature of Market Orientation	Global Market Leader	Domestic

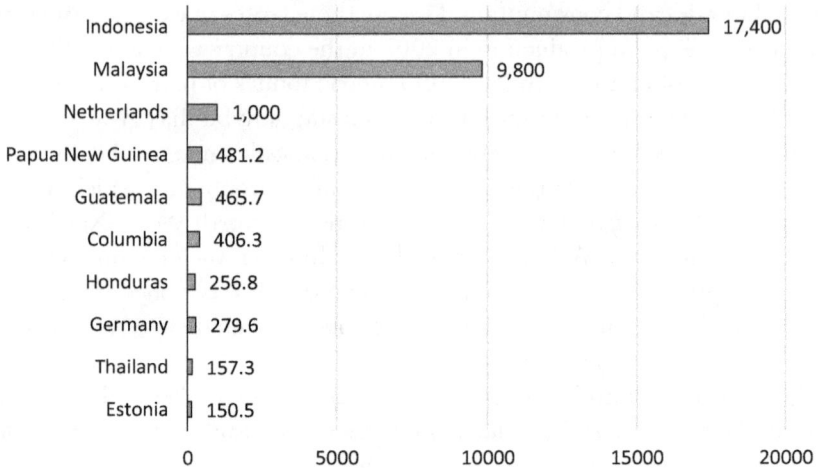

Figure 6.7. Leading exporters of palm oil worldwide in 2020 (in million US dollars). Source: Shahbandeh (2021).

the 1960s encouraged by the government's diversification policy to reduce the economy's dependence on natural rubber which was at the time facing competition from synthetic rubber and declining prices; (4) the expansion of large-scale planting in Sabah and Sarawak from the 1970s; and (5) expansion of upstream operations off-shore particularly to Indonesia where there existed an abundant supply of workers and land for plantation development, and a lower cost of production than in Malaysia.[42]

A significant driver of Malaysia's effort was the establishment of the FELDA in 1956, which was responsible for developing land for plantations for the rural poor and landless. The government had decided to focus on palm oil following recommendation from a World Bank mission in 1955.[43] Furthermore, from the 1960s, the Malaysian government introduced a major palm oil plantation scheme mainly to eradicate poverty. Each settler was allocated 10 acres of land to be planted with either palm oil or rubber, and they were given 20 years to pay off the land.[44]

Today, Malaysia is the second largest exporter of palm oil in the world, second only to Indonesia. Nigeria is not among the top 10 exporters (see Figure 6.7).

Historical performance of Malaysian and Nigerian oil palm and oil palm products industry

In this section, we compare the performance of the Malaysian and Nigerian palm oil industry along four criteria – production of palm oil, area of palm oil harvested, yields and export quantity from 1961 to 2018.

Area of palm oil harvested (Ha)

The area of palm oil harvested depicts the area from which palm oil was gathered and is measured in hectares. Between 1961 and 2018 the area harvested in Nigeria ranged between approximately 1.9 million Ha and 3.7 million Ha while in Malaysia the range is from 43,000 Ha to 5.2 million Ha.

Comparing the trends in the two countries as seen in Figure 6.8, we find that the area harvested in Nigeria has not even doubled over the past 58 years while Malaysia's has increased significantly over the years.

We see that although Nigeria started at a high value of 2.7 million Ha compared to Malaysia's 43,302 Ha, by 1997 Malaysia had caught up and was harvesting double that area by 2005.

The area harvested in Nigeria declined between 1967 and 1987. On the other hand, the area harvested in Malaysia is seen to increase consistently from 1961 to 2013, experiencing a slight decrease in 2015.

Yields of palm oil (Hg/Ha)

Palm oil yields refer to harvested production per unit of harvested area for crop products. Palm oil yields in Malaysia ranges approximately from 115,468 to 203,000 Hg/Ha and from 25,000 to 27,000 Hg/Ha in Nigeria between 1961 and 2018. The yield recorded in Malaysia fluctuated over the years while Nigeria's yield remained constant between 1961 and 1984 after which it fluctuated until 2018.

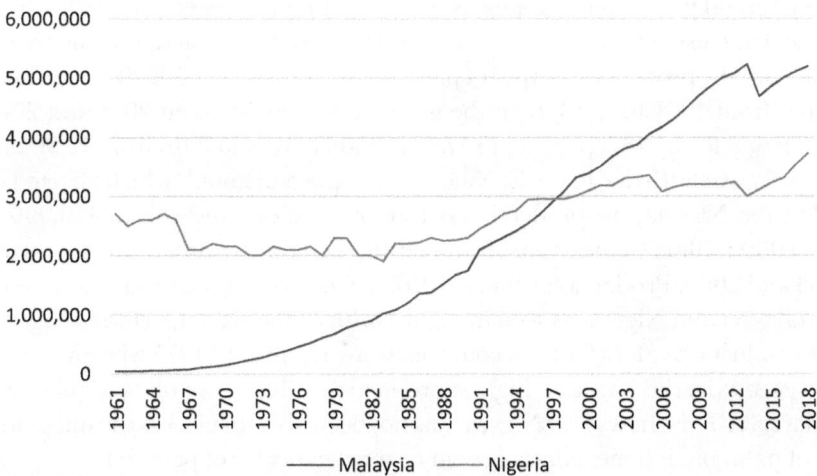

Figure 6.8. Trends on area of palm oil harvested in Malaysia versus Nigeria (1961–2018). Source: United Nations (2022).

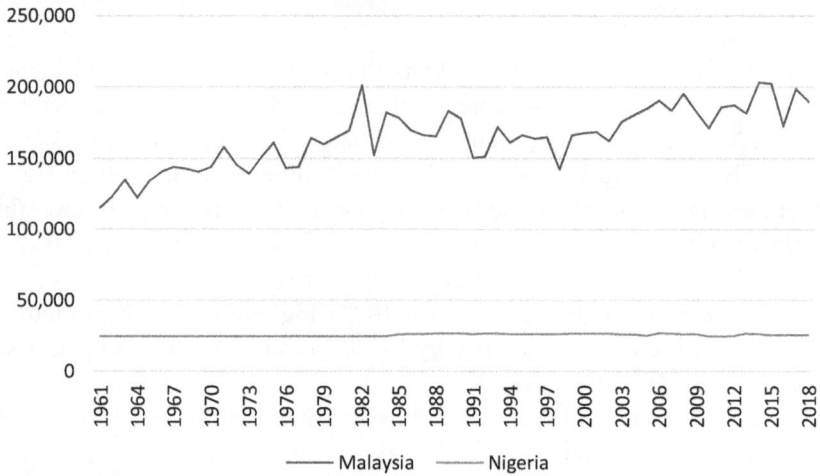

Figure 6.9. Trends on yields of palm oil in Malaysia versus Nigeria (1961–2018). Source: United Nations (2022).

The highest yield recorded in Malaysia was in 1982 and again between 2014 and 2015, while in Nigeria the highest yield was in 2006. Comparing the trend in palm oil yields between Malaysia and Nigeria as seen in Figure 6.9, we find that Malaysia outperforms Nigeria by a large margin.

Palm oil production trend (1000 tonnes)

The palm oil production data measures the actual harvested production from the field and excludes harvesting losses and those not harvested. We find that in Malaysia, the production output of palm oil ranges from 95,000 to 19.9 million tonnes from 1961 to 2018, with the greatest outputs between 2013 and 2018. Production fell by 13.2 per cent to 17.32 million tonnes in 2016 from 19.96 million tonnes in 2015 due to the El Nino weather phenomenon[45] which affected oil yields. For Nigeria, the production output of palm oil ranges from 430,000 to 1,330,000 million tonnes from 1961 to 2018, with the greatest outputs between 2003 and 2009. Production fell in the 1970s. Comparing the production trends in Malaysia and Nigeria as seen in Figure 6.10, Malaysia outperforms Nigeria. The production values for both countries were at par until 1971 when Malaysia surpassed Nigeria. Nigeria's highest production value is not up to a quarter of Malaysia's. This shows that Nigeria has not been able to harness the full potential of palm oil, if done; Nigeria could be a net exporter of palm oil.

Trends of oil palm export quantity: The palm oil production export data measures the quantity of palm oil exported and is measured in tonnes.

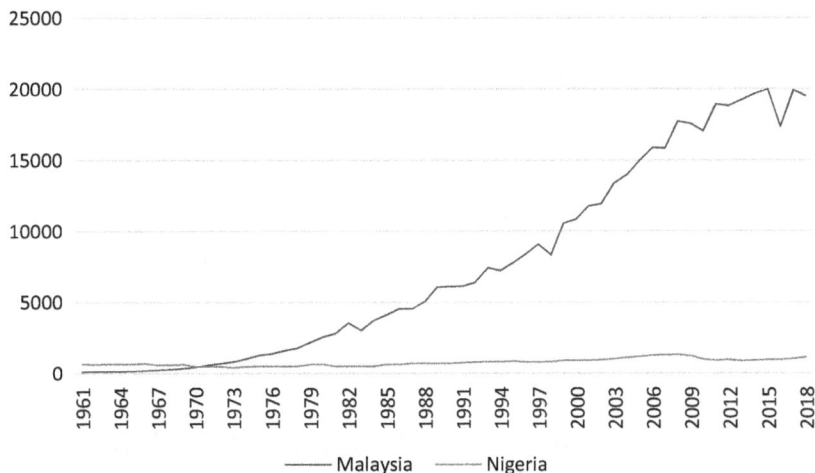

Figure 6.10. Trends on production of palm oil in Malaysia versus Nigeria (1961–2018). Source: United Nations (2022).

Between 1961 and 2018 the export quantity from Malaysia rises steadily from 96,000 to 18,000,000 million tonnes, while that of Nigeria ranges from 0 to 167,000. Between 1961 to 2009, Malaysia's export quantity has risen almost steadily. It experienced a decline in 2010 and again in 2016. The country's export quantity was at an all-time high in 2008 at 18 million tonnes.

Nigeria, on the other hand, has not had a positive trend in its export of palm oil. Nigeria was producing more palm oil than Malaysia from 1961 to 1965. Afterwards the country's exportation declined steadily until 1973 when it exported 0 tonnes of palm oil. Nigeria has not exported any palm oil for a total of 18 years between 1961 and 2018.

When compared, as seen in Figure 6.11, it is clear that Malaysia outperforms Nigeria. Nigeria will need to do more to position itself in the industry and earn major revenue.

Nigeria and Malaysia's oil palm and oil palm products – manufacturing value addition

In 2020, Malaysia accounted for 25.8 per cent and 34.3 per cent of world's palm oil production and exports, respectively, taking into account other oils and fats produced in the country. Its low production costs make it cheaper than frying oils such as cottonseed or sunflower. Malaysia manufactures several products from oil palm including foaming agent in virtually every shampoo, natural preservative in processed foods, liquid soap or detergent. It exports it as cheap raw material for biofuels, especially to the European

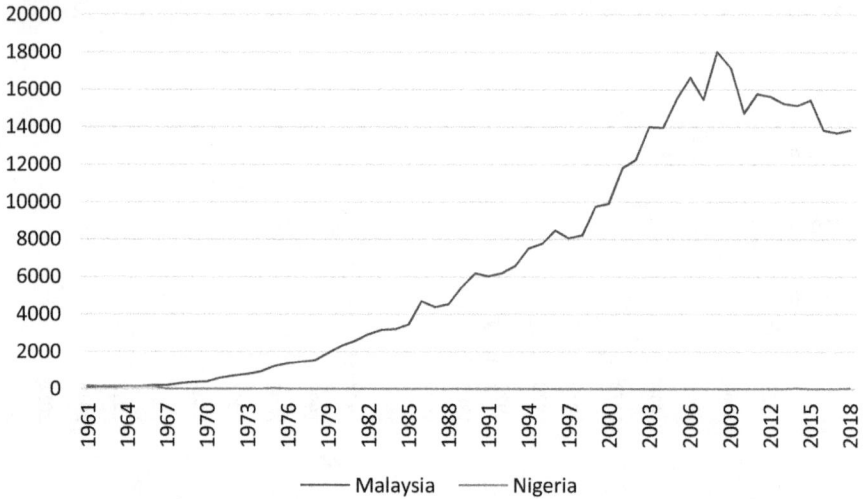

Figure 6.11. Trends on export quantity of palm oil in Malaysia versus Nigeria (1961–2018). Source: United Nations (2022).

Union. Other products from palm oil are as adhesives that binds together the particles in fibreboard. Oil palm trunks and fronds are made into everything from plywood to the composite body of Malaysia national automobile.

The success of Malaysia's oil palm industry has its origin in the national effort to promote the processing of crude palm oil (CPO) and subsequently its export. The emergence of the refining entities and as well the instruments and policies that triggered its success are important to understanding the industry. Export-oriented industrialization strategy was enacted in 1968 with the putting in place the Investment Incentives Act which led to considerable expansion of oil palm acreage arising from the settler schemes of the FELDA. The exemption of PPO from export duties after 1976 was an incentive to firms to switch from crude to PPO. For 10 years, between 1986 and 1996, stimulated by the industrial master plan, external markets expanded and firms invested in oleo-chemicals and other products. Post 1996, the firms developed new products and integrated into value chains and engaged other complementary products.

The production of CPO which rose from 1960 to 2000 was accompanied by the equally rapid production of PPO from the mid-1970s. The export diversification strategy also affected the production of crude palm kernel oil (CPKO), processed palm kernel oil and palm kernel cake, all of which recorded impressive growth from the mid-1980s. The growth of CPKO also furthered differentiation into the oleo-chemical industry, including in specialized and blended fats.

The first oil refinery, owned by a Dutch firm, was established in Kuala Lumpur in 1952. The second, owned by a Singaporean firm, was established 10 years later. These however catered mostly to the domestic market.[46] The eight first *export-oriented* refineries were established between 1969 and 1971. During the mid-1970s, the sector started expanding rapidly. In the early 1980s, the refining capacity had grown beyond the domestic supply of CPO. Malaysia thus became a net importer of CPO. The sector has since then grown to be one of Malaysia's most important export industries. In 2004, 20-billion-ringgit worth of refined palm oil was exported, which represented 5 per cent of Malaysia's added exports. In 2004, the exports earnings of refined palm oil even surpassed that of crude petroleum. Behind electronics, the palm oil industry has been Malaysia's premier post-World War II export success story.

The reason for the expansion in the late 1960s and early 1970s can be almost wholly found in a change in government policy. From 1960 until 1968, a single export duty was applied to all forms of palm oil, regardless of degree of processing.[47] However, from 1968, a 100 per cent export duty exemption was implemented for all forms of PPO. At the same time, PPO was placed on the promoted products and activities list, which made refining eligible for various tax rebates. In 1972, a more complicated export duty exemption formula was introduced, where the export duty placed on CPO was based on prices. Previous research has estimated that the duty differential between processed and CPO was between 9.8 and 39.3 per cent points during the 1970s, depending on the price of palm oil.[48] Due to this very large duty differential, and also due to the tax rebates, immense profit margins were created, and a large expansion of production and exports followed.

Nigeria and Malaysia's oil palm and oil palm products – success and failure factors

Malaysia and Nigeria were at the same production level in 1950. Nigeria was a major exporter at the time, but Malaysia caught up and surpassed it both in production and export. We consider the main success and failure factors that might have contributed to this divergence in outcomes.

Factors[49] that have come out prominently in explaining the divergence in the sector are role of government in providing policies and institutions, investment in scientific research and the nature of the markets in production and orientation towards export.

The sector in Malaysia enjoyed systematic investment including R&D spending, aggressive breeding and tissue culture developments[50] investment in science and technology. Malaysia's average spending per scientist grew from $175,000 in 1981 to $344,000 in 2002 and as at 2007 the figure has moved up to $500,000. Coincidentally, Nigeria has the largest number of FTE researchers in Africa (11 per cent of the region's total); however, its spending is only 7 per cent of region. Malaysia targets research areas under the scheme called Intensification of Research in Priority Area while Nigeria conducts significant public agricultural research, but there is little research capacity in the private sector.

In Nigeria, there was no significant institutional support for R&D and innovation in the sector. Nigeria established the Nigerian Institute for Oil Palm Research (NIFOR) where almost half of the research force 47 per cent had higher degrees such as master's and PhD. However, this did not translate to any significant effect on the country compared to its counterpart – Malaysia Palm Oil Board which had generated more than 300 technologies and products. The institute had filed 200 patents, and 30 per cent of patents are either sold or commercialized. NIFOR on the other hand has generated only five products aside from its well-known variety of planting material with no patents filed.

Funding for R&D and innovation has also been limited in Nigeria. For a period of 10 years, NIFOR only received 4 per cent of the approved budget of the institute. Even then, the sum of money released was only a fraction of the ideal funding requirement. For the period 1992 to 2002, no fund was released for R&D in the institute. Lack of finances not only put a ceiling on the capabilities required to conduct deep-impact research in a systematic way within the various PRIs and universities but sometimes also hindered the capabilities of organizations to install the required facilities even to perform the most basic research. The only exceptions were researchers who had succeeded in receiving individual grants to perform parts of their research in laboratories abroad, where the requisite technological capacities were available. Another group were those that secured institutional support to equip local laboratories. Second, efforts to enhance organizational capabilities through a competitive process have been unsuccessful due to lack of governmental funds and support. Partly due to the problems in providing up-to-date facilities and research funds, the most talented university graduates either do not show interest in pursuing research careers within Nigeria, or those who do and are very good choose to do so in developed countries. The problem of basic infrastructure exacerbates that of poor funding.

Another factor that explains the divergence in the outcomes of the two countries is a difference in their production and export orientation. Parallel with the increase in oil palm areas, production and exports of palm oil and palm oil products also increased from a share of only 7.7 per cent of agricultural exports in 1970, palm oil exports now accounted for more than 30 per

cent of all agricultural exports in Malaysia. Oil palm is the leading commodity export surpassing petroleum export. Nigeria does not export oil palm
because what is produced is a far cry from the local demand alone. Demand
outstrips the supply hence the companies do not export, and this is also partly
due to market price of the palm oil. A metric tonne of CPO sells for less than
US$900 at the global market while it sells at an average price of US$1,400
in Nigeria. Hence, there is no incentive to export the commodity as it has a
higher return on investment when disposed locally.

The Nigerian market is not as organized as the Malaysian one. For one,
Malaysia's oil palm industry is dominated by large-estate farming while that
of Nigeria is dominated by small-scale farmers. Large-estate farms are normally associated with higher productivity, better technology, and they thrive
on substantial investment. Again, an important challenge facing the Nigerian
market, like many developing countries, is the nature and types of markets
which is often small and highly fragmented. The mode of market exchange
in which productive agents are embedded is largely impersonal in traditional
societies using traditional techniques of production and often subject to high
levels of uncertainty due to the equally uncertain nature of relational contract.[51] Most markets in Africa have relatively small size (thrive on personal
exchanges of kinship relations, personal loyalty and social connections) and
fits situations characterized by low 'profitability, limited economies of scale
and low intensity learning that slows long run technological capability building'. Malaysia dealt with this structural constraint very early on using wide
instruments to foster export orientation by national enterprises.

Summing Up

The two case studies and the empirical analysis of sector trends again demonstrate the reversal of Nigeria's fortunes. Nigeria's lack of horizontal diversification due to poor governance of its resources led to significant regress and
lost economic opportunities. Again, the role of government and its policies
have been distinctive features of success and failure. Malaysia's government
enacted well-informed policies to drive the sectors. In Nigeria, the initial policies of the colonial government on oil palm development in Nigeria prevented
the participation of the private sectors, and it was limited until 2003 when
under the presidential initiatives scheme on vegetable oil in Nigeria saw a
new dawn in the industry with the ban of imported vegetable oil to enable
the indigenous industries to develop to a competitive stage. The policy also
encouraged the involvement of the private sector and a lot of privatizations of
the old government. Oil palm schemes are being bought over by multination-
als and private investors. The government had used policy as a coordination

mechanism to force all the actors to work together for a common goal. There are the dedicated funds (CESS) committed to targeted research areas in Malaysia and the establishment of Round Table Sustainable Palm Oil which has all the players in the industry as members.

The application of, and investment in, research and development financing was crucial to Malaysia's success and Nigeria falling behind. Sustained long-term focus defined industrial leadership in Malaysia while short termism, as we observed in the lack of support for Nigeria's rubber sector, characterized Nigeria.

Notes

1 Lall and Pietrobelli (2002).
2 According to a study cited in Oyelaran-Oyeyinka (2006) by (Yeats, 2002) for the World Bank, in 1962, Africa's exports of palm nuts and kernels accounted for 91 per cent of world total totalling $75 million. Exports fell to $3 million by 1999 while global market share was less than 10 per cent of 1960s. Also, global market shares for groundnuts, palm kernel oil and palm oil were between 51 and 83 per cent but have now fallen to only between 2 and 3 per cent, with the combined exports of these products now much lower than it was four decades ago.
3 Oyelaran-Oyeyinka (2006); Although in terms of macroeconomic indicators, divergent development is relatively recent because as late as 1980, average income levels in Africa and Southeast Asia were still similar (Aryeetey, Court, Nissanke and Weber, 1998).
4 We all collude in exploiting commodity-rich nations | Financial Times (ft.com), accessed May 8, 2021
5 Fortune Business Insights (2022); Industrial Rubber Goods (2022).
6 Find source.
7 Fortune Business Insights (2022).
8 Amuge (2021). Nigeria out of Global Rubber. Retrieved from https://www.pressreader.com/nigeria/business-a-m/20210816/281513639223295 on 23 June 2024.
9 Facts and Details (2015); Kawano (2018: 147).
10 Facts and Details (2015).
11 Kawano (2018).
12 The International Rubber Study Group (IRSG).
13 Kawano (2018).
14 See (ND).
15 See (ND); Kawano (2018).
16 Kawano (2018).
17 See (ND).
18 Kawano (2018).
19 See (ND); Kawano (2018).
20 See (ND: 4).
21 Ibid.
22 Mr Gbenga Ogundele, Chairman of the Kwara State Chapter of NARPPMAN.
23 Poku (2002).
24 Murphy, Goggin, and Paterson (2021).
25 Ibid.

26 CIRAD (2022).

27 Murphy, Goggin, and Paterson (2021).

28 Drackley (2010).

29 The Star (2014).

30 Balandrán-Quintana and Mendoza-Wilson (2019).

31 The Star (2014).

32 Murphy, Goggin, and Paterson (2021).

33 Kadandale, Marten, and Smith (2019).

34 Statisa (2020); Murphy, Goggin, and Paterson (2021).

35 This section draws heavily from the seventh chapter (Oyelaran-Oyeyinka, 2017). Book from Consumption to Production and Adebowale (Adebowale, Boladale O. Abiola (2009). Divergent Development: Technology and Innovation in the Oil Palm Sector in Malaysia and Nigeria. PhD Thesis submitted to the University of Malaya, Kuala Lumpur, Malaysia.) PhD dissertation which considered the reasons for the divergence in success between Nigeria and Malaysia's oil palm industry.

36 Oyelaran-Oyeyinka (2017).

37 Poku (2002).

38 Oyelaran-Oyeyinka (2017).

39 Drawing on various research in the oil palm zones of Imo and Akwa Ibom in the South-East region, Ondo and Osun States in the South-West region and Kogi State in the North Central region.

40 Oyelaran-Oyeyinka (2017).

41 Oil Palm India Limited (2017).

42 Harcharan (1976); Gray (1969); Teoh (2002).

43 Teoh (2002).

44 Oil Palm India Limited (2017).

45 This is a climate pattern that describes the unusual warming of surface waters in the eastern equatorial Pacific Ocean.

46 Lim Boh Ang, "An Evaluation of the Palm Oil Refining Industry in Malaysia" (unpublished master's thesis, Kuala Lumpur: Faculty of Economics and Administration, University of Malaya, 1979), p. 44.

47 Gopal, J. (2002). *The Development of Malaysia's Palm Oil Refining Industry: Obstacles, Policy and Performance* (Doctoral dissertation, University of London).

48 Ibid.; Lim, "An Evaluation of the Palm Oil Refining Industry in Malaysia".

49 This section draws heavily from the seventh chapter (Oyelaran-Oyeyinka, 2017). Book from Consumption to Production and Adebowale (Adebowale, Boladale O. Abiola (2009). Divergent Development: Technology and Innovation in the Oil Palm Sector in Malaysia and Nigeria. PhD Thesis submitted to the University of Malaya, Kuala Lumpur, Malaysia.) PhD dissertation which considered the reasons for the divergence in success between Nigeria and Malaysia's oil palm industry.

50 https://www.researchgate.net/publication/342245806_OIL_PALM_ECONOMIC_PERFORMANCE_IN_MALAYSIA_AND_RD_PROGRESS_IN_2019 accessed May 1, 2021.

51 Today's modern industrial societies evolved from a system of personal to impersonal exchange that is now build on complex institutions and highly knowledge specialized (North, 2005; Mokyr, 2002). 'As increased specialization occurred with the growth of markets, individuals exchanged increased specialized knowledge at the expense of less "general" knowledge' (North, 2005: 122).

Chapter 7

TEXTILES AND GARMENTS: THE CASE OF BANGLADESH AND NIGERIA

Introduction

The story of the textile and ready-made garments (RMG) industry is one of lost glory. Once a vibrant and dynamic sector in Nigeria, the sector recorded significant success and exported mostly to countries in the African region. It achieved an annual growth rate of about 70 per cent and constituted 25 per cent of the manufacturing sector's labour force between 1960 and the late 1980s. There were around 115 factories across the Cotton Textile and Garments (CTG) value chain which engaged in several stages of the value chain such as spinning, weaving and garment production in 1980. The textile industry in Nigeria was the country's largest employer, coming second after the government in 1985, with over 250,000 direct workers and over a million cotton farmers.[1] The sector ranked the third largest in Africa, after Egypt and South Africa, with products from local companies that are sold all over the Nigerian and West Africa markets.[2] According to a United Nations report of 2003,[3] the Nigerian textile manufacturing capacity was valued at N420 billion and investment worth US$3 billion in 1999. The textile industry engaged close to 30 million people when functioning at full capacity as 26 out of the country's 36 states grew cotton.[4]

Then came the reversal of fortune for this dynamic industry. By 2007, Nigeria had only 26 textile and ready-made garment companies in operation with employment of roughly 24,000 people. Closures were swift and persistent including the once-famous United Nigerian Textiles (UNT) among the many. The near demise of the industry in Nigeria coincided with the rise of Asian producers including China. Specifically, a dual process was underway: the growth of Chinese imports combined with a massive influx of Chinese company representatives to Nigeria, while Nigerian traders flocked to China to import garments and textiles into Nigeria. There were by 2008, 50,000 Chinese textile personnel in Nigeria and 20,000 Nigerians in China.[5]

Clearly, the import of cheap Chinese textiles into Nigeria was a trigger for the industrial reversal of its counterpart in Nigeria. However, there were other remote and immediate causes. A review of the state of the industry reveals that cheap labour, optimum firm size, product quality, aggressive foreign ownership, availability of local input materials that helped build backward linkages, new product development, preferential market access and working conditions are the major factors that help in gaining competitiveness in apparel exports during the post-Multi-Fibre Arrangement (MFA) period.[6] While the Nigerian industry relatively stagnated technologically, Asian firms leveraged cheaper labour cost and comparatively integrated industrial chain-making textile products Asia's and certainly China's and Bangladeshi's most competitive and sustained exports. Other factors that supported the rise of Asian countries included cheaper and abundant capital, continuous research and development (R&D), sophisticated branding and matured marketing channels.

We show in this chapter that while the textiles and garments sector regressed in Nigeria, Bangladesh, another low-income country, has succeeded in achieving export diversification, especially in garments and textiles around the same time. By 2022, Bangladesh had become the second-largest ready-made garment manufacturer and exporter in the world and the fastest-growing industries globally since the 1990s. There is a disturbing similarity in the export profile and pattern of both countries. Nigeria depends for over 80 per cent of its export revenue on crude petroleum while over 84 per cent of Bangladeshi total export earnings in 2018–2019 were derived from garment exports (BGMEA, 2021, ;). As with Nigeria's dependence on crude petroleum, Bangladesh's dependency on one source of foreign income could be a potential source of instability.

In the year 2021, Bangladesh marked its 50th Victory Day. This country's development trajectory has been controversial, described with the most unsavoury epithets, the same as many with Asian countries such as South Korea, which was once termed a 'basket case'. Today, South Korea has assumed a new status, it is no more an economic 'basket case' but a 'rising star'. It has become one of the world's fastest-growing economies and is one of the few least developed countries that graduated in the past 30 years. In 2019, its per capita income was US$1,856 – substantially higher than Pakistan's US$1,285 and only US$250 less than that of India.[7] In 2020, during the COVID-19 pandemic, while India's GDP shrank by 7.3 per cent, South Korea boasted a growth rate of 2.4 per cent. Impressively, the country is one of the few worldwide that maintained a positive rate of growth even during the pandemic year. A country with a GDP of over US$409 billion, it is forecasted that Bangladesh's current growth rate could double by 2030. The driving force for this previously agricultural economy is the ready-made garments (RMG) sector, as it provided job opportunities outside agriculture.

At the conclusion of Bangladesh's violent liberation war in 1971, the country lay in devastation, with its economy shattered and over 80 percent of the population living in dire poverty. Similar to Nigeria, Bangladesh soon faced numerous military coups, famine and persistent poverty. Amidst these challenges, the textile and clothing industries emerged as the sole drivers of growth in Bangladesh's rapidly developing economy, becoming the primary source of foreign exchange earnings. By 2002, exports of textiles, clothing and ready-made garments (RMG) comprised 77 per cent of Bangladesh's total merchandise exports. By 2016, Bangladesh had become the second-largest producer of garments globally, following China, and the second-largest exporter of apparel for Western fast fashion brands. Approximately 60 per cent of export contracts with Western brands are with European buyers, about 30 per cent with American buyers and 10 per cent with others. Notably, the majority of production is managed by local investors, with only 5 per cent of textile factories owned by foreign investors (Paul and Quadir, 2013; Latifee, 2016; Export Genius, 2022).

The growth of Bangladesh's GDP is equally impressive. In 1972, the World Bank estimated Bangladesh's gross domestic product (GDP) at US$6.29 billion. By 2021, it had surged to US$368 billion, with exports contributing to US$46 billion, and 82 per cent of that coming from RMG. During the 2016–2017 period, the RMG industry generated US$28.14 billion, accounting for 80.7 per cent of total export earnings and 12.36 per cent of the country's GDP (Latifee, 2016; Hossain and Latifee, 2017).

This chapter continues our narrative on Nigeria's industrial reversal in comparing its once-booming textile and garment industry that went into a precipitous decline with that of a relatively successful Bangladeshi industry that continues to flourish even in times of global crises.

We organize the rest of the chapter as follows. First, we provide a short outline of the global textiles and garments industry to situate our discourse in context. This is because international trade rules have, in large part, shaped the production trajectory of textiles and apparel. The MFA was in force until 2005, after which every country was forced to limit production as defined by the World Trade Organization (WTO). The year this arrangement was withdrawn by WTO, the production and trade of textiles and apparel experienced geographical dislocations. Firms that were operating in relatively cheap foreign locations shifted their bases to either home countries or even cheaper locations. This resulted in a relative advantage for a few and disadvantage for many. For instance, a few foreign firms were operating either out of Africa before 2005 but subsequently moved their operations to their home countries or to even cheaper locations resulting in a drastic reduction in exports from the region. The decline of textile and garment production and export from Nigeria is illustrative of the contrasting fortunes of countries. This is followed by a systematic analysis of selected countries including Nigeria. The sections that follow discuss the evolution of production and export of textiles and garments followed by the comparative sectoral growth of the two countries including the identification of the factors that influence sector evolution. The final section sums up the chapter.

The Global Textile and RMG Industry

Fashion and clothing emerged as the largest application segment globally with a value of US$712.3 billion in 2019 owing to the rapid rise in consumer spending on apparels and clothing. China is currently the world's largest textile producer and exporter of both raw textiles and ready-made garments, accounting for over half of the global textile output every year. The United States is the leading producer and exporter of raw cotton, while also being the top importer of raw textiles and garments.

The global textile industry triggered Britain's industrial revolution in the late eighteenth century and has been the source of early industrial growth in many countries. The global textile market size was estimated at US$993.6 billion in 2021 and is expected to reach US$1,032.1 billion in 2022 and US$1,522 billion by 2027. The industry as of today is estimated to be employing around global fashion industries employing more than 75 million workers worldwide. From a global perspective, the textile industry is an ever-growing market, with key competitors being China, the European Union, the United States and India.

The global textile industry growth continues to be driven by the world's largest textile-producing countries and the top textile exporters, mainly owing to their rising production and sales of materials such as cotton, yarn, fibre and other finished products or apparels. While China remains the world's largest textile producer and exporter, other major textile markets such as the EU, India and the US are also showing an impressive annual growth rate over the last few years. It is expected that the global textile industry will grow proportionally with the fast-changing fashion market around the world, meaning that the world's largest textile-producing countries and top textile exporters are still full of opportunities to flourish further over the near future.[8]

China undisputedly is the world's leading producer and exporter of both raw textiles and ready-made garments. Like Britain, China's first Industrial Revolution (1988–1998) was characterized by mass production of labour-intensive light consumer goods across China's rural and urban areas, relying mainly on imported machinery. During this period, China became the world's largest producer and exporter of textiles, the largest producer and importer of cotton and the largest producer and exporter of furniture and toys.[9] China's export value was approximately US$266.41 billion in 2020. The key success factors driving competitiveness are low-cost production, superior raw material, industrial infrastructure, advanced machinery, well-organized work processes in domestic as well as global markets, have led to the thriving textile industry. The eight major categories of China's textile and Ready-Made Garments (RMG) industries include cotton fabrics, silk fabric, chemical fabrics, wool fabrics, knitted fabric, textile machinery, fibre and garments. The industry is growing every day, and the government does its best to aid the growth.

China's agrarian revolution led to massive changes in the rural areas, raised living standards and subsequently the purchasing power of that population. This resulted in higher local demand for textiles and apparel which continued throughout the 1980s, owing to the income elasticity of these goods. China's huge market, in part, fuelled this relentless demand. The intense competitive pressure among small firms fostered demand-driven innovative changes and lowered prices. By China's own mass production standards, textiles and garments became a huge business; China's total production of yarn and cotton fabrics increased from 330,000 tons and 1.9 billion metres in 1985.

Not surprising, the textile and RMG industry became the largest manufacturing industry and major source of foreign exchange in China during its first industrial revolution between 1988 and 1998. According to Wen (2021), around 24,000 enterprises and about eight million workers were employed as early as the 1990s; RMG exports made up more than 20 per cent of China's total exports. China surpassed the United States and became the world's largest producer and exporter of textiles and clothing in 1995, six to seven years before joining the WTO, and has retained this dominant position ever since (see Wen, 2021).

The Chinese government under Deng promoted the textile and clothing industry for three key reasons: (i) This industry leveraged China's comparative advantage, especially its abundance in labour, (ii) the industry relies on low and well-established technologies and had relatively low entry costs and (iii) textiles and garments enjoy huge domestic and international markets. The Chinese government played a strong mercantilist role in the growth of this industry. It was directly involved in the import and storage of cotton nationwide to smooth fluctuations in domestic cotton prices and demand. Moreover, it established sophisticated organizations to nurture this industry[10] such as the China Cotton Textile Association, China Dyeing and Printing Association, China National Garment Association and the China Home Textile Association. The government facilitated several institutions that fostered the evolution of this industry (long before China joined the WTO) to supervise, regulate and assist the textile and clothing industry in coping with international textile market rules and competition.

The success of Chinese textile industry was a precursor to China's second industrial revolution in the late 1990s; this progression and sectoral sequencing is consistent with the pattern of the British Industrial Revolution. As earlier noted, the textile industry was the flagship industry during the first industrial revolution in Great Britain. From the 1760s to the 1830s, a series of inventions of simple yet powerful wood-framed tools and machines rapidly sped up spinning and weaving. However, markets are key. The British Industrial Revolution was not driven merely by these technological inventions alone, as the conventional wisdom often assumes. What drove growth and expansion was the massive overseas textile market created by British merchants heavily backed by the government. This was exemplified by trading relationships established through the British East India Company and its various incarnations in Africa.

BOX 7.1 THE MERITS OF SPECIALIZATION: EXPERIENCES OF OTHER INDUSTRIALIZATION COUNTRIES

The United States is the leading producer and exporter of raw cotton, while also being the top importer of raw textiles and garments. The US textile and apparel industry is a nearly US$70 billion sector when measured by value of industry shipments. It remains one of the most significant sectors of the manufacturing industry and ranks among the top markets in the world by export value: US$23 billion in 2018. At 341,300 jobs, the US industry is a globally competitive manufacturer of textile raw materials, yarns, fabrics, apparel, home furnishings and other textile-finished products.

With an export value of US$38.99 billion, Germany follows China as the second-largest exporter of textiles and ready-made garments in the world. The country excels in exporting synthetic yarn, knitted apparel cloth and man-made fibre. Most of the products in Germany are produced by medium and small-sized businesses. The country has been focussing on the production of high-quality textiles.

Italy's export value is US$36.57 billion, according to the 2020 evaluation. Italy has the advantage of a wide range of fibers: linen, cotton, wool and silk. Italy manufactures textiles that have a strong export orientation. The country is focussed on the technical performance of fabrics and yarns. The country has promising space and inclination for innovation and is likely to evolve further in the future.

Turkey is always able to meet high standards and cater to a wide range of products. As an important player in the global supply chain, Turkey is the seventh largest exporter of textiles and apparel in the world. The 2020 report mentioned Turkey's export value as US$27.56 billion. Turkey has a favourable atmosphere for textile manufacturing with high-tech solutions, design capacity and dynamic and flexible production.

Returning to our focus country, the question remains; How did Bangladesh emerge as a prominent competitor in the textile and apparel industry? The main driver of competitiveness in the Bangladesh case is low labour cost and a massive workforce. These two factors have enabled Bangladesh to become the third largest exporter of apparel in the world by 2020 (with an export value of US$38.73 billion in 2020) and the second largest RMG exporter of western fast fashion brands excelling in bulk orders. The vertical capacities of Bangladesh help global brands to maintain more coordination and transparency in their supply chain.

Following closely, Vietnam is the fourth largest exporter of textiles in the world, with a rich history of high-quality manufacturing. Vietnam is somewhat different from Bangladesh, with the advantages of a skilled labour force but relatively low wages. Vietnam mainly exports to countries like Japan, the USA, South Korea, and the EU. The export value of Vietnam as of 2020 is US$37.93 billion. The focus of the country is to produce high-quality items to keep up in the competitive market and to improve its supply chain.

Today India holds the fifth position in the global textile exporting business, with an export value of US$37.11 billion. One of the oldest textile industries in the world, India has the advantage of domestic supply of fabric, being the second largest producer of cotton in the world and producing some exclusive silk fibres. India has two textile sectors: the unorganized handloom and handicraft and the other is mechanized loom production. The former operates with traditional looms, tools, designs and techniques, many of which are centuries old, despite widescale improvements in technology, and its status as a global competitor in producing good modern textiles and RMGs.

Production and Export of Textiles and Garments

In this section, we move away from tracing the rise of different countries to proxying the production of the textiles using value added by sector to assess the factors that contributed to their successful performance over time. We depict success in terms of export performance of the textiles sector in

Figure 7.1. For example, in India and Turkey, among others, the removal of MFA impacted the sectors more positively. Many local companies from these countries, though previously located in foreign countries, returned to their countries with the capabilities and resources that helped boost domestic production and competitiveness (see chart 1 of Figure 7.1). China, in particular, benefitted enormously from the elimination of MFA after 2005. Due to the lack of availability of Chinese data before 2004, the graph shows growth of the sector after 2004, but it captures the effect of MFA on the Chinese Textiles sector. Vietnam has also made great strides in the production of the textiles sector, particularly post-MFA; it picked up considerable momentum after 2012

The figure also shows that the export performance of selected countries when compared with that of Nigeria. Turkey has been very consistent for the last three decades while the export of textiles witnessed a declining trend in China and India. An explanation is that instead of solely focussing on exporting textiles, these countries shifted to the export of RMGs in addition to, or rather than textiles, for which there has been a global growth boom as discussed earlier in the chapter.

The figure also shows that the export performance of Bangladesh has been highly volatile yet with overall growth, much like Nigeria. This is different from the sector's performance in Vietnam, where the export performance of Vietnamese textiles and apparel sectors has been steadily rising for the last two decades. A noticeable fact is that Nigeria exported more textiles than RMGs during the study period. In fact, Nigeria is the only country in the

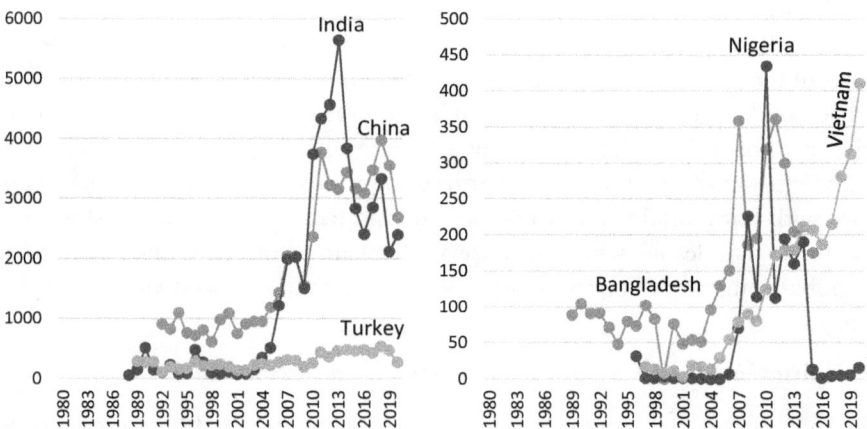

Figure 7.1. Export of textiles from sample countries. Source: Authors, calculated from WDI. Note: Export value is in million USD.

sample to do so, which might explain its relative decline. Even after the post-MFA era, the performance of these sectors of Nigeria failed to improve.

Ready-made garment exports

RMG manufacturing is a relatively low-tech industrial activity easily mastered by training and learning. But it remains an area of competitive advantage for developing countries given that it promotes value addition locally; most Asian garment firms have developed relative manufacturing competencies in this sub-sector. It is also within this context that the WTO eliminated the quota system in 2005 in order to induce global competitiveness in apparel manufacturing. However, this objective was achieved to a limited extent, partly due to a fallacy of composition, which led to several countries competing in the RMG sector solely based on low wages. The performance of the sector during the pre- and post-MFA period varied considerably depending on the country context, policy response and firm-level capabilities as shown in Figure 7.2.

Figure 7.2 now compares the export performance of the sample countries in different charts of Figure 7.1 for RMGs. There are, however, varying levels of export data. For instance, Chinese export performance varies from US$20 billion to more than US$180 billion while Nigeria's performance remains limited to US$4 million. From the graphs, the elimination of MFA had positive impact on export performance of Bangladesh, India and Turkey. As depicted in Chart 1, Figure 7.2, Bangladesh surpassed India and Turkey in 2010, but the export performance of Bangladesh has been lower than the other two countries during pre-MFA era. The growth of the Chinese RMG sector has outperformed that of Bangladesh, India and Turkey in post-MFA period, even though it has been declining since 2014.

The growth of Vietnamese apparel export has equally been impressive and could be compared with China though the volume of export has been much lower than China. The export performance of Vietnam in terms of volume of export is comparable to that of other Asian countries such as Bangladesh, India and Turkey. It may be inferred that Vietnam also benefitted from the removal of the quota system. Comparatively, the export performance[11] in the post-MFA period in Nigeria has not only been dismal but the sector has witnessed a decline in terms of employment and local production. It might be due to the fact that many foreign firms were operating in the country during the pre-MFA period and shifted their operations either to home countries or to even cheaper locations, the phenomenon witnessed by many African countries.

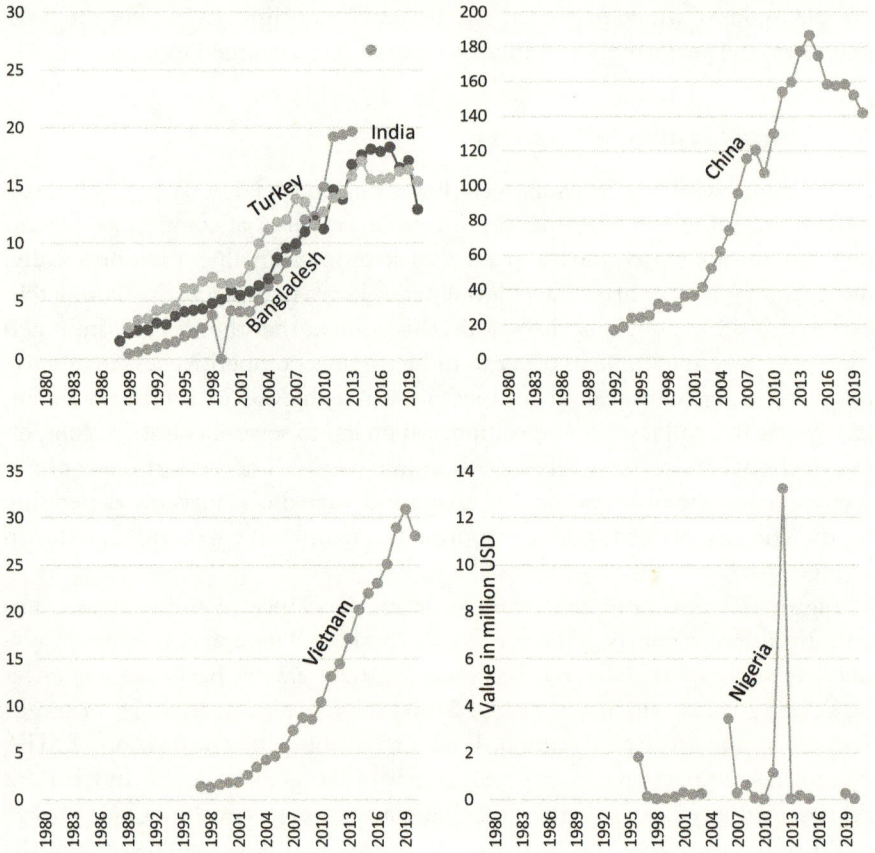

Figure 7.2. Export of RMGs from sample countries. Note: Export value is in billion USD except for Nigeria.

Sectoral Sources of Economic Growth in Nigeria and Bangladesh

In this section, we move away from the analysis of value added to disaggregate at length the growth dynamics and performance of the textiles and garments sectors for the two countries: Nigeria and Bangladesh.

As pointed out earlier in the chapter, in terms of industrial progress, the growth of shares has been moving in opposite directions in both sectors ever since the availability of data; evidently, the share of manufacturing has been higher than agriculture. The shares were 57.31 per cent and 27.85 per cent respectively in 1977. Since then, the manufacturing share has been growing and that of agriculture has been declining with the shares reaching 95.80

per cent and 0.75 per cent respectively in 2015. Export diversification in Bangladesh has been far more impressive than in Nigeria.

Depending on the degree of diversification, total merchandise exports will follow different trajectories. We analysed trends of both countries presented in Figure 7.3.

Figure 7.3 shows that, on the one hand, total merchandise exports of Bangladesh are lower than Nigeria; however, they have been growing at a steady pace, with less volatility overall. On the other hand, exports in Nigeria have witnessed a high level of volatility, normally detrimental to the development process. Moreover, oil exports rather than manufactured products or processed agricultural products have driven a high volume of exports in Nigeria. Due to the wide swings and crash of the oil market, exports of Bangladesh achieved the same value as that of Nigeria in 2019.

Textiles and RMG play a central role in the economic performance of Bangladesh in the last 25 years. A prime source of foreign exchange, the sector generates about US$5 billion worth of products each year from garment exports, comprising roughly 84 per cent of total exports and providing employment to around three million workers, of whom 90 per cent are women. While the ready-made garment (RMG) sector is not homogenous, Bangladesh has developed a highly advanced manufacturing ecosystem characterized by a high degree of entrepreneurship and innovative management capabilities. Detailed sector studies show that RMG firms have invested

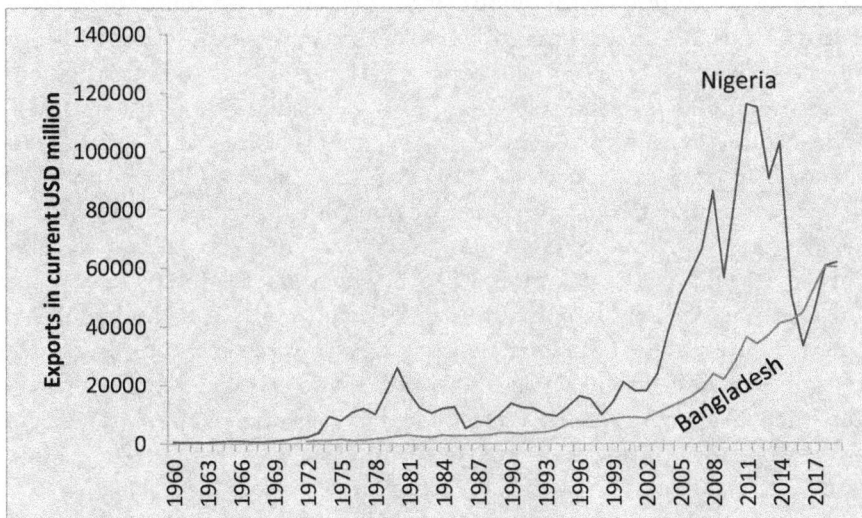

Figure 7.3. Export growth in Nigeria and Bangladesh. Source: Author.

significantly in productivity-enhancing technologies, automation, continuous improvement and digitization.[12]

The remarkable performance of the sector in international markets is partly a result of investments in manufacturing technologies in the garments sector, its lack of regulation and the low wages paid to its women garment workers. More importantly, the growth of Bangladesh's RMG sector has been as much a result of improved factory conditions and transparency as it is of the sector's growth through horizontal diversification over the past decade. Previously criticized for the treatment of workers, there have been several steps undertaken in the country to also improve the quality of workplace conditions. Although these remain contested in part, especially given the large-scale employment of women at lower levels of manufacturing, Bangladesh's success has been achieved through market diversification of its customer countries and upgrading into more complex products and value-added services. The sector has thrived by targeting a broader range of European customers and managing market risks through adaptation to the ever-changing demand patterns in the global fashion market.

Competitiveness of the RMG in Bangladesh

Bangladesh at 6.4 per cent has overtaken regional competitors in terms of its contribution towards the global RMG market share, namely Vietnam (6.2 per cent), India (3.3 per cent) and Turkey (3.1 per cent).[13] The low wage structure of the Bangladeshi RMG industry has been the main source of its competitiveness. It is a major attraction for foreign buyers mostly from Europe and the United States – the major exporting destinations. Other destinations for apparel products include Canada, Japan, Australia, China, India, Brazil, Chile, Mexico, Russia and Turkey.[14]

Despite its impressive performance, competitiveness and productivity of the sector continue to be constrained by poor infrastructure, weak research and development, scarcity of spinning facilities and diseconomies of scale. This is reflected in the country's 1.2 per cent negative growth rate in the global garment export share in 2019, while rival India and Pakistan enjoyed a positive growth rate of 2.2 per cent and 4.74 per cent, respectively, during the same period.[15] A focus on cheap prices has also translated into a range of labour law issues, particularly those related to wages and stable employment for the workers at the lower tiers of the sector.

Multi-Fiber Arrangement (MFA)

The MFA in the global textile trade in 1974 created quota restrictions on imports into the markets of the developed countries from several developing countries. Bangladesh, being a least developed country (LDC), was accorded a unique opportunity to export duty-free ready-made garments to the United States and European Union.[16] However, an Agreement on Textile and Clothing (ATC), reached with the WTO establishment in 1994, decided that all quota restrictions under MFA be phased out by 31 December 2004.

The MFA, which gave Bangladesh a quota-free status, led to significant foreign investors and the signing of several joint ventures in garment manufacturing in the early 1980s. In the MFA period, RMG exports from Bangladesh grew at an annual average rate of 19 per cent between 1990 and 2005; this impressive growth continued post-MFA at the rate of 21 per cent.[17] The sector was so successful post-MFA that it successfully navigated in 1985 the US and Canada imposed import quotas of their own, with no international agreement, on Bangladeshi textiles. However, Bangladesh was able to meet the demand for every quota each year and was able to successfully negotiate for higher quotas for subsequent years.[18]

To be sure, Bangladesh was naturally apprehensive of the post-MFA era when it was required to compete in an open market situation with other countries of the world. The move to concentrate on ready-made garments enabled the sector to utilize the comparative advantage of the country in abundant labour force. The RMG sector flourished, matured and created new opportunities in related fields of the national economy. The modern textile industry producing yarn equally grew and enhanced the rate of growth of the export-oriented clothing sector. Unlike the Nigerian counterpart, Bangladesh performed very well in the post-MFA period by maintaining a sustained and relatively elevated level of growth in its production and export. Belying all apprehensions, the garments export continued to grow at a steady pace. Over time, RMG export increasingly used fabrics produced by the local textile mills spawning the desired backward linkage within the economy.

However, the indigenous handloom sector (often called 'rural textile' or *khadi* industry) was somewhat affected by an uneven competition it faced from the flooding of RMG 'spill overs' into the domestic market. Inevitably, the traditional handloom industry was weakened a bit by the rapid occupation of a part of the domestic market by the RMGs and imported cloths. Nevertheless, it has also demonstrated remarkable resilience and survived the economic liberalization process since the 1980s, without any significant state patronage. In the early years, more than 50 per cent of the handloom producers lived below the poverty lines, especially those with fewer than two looms. This paints a rather high-contrast picture comprising two groups of entrepreneurs in the same industry. Nevertheless, the handloom industry not only supplies about half of the total clothing needs of the population; some of its products are also exported. The asymmetric impact of growth points to the need to reduce disparity between different actors in the textile and clothing sector through increased integration of the relevant sectors. This is clearly important for an equitable development process of the country to promote increased coordination and synergies between the related sectors and sub-sectors in the clothing and textile industry.[19]

Overall, the MFA's application especially in North America and Asia particularly favoured Bangladesh and worked to the detriment of the Nigerian textile industry. Right from 1974 the MFA, trade in textiles and garments could be seen as the most institutionally regulated in the North American market. While the MFA set quotas on garments exports from the newly industrializing countries of Asia, Bangladesh was exempted from these stringent limits given its status as a Least Developed Country (LDC). The country's location within the Asian region gave it proximity to more advanced industrial nations like South Korea that were once again quota restricted. These countries, like South Korea, adopted a strategy of 'quota hopping' seeking quota-free countries that could become quota-free manufacturing sites. This shift in strategy helped the export-oriented ready-made garment industry in Bangladesh through the re-location of Korean firms such as Daewoo of South Korea.[20]

At the macro-economic level, the sector has been instrumental in creating significant stability by persistently raising the GDP growth rate (to 5 per cent point by 2000), while at the community level it became an important means of livelihood for a large section of mainly poorer households. It has also caused re-location of a large section of the labour force (mainly women) to urban centres causing an overall change in the lifestyle of many people. An increased number of women going out to work earning decent income caused a change in the fortunes of households including improvements in living standards. Changing urban lifestyle for about 2 million low-income households evidently drove a changed habit of food consumption. This had several ripple effects, making small-scale food processing a lucrative occupation and an employment source for a large section of people.

The rising economic growth evidently led to significant socio-economic changes including backward–forward linkages. This leads to an array of ancillary services and products for people at every level of the economic ladder.

Another important policy step was the combination of de-nationalization, privatization and the establishment of export processing zones (EPZs). By 1981, up to 300 textile companies, many of them being small ones, had been denationalized and often returned to their original owners (Klaus, 1991).[17] In 1980, Bangladesh officially established an export-processing zone at the port of Chittagong. In 1982, the then President, Hussain Muhammad Ershad introduced the New Industrial Policy (NPI), the was significant for its privatization process. This policy denationalized much of the textile industry, created EPZs and encouraged direct foreign investment. As part of the NPI 33 jute mills and 27 textile mills were returned to their original owners (Nurul, 2007). Due to these and other government incentives, the export of ready-made garments (RMG) surged from US$3.5 million in 1981 to US$10.7 billion in 2007. While apparel exports grew, it took time for national-level actors and various sub-sectors of the domestic supply chain – such as spinning, weaving, knitting, fabric processing and accessories industries – to establish the productive linkages that fully maximize the potential of the ready-made garments industry (Aman Tex, nd).

Textiles and RMG Industry in Nigeria

The textiles industry has a long history in Nigeria with the first Textile Millestablished, Kano Citizen Trading Company, in 1951. Churchgate of Bolton, England, established the second Mill (KTL) in Kaduna in 1957. The peak number of textile mills (including the small mills) was up to 300+ in 1992.

The decline of the sector in Nigeria began around 1996, coinciding with Nigeria's accession to the WTO agreement. By 2022, there were fewer than 25 surviving textile mills in Nigeria from its peak of over 300 in the early 1990s. The main factors responsible for the decline and near-total collapse of the textile sub-sector include, but are not limited to, the following: the perennial inadequacy of power supply, high power tariff, obsolete machinery, smuggling and influx of second-hand clothing into the country, among others. In addition to infrastructure challenges, several trade-related factors, such as lock-out from the African Growth and Opportunity Act (AGOA), WTO agreement, have been responsible for the influx of cheaper textiles into the Nigerian market.

The RMG sector in Nigeria consists largely of small-scale fashion designers, tailors and artisans. This sub-unit currently appears to be the 'weak link' in the Cotton Textiles Garment (CTG) value chain in Nigeria. From 2018 to 2022, Nigeria's RMG market was projected to grow at 6 per cent (fastest in Africa). The value of total local production of the textiles and garments in Nigeria was about 40 million dollars while the estimated value of imported textiles and apparel (was about 4 billion dollars per annum (Vanguard, 2019). The estimated yearly value of textiles and garments smuggled into Nigeria is about 2.2 billion dollars, while the value of apparel demand per annum is about US$6.2 billion (Fawehinmi, 2015). In other words, projected yearly revenue lost (Import Duty and VAT) is about US$325 million dollar. The entire Nigerian CTG value chain is therefore a potential 'gold mine'.

A particularly heavy criticism has focussed on the claims that Chinese imports have completely undermined the textile and RMG sectors. In the case of textiles, both China and Nigeria have long histories of textile production, which dates back to hand weaving in the eighteenth century in the Yangtze valley in China under the Qing dynasty and the city of Kano under the Sokoto Caliphate which began in 1804.[21] Both were affected by colonialism, foreign ownership and mechanization in the twentieth century. In China, cotton textiles rapidly expanded after the nationalization following World War II.

In Nigeria, the modern history of textiles began in the 1940s and 1950s as part of the textile development scheme centred in Kano and Kaduna with support from overseas capital. The first indigenous factory was commissioned in Kano in 1952. Later, several factories were opened by the Emir of Kano with the financial support of Lebanese businessmen. Other factories were opened in the 1960s with capital from Britain, Sudan and the Hong Kong-based CHA group which provided financial support for United Nigeria Textiles Ltd (UNT). The first textile mill established in Nigeria was in Kaduna state in Northern Nigeria, the Kaduna Textile Limited, in 1957 under the protection of 'customs tariffs' to prevent the importation of textile products from Europe and Japan. The tariff system remained in place until 1977 when a ban on foreign textiles replaced it. The Kaduna factory produced about 8 million metres of belt materials woven with Nigeria-grown cotton. By the early to mid-1960s, six more textile mills were established in Kaduna, including the United Nigeria Textiles Limited, Arewa Textiles and Nortex.

In the 1980s, Nigeria had 175 textile plants employing 250,000 people with many more employed as traders and suppliers of cotton and other inputs including thousands of cotton farmers, and by the mid-1900s, Kaduna state had nine large textile mills.[22] The state of Kano, a regional industrial and commercial hub, has been arguably the second most important industrial location in Nigeria. Overall, Nigeria's textile production accounted for around 25 per cent of manufactured value added with roughly 35 per cent exported to West African countries in the mid-1980s. However, production thereafter began to decline while production in China led by FDI in the SEZs dramatically increased.

The reversal of fortunes for Nigerian textiles manifests in several ways at both the macro and the micro level. While 19 small- and medium-sized mills were already operating within the city in the 1960s right up to mid-1980s, by 2010 only 24 mills were operating in all of Nigeria, with 175 factories closed.[23] In Lagos, only three textile-manufacturing firms out of the 15 textile firms survived; they are Wollen and Synthetic Textile Ltd, Nichemtex Textile Ltd and Sunflag Textile Ltd. In Kano, after Lagos, textile production and trade provide around 30 to 35 per cent of output and employment opportunities for the Kano state workforce even today.[24]

Contrary to the Bangladeshi story where firms thrived during and post-MFA, the story of the textile industry decline in Nigeria is a result of the MFA as well as a lack of focus on value addition. In many ways, one could even argue that the quota restrictions of the MFA prevented Nigerian firms from focussing on the RMG sector, thereby taking away a critical next step in the textile manufacturing industry. As discussed earlier, the MFA was a set in 1974 that allowed both developing and developed countries to control and restrict foreign textiles' importation to protect home industries. Nigeria adopted this policy on foreign textiles importation, being a GATT member since November 1960 before it was replaced by the World Trade Organization (WTO) in 1995. Then, the introduction of the Structural Adjustment Programme (SAP) in 1986 by the Nigerian government was designed under the guidance of the International Monetary Fund (IMF) to stimulate domestic production, correct the balance of payment deficit, relieve debt burden, control inflation and attract foreign investors.

By 1993, after seven years of implementing the SAP, high inflation and interest rates persisted, along with high consumer goods prices like cloth. The removal of all trade barriers and the adoption of an open market policy further intensified competition from abroad, especially from Asia. This was due to the SAP crises coinciding with the boom in China's textile industry in the 1990s, leading Chinese firms to seek foreign markets. Renne (2015) noted increased cooperation in the 'Chinese-Nigerian textile trade' during the 1990s, with Chinese companies opening offices in Lagos and Kano, and Nigerian personnel doing the same in Guangzhou, China. The challenges with the SAP may not be solely due to the IMF policy or the program; the prevailing political situation and leadership responsible for formulating Nigeria's trade policy also played a potential role. Historically, the textile industry in northern Nigeria was centered in the Kaduna and Kano mills, but much has changed over the past fifty years. By 2014, Chinese textiles made up 90 per cent of all textiles sold in the Kaduna and Kano markets (Maiwada and Renne, 2013; Murtala M. et al., 2018; Sola and Olukoya, 2008). Maiwada and Renne (2013: 188) found that Chinese personnel were 'acting as suppliers, distributors, and retailers' of Chinese goods in Kano and Kaduna markets. In 2015, nearly US$3.5 billion worth of textiles were reportedly smuggled illegally into the Kano market, mainly from China through Cotonou, Benin, to the Niger Republic (Murtala et al., 2018). The influx of Chinese companies and their textiles marks a significant shift from the establishment of the first mill in Kaduna in 1957, which aimed to reduce the country's dependence on foreign textiles.

The influx affects both domestic production and consumption of quality textiles. While some Nigerians may enjoy buying cheap textiles imported from China, the impacts on jobs lost from the moribund factories have been less explored.

Issues arising from the divergent development of two countries

The premise of this book is that industrial manufacturing is subject to increasing returns; it has higher income elasticities compared with agriculture and services and generates widespread employment. Additionally, we argue for explicit policies that foster economic diversification. We discuss the issues in the section that follows.

Effectiveness of policy support to textiles and garments sector

In general, the policy support for the textiles and RMG sector has been insufficient and ad-hoc. Specifically, it has not corresponded to the challenges faced by the producers at different stages of Nigeria's development trajectory. In 2014, the National Industrial Revolution Plan (NIRP) was launched with the aim to expand the country's industrial capacity through agricultural-related industries, metal and mineral processing, oil and gas, construction and light manufacturing. Yet, it has not had the impact of boosting RMG production in the country in a manner similar to its Asian counterparts. The federal government also initiated the National Cotton, Textile and Garment Policy under the NIRP. The policy was aimed at reducing the US$2.0 billion bill on imported textiles and garments. It was also targeted at increasing export earnings of at least US$3.0 billion annually, attracting FDI and expanding the country's seed cotton production capacity from 300,000 MT in 2013 to 500,000 MT in 2015. Policies used in support of the goals were two-year duty and VAT waivers for textile manufacturing between 2015 and 2019, as well as a three-year tax holiday. But change has been slow.

The textile sector received further support in 2015 with the constitution of a special committee in the country's ailing cotton and textile industry. The Nigeria Investment Promotion Commission (NIPC) partnered with the National Cotton Textile and Garment (CTG) Policy Committee to promote Made-in-Nigeria products. The CBN committed to providing a concessionary loan, under the Real Sector Support Facility (RSSF), to operators in the sub-sector. The Bangladesh policy framework, in contrast, provided sustained production and export support for the textiles and RMG sector, including duty-free import of capital machineries and spare parts up to 10 per cent of the value of such capital machinery.

a) Bonded Warehouse and back-to-back L/C facility
b) Facilities and benefits at prescribed rates given to export-oriented (RMG) industries using indigenous raw materials
c) The export-oriented industries which are identified by the government as 'Thrust Sector' are provided special facilities and venture capital support.

Promoting Different Types of Diversification: Countries such as South Korea, Malaysia and Vietnam have succeeded in diversifying away from resource-based products, garments and footwear within two decades. These countries have developed capabilities that turned them into exporters of complex manufactured products including steel, machinery, chemicals, transport equipment and consumer electronics. Bangladesh, on the other hand, similar to Nigeria, is stuck in a narrow range of relatively low-value garments and crude petroleum respectively more than 40 years after their industrialization drives began. Bangladesh's reliance on low prices has thwarted the growth and expansion into value addition in this sector, much unlike its performance in the pharmaceutical sector, where local companies now cater to 97 per cent of the local market estimated to be just above US$2.5 billion in 2018 (Gehl Sampath, 2019).

On the whole, Bangladesh still remains weak in other manufacturing sectors. When we look at Bangladesh from regional comparative perspective with other Asian countries like Malaysia, Korea and lately Vietnam, these have diversified significantly despite possessing significant deposits of natural resources. Malaysia's GDP and exports comprise significant manufacturing activities that drove the increase in GDP per capita. Over time, the share of low technology industrial outputs such as food and textiles in these countries has reduced progressive electronics and now machinery account for a very significant share.

Malaysia through deliberate policy actions diversified its exports over the last five decades while a country like Nigeria with very similar agricultural endowment did not diversify (as shown in Chapter 6 of this book). Exports of manufactures by Malaysia reached 80 per cent of total exports by 2000 with the electronics sector accounting for a large share of the country's manufactured exports. Additionally, it succeeded with horizontal diversification of its rich agro-business sectors namely, rubber, palm oil and petroleum industries that contributed to its dynamic industrial base.

Vietnam is endowed with considerable natural resources such as coal, phosphates, rare earth elements, bauxite, chromate, copper, gold, iron, manganese, silver, zinc, offshore oil and gas deposits, timber and hydropower. Natural resources contributing to GDP diminished after 1980, and their contribution to GDP fell substantially. Subsequently, the country's focus shifted to manufacturing and services from agriculture and crude oil exports; it succeeded in diversifying economic activities rather than depending on natural resources. Subsequently, the percentage of GDP contribution of mineral and oil resources gradually reduced and is now relatively smaller. The GDP contribution of natural resources was highest (14.18 per cent) in 2008 while in the case of crude oil, it was less than 10 per cent (8.98 per cent in 2006).

Bangladesh's share of exports in GDP fell to 15 per cent in 2019 from a peak of 20 per cent in 2012, far short of Vietnam's ratio of 107 per cent. In addition, the economic complexity of Bangladesh's trade has also slipped (that ranking is down from 77 in 1991 to 123 in 2017). Not surprisingly, on the 2022 Global Innovation Index (GII), the following are the rankings: South Korea (10), China (14), Malaysia (33), Bangladesh (116) and Nigeria (117). Nigeria and South Korea were at the same level of per capita income in the 1960s. On the one hand, Korea, a non-resource-based economy, has performed incredibly strongly through export diversification and growth since the 1960s. It devoted considerable energy to the accumulation of industrial manufacturing technology and innovation that propelled its remarkable growth. The country is now ranked the 'most innovative country on earth' followed by Germany, Finland, Switzerland and Israel. In other words, both countries under study have relied on the most basic competitive factors in driving economic growth.

While Bangladesh RMG has thrived on low labour cost, its diversification drive has been unimpressive just like Nigeria slowed in part by domestic constraints such as limited availability of credit, especially to small and medium enterprises. The entry and growth of firms are also hampered by the deterioration of the business environment: Bangladesh was ranked 65th of 155 countries in 2006 in the World Bank's Doing Business index. By 2020, it was in 168th place of 190 countries. Ease of Doing Business in Nigeria was 128.00 by the end of 2020, and it is projected to trend around 133.00 in 2021 and 135.00 in 2022.[25]

Bangladesh was ranked 105th by the World Economic Forum's Global Competitiveness Index for 2019, down two places from 2018 while Nigeria is ranked 115 out of 140 countries in its 2018 Global Competitiveness Index. Bangladesh is ranked low on the World Bank's Logistics Performance Indicator (LPI), which has a bearing on a nations' export prospects. It slid to 100th place in 2018, Nigeria (110), while a competitor, Vietnam, ranked 39th and scored higher on every sub-indicator. Exporters and importers face transaction costs much higher in the two countries than those of competitors in Southeast Asia. The manufacturing environment in both countries is made difficult by the poor and unreliable electric power, in spite of private investment in generating capacity, because transmission and distribution infrastructures have been neglected. Corruption is pervasive, reflected in Transparency International's ranking. In 2020, Bangladesh had the dubious distinction of occupying the 146th slot between Angola and the Central African Republic, a drop of three places from 2010. According to the 2020 estimation, Indonesia ranked and scored 102/180 and 37/100 respectively while Nigeria ranked and scored 149/180 and 25/100, respectively.[26]

Socio-economic impacts

Both countries face severe challenges of inequality. In Bangladesh, close to 30 per cent of the population are living in poverty in 2020; income inequality is on the rise (the Gini coefficient rose from 0.458 in 2010 to 0.482 in 2016). In short, while it enjoys growth momentum driven by RMG, its growth fortunes are fragile as it depends too closely on a single, low-tech industry and on overseas remittances. The failure to use garments as a springboard to diversify into more complex products, as Korea did; to nurture world-class firms with brand recognition, as several East Asian economies have done; to improve the business environment and governance; and to raise factor productivity, which determines whether a country moves steadily up the income ladder, warns of troubles ahead.

Nevertheless, following the sustained industrial growth in Bangladesh, human living standards have improved dramatically: life expectancy in 2019 was 72.6 years, a gain of over 7 years since 2000; mean years of schooling were up from 4.1 to 6.2; and the country's human development index (HDI) value had climbed from 0.478 in 2000 to 0.632 in 2019. The growth headwind of around 8 per cent for years that was propelling the country's economy before the onset of the coronavirus pandemic helped to sustain rapid economy growth when many countries suffered contraction.

Another remarkable success is that Bangladesh currently grows enough food now to feed its 167 million people. The country shares striking similarity with Nigeria in their initial conditions. After independence, the agricultural sector like Nigeria was Bangladesh's main economic driving force. Its contribution to GDP was around 60 per cent and an important source of people's livelihood and employment. Over the past decades, as industrial and services contributions to GDP rose, agriculture's contribution reduced from 17 per cent in 2010 to 12.6 per cent in 2020.

In terms of human capital, Bangladesh has recorded a significantly reduced maternal and infant mortality, raised income, and by 2015, it achieved the status of a lower middle-income country. The country's educational achievement has been impressive, with 98 per cent primary school completion rate and remarkably, with more girls in secondary school than boys in a majority Muslim nation. This contrasts with Nigeria, especially, Muslim-dominated Northern Nigeria where school enrolment is poor, investment in women and girls is poor and progress in combating child malnutrition and reproductive health has been slow. Northern Nigeria has one of the highest maternal mortality rates in the world, with approximately 1,012 maternal deaths per 100,000 live births. Pregnant women in northern Nigeria also have limited take-up of health services. Nigeria, the eighth most populous country in the world with over 200 million population, accounts for 20 per cent of all global maternal deaths with a depressing maternal mortality ratio of 800 maternal deaths per 100,000 live births. Northern Nigeria has been the epicentre of the disease burden, it has suffered devastating attacks of banditry and terrorism turning the region into a centre of poverty, diseases, joblessness, illiteracy, early/child marriage, maternal mortality and terrorism.

Sectoral Policy and Programmes: The government of Bangladesh has also taken major steps to enhance the economy through liberalization policies and reforms that brought in foreign investment in the RMG manufacturing industry (Hossian et al., 2019; Rasel et al., 2020; Hasan et al., 2020). A bonded warehouse is one of the facilities that has been provided by the Bangladeshi government on which RMG firms can import raw materials without paying any import duty (Ahmed, 2009; Akter, 2020). The government of Bangladesh also established the Export Processing Zone (EPZ) to help the RMG manufacturing industries to grow (Rahman, 2021).

Additionally, product diversification and export market diversification helped Bangladesh to become a powerhouse in RMG exports. The availability of domestically produced raw materials for knitwear has boosted knitwear exports for Bangladesh, whereas the export firms have to rely on imports for manufacturing woven products (Mottaleb and Sonobe, 2011; Hossian et al., 2019; Rahman, 2021; Lavassani and Movahedi, 2021).

Progress depends on Continuous Learning and Capabilities Acquisition

With little variation, most developing countries started from agrarian beginnings, they earn foreign exchanges through exports of basic agricultural primary commodities, minerals or low technology manufactures. Over time, economies are unable to sustain the living standards of their citizens by this trade regime as the competitiveness of basic raw materials deteriorate. Again, as urbanization intensifies, citizens began to demand more sophisticated goods that require more complex technologies (Palma and Guimard 2015). Two avenues open for low-income countries to address their trade deficit: the diversification of production structure, which has two directions namely, 'horizontal' and 'vertical' diversification. The former means an expansion of other primary commodities or basic manufacturing goods; but far more demanding is 'vertical' diversification, which requires a country or firm to master new technological capabilities. This diversification is accompanied by movement towards medium and high technology-intensive industries.

The cases of Bangladesh and Nigeria on the one hand, and that of the more successful ones show clearly a number of lessons for follower countries on the pathway to a competitive economy. First, Bangladesh, despite its socio-economic challenges, has established a globally cost-competitive garments industry that is closely integrated into the global value chain (GVC). Scale definitely matters and this is precisely where the sector faltered and failed in Nigeria. Bangladesh had 4,600 factories producing garments in 2019 and exports amounted to over US$33 billion. These firms built the capabilities over several decades. The ability to continue to compete with more advanced and established producers such as Bangladesh, Vietnam, Cambodia, Pakistan, and Ethiopia, not to mention China and Turkey, demands explicit investment in technological capacities. Integrating a country like Nigeria into the apparel GVC and achieving scale has become a lot harder and with automation, the advantages of low-cost labour are less compelling. Presumably, Bangladesh will find it relatively less hard.

Second, the experience of Korea and other East Asian economies demonstrates the need for early diversification into higher-value manufacturers. All these countries began their ascent up the income ladder by producing light manufactures but then quickly branched out into complex products. That sort of structural transformation now looks forbiddingly difficult for developing countries like Nigeria and Bangladesh. There are technological barriers to entry, high-value GVCs are harder to integrate with for newcomers, manufacturing is automating and becoming servitized, and the share of manufacturing in GDP and its contribution to growth is diminishing. As we can see from the Bangladeshi case, the Korea/Taiwan-type manufacturing and export-led growth stories are not being easily replicated – not by Bangladesh, or emerging markets such as India, Brazil, and Mexico.

Export diversification not only protects an economy from volatility and external shocks, it alleviates Balance of Payment (BoP) pressure by making the export basket more 'demand-dynamic', thereby generating more foreign exchange than it would otherwise. Technological upgrading is a necessary condition for export diversification. Clearly, industrialized economies have upgraded the most – with high- and medium-technology goods dominating their exports. At the same time, no country which has upgraded only moderately has experienced significant industrialization success. Furthermore, the experiences of China and Vietnam support the idea that countries which upgrade aggressively at relatively low-income levels subsequently experience faster rates of economic growth. These countries moved from primary commodity dependence in 1965 to the dominance of mostly high-tech products in 2016. Countries like the Philippines, Malaysia, and Thailand have an even higher concentration of export share in electronic products. However, they, including Malaysia, still significantly depend on primary commodities.

What is evident is that industrializing and diversification, especially in competitive sectors, must undertake explicit technological learning in order to climb the industrial technological ladder from low-technology to high-technology regimes. This requires sustained investment in knowledge and skills upgrading required to master new technologies. Second, national-level policies are key to development outcomes that originate from firms and sectors.

Third, Bangladesh unlike Nigeria enjoyed considerable foreign direct investment (FDI) in the RMG sector. From studies earlier cited, while Chinese textile and garment companies (mostly traders it turned out not manufacturers) flooded Nigeria from late 1980s, the outcome was very different from what was obtained in Bangladesh. The sector in Nigeria collapsed as foreign Chinese finished products flooded the market. The success of Vietnam, the only country that appears to be following the East Asian playbook, highlights the importance of foreign direct investment (FDI) in firmly placing a country on the path to rapid and sustainable growth. These are pertinent lessons for Nigeria, it is important to attract the right kinds of FDI that would accelerate the process of diversification.

Building industrial capabilities means at the base, nurturing human skills to ensure rising factor productivity year after year. Firm performance is highly associated with learning capabilities, levels of technology, and a host of firm-level knowledge, skills, and experience. In developing countries and sectors, non-formal learning is the dominant form of mastering new technologies. However, both formal local and overseas training have been deployed and associated with increasing technological complexity. There is also a close correlation between technical complexity of firms' internal ICT tools and available telecommunication infrastructure.

Combined with continuous firm-level capability building, the macroeconomy is extremely important to ensure a thriving private entrepreneurship and investment. A stable and predictable policy environment is extremely important to building dynamic sectoral systems.

Summing Up

The analysis presented in this chapter suggests that export diversification results in higher foreign earnings. However, if the manufacturing base is strong and products are competitive in global markets, there is a greater possibility that export diversification may take place. This kind of diversification leads to income growth and employment generation.

The recent empirical evidence suggests that economic diversification has become pivotal to the sustainability of growth and economic development in all the countries irrespective of the richness in natural resources. In fact, the evidence presented in the chapter suggests a strong association between export diversification and better economic performance, thus, resulting in improvements in development indicators. On the other hand, the countries that could not diversify faced unstable income and reduction in employment resulting in poor economic performance. In general, Asian countries are more diversified compared to their African counterpart.

The manufacturing sector has witnessed more diversification compared to other sectors. Consequently, the export share of manufacturing in total exports from leading countries is around 80 per cent in 2019 in Asia compared to less than 50 per cent in Africa. The evidence presented in the chapter suggests that there is a strong association between export diversification and employment creation. The chapter concludes that export diversification is one instrument that could be applied for better economic performance.

Notes

1 Murtala M., et al. (2018: 42).
2 Kenneth et al. (2019: 4).
3 The United Nations Industrial Development Organization review (2003).
4 Murtala M. et al. (2018: 42–3).
5 Muhammad et al. (2017), Umejei (2015), Renne (2015).
6 https://www.google.com/search?q=competitiveness+of+Chinese+textiles+industry&rlz=1C1GCEB_enDE819DE819&oq=competitiveness+of+Chinese+textiles+industry&aqs=chrome..69i57j33i16013j33i22i29i30.26004j1j7&sourceid=chrome&ie=UTF-8, accessed May 20, 2022.
7 Yusuf Shahid, "Bangladesh: Growth Miracle or Mirage?" June 16, 2021. https://www.cgdev.org/blog/bangladesh-growth-miracle-or-mirage, accessed March 8, 2022.
8 https://blog.bizvibe.com/blog/top-10-largest-textile-producing-countries, accessed March 13, 2022.
9 Yi Wen (2016).
10 To promote the textile industry, the government launched a policy called 'Six Priorities', which favoured the textile industry in six areas: supply of raw materials,

energy and power, bank loans, foreign exchange, imported advanced technology and transportation (see, e.g., Qiu, 2005).

11   Export data for 2012 is very inconsistent with other years. It might be a data error but this is what is reported in the UNCOMTRADE database against Code '84' for 2012.

12   https://www.mckinsey.com/industries/retail/our-insights/whats-next-for-bangla-deshs-garment-industry-after-a-decade-of-growth, accessed July 19, 2021.

13   Hasan et al. (2020); Islam (2021).

14   Menzel and Woodruff (2021).

15   Islam (2021); Rahman (2021); Zaman (2021).

16   About 96 per cent of all RMG exports went to the buyers in the USA and EU (WB, 2005).

17   Export Promotion Bureau (2019). Retrieved from Export Promotion Bureau of Bangladesh: http://www.epb.gov.bd/.

18   Export Genius (2022); Latifee (2016); Paul and Quadir (2013); Hossain and Latifee (2017).

19   Source: Compiled from the following:
     P. Gehl-Sampath (2007), UNU-MERIT.
     P. Paul-Majumder and A. Begum (2006), *Engendering Garment Industry: The Bangladesh Context* (Dhaka: UPL).
     Muhammad A. Latif (1997), *Handloom Industry of Bangladesh 1947-90* (Dhaka: UPL).
     Sadequl Islam (2001), *The Textile and Clothing Industry of Bangladesh in a Changing World Economy* (Dhaka: Centre for Policy Dialogue and the University Press Limited).

20   An early entrant in Bangladesh, it established a joint venture in 1977 with Desh Garments Ltd., making it the first export-orientated ready-made garment industry in Bangladesh.

21   Omolade Adunbi and Howard Stein Prepared for AFEE Panel "The Political Economy of State Capitalism", An earlier version of this paper was first presented at a workshop in Addis Ababa, August 2019.

22   Maiwada and Renne (2013: 172).

23   Salihu Maiwada and Elisha Renne (2020), *Textile Ascendancies: Aesthetics, Production, and Trade in Northern Nigeria (African Perspectives)*, ed. Elisha Renne and Salihu Maiwada (Hardcover, 2020).

24   Ibid. Murtala et al. (2019).

25   This section draws heavily from Toye (2021). China-Africa Relations: The Northern Nigeria Textile Industry. https://digitalcommons.chapman.edu/cgi/viewcontent.cgi?article=1007&context=international_studies_theses. Accessed 1 July 2023.

26   Transparency International. "Corruption Perception Index." July 27, 2021 from https://www.transparency.org/en/countries/nigeria, accessed 27 July 2021.

Part III

Chapter 8

LEADERSHIP AND ECONOMIC DEVELOPMENT

'In explaining South Korea's macroeconomic take-off Park Chung Hee's leadership was one of many factors. By contrast, in the development of POSCO (the Pohang Iron & Steel Company), his leadership was the pivotal variable, to recount the story of POSCO is to retell the story of Park as the soldier and the modernizer.'

Chinua Achebe, 'Nigeria's problem is simply and squarely that of leadership'.

Introduction

This chapter asserts the pivotal role of leaders, leadership and the elite in national development. In the previous chapters, we analysed a few of the several factors and variables that determine the rate and direction of economic growth. It focusses on the role of leadership, a subject that is not frequently related to economic growth in the large body of research explaining development. According to Howard Gardner in his book *The Leading Minds:*[1] *'In the grip of an ideology, postmodern critiques of leadership-critiques that question the role of the leader or any claims of extraordinariness-risk obscuring a vital enduring fact of life.'*

We will demonstrate that the character, commitment choices and actions taken by those in political positions, the 'leaders' and 'elites' especially in developing countries where governments and their leaders hold and control the levers of power, tend to trump all other factors. Their interests and predilections in a weak institutional regime which characterize post-colonial nations could push their nation into a trajectory of a positive or negative economic development pathway. In post-colonial states with weakened or absent institutions and poor coordination across the economic system, the evolution of a capable state is critical to the long-term emergence of nations. In other words, leadership in some form needs to be in place to prevent chaos and to manage the process of nation-building. Nation-building necessitates that a 'builder' or a collection of builders devotes explicit and deliberate effort to the process of nation-building. For most African countries the end of colonialism was abrupt, chaotic and disorderly. Nation-building process requires complex and difficult long-term investment in diverse capabilities to create an equitable society and engineer fast economic growth. Leadership is essential to providing purpose and direction during the process of nation-building. A new nation may falter without capable, legitimate and visionary leaders.

The chapter will examine the key role that leadership and social capabilities play in managing industrialization, as well as the investment necessary for human and physical capital formation. We posit that leadership and capabilities are critical to efficient institutions, especially in navigating complex industrial systems, in terms of defining structures and functions ensuring necessary financing and creating a coherent management system. Additionally, good leadership gives direction in promoting good institutions to administer transparent sanctions, incentives and authority while bad leadership corrupts their institutions. More crucially, leadership influences the role of individual actors be they politicians, bureaucrats or scientists, as these actors run organizations and therefore transmit the effectiveness of institutions. The behaviour of governments plays an important role in stimulating or discouraging economic activity, as does the behaviour of entrepreneurs, parents, scientists or priests.

The rest of the chapter is organized as follows: the next section briefly examines a large and complex subject of how leaders function within the context of state capacity in development. This is followed by a review of the nature and functions of leadership.

A Review of Leadership in Development

There are two broad views of the influence of leaders.[2] Thinkers like Marx and Tolstoy and others believe individual leaders matter little. Scholars, especially in the field of psychology literature, believe the notion of a powerful leader influencing the fate of nations is a social myth embraced to satisfy citizens' psychological expectations. In contrast, the absolutist takes the extreme view in which the larger-than-life individuals are responsible for decisive historical changes – the so-called 'Great Man' view. This perspective presents the evolution of a nation's history as a phenomenon ascribed purely to the causative influences of certain powerful leaders or a very small number of elites in society. This is the thesis espoused by Thomas Carlyle in his study of the French Revolution and further expanded in his later works (Carlyle, 1837, 1859). This concept of leadership is broadly popular among military historians, who tend to see the individual leader as the key to military outcomes. The British historian John Keegan sees the political history of the twentieth century in the leadership of six men: Lenin, Stalin, Hitler, Mao, Roosevelt and Churchill (Keegan, 2003).[3]

Recent findings that look beyond especially evolutionary and institutional literature emphasize the role of institutions and social context in shaping economic outcomes. This is where the role of national leaders and the elites matter as humans ultimately manage organizations and determine the evolution of institutions. This is critical where individual influences for the most part substitute for formal institutions and consequently exert personal influences on growth.[4]

The study by Bragg (2016) explicitly identifies the deterministic view of leaders as incidental actors to the evolution of their national economies and the influence they exert is proportional to institutional effectiveness that constrain their exercise of power. According to Fukuyama (2001), while scholars remain focussed on institutional evolution, institutions can be shaped by human agency and learning, and leaders influence development at every level. Deng Xiaoping's ideas shaped the organization of the Chinese state in ways dramatically different from that of Mao Zedong, a move that had deepgoing consequences for the country's economy and society.

This chapter suggests that while political institutions may matter, their impact is not deterministic. Rather, one important effect of political institutions is to constrain the power of individual leaders. The ideal parliamentary oversight that evolved in more advanced nations is yet to develop in most postcolonial states. In some cases, nascent democratic oversights are rendered redundant in an environment of autocracy which is prevalent in developing countries. A leader's role therefore becomes critical, especially in developing countries that face multidimensional and many concurrent challenges.

Defining political leadership and the elite

An important concept in the discussion of leadership is the notion of political *power elite*, defined as a small group of people who control a disproportionate amount of wealth, privilege and access to decision-making of global consequence.[5] The power elite describe the relationship between individuals at the pinnacles of political, military and economic institutions, who share a common world view of governance and tend to be disposed to satisfying group interest. The power elite in a modern society consist of the highest-ranking members of the corporate community, academia, politicians, the bureaucracy, media editors, military service personnel and high-profile journalists.[6]

According to Mills (1956), the power elite refer to 'those political, economic, and military circles, which as an intricate set of overlapping small but dominant groups share decisions having at least national consequences. Insofar as national events are decided, the power elite are those who decide them'. Drawing on this concept of the power elite, the political elite in the present-day Nigeria have emerged from the four disciplines and institutions:

(i)   The highest political leaders and a handful of key cabinet members and close advisers;
(ii) Major corporate owners and directors particularly in the oil, banking, telecommunications and other key sectors;
(iii) High-ranking military officers, in the most part, retired military officers who have transformed into civilian politicians; and
(iv) Top-level bureaucrats who are for the most part faceless but very rich and powerful.

These groups overlap, and elites tend to circulate from one sector to another, consolidating power as they do so. A new economic elite emerged with the advent of the democratic order although they have always existed since the military era, particularly from the early 1980s. The economic order that developed gradually during the period threw up an economic and social elite.

The most powerful elite is the one who holds political power and exerts authority over the national rather than corporate segments. Since government remains the biggest spender at both federal and state levels and because institutions of control over national resources are so weak or non-existent, this group treats national resources as personal assets, its interest is the national interest. They occupy the executive and legislative arms and tend to have developed immunity to public criticism of corruption, poor governance and poor service delivery.[7] While the media has found the courage occasionally to call attention to the cost of governance and the recklessness of squandered wealth of the common heritage, the group seems rather unmindful of public opinion. Public opinion, on the other hand, is largely controlled and shaped by some of the power elite in charge of the media and communication sectors. Through the exploitation of mass illiteracy, weakened civil society and exploitation of ethnic sentiments, many within the power elite have managed to perpetuate themselves in office. They have instituted systems of patronage where the patrons (political parties) supply clients (voters) with material advantage in exchange for support, essentially sidestepping the need for performance once power is accrued. Not surprisingly, many, including their children, are working the system to self-perpetuate the space soon to be vacated through death and natural attrition by the extant political elite.

The current Nigerian power elite is therefore a continuation of a political institution with its quotidian routines and practices that were instituted way back in our history, a successor to the colonial regime with its structures of repression that limited private liberties and curtailed opportunities for the powerless.[8] The inherited institutions of governance, taking its cues from the initial conditions persist, as it continued its normative and largely informal rules of governance.

In sum, the most distinguishing feature of the different power elites is the concentration of extreme and unproductive wealth in the hands of a tiny elite, and their most notable identity is the unusual lack of concern for the suffering of the majority, the growing levels of poverty and inequality and the heating angst of the silent majority who bear the brunt of multidimensional deprivations. Despite the enormous oil wealth accruing to Nigeria, we are ranked very low on prosperity scales and prominent among the counties rated poor.

According to Ake (2001: 1), African economies have been 'stagnating or regressing'. Africa has been grappling with the issue of development for over four decades, and the result has not been very promising despite the recent resource-induced growth. While the development regress could be attributed to a negative colonial legacy, the corruption of the leaders, inappropriate policies, poor planning and incompetent bureaucratic management remain key challenges. Evidently, while there has been a failure of development for the most part, the problem is not so much that development has failed as it was never really on the agenda in the first place.

There is a wide and complex relationship between governance, public service and policy processes, but at the heart of it all is the quality of political leadership. Without the explicit support of the political leadership, the state is rudderless. As an African saying goes, 'the fish starts to rot from the head'. The head controls all the essential organs of the body, as the political leadership affects the rest of the government, so if there is a problem with the head, it eventually affects the remaining part of the body.

In developing nations, state building succeeds with a determined and competent leader, or in Cyril Black's term 'modernizing leader'. Considering the challenging leadership environment and daunting leadership tasks in third-world states, several criteria for the evaluation of political leaders of developing nations are suggested. First, a leader of a new nation needs to provide a vision for the future of that nation. An inspired vision serves to strengthen national unity and galvanize popular support for, and participation in, nation-building. Second, with limited political and economic resources, major tasks of nation-building cannot be solved concurrently. Therefore, agenda and priority setting are crucial to successful leadership. Third, a successful leader requires qualities that guarantee the successful implementation of nation-building policies. Such qualities include the ability to make sound appointments, managerial skill and personal commitment. In addition, nation-building, which in the West was accomplished over centuries, must be completed in a few decades and under challenging conditions. To overcome the inertia and resistance of existing institutions, a successful leader must be highly motivated and forceful, one who can mobilize and concentrate resources to effectively implement his policies. Fourth, skill in crisis management is a critical quality, as internal and external threats to stability can be both sudden and lethal. Finally, in developing nations, where legitimacy and loyalty are not deeply rooted, integrity can cement popular trust and support for the leader.

Cases of Leadership in Development

South Korea: Transformational leadership role in industrial progress

Let me start with the below quotes.

> During the most difficult and challenging period in its history, South Korea produced some extraordinary leaders. Together, they preserved the nation from Communist rule, created 'the miracle on Han', and built a dynamic democracy. Within a half-century, South Korea was transformed from a country of dire poverty to one of relative wellbeing, from post-colonial chaos to dynamic democracy, from an underdeveloped society to a post-industrial one, and from a client state to a key economic and political powerhouse in East Asia. (p. 12)[9]

> Park Chung Hee wrote in his book *To Build a Nation*:

> When I took over power as the leader of the revolutionary group on 16 May 1961, I felt, honestly speaking, as if I had been given a pilfered household or a bankrupt firm to manage. Around me I could find little hope or encouragement. The outlook was bleak. But I had to rise above this pessimism to rehabilitate the household. I had to break, once and for all, the vicious circle of poverty and economic stagnation. Only by curing the abnormal economic structure could we lay the foundation for decent living standards. But I soon came to realize the difficulty of simultaneously achieving our goals of social stability and economic development and the goal of efficient government. I was also aware of the fact that economic development in the capitalist manner requires not only an immense investment of money and materials but also a stable political situation and competent administrators.[10]

In explaining South Korea's miraculous development and industrial takeoff, Park Chung Hee's leadership was one of many factors.[11] The book's authors gave a detailed account of his role in the development of Korea's

Heavy Chemical Industry and critically the Pohang Iron & Steel Company (POSCO). His leadership was the pivotal variable, dwarfing all other factors, in determining the scale and speed of the effort. Evidently, the history of POSCO cannot be correctly told without the leadership of Park, both as the soldier and the builder of modern Korea. His perception of the longer term was acute. In the midst of hunger and acute deprivation of the Korean people, Park envisioned the building of an industrialized nation. His focus was the more enduring industrial Korea.

Park graduated top of his class from the Japanese military academy in Manchuria at the age of 28 during World War II. Shortly after in 1948, Park was arrested on allegations that he joined a Communist organization. He faced a military junta and was sentenced to death for his connections with Communists, but he was rescued by other military officers and a senior general.[12] In the May 1961 coup, the South Korean armed forces seized power in a bloodless coup and established a military junta headed by General Park Chung Hee. As the earlier quote demonstrates, the military government faced a monumental challenge. The economy was not just on a downward spiral, it suffered from mismanagement and corruption.

General Park, a man driven by a singular vision, once remarked: 'a fire burns inside me.' His work ethics was well known; he was well known for working 18-hour daily. An institution is the lengthened shadow of its leader and not surprisingly the country's economy at the time seemed to follow his example. During the Park era, the South Korean economy grew in some years at a phenomenal rate of 14 per cent, with exports increasing by as much as 40 per cent annually. Under what was known as Korean capitalism, the Korean labour force worked hard under harsh conditions for little money. Soon, the frenetic pace of industrialization led to massive structural transformation. The South Korean landscape changed as rural-urban divide narrowed. Farmlands gave way to highways and factory sites sprang up which profoundly altered society's social structure, social values and behaviour. In mid to late 1960s, around 60 per cent of the labour force was engaged in agriculture and fishery, but the percentage declined to 50.4 per cent in 1970 and 38.4 per cent in 1978. Concomitantly, the percentage of workers engaged in the industrial sector, including mining and manufacturing, rose from 10.3 per cent in 1965 to 35.2 per cent in 1970 and 38.4 per cent in 1978. Industrialization led to a rapid increase in South Korea's urban population, which rose from 28.3 per cent of the total in 1960 to 54.9 per cent in 1979. Rapid urbanization compounded the problems of housing, transportation, sanitation and pollution and exacerbated other social problems.[13]

Improved living standards and ever-increasing job opportunities accelerated the desire among South Koreans for education, particularly at secondary schools and institutions of higher learning. In 1960, about one-third of children between 12 and 14 years of age attended middle schools; that proportion increased to 53.3 per cent in 1970 and 74.0 per cent in 1975. Rural villages also underwent changes of revolutionary proportions, particularly after 1971. As the government had emphasized industrial growth and slighted the agrarian sector, agricultural production lagged; its annual rate of growth during the 1967–72 period was only about 2.5 per cent. With overall GNP growing at over 10 per cent a year during the same period, the rural economy steadily lost ground, until by 1969 farm income was only a little more than half that earned by urban workers. This situation contributed to the high rate of migration to the cities and eroded political support for the president.

The seeming neglect of the rural areas led to a change in government policy. It took active measures to modernize the agriculture sector that led to a rise in farm productivity and a rise in income from 1970. The steps taken include targeted increased subsidies to farmers which led to the setting of relatively high prices for grains. Higher-yield rice varieties were introduced. Advanced agricultural technology was made more widely available through extension services, and more fertilizers and credits were provided. As a result of these measures, farm productivity and farm income increased very rapidly during the ensuing years, and the rate of emigration to the cities tapered off.

Harvard scholar, Ezra Vogel, wrote in his book *The Park Chung Hee Era: The Transformation of South Korea* that Park was one of only four 'outstanding national leaders in the 20th century' who successfully modernized their country. Choe Sang-Hun wrote in the *New York Times*:

He was a beloved president of South Korea; he was a hated dictator. He banned miniskirts from streets but held late-night parties with young women. He served in the army of his country's colonial ruler but dreamed of building atomic bombs to check neighboring superpowers. His 18-year rule was the best of times when South Korea cast off centuries-old poverty and roared as an 'Asian tiger' economy; it was the worst of times when spies monitored classrooms and dissidents languished in prison.[14]

Korean industrialization followed the classic Asian model; its major export in the early years was textiles and garments. The cotton textile spinning and weaving industry had engaged, as in many countries, the first 'modern' industry in Korea even prior to the Park years.[15] In 1961, textiles accounted for about 25 per cent of Korean exports totaling US$5.7 million. In 1965, four years later, total exports had risen to more than US$106 million, of which textiles made up 41 per cent. Firms that would eventually become the largest of the chaebol figured in this dramatic growth.

While the export performance of the textile industry and of certain other light industries (e.g. footwear) created the first major spurt of growth in the Korean economy, Park was focussed on bigger goals. He dreamed of a time when Korea would be a major international producer of such products as steel, ships, heavy vehicles and heavy machinery – products that Park associated with national strength (an association that dated to Park's years with the Japanese military).

Clearly, Park fits into the category of visionary leaders. This is an individual with a clear idea of what they envision the future to be. He/she sets concrete goals and takes definable steps to plan and implement this vision and persuade a team towards accomplishing these goals. Despite persistent opposition from international development agencies such as the World Bank Park did waver in his single-minded goal. Due to the significant size of the financing to achieve capital formation in the early Park years, Korean firms made a recourse to what was then limited overseas financing. Foreign lenders declined to take the risk to lend money to build steel mills or shipyards to Korean firms with little or no experience in the heavy industries. For example, whereas the first five-year plan, at Park's insistence, called for the development of an integrated iron and steel complex in Korea, the World Bank blocked the idea. This requirement for foreign finance initially threatened Park's ambitions.[16]

Park's life and leadership fit the textbook definition of a visionary leader. These are people who see things far off and make sense of them before most others are able to. He was able to imagine a future that was impossible to conceive. Despite the financial obstacles aided by the international system General Park was unmoved from his predetermined agenda. The success and the resounding performance of the iron and steel plant, POSCO demonstrated success of Park's Heavy and Chemical Industry (HCI) plan. Again, it showed another trait of leadership which is the willingness to take risk. The steel industry required huge, whose development required a huge front-end investment (i.e. the resources had to be committed prior to any commercial output being achieved), the plan called for a state-owned firm to be created: the POSCO. This investment proved to be the most successful of all the HCI programs in that era. POSCO currently is one of the world's most efficient and profitable steelmaking firm.

'POSCO was established in 1968, and another former general in the Korean army who had been trained in Japan (at the prestigious Waseda University) was put in charge of the firm. This general was Park Tae-Joon, who was to run POSCO as though it were a military operation until he retired in 1992' (p. 18).[17] The plant which became a 9 million tonne per year mill was completed and was operational within three years in Pohang in 1972.[18] The greater success of Pohang was that its output would provide input for other HCI firms and foster that country's entries into large-scale shipbuilding and automobile. Twelve years later an even larger complex was opened on an artificial island in Kwangyang Bay, in southwestern Korea.

Consistent with Park's vision of 'Steel is national power', the industry assumed a central position at the heart of this emergent industrial country. The multiplier effect of the steel industry made it the engine of economic growth. Steel production engendered a local production network and contributed to value-added manufacturing. Globally, for any additional demand for steel, the value of industrial production increases by several factors. The multiplier factor for employment is even greater between 6 and 10; the output and employment multipliers of the steel industry are far greater than in most other industries. This is because a large number of industries are connected to steel production – from the business services sector on trade and energy to secondary raw materials. With steel production so wide, the spillover effects on various sectors of the economy are large.

Steel therefore provided inputs for the rest of the Korean heavy and chemical industries, from machinery, automobiles, shipbuilding to the defense industries. The industry led the way in lifting South Korea out of its poverty and military insecurity. The establishment of an integrated steel mill exemplified by POSCO fulfilled Park's strategy of legitimization based on performance. Steel was a measure of military.[19]

Nigeria's Contrasting Experience in Iron and Steel Development

Misallocation of investment: the case of Ajaokuta Steel Company

The Early Phase of Start-up: The Constraints and the Atmosphere. In April 1971, the Nigerian Steel Development Authority (NSDA) was established by a military Decree (No 19 of April 14). This birthed the first formal body to be charged directly with the actualization of the steel programme. NSDA was charged with the following objectives:

(a) planning, construction and operation of steel plants; and
(b) carrying out geological surveys, market studies and metallurgical research.

The authority was to examine various process routes, including natural gas-based direct reduction processes that required high-grade iron ores which were not known to be available in Nigeria. The presence of high-grade iron at Itakpe was confirmed in 1973, and NSDA then commissioned TPE to prepare a preliminary project report (PPR) for the proposed BF/BOP plant. The PPR was submitted in 1974, scrutinized and finally accepted in 1975. With Itakpe confirmed as the source of iron ore, coal was expected to be used in the ratio of 35 per cent Enugu coal and 65 per cent imported coal. The initial product mix proposal suggested 50 per cent of long products and 50 per cent flats. This was based on the product demand profile revealed by market surveys. Curiously, the government ruled that Ajaokuta should produce only long products in the first stage. This decision would later be seen to have had one of the most profoundly negative and far-reaching consequences on the future of the steel industry in Nigeria. The major aspects of the PPR recommendation were as follows:

1. The plant would produce 1.3 million tonnes of long products only in the first phase
2. Expansion to 2.6 million tonnes would continue immediately after the completion of the first phase. This would incorporate 1.3 million tonnes of flat steel sheets.

In the same year, V/O Tiaj Prom Export (TPE) of the USSR was commissioned to prepare a detailed project report (DPR) based on the earlier recommendations.

Parallel efforts – genesis of the DR system and the inland rolling mills

While negotiating with the Soviets, a parallel effort was made in the Federal Ministry of Industries (which was then overseeing the steel project) to explore the establishment of a Direct Reduction (DR) plant. The impetus for this came from the abundance of natural gas, the major energy source in the DR process, which is available in Nigeria. By 1975, a detailed blueprint had been prepared and presented to the government. The proposal called for the setting up of two DR plants, both based in the two coastal towns of Warri and Port-Harcourt.

In 1976, the decision was taken that a DR plant on MIDREX technology be sited in Warri; the Aladja Steel Plant after international tenders had been examined. On the 3 October 1977, the Federal Ministry of Industries, on behalf of the federal government, signed a contract with an Austro-German Consortium (CSA) for engineering supply, erection, civil works and supervision of commissioning, phases for a turnkey integrated steel plant. The plant would be a Direct Reduction/Electric Arc Furnace (DR/EAF) with a liquid steel production capacity of 1 million tonnes of steel. Delta Steel Company

(DSC), the operating entity for the Delta Steel Plant (DSP) was established by the government in 1979 the same year as the contract for the construction of Ajaokuta was signed with the Soviet Union.

Also, that year, the NSDA was dissolved, giving rise to different companies which became responsible for various aspects of the steel programme. The Ajaokuta Steel Plant (ASP) simultaneously came into being. Nigeria, with an agrarian-based economy, and a weak industrial sector, dominated by consumer goods industries, thus embarked on the development of two capital-intensive and technology-intensive steel factories at the same time. Since ASP, DSC and all the rolling mills were designed to produce long products, they were restricted to only about one-half of the steel products market. Sales, however, improved in 1986 with the resumption of work by the civil engineering contractors who bought the bulk of the long products. Product diversification into other profiles, especially plain and ribbed bars, brought greater demand.

Performance of the steel plants

With support from the technical partners during the Performance Guarantee Test (PGT) period, workforce deficiency did not constitute a major problem. Technical deficiencies led to major setbacks in the achievement of rated capacities. Even though DSC was built on a turnkey basis, it still had to build up supply networks from scratch. Basic raw materials such as iron ore were imported. DSC therefore had to get involved in setting up, for instance, a crushing and screening plant to exploit and transport limestone to the DSC plant site. The plant was built close to the sources of electrical energy and natural gas, and although both were not expected to be part of the hindrances to production, this in fact proved to be a wrong expectation. The 330kv electric feeder lines from Sapele that were supposed to supply the plant were not completed on schedule. An alternative 33kv line had to be installed in a hurry to provide electrical energy to commission the materials handling system in March 1981.

Coupled with these exogenous factors, the plant had the usual startup problems of electrical, mechanical and operational malfunctions and modifications. None of the primary plants produced above 20 per cent of installed capacity until 1986 despite high initial optimistic projections. However, this was not enough to take total tonnage steel output above 10 per cent because of the linear sequential nature of an integrated steel plant. In other words, if the DR plant produces at 100 per cent but steel making shop (SMS) is idle, no steel will be made. The overall performance of the plant however may not reflect the efficiency of the individual units and may conceal the root of the problems of the linear sequential nature of an integrated steel plant explained above. The lime plant for instance will be forced to shut down if its products are not being utilized in the consumer units, or the DR plant could shut down if the pellet plant could not meet its production demand, or because the SMS had broken down, and could not take all the direct reduced iron (DR) coming from the DR plant. This indeed was a frequent phenomenon at DSP where all the inputs were never available adequately and simultaneously. The combined effects of these constraints led to lost tonnage capacity of about five metric tons in ten years. This means that DSP on the average only produced about one-sixth of its installed capacity in six years.

This section considers the start-up performance of the two integrated steel plants in Nigeria. The most reliable and consistently recorded indicators were the data on tonnage output from individual units and plants. This suggested the use of capacity utilization as a useful concept to understand plant behaviour. Overall, capacity utilization was extremely low for both integrated steel plants. In 12 years, the DSC consistently produced at one-tenth of its installed capacity – meaning that the plant may well have been idle for almost ten years in another environment where it could have operated at full capacity. Ajaokuta rolling mills did not do any better. Constraint categories are not very different from those found in other developing countries.

In the two plants, the following factors were prominent:

(i)   lack of material inputs
(ii) lack of replacement capacity
(iii) lack of working capital
(iv) shortage of foreign exchange on which items 1 and 2 mostly depend; and,
(v)   Start-up problems associated with the early months of manufacturing plants.

The findings suggest that all the components required for plant operation should be available simultaneously for the plant to function efficiently. This was, however, not the case. This phase is critical in that it sets the pace, defines the character and suggests the broad evolutionary trajectory of the plants. Failure to take advantage of this learning opportunity may well deny the firms the chance to acquire technological capability. For most of the years since they were established, the two plants were largely idle.

Summing up the mechanics of industrial failure in this context, it is evident that technological capability mastery is a critical factor of success, and it is achievable only through continuous technological efforts. However, technological knowledge is not shared equally among firms, and it is not easily imitated or transferred. Technical expertise is required to draw up pre-feasibility documents, in the investment and operational phases, and in human capital and technology acquisition process. The lessons from the collapse of these industrial firms and failures of performance reveal that socio-political management of public investments is crucial for desired results. The political and bureaucratic support pillars were absent. Politicians were more interested in skimming rents from large-scale investments rather than setting goals for completion and performance. Learning from the technical problems of the Federal Fertilizer Company, industrial success requires technology choice capacity, technical management, effective communication and technological innovation/transfer, infrastructural support, auto-generative skills acquisition and effective training/participation.

The case of the Nigerian steel adventure shows the challenges inherent in large-scale technological investment and the implementation difficulties revealed the complex technicality of the investment phase. More importantly, the failure of the program shows the lack of strategic and visionary leadership at the critical junctures. We see those decisions taken at the beginning of the project life often become irreversible and define the character of technical systems for a long time. Also, the overall costs of the project and other key issues such as the structure of the firm are negotiated at this phase. These further stress the importance of strong knowledgeable technical management leadership as the consequences are dire with implications such as industrial failure and loss of investment. The Case of Ajaokuta Steel Company reveals a situation of misallocation of investment where investment decisions inhibit productivity, capacity utilization, output and industrial success.

Deng Xiaoping and the transformation of China

Deng Xiaoping like Park represents that transformative leader in the case of China. The dramatic economic extremes experienced in China in the last 70 years highlight the impact ruling elites and leaders can have on the economic welfare of states. China experienced massive declines in economic growth because of Mao's forced collectivization of agricultural and the Cultural Revolution. Millions of Chinese people starved to death with the failure of Mao's agricultural reforms and his attempts to create a new society. However, Deng was the man who envisioned a new direction for China towards more market-orientated policies. This led to meteoric industrial expansion and economic growth since 1978.

Ezra Vogel used the corporate management model as a useful metaphor to explain the leadership role of Deng who was like a manager in a large corporation. Deng as general manager 'helped package the ideas' and led his team to get them accepted; he 'provided a steady hand at the top' to give people confidence through trying changes; he oversaw the selection and guidance of 'the team of colleagues that worked together' to manage China's complex transformation. 'Deng was a problem solver who helped forge a robust and capable administration that could implement plans and survive political and popular challenges. He led in setting priorities, but he delegated; he articulated the core ideas, but in a way the public could appreciate. When controversies arose, Deng managed the process to minimize cleavages'[20] (p. 2). According to a reviewer of Vogel's biography of Deng, so transformational and deep-going was the leadership role of Deng. 'Deng succeeded where all other generations of modernizing leaders floundered for more than 150 years, making him one of the most important personalities in Chinese history over the past two centuries and of world history from the latter half of the twentieth century to the start of the twenty-first'[21]

For example, 35 years ago, China's per capita income was only one-third of that of sub-Sahara Africa. Today, China is the world's largest manufacturing powerhouse. It produces nearly 50 per cent of the world's major industrial goods, including crude steel (800 per cent of the US level and 50 per cent of global supply); cement (60 per cent of the world's production), coal (50 per cent of the world's production), vehicles (more than 25 per cent of global supply) and industrial patent applications (about 150 per cent of the US level). China is also the world's largest producer of ships, high-speed trains, robots, tunnels, bridges, highways, chemical fibres, machine tools, computers, cellphones, among others.

China's industrial revolution started in 1978 under the leadership of Deng Xiaoping. Deng Xiaoping worked alongside Mao Zedong through the political, social, and economic strife from the 1950s through the 1970s, including the Great Leap Forward. Deng developed a reputation for inner strength and philosophical flexibility, and Mao once described him as 'a needle inside a cotton ball' (Vogel, 2013: 26). Ultimately, Deng Xiaoping's pragmatic and patient reforms led to a sustainable industrial revolution in China and paved the way for continued economic growth. After observing major political upheavals and miscalculations based on ideology, Deng established fundamental principles behind his approach to economic reform: No socialist economy can achieve sustainable growth without market elements; but no market economy can flourish and continue to prosper without state-led industrial policy, social order and political stability, which, in China's case, would be established by a strong state government. Deng's reforms were enacted, modified, and supported by high-ranking central government officials and implemented by local-level officials in the counties and countryside. China would 'cross the river by touching the stones' and 'seek the truth from its own practice': that is, China would not adhere to a strictly dogmatic approach, but rather would embrace persistent pragmatism, step by step.

China's industrial revolution started in 1978 under the leadership of Deng Xiaoping. The country repudiated advice from Western economists (unlike what Russia did in the 1990s) and instead took a very humble, gradualist, experimental approach with its economic reforms. Central to Deng's reform was the creation of China's Special Economic Zones. Created after Deng Xiaoping's economic reforms were implemented in China in 1979, the Special Economic Zones are areas where market-driven capitalist policies are implemented to attract foreign businesses to China. The first four SEZs were established in 1979. Shenzhen, Shantou, and Zhuhai are in Guangdong province, and Xiamen is located in Fujian province.[22]

Shenzhen became the model for China's Special Economic Zones when it was transformed from 126 square miles of villages known for sales of knock-offs to a bustling business metropolis. Located a short bus ride from Hong Kong in southern China, Shenzhen is now one of China's richest cities. The success of Shenzhen and the other SEZs encouraged the Chinese government to add 14 cities plus Hainan Island to the list of SEZs in 1986. The 14 cities include Beihai, Dalian, Fuzhou, Guangzhou, Lianyungang, Nantong, Ningbo, Qinhuangdao, Qingdao, Shanghai, Tianjin, Wenzhou, Yantai and Zhanjiang.[23]

Sector-Level Transformational Leaders

Norman Borlaug, the Green Revolution and the Mexican connection

The Green Revolution was a momentous event in the agricultural transformation which occurred in the 1960s. This resulted in a change of activities that resulted in the conversion of India's agriculture into a modern industrial system by the adoption of technology. Technological change made possible the adoption and use of high-yielding variety (HYV) seeds, mechanized farm tools, irrigation facilities, pesticides and fertilizers. Specifically, the Green Revolution led to high productivity of crops through adapted measures, such as '(1) increased area under farming, (2) double-cropping, which includes planting two crops rather than one, annually, (3) adoption of HYV of seeds, (4) highly increased use of inorganic fertilizers and pesticides, (5) improved irrigation facilities, and (6) improved farm implements and crop protection measures' (John and Babu, 2021:1).

The path to India's Green Revolution came through Mexico. Mexico experienced an agricultural crisis in the 1930s and 1940s.[24] The country's crops were blighted by *rust*, a parasitic fungi plant disease; for this reason, farmers were harvesting less than half the crops necessary to sustain the population. For three years between 1939 and 1941, all new wheat varieties created by Mexican scientists were devastated by the rust. When American scientists approached the Mexican farmers with newer varieties of wheat, the Mexican farmers treated them with understandable suspicion.

This period coincided with the time Borlaug was completing his PhD in plant pathology from the University of Minnesota, graduating in 1942. He was hired by DuPont Corporation to work on research beneficial to the US armed forces fighting World War II. Few years into this, he joined the Rockefeller Foundation on a project in Mexico focused on soil development, plant pathology, maize, and wheat production. He took it and changed history.

The nature of this work was laborious and demanding. The essence was to check for wheat stems for rust in the scorching sun. Borlaug made a breakthrough that was near revolutionary after nine years of backbreaking research. Borlaug's team developed 6,000 individual crossings of wheat. By 1956, Mexico's wheat production had doubled.That Norman Borlaug's efforts were successful is undeniable as by 1948 Mexico was self-sufficient in grain and by 1965, despite a dramatic population increase, had become a net exporter of wheat. The new wheat varieties were made available to other countries notably the Indian sub-continent. Chief architect of the Indian 'Green Revolution' was Dr Monkombu Swaminathan, who was awarded the World Food Prize in 1987.[25] In 1970 Dr Borlaug was awarded the Nobel Prize for his towering achievements. The success of the Mexican programme prompted the setting up of a similar programme for rice. It was based at purpose-built research centre, the International Rice Research Institute (IRRI) in The Philippines and funded jointly by the Rockefeller and Ford Foundations. The Green Revolution resulted in increased production of food grains (especially wheat and rice) and was in large part due to the introduction into developing countries of new, HYV, beginning in the mid-twentieth century with Borlaug's work.

Swaminathan: Father of the Green Revolution

Following Borlaug's success in Mexico, the Indian and Pakistani government requested his assistance, and with the support of the Rockefeller Foundation and the Food and Agriculture Organization of the United Nations (FAO), Borlaug began his agricultural revolution in Asia. With India and Pakistan facing food shortages due to rapid population growth, the importation of Borlaug's dwarf wheat in the mid-1960s was responsible for a 60 per cent increase in harvests there, helping both countries to become agriculturally self-sufficient. His work in developing countries, especially on the Indian sub-continent, is estimated to have saved as many as one billion people from starvation and death.[26]

In India, Swaminathan was the visionary leader who championed the Green Revolution. Swaminathan is a well-recognized global leader of the Green Revolution and the main architect of the Green Revolution in India for his leadership and role in introducing and further developing HYV of wheat and rice. Swaminathan's collaborative scientific efforts with Norman Borlaug, spearheading a mass movement with farmers and other scientists and backed by public policies, saved India and Pakistan from certain famine-like conditions in the 1960s. His leadership as Director General of the IRRI in the Philippines was instrumental in his being awarded the first World Food Prize in 1987, recognized as the Nobel or the highest honours in the field of agriculture. United Nations Environment Programme has called him 'the Father of Economic Ecology'.

Born four decades before the famine crisis, on 7 August 1925, in Tamil Nadu, his father taught Swaminathan from an early age that the word impossible exists only in our minds, and this would be evident in how he tackled complex problems for the rest of his life. His father, Dr. M.K. Sambasivan, was a surgeon and loyal follower of Mahatma Ghandi. He, like his son after him, believed in empowering the Indian nation from within, and was one of the early leaders in Kumbakonam, the 'burning of foreign clothes', in support of the Swadeshi movement, which emphasized made in India cloths. Swaminathan's devotion to making India great was clearly fostered from an early age and made evident when he refused a full-time role at the University of Wisconsin to return home in 1954. The only surprise was the degree he held.

Coming from a family of doctors, the young Swaminathan was initially determined to follow a similar path and was already enrolled in medical studies when he witnessed the great Bengal Famine at the age of 18. It was estimated that between two and three million people died, and Swaminathan was so affected by this that he decided to switch his focus to Agriculture and devote his life to eradicating hunger in India.[27] He would spend the next couple of decades learning and researching across Europe and the United States until his return to India in early 1954. His first decade back was spent searching for solutions to the recurring famines, but the big breakthrough would come almost a decade later. In 1963, Borlaug would visit India at the request of the Indian government, under the urging M.S. Swaminathan.

Swaminathan strongly believed in Borlaug's research and would immediately implement his findings to address the food shortages, planting four of the most promising strains of seeds that Borlaug brought with him in different locations across North India. However, India's agricultural landscape was complex, the nightmares of his late teens would still return between 1964–65 and 1965–66, as the country experienced severe droughts resulting in widespread famines. The conditions were tough for farming, and it was not an easy landscape for farmers as they also suffered credit shortages. Banks and government were not providing financing at economic viable rates so many were forced to resort to money lenders, resulting in mass exploitation across the farming sector. This is where the role of institutions becomes important, as the financial institutions were failing the farmers in safeguarding the wealth of the collective, exacerbating inefficiencies instead of providing solutions.

In addition to weak state support structures, India's agricultural yield given its population size was woefully insufficient, and more severe than other developing countries. As a geneticist, solving this last problem was the most appealing to Swaminathan, and he believed his collaboration with Borlaug in developing HYV of wheat would lead to self-sustenance. He was right, getting much acclaim for this, and later promoting sustainable development, which he called the 'evergreen revolution'. While Swaminathan was bold in implanting his plans, he anchored his policies not in blind faith, but in lessons he derived from what Borlaug's team had done in Mexico.

India's Green Revolution

The system championed by Swaminathan would usher in the era known as the Green Revolution in India when Indian agriculture was converted into an industrial system with the adoption of modern methods and technology such as the use of HYV seeds, tractors, irrigation facilities, pesticides, and fertilizers. It was part of the larger Green Revolution endeavour initiated by Norman Borlaug, which leveraged agricultural research and technology to increase agricultural productivity in the developing world (CGIAR, 2019). Although the Indian Green Revolution technically began in 1965 under the premiership of Congress leader Lal Bahadur Shastri, with immediate gains in food grain production, especially in the Punjab, Haryana, and Uttar Pradesh regions, it would really take off under the premiership of Indira Ghandi, with major milestones recorded in the development of high-yielding and rust resistant strains of wheat.

In 1966, India imported 18,000 tonnes of seeds for planting, and the impact was immediately apparent. In 1965, the harvested wheat was 12 million tonnes but by 1968, India's yield had grown so much that schools had to be used as temporary granaries. By 1974, India was self-sufficient in cereals. By the turn of the millennium, they were up to 76 million tonnes. According to the Food and Agricultural Organization (FAO), between 1961 and 2001,

India more than doubled its population, from 452 million to more than one billion. At the same time, it nearly tripled its grain production from 87 million tons to 231 million tons. It accomplished this feat while increasing cultivated grain acreage by a mere 8 per cent.

All of this, a nation on the brink of starvation to self-sufficiency in a decade achievable because of the work and belief of a couple of men. The systemic problems that plague many institutions often need a visionary leader to instill a new culture and outlook, showing those around him the true potential of their resources and inspiring them to achieve more.

Lessons from the Leaders and Leadership in This Chapter

Political leadership and transformational leadership

The term leadership has no set definition, as the most qualities of successful leadership can vary greatly. However, the role, motivation and the agenda pursued by leaders usually depend on the historical and development contexts. To a large degree, however, leadership is about controlling and directing an organization or group towards predetermined goals. This could be accomplished through a vision, communicating the vision and motivating the group to achieve the vision. Leaders make the difference in the performance of organizations and in the development of nations. The right leader translates resources or assets to production, which ultimately determines the survival or success level of the entity. The overall organizational effectiveness and performance may not be due to poor administrative system, but poor organizational leadership. Therefore, leadership is about 'doing the right thing'.

Clearly at this historical juncture, when Nigeria faces monumental challenges of governance and development, the country requires the kinds of leaders who are not only committed to ensuring high- performing public sector institutions and organizations but those who seek to transform society through both vision and action. 'Transformational Leaders (TL)' are motivated by strong values, including commitment to a clearly vision and mission, focus on quality services, empowerment of followers. A transformational leader puts forward core values that is practiced both in private and in public, he/she celebrates the diversity of the nation and effectively communicates his ideals. He/she thinks in strategic terms and demands commitment to excellence and innovation, sensitivity to ethical and cultural values of the society irrespective of an inevitable globalizing world in which nations must compete for investment and resources. It is within the power of a leader to initiate and promote commitment to these strong values through the design of reward schemes and monitoring and accountability mechanisms that reduce the opportunities and incentives for rent-seeking.[28]

There are several dimensions to transformational leadership with respect to style, vision and motivation. A transformational leader uplifts the followers through the inspiration and passion that this leader brings to the assignment. The followers draw on the energy of the leader and works for the team to succeed. Transformational leadership is characterized by a compelling vision, a strong accent on a changed future by which the followers are guided in their actions and conduct; such leadership style excites and convert potential followers. This vision may be developed by the leader, by the senior team or may emerge from a broad series of discussions. The important factor is the leader buys into it and puts his/her weight behind such a vision without equivocation.

Once a vision of society is fully formed the leader strives to constantly sell the vision. This takes energy and commitment, as few people will immediately buy into a radical vision, and some will join the show much more slowly than others. The Transformational Leader thus takes every opportunity and will use whatever works to convince others to climb on board the bandwagon. Committed followership in the context of transformational leadership carefully creates trust, and for this reason the personal integrity of a leader becomes a critical part of the package that they are selling. In effect, transformational leaders sell not just a vision but themselves.

As well as promoting the vision and the activity this sort of leader draws followership by force of knowledge and clarity of mandate and as such followers tend to simply trust their judgment in seeking the way forward. Some Transformational Leaders know the way, and simply want others to follow them. Others do not have a ready strategy but will happily lead the exploration of possible routes to the Promised Land. The route forwards may not be obvious and may not be plotted in detail, but with a clear vision, the *direction* will always be known. Thus, finding the way forward can be an ongoing process of course correction and the Transformational Leader (TL) will accept that there will be failures and blind canyons along the way. If they feel progress is being made, they will be happy.

Another critical dimension of the TL is that they are always visible and will stand up to be counted rather than hide behind their troops. They show by their attitudes and actions how everyone else should behave. They also make continued efforts to motivate and rally their followers, constantly doing the rounds, listening, soothing and enthusing. It is their unswerving commitment as much as anything else that keeps people going, particularly through the darker times when some may question whether the vision can ever be achieved. If the people do not believe that they can succeed, then their efforts will flag. The transformational leader seeks to infect and re-infect their followers with a high level of commitment to the vision. Overall, they balance their attention between action that creates progress and the mental state of their followers. Perhaps more than other approaches, they are people-oriented and believe that success comes first and last through deep and sustained commitment. While the TL seeks overtly to transform the organization, there is also a tacit promise to followers that they also will be transformed in some way, perhaps to be more like this amazing leader. In some respects, then, the followers are the *product* of the transformation. TLs are often charismatic but are not as narcissistic as pure Charismatic Leaders, who succeed through a belief in themselves rather than a belief in others. Finally, TLs, by definition, seek to transform. When the organization does not need transformation and people are as happy as they are, then such a leader will be frustrated. Like wartime leaders, however, given the right situation they come into their own and can be personally responsible for saving entire companies.

The extent to which a leader is transformational is measured first, in terms of his influence on the followers. The followers of such a leader feel trust, admiration, loyalty and respect for the leader and because of the qualities of the transformational leader are willing to work harder than originally expected. These outcomes occur because the transformational leader offers followers something more than just working for self-gain; they provide followers with an inspiring mission and vision and give them an identity. The leader transforms and motivates followers through his or her idealized influence (earlier referred to as charisma), intellectual stimulation and individual consideration. In addition, this leader encourages followers to come up with new and unique ways to challenge.

A democratic leadership style presupposes that the power of leaders is granted by the group they are to lead, and that people can be basically self-directed and creative at work if properly motivated. This type of leadership is participatory and encourages individual involvement in decision-making and problem-solving. There is a high element of trust between leaders and followers which fosters cooperation and high morale. Ideally democratic governance is participatory largely through their representatives in the parliament, House of Assembly, Senate, civic societies, etc., who are appointed, responsible and directly accountable to the people. In a democratic government, the leader places the will of the people above himself and public policies are transparent and open. The leader is receptive to the people because the people freely vote to elect him/her. Measured by the yardstick of ideal democratic and transformational leadership, clearly leadership has failed the people in Nigeria.

Summing Up

Our overall proposition in this chapter is that leadership and governance in Nigeria became dysfunctional, in large part due to the corrupting influence of a rentier economy.

The development agenda must be driven largely by a state; as described by Fukuyama: 'one that is limited in scope but strong in its ability to enforce the rule of law, competent and transparent in the formulation of policy, and legitimate enough to have the authority to make painful economic decisions.'[29] This notion of the developmental state, routinely associated with East Asia is less of a phenomenon in Africa. Evidently, the Nigerian state does not answer to this description: it is not small or strong, it is neither capable nor accountable. A 'Developmental' state is one that 'establishes as its principle of legitimacy its ability to promote sustained development, understanding by development the steady high rates of economic growth and structural change in the productive system, both domestically and in its relationship to the international economy'.[30]

The development agenda is thus intimately connected with and dependent on governance and the institutional context. However, governance is frequently cited as the most significant obstacle to development in Africa. In 1989 the World Bank acknowledged the positive role of the state following their assessment of the structural adjustment programs in Africa, but yet in the same breath identified the single most important challenge facing African countries as a 'crisis of governance'.[31] This concern is often voiced in speculations that development of the African state along East Asian lines is not possible due to a lack of state capabilities.

Patrimonialism or Prebendalism tends to shape the evolution and implementation of public policies and programmes in Nigeria. The comparative cases of POHANG and the Nigeria Steel projects clearly illustrate how policies that work under a strong leadership direction failed spectacularly in another environment. Several federal projects including the Ajaokuta steel company, Katsina rolling mills, Iwopin paper mills, Bacita sugar industry and fertilizer plants became White Elephants. There are several factors but top of the list is corruption of the different levels of political and bureaucratic leadership leading to mismanagement of public finance. Ethnic and self-interest rather than commercial and economic, in some cases, determined locational decisions of complex and capital-intensive projects. While some project locations were due to the influence of some influential persons, some serve as 'political compensation' for election support or a demonstration of political importance in the community. This is the hallmark of Prebendal politics that has set the country on a path of continuous regress. As well, most of the time, project management is left in inept hands. All the elements of good public policies that help establish good governance are thereby lost. Hyden and Braton (1992: 7) identified four fundamental elements of governance as level of trust, mutual relationship between the government and civil society, level of accountability, and the nature of authority exerted. These fundamentals tend to be missing at different levels of governance in Nigeria. Elements of patrimonial and prebendalism are also experienced at the state level. Sometimes, relatives and the party faithful receive contracts and consultancy positions, despite their incompetence to do the job. This situation contributes to shoddy work or abandonment of such projects.

Nigeria is a nation endowed with tremendous resources ranging from natural to human and capital resources, which should have placed it among the fast follower industrializing countries such as Indonesia, Malaysia and Thailand. For instance, "Nigeria has received, and somewhat squandered over US$300 billion from oil since early 1970s. At present, it has proven oil reserves estimated at about 36 billion barrels, while natural gas reserves are somewhat larger, estimated at over 100 trillion cubic feet" (Orngu, 2012: 216). The government of Nigeria and its leadership should aim for a transformational agenda by facing squarely the development agenda deficit identified in the different indices. The key agenda is a focus on achieving poverty-reducing growth, which would involve tackling corruption and improving security in the country. Nigeria needs to create an enabling environment for private sector development that would generate jobs for its people and boost the economy. The government should reduce the cost of governance and focus more on effectively delivering public services to the people. This would improve the lives of Nigerians and help to address issues such as group grievances and deteriorating public services mentioned in the index. Finance is inseparable from the nature and dynamic of political power in the same manner that one can define finance as a set of contracts that are inextricably linked to the legal system, the entire financial, contractual and legal apparatus is embedded in a political system. The political system is, in turn, shaped by the distribution of power among members of society – and that distribution of power is in no small part an outcome of the distribution of human capital. Inequality and poverty can be traced to the complex ways in which human capital, the labour market and power become embedded in political and economic institutions.

Notes

1 Howard Gardner (1995), *The Leading Minds: An Anatomy of Leadership* (New York: Basic Books).
2 This section draws on https://www.academia.edu/25478696/ECONOMICS_AND _LEADERS_AND_THE_21ST_CENTURY, accessed 20 September 2022.

3 Outside of military history, the great man view fell out of fashion for many historians in the twentieth century, its demise related to the seeming inevitability of World War I and Herbert Butterfield's broad attack, *The Whig Interpretation of History*, on earlier historical reasoning (Butterfield, 1931).

4 If the economics literature takes the idea that individual personalities matter seriously, it is primarily in the management literature, which has seen many studies of the impacts of particular CEOs, with notable contributions by Johnson et al. [1985] and Bertrand and Schoar [2003], who estimate leader effects on firm behaviour. In the micro-development literature, recent work by Duflo and Chattopadhyay [2004] also examines leader effects at the village level in India.

5 The term power elite was coined by C. Wright Mills in his 1956 book, *The Power Elite*.

6 This section draws on Banji Oyelaran-Oyeyinka (2014), R*ich Country Poor People, Nigeria's Story of Poverty in the Midst of Plenty*(Lagos: Technopol).

7 The recent brave efforts of the house in confronting the oil subsidy scam suggest that even in thick darkness there is light.

8 The origins of the military in Nigeria, are embedded within colonial rule and conquest (Yusuf, 2018), for the British had a colonial army, the police, the judiciary and prison services, as instruments of coercion. The West African Frontier Force (WAFF), created in the 1880s by the British, was used in the subjugation of local peoples, and after colonial conquest, the WAFF was engaged in the so-called 'pacification patrols' to cover areas of dissent. The WAFF later became the colonial army, and then the Nigerian army (Njoku, 2001). During the military rule in the country, it was common for 'dissent' persons to be put in prison or even assassinated.

9 https://ciaotest.cc.columbia.edu/journals/ijoks/v11il/f_0013268_10765.pdf, accessed 20 September 2022.

10 "To Build a Nation" (1971) By Pak Chonghŭi (Park Chung Hee), pp. 101–114; "Sources of Korean Tradition", edited by Yong-ho Ch'oe, Peter H. Lee, and Wm. Theodore de Bary, vol. 2 (New York: Columbia University Press, 2000), 396–8.

11 From the book *The Park Chung Hee Era*, Sang-young Rhyu and Seok-jin Lew (Published by Harvard University Press, 2013), https://doi.org/10.4159/harvard .9780674061064.c11

12 Compiled from https://factsanddetails.com/korea/South_Korea/Modern_History/ entry-7182.html, accessed 21 September 2022.

13 Source: Andrea Matles Savada and William Shaw, Library of Congress, 1990*.

14 Choe Sang-Hun, *New York Times*, 27 January 2005.

15 A. H. Amsden (1989), *Asia's Next Giant: South Korea and Late Industrialization* (New York and Oxford: Oxford University Press).

16 Ibid: https://www.piie.com/publications/chapters_preview/341/2iie3373.pdf

17 ibid.

18 Institute for International Economics. HTTP://www.iie.com, Economic development under Park Chung-Hee, 2003.

19 https://www.degruyter.com/document/doi/10.4159/harvard.9780674061064.c11/ pdf

20 https://cross-currents.berkeley.edu/sites/default/files/e-journal/articles/final_cheek _0.pdf

21 Jean-François Huchet (2014), Ezra Vogel, *Deng Xiaoping and the Transformation of China* (Cambridge, MA, and London: The Belknap Press of Harvard University Press)2011, 876pp, China Perspectives. Retrieved from https://www.cefc.com.hk/article/book -reviews-pdf-version-5/, 6 July 2024.

22 https://www.thoughtco.com/chinas-special-economic-zones-sez-687417
23 China is now home to more than 2,500 SEZs. They range from small business parks
    to full-fledged cities with populations in the millions. The World Bank estimates that
    China's SEZs contribute 22 per cent of GDP, 45 per cent of its FDI and 60 per cent of
    its exports.
24 Compiled from the following: http://www.agbioworld.org/biotech-info/topics/bor-
    laug/green-revolution.html, accessed 1 December 2022.
25 G. N. Hariharan and P. C. Kesavan (2015), "Birth and Growth of M.S. Swaminathan
    Research Foundation, Chennai." *Current Science*, 109(3): 502–12. JSTOR 24906104;
    Glenn Denning (2015), "Fostering International Collaboration for Food Security and
    Sustainable Development: A Personal Perspective of M. S. Swaminathan's Vision,
    Impact and Legacy for Humanity." *Current Science*, 109(3): 447–55. JSTOR 24906099;
    Rudy Rabbinge (2015), "M. S. Swaminathan: His Contributions to Science and
    Public Policy." *Current Science*, 109(3): 439–46. JSTOR 24906098.
26 https://www.britannica.com/biography/Norman-Borlaug, accessed 1 December
    2022.
27 SGI Quarterly, A Buddhist forum for peace, culture, and education.
28 Olowu (2009: 18).
29 Fukuyama (2002: 25).
30 Castells (1992: 55).
31 World Bank (1989: 60).

Chapter 9

STATE CAPACITY AND DEVELOPMENT REVERSAL IN NIGERIA

Introduction

I start this chapter with a few vignettes. At the onset of the Russian–Ukraine war, the price of oil, Nigeria's main export commodity, increased from a low pandemic-induced crash of US$10 in 2020 to a high of US$85 in 2021 and now around US$120 in 2022. The oil price at a point rose to a record US$139 per barrel. According to the Nigerian National Petroleum Company (NNPC) Limited, it uncovered among hundreds of others, an illegal oil connection from Forcados Terminal that operated for nine years with about 600,000 barrels per day of oil lost in the same period. Oil theft and pipeline vandalization have become major drains on this important sector of the Nigerian economy.

Besides oil theft, Nigeria has been unable to benefit from the oil boom due to the lack of capacity of Nigeria to refine its own crude oil. Despite its huge oil reserves, Nigeria has one of the lowest production per capita among oil-producing countries in the world, producing less than a barrel per 100 people. In Saudi Arabia, for instance, it is about 28 barrels per 100 people, in Kuwait it is roughly 60 barrels per 100 people, while in the United Arab Emirates (UAE) production per capita is 32 barrels per 100 people. According to Nigeria's petroleum minister, the optimal situation for Nigeria as the leading crude oil producer in Africa is to attain a production level of 2.6 million barrels per day (bpd) and in the long run boost it to 3 million bpd. This has not been the case due to the nexus of insecurity and weak technological capability to maintain a high level of crude oil production and to refine the same. The twin challenge of the oil sector is the massive crude oil theft that at a point in 2022 reduced daily production to under one million barrels per day. In other words, Nigeria's economic growth has been a direct result of a lack of state capacity and governance failure to deal with national security and technical issues.

Over 50 years ago, Nigeria established the first fertilizer firm, the Federal Superphosphate Fertilizer Company (FSFC) Limited, Kaduna to produce Single Super Phosphate (SSP) fertilizer among other products. The construction and installation of equipment started in 1974 and was completed in 1976 immediately after which production started. Between 1985 and 1991, the textile sector in Nigeria recorded an annual growth of 67 per cent, and in 1991 it employed about 25 per cent workers in the manufacturing sector. At the time, 180 textile companies employed about 1 million people; we have detailed the history of Nigeria's textiles in a previous chapter.

As part of its strategic plan for pulp and paper production for domestic and export markets, the Nigerian government commissioned the Nigeria Paper Mill, Jebba, Kwara State, in 1969; Iwopin Pulp and Paper Company (IPPC), Ogun State in 1975 and Nigeria Newsprint Manufacturing Company (NNMC) in Oku-Iboku, Akwa Ibom in 1986. The government's plan was for the three pulp and paper mills to provide tonnes of different papers in their thousands every year and, of course, their performance was encouraging and promising. As of 1985, the Jebba mill, which was to be the largest in West Africa, was producing 65,000 tonnes of Kraft paper, liner and chipboards, sack Kraft and corrugated cartons per annum. These plants have ceased to exist.

These factories did not break even, not to talk of re-investing their surplus cash and profit in the acquisition of technological capabilities and skills required to adapt, operate and maintain the imported technology in use. Within 10 years, 80 per cent of trained technical staff of FSFC had left. The same fate befell Ajaokuta and Aladja Steel complexes, Nigeria's Aluminum Company, Aluminum Smelter Company of Nigeria (ALSCON) and several state-owned projects. All are moribund. These examples count among the thousands of White Elephants that litter the industrial wasteland in Nigeria. Former Nigerian president, Goodluck Jonathan, 2011, set up the Presidential Committee on Restructuring and Rationalization of Federal Government Parastatals, Commissions and Agencies, under the leadership of Steve Oronsaye. The committee submitted an 800-page report on 16 April 2012, which recommended the abolition and merger of 102 government agencies and parastatals, while some were listed to be self-funding. The report revealed a high level of competition among several overlapping agencies, which had not only created ill feelings among government agencies but also brought about unnecessary wastage in government expenditure. There were no fewer than 250 additional agencies, commissions and parastatals created through new legislative bills in the National Assembly. For instance, according to the 2012 Oronsaye report, there are 106 public-funded core research and quasi-research centres spread across the country, including a full-fledged institute for the study of Trypanosomiasis. Only about 10 per cent of their funds is expended on core research work with the rest going to staff salaries and procurements.

The report also identified 50 agencies without any enabling laws as well as 55 others not under the supervision of any ministry! This phenomenon results in high personnel costs as 'many of them receive more budgetary allocations for personnel than they require because that component of their budget is usually inflated'. Several of them are also 'obvious duplications of existing bodies' which then underscores the fact of 'overlaps and enormous wastage of scarce resources'. Four of these agencies are beyond scandalous: National Agency for Population Programmes and Development, Population Activities Fund, Population Fund Activities Agency and Population Research Fund![1]

The above vignettes demonstrate the nature and capacity of the Nigerian state and set the stage for our treatment of the issue. These examples illustrate what the literature conceptualize the term 'state capacity' and its reference to the state's ability to get things done; 'the capacity to implement state-initiated policies' (Geddes, 1994: 14). The lessons from the above opening examples: dysfunctional bureaucracies, collapse of industrial programs and failures of the state to see national visions to completion, reveal the paucity of state and bureaucratic capacity. The political and bureaucratic support pillars were absent or weak. Politicians were more interested in skimming rents from large-scale investments rather than setting goals for completion and performance.

In this chapter we discuss the challenges of state capacity that manifest in widespread and costly industrial failures, insecurity and slow economic growth. Nigeria is organized into 36 states or provinces and the Federal Capital Territory (FCTA). All state governments are modeled after the fed-eral/central government and consist of three branches: executive, legislative and judicial. Clearly, state capacity (executive, legislative and judicial) and state institutions exert significant influence on outcomes such as economic development, civil conflict, democratic consolidation and international security.

The rest of the chapter is organized as follows. In the section that follows, we selectively review the literature focussing on the definitions and various aspects of state capacity followed by a discussion of the state and its role in promoting industrialization. The final section presents a historical narra-tive of Nigeria's industrial plans and programs. The final part sums up the chapter.

A Framework for Understanding State Capacity

We define a state as either weak/fragile or strong. Fragile states are also known as weak states. A state is fragile when it is incapable of meeting the key needs of their citizens, especially their security and economic well-being. We code the shortcomings as *gaps*, with three prominent core gaps: *security gap*, *capacity gap* and *legitimacy gap*. Fukuyama presents two notions of the state: state strength and state scope.[2] The former is defined as the capacity of the state to command loyalty – the right to rule legitimately – to extract the resources necessary and provide services, to maintain that essential element of sovereignty, a monopoly over the legitimate use of force within defined geographic boundaries. The state or government be it federal or provincial/state has a defined scope, which are the key functions it performs including education, health and security for example.

State capacity is the ability of a government to accomplish its planned programs and realize policy goals, which underpins economic development. A strong state capacity has been strongly associated with long-term economic development. This includes the capacity to establish law and order, enforce private property rights, defend a country against external threats, as well as support development by establishing a competitive market, transportation infrastructure and mass education. The latter is the focus of this chapter, especially the ability to foster industrialization and long-run economic diversification.

In this chapter, we articulate state capacity as an important explanatory variable that underpins Nigeria's abysmal socio-economic conditions reflected in the historical regress in comparison with the developmental states of East Asia with which it started the development race together. It situates the Nigerian reversal within the theoretical matrices of the failing or failed state. Scholars notably Richard Joseph (1987) in a seminar book on the Second Republic, explained it within the theory of Prebendalism.

We posit in this chapter that the concept of 'state capacity' is critical for driving a development agenda. Political evolution has three components, namely, state building, rule of law and accountability.[3] State building aims at building a society organized by strong institutions that promote political regimes beyond family ties and create a neutral and accountable system of governance. A modern state concentrates and deploys power to enforce rules on an impersonal basis. The objective of the rule of law is to create checks and balances that limit the power of government through accepted system of justice, which is higher than any individual who currently holds political power. An accountable government is responsible to the people it governs. The three components evidently work together and clearly there are direct and indirect associations between different aspects of development. The rule of law and state-building have been positively linked to economic growth, while social mobilization can lead to greater public accountability. Yet these connections are not automatic, and the most fundamental aspects of development can also be the hardest to create. For instance, it is much easier to hold elections than to build a functioning judiciary, noted Fukuyama.

Where a capable state is absent, violence and insecurity tend to be the order.[4] Literature shows that the level of violence – used as a proxy for security of person – is one of the more important factors in differentiating among developing countries with respect to the rule of law and economic growth. Some developing countries have managed to control social violence while others have not.[5] Prominent among the proxy measures of the rule of law is the corruption factor, which characterizes predatory governments.

The tendency to autocracy is strong, especially in developing countries; therefore institutional checks and balances are necessary for the society and the economy because leaders and governments tend to routinely renege on their commitments. The usage of the term state capacity varies considerably across disciplines not just in political science but in science, technology and related disciplines. For example, evolutionary economics articulates the concept of 'Productive capabilities'. Productive capabilities refer to personal and collective skills, productive knowledge and experiences embedded in physical agents and organizations that firms need to perform different productive tasks.[6] Further analytical uses of the concept refer to other closely related attributes of states: strength, fragility, failure, effectiveness, efficiency, quality, legitimacy, autonomy, scope and so on.

Related to the above postulation is the concept of state capacity conceived as the required capability for a state, not just to design but to implement and follow through public policy in the context of state–society relations (Gomide, 2018). Obviously, the concept is related to the healthy functioning of institutions of the state, especially merit-based bureaucracy, the retrenchment of corruption in public life, as well as rule-based structures. Sometimes, the concept is defined in such ways that conflate it with governance, although governance is a much broader concept. Governance, following Mabogunje and Kates (2004), is conceived as the myriad ways in which key actors, as well as institutions, take part as well as 'own' the design, management and implementation of national policies and affairs. It is also useful to view the concept of governance as it has emerged in the literature from the perspective of structure, process, as well as strategy.

Structure refers to the ensemble of institutions, state and non-state; process speaks to the policymaking dimension, while strategy denotes efforts of bureaucrats and politicians to manipulate and design policies at systemic levels to bring about desired results (Adeyeye, 2017). Useful, if a little too broad, is the definition of Governance by the World Bank Study Group (Kaufmann, Kraay & Mastruzzi, 2010) as, 'the traditions and institutions by which authority of a country is exercised. These include the processes by which governments are selected, monitored, and replaced; the capacity of a government to effectively formulate and implement sound policies, and the respect of citizens and the state for the institutions that govern economic and social interactions among them. The advantage of this definition is that it emphasizes state–society interactions, as well as institutions in a dynamic context.

We adopt the simple notion of state which relates to the state's ability to implement its goals or policies (Cingolani, 2013). We consider two key areas of divergence about what it means for states to possess such abilities like Fukuyama's framing. The first relates to the nature of the state's power or its strength. The second involves defining the set of functions on which state capacity should be assessed. State capacity embodies state power, as in the ability of one actor (the state) to get another actor (members of society) to do things they would not otherwise do (Dahl, 1957). Our conception of state power relates to those instruments that constitute a legitimate exercise of state power.[7] According to Mann's notion of infrastructural power, it is the capacity of the state to penetrate society and 'to implement logistically political decisions throughout the realm' (Mann, 1984: 189).

Soifer (2008) describes infrastructural power in three ways: the state's material capabilities, its effects on society and its territoriality. In a seminal piece, the author distinguishes among three analytical approaches to state capacity, which he calls the 'national capabilities approach', the 'weight of the state approach' and the 'subnational variation approach'. According to the national capabilities approach, state capacity can be equated with the stock of resources that are available to the central state, which is seen as 'invariable within a particular country' (ibid., 236).

Some scholars articulate specific and narrow approaches to define state capacity. They include defining state capacity as 'the organizational competence of the bureaucracy'. Others define it as the capacity with 'extractive' or 'fiscal' capacity, including the collection of taxes.[8] A third starts from Scott's (1998) idea of 'legibility' and equates state capacity with the informational capacity of the state (Lee and Zhang, 2017; D'Arcy and Nistotskaya, 2017). Others combine all these dimensions, namely: the quality of the bureaucracy, revenue extraction and information capacity as factors that together contribute to the effective implementation of public policies.[9] In this book, we take account of the various capacities embedded within the state's organizational structures, the bureaucracy and the territorial reach of these capacities in promoting industrial dynamism and economic growth.

State capabilities include material resources and organizational competencies internal to the state that exist independently of political decisions about how to deploy these capabilities. Giddens observes, for example, that 'resources are the media through which power is exercised'. Again, state power is described as arising from access to monetary, human and informational resources.[10] Others direct attention to the organizational and bureaucratic competence of state institutions (Oyelaran-Oyeyinka and Gehl-Sampath, 2010; Centeno et al., 2017: 4–7), which itself flows from resources, expertise and professionalism. The capabilities of a state in terms of its territorial reach are critical to its ability to secure its citizens from external aggressors.[11]

The second issue in defining state capacity relates to the question of what functions a capable state should have the capacity to perform. The capacity to do what? Connected to this question of scope is the issue of whether we can conceive of capacity as a general characteristic of states that relates to core state functions or whether a disaggregated approach is required. In our use of the related issue of state functions, we go beyond the Weberian definition of the state as an entity holding a monopoly on the legitimate use of force in its territory; an idea sometimes used interchangeably with state capacity.[12] The concept of the state as an organized compulsory political community possessing a central government within a specified territory, which features a monopoly of legitimate violence, is central to political science. This definition will be too narrow given the widening and complex assignments of modern states.

We will rely on approaches that articulate a much broader range of functions including economic, administrative and regulatory functions. Work in this perspective describes states as serving a potentially large number of roles such as the development and maintenance of economic systems, the provision of public services to the population and the administration of justice; others include a wide range of fiscal, administrative, public service delivery and legal capacities in their definition.[13] We are focussed on the ability of the state to promote industrial dynamism and long-term economic growth.

In other words, states that will successfully promote structural change must be capable of fashioning the institutions with the capacity to foster interactive learning through systemic coordination. Incentive systems tend to develop from more fundamental institutional roots such as labour laws and even national constitutions. Terms of employment and work environments, both tangible (research and teaching facilities) and intangible (possibilities for institutional collaboration, quality of networks and colleagues), play a pivotal role in retaining skilled professionals.[14] States in Western societies have been involved in promoting academic-industry exchange by encouraging channels of learning, such as: joint publications, mobility of scientists and engineers, cooperative R&D, facility sharing, research training (e.g. capacity development at PhD level, international and local exchange of staff), IPRs (licenses, patents, copyrights) and academic entrepreneurship (spin-off firms) (Brennenraedts, Bekkers, and Verspagen, 2006).

State Capacity and Industrial Technological Capacity

Structural change demands the building up of new capabilities through learning, and it is primarily the hallmark of developing economies (Amsden, 1989). More importantly, it is fostered and implemented through state policies and actions. The main challenge is how the state should play its role, and what sorts of capacity will be needed for such roles to be effectively played. This book addresses the advancement of industrialization. We understand industrial dynamism as the transition from the agricultural sector to the industrial sector, specifically, manufacturing industries, which we take as central to development. We conceptualize industrialization as occurring within a process of structural transformation mediated by the expansion of the industrial sector. Productive capabilities are also termed technological capabilities. These are capabilities needed to generate, absorb and manage technological and organizational change which may differ substantially from those required to perform in existing production systems.

To address market imperfections, states in East Asia and Latin America employed industrial policies extensively in the catching-up process as a means to remove obstacles to structural transformation. State capacity and effectiveness in performing its functions are critical because of the severity of structural challenges poor countries face. The challenges of industrial and economic backwardness manifest in several ways: the absence of strong and competent state institutions, weak entrepreneurial business firms, relatively low level of skilled engineers and technical personnel and a lack of well-educated and abundant low-cost managers.[15]Paradoxically, the weaker an economy, the greater the required coordination role of public agencies; and as Amsden and Chu (2003: 13) observe, market forces are unkind to the weakly organized economies ('the more backward the country, the harsher the justice meted out by market forces') with its inherent and often contradictory requirements. In this chapter, we argue the point that poor countries tend to require far stronger state support that is often in short supply (which is not necessarily anathema to free trade) in terms of innovation policies that address the present institutional gaps in their local contexts.

This section reviews the roles as well as the broad and specific instruments available to states[16] in influencing structural change. The development agenda will of necessity be driven largely by a developmental state, described by Fukuyama as 'one that is limited in scope but strong in its ability to enforce the rule of law, competent and transparent in the formulation of policy, and legitimate enough to have the authority to make painful economic decisions'.[17] The development agenda driven by structural change is thus intimately connected with, and dependent on, governance and the institutional context.

In the theoretical literature, the following stylized facts describe the approach taken by institutional as well as the comparative institutional analysis of the state.[18] 1. The state is considered a social construct that is historically rooted and not simply a collection of self-interested individuals. Therefore, decisions and policymaking processes are not made in a vacuum but shaped by an institutional context shaped over a long historical period. 2. Horizontal integration mediated through interaction between economic actors is critical to building a strong economic system and as such patterns of state–society relationships, particularly the relations between state and entrepreneurial groups need to be understood and developed. 3. Both markets and the state are important institutions and form the fulcrum of economic systems and efficiency. 4. Finally a wider set of economic and non-economic actors and institutions drive the economic system therefore the state has a strong coordination role to play in ensuring harmony and effectiveness of the system.

From the above, an enduring, important and continually relevant insight that emerged from the earlier development economists was that underdevelopment resulted from poor coordination failures that foreclose complementary investments. It therefore called forth the function of the state as an entrepreneur in addition to its role in attenuating uncertainty and in conflict resolution.

There are fundamental risks in attending a country's industrialization program and projects new to them requiring innovation (risk and uncertainty). These include problems of incompleteness of contracts that are deeply inherent in large-scale industrialization efforts. Industrialization involves the execution of large-scale projects such as heavy chemicals, iron and steel, and electronics industries; it involves the participation and in ideal situations the collaboration of several actors all of whom might not be willing participants. This could happen when powerful actors in an economy with vested interest stand to lose influence, profits and markets because of emerging new sectors and industries. In other words, some actors might potentially gain while others potentially lose; and more invidious is the uncertainty of the extent of gains and losses. This raises the prospects for conflict. Where then is the platform for bargaining and mediation? In this scenario, the state could act as the *overall coordinator* with the mechanisms of institutions.[19] This is not to say that the state in question would always have all the requisite capacity and the willingness to undertake such a task.

State Capacity and Nigeria's Development

In October 2022, Nigeria had existed as a sovereign state for 62 years, having won its independence from Britain in October 1960. Despite its chronological age and possession within its borders of several artefacts of development, the country remains very much underdeveloped. Some scholars and analysts fashionably refer to it as the Nigerian predicament; it is not necessarily the absence of growth and development alone but a crisis which can be termed a governance arrest, the failure to develop in its public institutions, a culture of performance, productivity and transparency. It includes state dereliction in the provision of social services, as well as dysfunction in its political, social and economic life.

This Nigerian dilemma is articulated in several publications among which are *Why Nigeria Is Not Working*[20] and *The Crippled Giant*.[21] The quandary is how an incredibly resourced country which possesses the most educated immigrant group in the United States and according to records is the sixth country with the largest number of medical doctors in the United Kingdom has managed to accumulate so much disorder, bedlam and lack of productivity at home.

In Figure 9.1 we provide an empirical measure of Nigeria's state capacity. From the figure, fragility index and governance effectiveness are inversely related to each other suggesting that the higher the fragility index, the lower the governance effectiveness. For instance, the fragility index of the Republic of Korea, clearly a highly industrialized country, is the lowest among sample countries for the study period while its governance effectiveness is highest. On the other hand, fragility index is highest in Nigeria while governance index is the lowest for most years. China maintains its third position in terms of governance effectiveness as well as fragility index. Notably, governance effectiveness did not change over time in sample countries except in the case of China

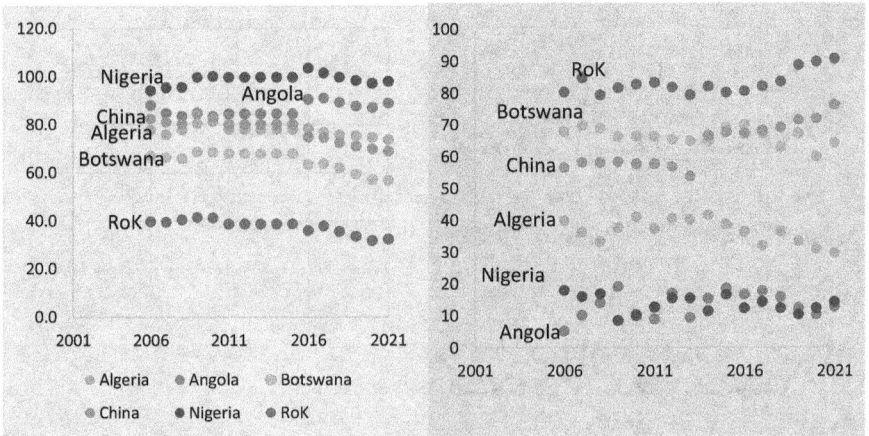

Figure 9.1. Nigeria: Comparison of fragility index and governance effectiveness. Source: Calculated from WDI.

which improved to second position and reached just below the Republic of Korea since 2017. The findings confirm a pattern of weak state capacity in Nigeria leading to persistent fragility over time. It confirms the metrics in Chapter 2.

We further examine the ranking using the Fragile States Index, formerly called the Failed States Index, published annually by the US-based The Fund for Peace and the American Magazine, *Foreign Policy*, since 2005. While there are scholarly debates around the scientific status and methodology of the Fragile States Index, it offers an acceptable way to understand the phenomenon in comparative contexts of state decay and vulnerability. At any rate, the indices employed by the Fragile States Index are not significantly different from the worldwide governance indicators of the World Bank, which measures state effectiveness from a political perspective, along such lines as voice and accountability, political stability and absence of violence, government effectiveness, and regulatory quality, rule of law and control of corruption.

Revealing, in this connection, is Table 9.1 showing the 2019 ranking of Fragile States in selected African countries. The table was chosen because it is more comprehensive than the 2020 and 2021 editions. It shows countries like Kenya, Ethiopia, Uganda and even former war-torn Burundi coming ahead in terms of state capacity which is the opposite of state fragility. Interestingly, too, are the relative scores on the viability and functionality of the security apparatus, which shows that Nigeria, with a score of 9.0, is behind the other selected countries in Africa.

The State and Industrial Progress in Nigeria

Nigeria's attempt at catching up has resulted rather in development reversal. Development is a mountain climbing metaphor as it is a marathon challenge where firms and countries practically run the gauntlet. Failure is costly. Nigeria is not alone, and several countries on a supposedly sound industrial catch-up path often do not move as predicted or regress along this path mainly due to the inability of these countries to manage the coordination efforts required in setting up a sound basis to move to the next knowledge domain. In what follows, we provide a narrative of learning and industrialization failure in Nigeria. At the end, we would interrogate our narrative of state capacity by probing if the Nigerian state played its proper state roles and had the state strength for the journey it embarked upon.

Context and consequences of Nigeria's failed industrial efforts

In order to give a background, we recall that Nigeria invested billions of dollars in building what constitutes the foundations of a modern economy,

Table 9.1. Ranking of fragile states in selected African countries (2019).

S/N	Country	Rank	Overall Score	C1: Security Apparatus	E1: Economy	P1: State Legitimacy	P2: Public Services	S2: Refugees and IDPs	Change from Previous Year
1.	Kenya	25	93.5	7.9	6.6	8.2	8.0	7.7	-3.8
2.	Ethiopia	23	94.2	8.2	6.4	8.0	8.3	8.7	-5.3
3.	Mali	21	94.5	9.5	7.4	6.5	8.5	8.4	1.0
4.	Uganda	20	95.3	7.5	6.3	8.6	7.8	9.1	0.2
5.	Guinea Bissau	19	95.5	8.3	7.7	8.9	8.9	6.7	-2.6
6.	Niger	18	96.2	8.7	7.1	7.3	9.3	8.3	0.1
7.	Eritrea	17	96.4	6.6	7.7	9.4	7.8	7.7	-0.8
8.	Cameroon	16	97.0	8.5	6.5	9.2	8.2	8.3	1.7
9.	Burundi	15	98.2	8.6	8.4	9.0	8.2	8.4	0.8
10.	**Nigeria**	**14**	**98.5**	**9.0**	**7.8**	**8.0**	**8.9**	**7.2**	**-1.4**

Source: The Fund for Peace (2019).

namely iron and steel plants, petrochemical (Eleme), fertilizer plants (Onne and Kaduna), refineries (Port Harcourt, Warri, Kaduna), among others, much of it run by highly educated Nigerians, but currently the country has little to show for all these in terms of industrial outputs and structural transformation. Again, after more than four decades of industrialization and development efforts, Nigeria's economy is still dominated by low-productivity agriculture and petty service activities compared with her Asian comparators (e.g. Malaysia, Thailand) that have become centres for global production. Industrial activities and services have expanded but are composed largely of mining, the exploitation of crude oil and telecommunication made up mainly of the telephone segment. The share of manufacturing value added to total GDP remains very low. Crude oil exports account for approximately 70 per cent of total exports during the last four decades, a clear manifestation of a lack of significant structural change, low sector dynamism and over-dependence on a single commodity.

There has been consistent economic growth in some key sectors over the last few years; however, the growth has not translated into appreciable change in the life of the average Nigerian. Oil and gas continue to dominate overall revenue generation despite the emergence of telecommunication and the resurgence of agriculture. The quantum of wealth from subsistence agriculture has not transformed the rural areas because it operates in large part with poor technologies and with low-skill base. Between 1980 and 1996, Nigeria's poverty level rose from 28 to 66 per cent. According to Nigeria Bureau of Statistics (NBS), the 2022 Multidimensional Poverty Index survey reveals that 63 per cent of persons living within Nigeria (133 million people) are multidimensionally poor. The national MPI is 0.257, indicating that poor people in Nigeria experience just over one-quarter of all possible deprivations. Chapter 2 provides detailed analytics of reversal.

Poverty and inequality have worsened and, while relatively less well-endowed countries are lifting large populations out of poverty, Nigeria sink deeper into poverty.[22] The designation of Nigeria between 2018 and 2022 as the world's poverty capital points to a sea change of reversal in an effort to reduce poverty and inequality. However, as Table 9.2 shows, in terms of commitment to social spending, Nigeria ranks the lowest for the year 2018. This suggests that despite the policy declaration by the current administration of lifting 100 million Nigerians out of poverty in 10 years, on present terms, given low spending on social services, that is unlikely to happen. Indeed, the World Bank predicted in its 2019 Biannual Economic Update that, with the economy projected to grow by 2.1 per cent in 2020 and 2021, in the face of an annual population growth rate of 2.6 per cent, many more people, close to 30 million, may fall into extreme poverty by 2030. It should be noted that

Table 9.2. CRI index on commitment to social spending: bottom 10 countries.

Country	Rank	
	2018	2022
Bangladesh	148	107
Singapore	149	79
Lao PDR	150	143
Madagascar	151	156
Bhutan	152	116
Sierra Leone	153	153
Chad	154	150
Haiti	155	158
Uzbekistan	156	61
Nigeria	157	159

Source: Development Finance International/Oxfam Research Report (2018, 2022);Lawson, M., & Martin, M. (2018). The Commitment to Reducing Inequality Index 2018: A global ranking of governments based on what they are doing to tackle the gap between rich and poor; Walker, J., Martin, M., Seery, E., Abdo, N., Kamande, A., & Lawson, M. (2022). The commitment to reducing inequality index 2022.

this was a prediction that was made before the crash of oil prices occasioned by COVID-19, which first broke out in China. One can only imagine what the outlook will be now. In other words, the capacity of the state to deliver social goods may further weaken because of not just low social spending but diminishing resources in an oil-dependent economy.

In Nigeria, several reasons were given for the widespread investment in public enterprises. First, large-scale technology projects were to generate domestic technological capacity (increase in physical capital); second was to develop endogenous technological capabilities (human knowledge and resources) in design, production and innovation; and third was to generate employment. The overall aim might have well been to deepen the industrialization process and to hasten development. By the end of 1990s, total federal government investments were worth over 36 billion Naira at their historical book values. Nigeria's Bureau of Public Enterprises (BPE) survey, (1991), showed the magnitude of state intervention in Nigeria, in that there were more than 600 public enterprises at the federal level alone and several smaller ones at the state level that accounted for between 10 and 40 per cent of fixed capital and formal employment. However, over time the huge investment and continued state participation in industrial production came under intense questioning.[23]

Public ownership of industry in Nigeria achieved minimal success and many of the projects failed; failure in the context of this narrative being when a project encounters severe cost and time overruns, operates persistently below design or nominal capacity and, due to the above factors, cannot build up technological capabilities, operates at a financial loss and in the end falls short of meeting social and economic objectives. This was in large part the fate of many of the projects which despite huge investments by the government failed. For example, the Federal Superphosphate Fertilizer Company in Kaduna completed in 1973 to produce superphosphate fertilizer and sulphuric acid for the Nigerian market collapsed within 10 years of commissioning. The fate of the Delta Steel Company in Warri was not much different. The company was operating at about 4 per cent capacity after 14 years in operation. The same can be said of the Machine Tools Company in Oshogbo which suffered several years of delay and cost overruns. The Iwopin Paper Mill was uncompleted, while Oku-Iboku Paper Mill closed.[24] These were companies that were of strategic importance to the Nigerian economy. The fertilizer companies were expected to contribute to increased agricultural productivity and supply of food. The machine tools company was expected to service the informal sector as well as the large- and small-scale industries whose contributions to the economy are enormous while the paper mill was expected to facilitate literacy in the country. There are many more examples of large technological projects that failed in Nigeria. Clearly, the failure of these strategic projects contributed significantly to the poor state of the Nigerian economy today. In the next section, I provide an outline of the underlying causes of the failed industrialization policies and implementation.

Policy and technical challenges leading to public industrial pathway failure

The state enterprises which were largely import-substituting were grossly inefficient. They were generally plagued by excess capacity because of the inability to maintain plants locally, to substitute local for foreign materials and to provide basic technical management skills. Most of the spare parts and components needed for repairs and maintenance in the plants had to be imported mainly from Europe. They were therefore faced with perpetual shortages of these parts, which were commonplace items within the industrial system of advanced economies.

Again, large scale projects are often very capital and technology-intensive requiring multiple technology mastery efforts in implementation, and the management requirements of such projects are usually far beyond what most developing countries like Nigeria possess. For the Nigerian government though, domestic participation in technological acquisition was a key objective. This constituted a significant drag on the speedy completion of projects, although the general reasoning was that it was a worthwhile price to pay. Public servants, withthe advice of young engineers relying on no more than theoretical knowledge of how industry works, assumed the enormous responsibilities of planning and managing large-scale process plants, roles for which they were ill-prepared. Furthermore, in order to encourage local participation in the project, civil and construction works were reserved for Nigerian contractors, which also caused a lot of problems in implementation. For many of the projects, the commissioning dates were never met. This caused a lot of unnecessary delays and internal wrangling between foreign contractors and national bureaucrats.

Lack of institutional infrastructure leading to public industrial pathway failure

Nigeria's institutional infrastructure was and remains to a large extent structurally weak. Technology infrastructure including research and development institutions, quality assurance and testing, technology information is evidently ineffective. A vibrant system of production, which would guarantee a minimum interdependent relation among economic agents, is completely absent. While some technology institutions certainly exist in Nigeria, there appears to be limited interaction between them and the industrial sector. They thus operate in isolation from the productive sectors. In addition, many are not only poorly funded and given conflicting objectives but also have inadequate equipment and unmotivated staff. Further, poor coordination among agencies competing for relevance, the limited skills of policymakers, together with the paucity of scientific and technical personnel with the requisite understanding of the science and technology system jeopardized development objectives. Moreover, there seems to be a paucity of institutions that are critical to the industrial initiatives.

In addition, the ubiquitous lack of efficient physical infrastructure such as electricity for industrial purposes has been and continues to be a drag on the economy. During the initial stages of operation of many of the plants, there were frequent interruptions of power supply by the now defunct National Electric Power Authority (NEPA). The issue of power supply, which should have been taken into consideration during the planning stages of the plants, had unfortunately been overlooked.For most of the plantswhen commercial production started in 1970s, the electrical power problem became more severe and was not rectified. By the mid-1980s, standby power generating sets were purchased to supplement the power supply from NEPA; this practice became widespread in practically all industrial installations.

Understanding failures of state intervention

Why has the Nigerian state failed on almost all counts? Analysing what could be the role of the state in view of the narrative of failed industrialization in

Nigeria points attention to six important issues.We try to understand why despite plans and investments, the state in Nigeria failed to benefit from policies that worked relatively well elsewhere in fostering structural trans-formation. The first duty of the state, as we suggested in Chapter 8, is about a definite vision; the question is: Did the Nigerian government articulate a vision of what the future of the industrial landscape might look like? The much we can answer is that while there were several 'development plans' starting in the 1970s, there was no guiding 'vision' collective by the leader-ship. Such awareness of the industrial imperative was not too common among the leadership at the time emerging from a Civil War (1969–1972) and preoc-cupied with uniting a fractious nation. The first attempt at a Nigerian vision was undertaken almost 40 years later named Vision 2010 that was initiated by the military government of the time. As such because there was no such overarching vision, the national plans fell victim to the traps of *involuntary entrapments of entrenched institutions* that shaped and subverted the entrepreneur-ial role of the state.

Second, the Nigerian economy just as with other African economies in the 1970s did not possess an elaborate institutional bureaucracy as with the East Asian economies that were credited to be largely responsible for their indus-trial success. Institutional changes were required but in a situation of rela-tive economic backwardness, desired changes to institutions and institutional expansion have been just as rare as technological innovation itself.[25] Poor state capacity in African countries is as much a result of low-level information regimes as much as it is of low-level knowledge and skills for policymaking choices. Third, we consider the custodial interventions of institution-building which relate to the creation and enforcement of rules and regulations. These rules are meant to prevent private factors from deviating from accepted norms of behavior as well as induce them to act in ways to promote develop-ment. However, my conclusion is that the *rule-makers* of state polity as well as bureaucrats were just in need of the same types of rules to prevent them from subverting national vision and policies. While conventional wisdom focusses on the capability of the state to design and implement rules and regulations, the experience we share shows that regulations for private actors alone are not only inadequate but remarkably flawed in enforcement and too weak to sustain a long-term vision to the point of jeopardizing the most well laid out plans required for fostering industrial transformation.[26]

Fourth, was the state able to guarantee risks as insurance for innovation? The core elements of state intervention which aimed at 'midwifery' – the tech-nique of inducing domestic entrepreneurs to make investments in targeted sectors – were equally not successful given that the fundamental capabili-ties of human and infrastructure were absent, and institutions were too weak to reduce the risk and uncertainty of such private investments. For example, a very important instrument is subsidies, complemented by protection.[27] However, in the absence of strong bureaucratic capacity to enforce performance standards in terms of output, exports or other relevant variables, even this instrument failed and became subject of destructive rent-seeking. Simply put, in the 1970s and early 1980s when there was a profusion of national plans and huge ambition, there were simply not enough capabilities to deal with the large-scale, capital and technology-intensive projects that were started all at once by Nigeria.

Fifth, the traditional state capacity discourse needs to be widened to capture a wider array of issues than those simulated by the East Asian experiences. Much of the East Asian and Japanese experiences of state-led development have focussed on the conduits of credit-based financial structures and financial policy, with some labour-related issues on the side (Woo-Cumings, 1999).[28] In the context of African development, this needs to be broadened to include labour and human skills, land reforms and social coalitions that may often have their basis in unequal distribution of wealth over time but are powerful enough to induce socially sub-optimal policy choices in order to retain undesirable status-quo. In other words, the distribution of power among various interest groups in relatively poorer societies may not be one conducive to a 'developmental embeddedness'. As Evans (1995) argued, for the state to be called 'developmental' it should be embedded in the society and share a set of connections that 'link the state intimately and aggressively to particular social groups with whom the state shares a joint project of transformation'.

Sixth, one prominent factor that jeopardized Nigeria's economic progress is the near perversion of the role of the state. Rather than act as regulator and promoter, the Nigerian state assumed the role of the controller of economic and financial assets that seized all power unto itself, especially in the critical oil sector. From our earlier analysis, the state–business relationship has been less than harmonious. The state has not developed the capacity to promote stronger domestic economic integration. The institutions needed to promote knowledge-based and innovation-driven development have not evolved. The policies set out in national plans to foster institutional capacities were never implemented.

Summing Up

We have shown in this chapter that the Nigerian state has weak or no capacity, which explains its industrial backwardness relative to Asian comparators. The country, despite its abundant human and natural resources, lacks fundamentals of state capacity or has a weak state capacity to foster such change. We demonstrate that state capacity has been a critical component of sustainable development for successful countries. In this chapter, we conceptualize development in the broadest term to mean a shift away from agriculture to engagement in high-value manufacturing production and export and such changes, driven largely by skilled manpower (technicians, engineers and scientists).

This chapter sought in large part to juxtapose state capacity and development in Nigeria's quest for structural transformation. At a broader level, we have contextualized the Nigerian state's laggard and failing status. Its resource profile and the abundance of human capital would suggest a country deserving of the epithet, 'Giant of Africa'. On the contrary, Nigeria qualifies to be called the 'The Crippled Giant'. We show with empirical data that Nigeria is increasingly a fragile and failing state.

Nigeria qualifies to be referred to as a weak or fragile state, based on governance arrest in such areas as social services, legitimacy, poor economic growth characterized by rising debts, oil-dependence pathology, widespread insecurity and failure to overcome a protracted multifaceted insurgency. In broad conceptual terms, there are two aspects of state fragility that tend to define Nigeria's reversal, namely, the failure to provide public and social goods, including security, and secondly, a legitimacy gap to the extent that important actors in society differ on the extent to which state power is exercised on behalf of the entire nation.

Nigeria's increasing state of fragility has to a large extent been a result of monumental corruption which has robbed Nigeria of its development potential, setting it in a tragic race to the bottom. As we show systematically with several metrics, in Chapter 2, the country for decades has performed sub-optimally and in comparative perspective with other African and Asian countries. Any programme for the reinvention of the Nigerian state must deal with ways and strategies of overcoming the capability deficits which have in turn led to developmental and governance stagnation. The Nigerian state must be able to do what the Indonesian state which has a similar topography in terms of religious and ethnic divisions but managed through effective leadership provided by a dominant ethnic group to prevent the wild play of centrifugal forces from devouring the country's fortunes. Undoubtedly, not much progress can be made until Nigeria overcomes the corruption in public life, the ineffectiveness of institutions, the cronyism in politics resulting in state capture as well as the neo-patrimonial ways of the elite class.

Importantly too, the sense of entitlement which treats public resources as a bonanza to be shared by competing elites must be replaced with transformational leadership that will reform the state, not just in precepts but by example.

Notes

1 https://www.theconclaveng.com/when-budget-becomes-racket-by-olusegun
-adeniyi/
2 Fukuyama.
3 Fukuyama, F. [...], Governance and World Order in twenty-first century.
4 Collier (2007).
5 https://law.utexas.edu/conferences/measuring/The%20Papers/ruleoflawconfer-
ence.Haggard&Tiede.Rule%20of%20Law.March13.2010.pdf
6 United Nations Industrial Development Organization (UNIDO) (2012), Productive
Capabilities Indicators.
7 Centeno et al. (2017); Lindvall and Teorell (2016).
8 Centeno, Kohli, and Yashar (2017: 5); Levi (1988).
9 https://lucris.lub.lu.se/ws/portalfiles/portal/102775891/WP_1_Lindvall_and
_Teorell_State_Capacity_as_Power_A_Conceptual_Framework.pdf, accessed
November 23, 2022.
10 Giddens (1979 141); Lindvall and Teorell (2016).
11 Foa and Nemirovskaya (2016); Harbers (2015); Harbers and Steele (2020); Soifer
(2008).
12 Møller and Skaaning (2011).
13 Bersch et al. (2017); Besley and Persson (2011); Rauch and Evans (2000). For example,
Besley and Persson (2011).
14 Countries have other incentives such as those in German law confer ownership of patents on individual researchers thereby, they have full intellectual property to inventions (Giesecke, 2000).
15 Amsden (1989); Oyelaran-Oyeyinka and Gehl-Sampath (2010).
16 The state is hereby conceptualized as a 'set of organizations invested with the authority to make binding decisions for people and organizations located in a particular
territory and to implement these decisions, if necessary, by force' Rueschemeyer and
Evans (1985: 46).
17 Fukuyama (2002: 25).
18 Chang (1994) and Chang and Rowthorn (1995); Amsden (1989).
19 'The point is that efficiency may require that the parties can contract on an extremely
wide set of variables [...] the structure of transactions and property rights may, however, rule out such bargains' (Vartiainen, 1999: 211).
20 Paul Irikefe (2013).
21 Eghosa Osaghae (1998).
22 Materials from this section is fully developed in Oyelaran-Oyeyinka (2014), *Rich
Country Poor People*.
23 This led to the setting up of several study groups that reviewed the activities of public enterprises. In 1988, the government established the TCPC to carry out deep-
going restructuring of the public ownership by privatizing and commercializing the
enterprises.
24 For a full account of the history of the projects cited and the broader industrialization,
see Oyelaran-Oyeyinka et al. (1998), *Ailing Public Enterprises: Technological Project Failures
and Prospects for Industrial Renewal in Nigeria*. Obafemi Awolowo University Press.

25 Nelson and Sampat (2001) cite North's (1990) re-articulation of the 'institutional obstructionist' notion of economic backwardness as being responsible for the failure of poorly performing economies to adopt productive technologies.

26 This type of intervention is central for the minimalist neoclassical state. In fact, the ability of the state to implement policies of liberalization and deregulation ironically depends on its relative capacity as custodian.

27 Amsden (1989, 1992).

28 For example, strong financial incentives were used by Korean governments as instruments to deepen technology and to foster export growth (Chang, 1994).

Part IV

Chapter 10

CONCLUSIONS AND PROPOSALS FOR REVERSING DEVELOPMENT REVERSAL

Introduction

This book explores as its central question the wide divergence in income between Nigeria and four Asian countries namely Malaysia, Indonesia, Vietnam and Bangladesh. Additionally, these countries achieved a significant reduction in poverty and recorded equitable growth, especially after the 1970s. Nigerian citizens by contrast became poorer, and the country became more unequal over time. For example, Indonesia, Vietnam and Malaysia all had considerable natural resources and benefited from the enormous oil windfall during the 1970s/1980s. These Asian countries have prospered while Nigeria faltered due in large part to the ways these nations managed their resource wealth. The policy and institutional differences that shaped the development evolution of these countries were critical to, and ultimately defined, the differences in outcomes.

While these four countries used oil income to build infrastructure and invested in productive assets, Nigeria's oil income was largely lost to official theft or wasted on White Elephant projects. According to a report from the Abandoned Projects Audit Commission president Goodluck Jonathan set up in 2011, it stated that 11,886 federal government projects were abandoned in the past 40 years, from 1971 to 2011, in Nigeria.[1] According to one commentator, 'Nigeria has become the world's junkyard of abandoned and failed projects worth billions of naira.'[2] In stressing the economic implication of project abandonment to the society and the nation, the committee cited the case of Ajaokuta Steel Complex. This project commenced in 1979 with an estimated project cost of US$650 million but remains uncompleted after spending over US$5 billion.[3] During this period, the country spent about ₦2.1 trillion, an equivalent of US$10.5 billion, in importing steel into the country.[4]

While most Asian and African countries were on the same levels of economic and industrial development in the 1950s to early days of independence in the early 1960s, there had been a significant divergence of income starting in the late 1960s. The onset of the most recent developmental reversal coincided with the 1970s oil crisis and had persisted ever since. The large windfalls from the oil price rises first in 1970 and then in 1980 benefitted oil-producing countries such as Nigeria, Gabon and Angola, but prices of most tropical cash crops and minerals collapsed at the same time. When the oil prices crashed in the 1980s, the terms of trade declined in virtually all African countries. This setback continued until the mid-1990s, when a new cycle of commodity price rises set in, which levelled off around 2015. Although the dominant pattern of specialization was in primary resource-intensive or land-extensive commodities, there were major shifts in the direction and composition of trade, two of which are worth highlighting. First, in the export mix, the relative share of tropical cash crops, such as palm oil, rubber, sugar, cotton, coffee, tea, tobacco and cocoa, declined with the surge of highly valuable mineral resources such as gold, diamonds, copper, tin and, above all, crude oil. One of the main causes of development reversal is the reliance on volatile oil, mineral and commodity exports that foreclosed industrial progress. The boom in trade in Africa in the two decades between 1995 and 2015 had its source in elevated oil prices. In Nigeria and Angola as well as other oil-dependent African countries, income growth and fiscal health were tied inextricably with oil revenues. Every cycle of oil crisis directly affects government revenue and channels into public service delivery including health and education, the fulcrum of human capital.

This book focusses on Nigeria and how it has undergone a reversal of fortune or a development reversal. While most African countries fit this description, we will systematically examine the case of Nigeria, the so-called *Giant of Africa*. We analysed the phenomenon in all aspects of development, namely: social, economic, political, industrial/technological using available indicators. The observed developmental reversal in economic and social outcomes almost often triggers concomitant political outcomes including social upheavals, violent conflicts, street demonstrations as we recently observed in Sri Lanka.

There is a close correlation betweenf the secular trends in trade and GDP growth. Over two decades between 1995 and 2014, several African economies grew and ranked among the fastest growing in the world, with annual growth rates of 5–10 per cent being no exception. The aggregate average annual GDP growth rates for sub-Saharan Africa (including South Africa) stood at an estimated 5 per cent since 1995.[5] Due to several structural and other factors, including faster population growth, total GDP growth and per capita growth rates post-1995, slowed and regressed to return to levels that were observed in the 1950s and 1960s. While most countries were affected, a few countries were worse off especially commodity and oil-dependent countries. This was particularly so in the years 1985–95. These countries suffered further setbacks in the second half of the 2010s, when world commodity markets – especially the oil markets after 2014 – crashed; predictably growth rates fell back to very modest rates. Then came the synchronous impact of the COVID-19 pandemic, the financial meltdown and the extenuating Russia–Ukraine war, all between the years 2020 and 2022. The health crisis pushed an estimated 120 million people into extreme poverty and exacerbated the African economic conundrum. However, the recent pandemic and food security crises merely compounded and accelerated the simmering reversal that had set in much earlier.

We take our starting point for Africa's and specifically Nigeria's regress from the 1970s. However, this is not an uncommon phenomenon. The literature suggests that countries have quite frequently experienced sudden and dramatic reversals in growth, such that gains of decades of a country's growth can be wiped out in a few weeks and patterns in one decade are often little related to growth in the next.[6,7] These cyclical phenomena contribute to the totality of the explanations that we code as *reversals*. Moreover, the full explanations for such reversals are likely to be more complicated and nuanced. These include external shocks and/or other country-specific events.

In what follows, we summarize the key ideas based on the chapters.

Understanding Development Reversal

Several reasons explain the nature and processes of development and underdevelopment. As we show in Chapter 2, our dominant explanation is that poor nations, and in the case of Nigeria, are poor, because of their technological backwardness.There has emerged a wide and growing income gap between Asia, represented by the four country cases, and Nigeria. Pointedly, the gap in knowledge, especially scientific and technological knowledge, has widened even as the wealth gap widened. Evidently, the focus on crude oil for its foreign exchange revenue has been a counterproductive development strategy.

The Asian countries emulated the early industrializers which have had a long history of *learning* and acquisition of knowledge and using this knowledge to master nature and in transforming natural resources to high-value goods. Nigeria possesses enormous crude oil and natural gas resources but lags far behind in the technological knowledge necessary to transform these into high-value goods. The cost of overcoming the knowledge gap built up over centuries is huge.

Worse, those countries blessed with oil and minerals are unable to add value to these precious gifts of nature, and on the contrary, oil for example has been associated with the phenomenon of 'resource curse'. In the face of acute shortages of vaccines, for example, African countries looked on helplessly while individuals in Western nations received multiple booster vaccine shots. It was not about money. When these nations had money to buy vaccines, they were pushed to the end queue in the global supply chain. Vaccine nationalism ensured that as of July 2022, only 16 per cent of Africans on average had been vaccinated. While much of the developing world begs and complains about the lack of global collaboration, a half dozen Western pharmaceutical companies dug into their arsenal of scientific and technological banks and came up with the mRNA vaccines. Technological capacity of nations has always trumped resource abundance.

Human Capital Is the Key to Economic Growth

We established that the source of wealth is technological change, and progress is advanced by the embodied human capital made of scientists and engineers and so on. For this reason, human capital is the largest component of global wealth, accounting for two-thirds of total wealth globally. While rich technologically advanced nations prioritize human capital, poor countries have developed a chronic affinity with natural capital which accounts for 9 per cent of wealth globally but makes up nearly half (47 per cent) of the wealth in low-income countries. The more successful Asian resource-rich countries in our book found the key to sustainable development using resource wealth to build their infrastructure and human capital.

Technological Capabilities of Earlier Industrializers Underpinned Successful Resource-Based Development

Historically, natural resources (NR) played significant roles in the rate and direction of economic growth of industrialized countries. The conventional wisdom was that a country's natural resources should naturally affect its economic growth positively. Several authors[8] put forward the notion that natural resources – notably coal as a source of energy – were among the primary drivers of the Industrial Revolution. The unstated fact was that the countries that profited from resource abundance were equally advanced technologically at the time. In other words, unlike the low levels of scientific and technological human capital, and weak knowledge systems with which poorer resource-dependent African countries started at independence, the experiences of more advanced resource-rich countries that had accumulated pertinent technology, skills, knowledge were different. The existing capabilities within these countries enabled the NR sector to lead the industrialization drive. By these, the technologies fostered backward and forward linkages of the natural resource sectors through new oil and mineral discovery, extraction and resource processing technologies and processes, as well as moved the countries into new industries related to the resource sectors.

Post-independence Nigeria, as with other colonized countries, did not have the scientific base to replicate what these countries did. The failure of resource-dependence strategy led to the now widely held view known as the 'resource curse' hypothesis originally coined by Richard Auty (1993).

The association of natural resources dependence with the resource curse is a relatively recent phenomenon, specifically after the 1950s. This book specifically identifies resource dependence as a fundamental reason for poor industrialization and economic diversification of developing countries. Of the 15 least diversified countries in the world, eight are in Africa. At the current estimation, natural resources account for more than one-fifth of GDP in 5 of the 10 African countries with GDP per capita of more than $5,000. We also show that oil dependence has a negative relationship with GDP. Historically, this has not always been the case as several countries, especially the most industrialized countries, prospered based on adding value to minerals and commodities for the most part of the nineteenth and twentieth centuries.

The country experiences outlined in this book show that investment in domestic technological capabilities underlined the success of resource-based industrialization (downstream, upstream and horizontal). Investment in education and training especially engineering and vocational skills, strong public–private partnerships and alignment of different policy tools, including industrial strategy ones, emerge as recurrent factors. Ultimately, these depend on the countries' policy frameworks and institutional capabilities.

Economic growth experienced by several developing nations is tied to the income generated from rents and sales of resources in the international markets. However, exports of fossil fuels and minerals even when it leads to annual growth in GDP do not translate to improved human capital and manufacturing value added (MVA). Africa's industrial performance, measured in terms of industry value added (IVA) and MVA in GDP, has been lagging far behind comparator countries in Asia. MVA, which measures the degree of industrial processing, remains low in Africa, signifying the lack of industrial dynamism. This is consistent with the continent's reliance on exports of its abundant natural resources, especially mineral and agricultural resources, UNCTAD (2011). We demonstrate that the phenomenon of the Dutch disease only in part explains poor industrial growth. This is because whenever there is a resource boom, the extra revenue accruing from the sale of natural resources (oil and minerals) triggers appreciation of the real exchange rate and subsequent contraction of the traded sector. This is however a short-term phenomenon but with impacts that are long term in nature; the most insidious being the displacement of policy focus from tradeable sectors, particularly industrial manufacturing, which requires long-term vision, planning and consistent investment.

Natural Resource Dependence Undermines the Industrialization Process

A key finding resonating in the literature on resource abundance is the role of institutions in explaining resource blessing or curse. Within strong institutional contexts, it is possible for policies to prevent the Dutch disease effect; however, this has been very rare in the experience of developing countries and hardly so in the African experience except for Botswana.

The conventional wisdom on resource abundance much earlier was that of a 'blessing' not a 'curse'. Several scholars attributed economic development of earlier industrial nations to their mineral and commodities abundance as the driver of economic development.[9] Latecomer countries that pursue technology-driven horizontal and vertical diversification especially at the low-income stage such as Malaysia and Vietnam have proved that *resource abundance*, as opposed to *resourcedependence*, could supply the needed investment capital for latecomer economies to achieve sustainable growth.[10] In other words, the development outcome of a country possessing abundant natural resources including improvements in economic and human development is not as a result of the asset itself but rather on the rate and direction of technologies applied, the structure of knowledge institutions and the technological capabilities that a country explicitly invest in.

In regional comparative perspective with Africa, Asian countries like Malaysia, Republic of Korea and lately Vietnam have diversified their economies significantly despite possessing significant deposits of natural resources. The same with Malaysia, it's GDP and exports comprise significant manufacturing activities that drove an increase GDP per capita. Over time, the share of low technology such as food and textiles in this country reduced while machinery accounts for a very significant share, and both machinery and other manufactures comprise a large majority of the added value originating from the manufacturing sector.

Clearly, resource-rich economies may turn such assets into a curse by relying exclusively on these commodities as sources of export revenue, which exposes them to a regime of volatility and foreign exchange shocks. The blessing is lost when countries fail to develop autonomous capabilities for processing, such as oil refining, by which systemic learning is foregone.

In sum, the prevalence of resource curse is a peculiar feature of some but not all countries, especially developing countries that discovered minerals and oil resources in the absence of the pertinent technological and human capabilities to explore, extract and process them. Second, the phenomenon of resource curse is, in terms of time frame, prominent only in the last 50 years which correspond roughly to the period when most of these countries that bear the burden of a 'curse' attained independence. We suggest that a combination of a relatively strong knowledge system including universities and vocational education assets, legal and political institutions and the right technologies underpinned the resource blessing of the older nations.

Institutions in Africa exhibit profound ineffectiveness in responding to development challenges.[11] The most telling recent examples have been the current and past outbreaks of pandemics, commodity price booms and bursts, locust invasions, among others. The devastating impacts of these profoundly damaging crises could not trigger short- and longer-term strategic solutions as there have been no institutions for responding to crises including production of medicines and vaccines. It is hard to find scientific organizations and institutions with comparable capacity as comparators outside the continent. When coupled with poorly functioning policymaking bureaucracies, Africa can be said to be characterized by a lack of both broad and specific competencies in their coordination functions. For the most part, we have a situation in which policy coordination is largely politically driven in the absence of strong market coordination.

A critical institutional gap is the lack of industrial and development finance structures dedicated to long-term industrial development. Poor financial commitment to meeting organizational goals results in disillusionment of scientists and policy researchers over time, leading to migration and brain drain. We also have here a lack of private sector trust in collaborations with public sector institutions; this has jeopardized the rise of a vibrant private sector since organizations that promote the growth of private sector firms are missing. Their inefficiencies give rise to the poor coordination of knowledge and economic production functions, leading to imbalances in the demand and supply for skills of the right kinds, quantity and quality mix at sectoral levels and over time.

Measuring Nigeria's Reversal of Fortune

In the second chapter, we deploy different metrics of development to measure the reversal of fortune. Our basic assumption is that the long-term development patterns of countries are driven by the rate of industrialization measured by increases in the share of manufacturing and the share of manufacturing employment in GDP. A key feature of industrialized nations and those that achieved rapid growth in the last five decades is the attainment of high rates of industrial growth. What sets these countries apart from laggard countries, especially in Africa, is the markedly higher rates of industrial development. We used available indices of the industrial manufacturing sector of countries under examination in the book. We take the manufacturing sector as '*the main engine of fast growth*' (Kaldor, 1967: 48); this assertion is taken as causal as it characterizes not only the current most industrialized nations but also catching-up countries that have experienced rapid, sustained growth.

The countries that made sustained efforts to acquire industrial technologies attained fast rates of economic growth while the other set of countries is poor and dependent on subsistent agriculture and natural resources. Industrialization became the main driver of economic development for the rich while resource dependence, weak technological base, among others, jeopardized the long-term growth of poor nations.

Our point of departure in measuring the divergence is the period after African countries attained political independence. It is after these countries gained independence that they can reasonably be expected to have the autonomy in deciding their own development agenda and in formulating supporting policies towards achieving development objectives.

Measuring reversal

Economic reversal

We measure development of economies using comparative national income measures, the performance of the GDP. We track the trend in the GDP per capita and annual growth in GDP for Nigeria compared to other countries from 1960 to 2022. Nigeria's reversal of fortune manifests in several dimensions, namely: economic, social, technological and industrial conditions. We examine the wide disparities in development metrics, particularly the levels and rates of growth of national incomes and Human Development Index. For example, among the countries we are examining in this book, the Republic of Korea had the highest GDP/capita in 2022 (US$28,075), almost double that of the year 2000 (US$15,414.29), two decades earlier. The figure increased sevenfold in 40 years from 1980 (US$3,679.11). On the contrary, the GDP/capita for Nigeria was US$845 in 1980, declined to US$290 20 years later and then rose to US$2,424 in 2019.

Industrial indicators

We include several countries for comparison. To analyse industrial progress and regress, we use the Productive Capacities Index (PCI) developed by UNCTAD as a proxy of industrialization. PCI has eight dimensions that encompass the contribution of natural resources as well as aspects based on acquired advantages. The results show a strong positive association between PCI and income levels of sample countries. Data for the analysis derive from WDI from 2000 to 2018.

All indicators taken together, Nigeria has evidently suffered a reversal in the industrial capacity to produce, process and add value compared to its comparators. For example, Nigeria ranks 99th on UNIDO's Competitive Industrial Performance (CIP)index while South Africa ranked 52nd in 2020. The CIP index measures industrial capacity on three metrics, namely: (i) the capacity to produce and export manufactured goods, (ii) technological deepening and upgrading and (iii) world impact. On average, industry in Africa generates merely US700 of GDP per capita, less than a third of Latin America's output (US$2,500) and barely a fifth of East Asia's ($3,400). Nigeria's industry contribution to GDP is US$650, while manufacturing contribution is a mere 14.1 per cent (US$326).

The export of fossil fuels and minerals, even when it leads toannual growth in GDP, does not translate to improved human capital while resource-dependent nations tend to do very little manufacturing value addition. Africa's industrial performance, measured in terms of IVA and MVA in GDP, has been lagging far behind comparator countries in Asia. MVA, which measures the degree of industrial processing, remains low in Africa, signifying the lack of industrial dynamism. This is consistent with the continent's reliance on export of its abundant natural resources, especially mineral and agricultural resources. The phenomenon of Dutch disease only in part explains poor industrial growth. This is because whenever there is a resource boom, the extra revenue accruing from the sale of natural resources (oil and minerals) triggers appreciation of the real exchange rate and subsequent contraction of the traded sector. This is however a short-term phenomenon but with impacts that are long term in nature; the most insidious being the displacement of policy focus from tradeable sectors, and in particular, industrial manufacturing, which requires long-term vision, planning and consistent investment.

Not surprisingly, Nigeria ranks equally low on the Global Innovation Index at 118th with South Africa ranking the highest on the continent but only 58th worldwide.

Why Nigeria Fell Behind Asian Counterparts?

Throughout the history of capitalism – in both the near and the distant past – practically all countries that have transformed their economies from low to high income have done so through a process of industrialization. In 1750, Europe, North America and Japan constituted only 27 per cent of manufacturing production in the world. However, by 1900, those regions made up 90 per cent of world manufacturing production. Unsurprisingly, economic growth rates between the West and 'the rest' started diverging as well.

By the early twentieth century, the world had been divided into two groups of economies: one was rich and industrialized; the other was poor and dependent on subsistent agriculture and natural resources. Industrialization became the main driver of economic development. After World War II, the world's manufacturing landscape started to change. As developing countries gained independence and had more autonomy in formulating policies towards their own development objectives, they implemented policies to promote industrialization. Over time, a significant share of global manufacturing production relocated to these countries, particularly to East Asia.

According to a study of 'growth miracles' by the World Bank in 2008, only 13 countries in the world have been able to sustain an annual growth rate of 7 per cent or higher since 1950. Only two countries, both with small populations and highly idiosyncratic economic structures – Botswana and Oman – are among the group of 13 that have not grown because of industrialization.[12] Additionally, countries and regions that have de-industrialized or prematurely de-industrialized have experienced a slowdown in economic growth or, at worst, declining economic growth.

The quantum of learning and skills required to move from the lowest domain of artisanal and indigenous manufacturing to the second lowest knowledge domain of modern manufacturing is embedded in primary and secondary schooling capacities, apprenticeship training, training to read engineering designs and blueprints and organization of production. Several of these aspects that are missing in developing countries – foundry making, metal cutting and so on – are essential skills to move to the next higher level but a hiatus in several developing countries since they constitute 'nodes of learning' (Rosenberg, 1982). To move their economies to a higher knowledge domain and to master the design and re-engineering of products and innovate, these countries need to invest beyond primary and secondary schooling. Industrial progress requires strong science and technology tertiary education that equips individuals with technical and analytical skills and public sector investments in building basic R&D capabilities for standards, metrology and other infrastructure. To operate in this domain, a country also requires significant entrepreneurial capabilities that act on the 'demand side' of the market and act to stimulate demand. The learning associated with transitioning to this knowledge domain is more systematic, systemic and rigorous; this must be sustained over a long period and capable of replication across several sectors. It also requires an unlearning of much of the conventional ways of conducting the innovation business in these countries. This means new perspectives on collaboration, public–private partnerships, education system design and administering of courses, as well as new entrepreneurship models. For a country to move to the final knowledge domain, learning becomes concentrated in R&D activities and can be measured using conventional indicators, such as patents, skilled employees and so on. At this level, the absorptive capacity of firms/entities relies on concentrated efforts in key facilities by highly specialized individuals who conduct research and design activities. This is the level where the orthodox measure of R&D as a source of national knowledge begins to apply.

Again, economic history shows that whereas countries move easily from the lowest knowledge domain to the next higher one, moving further up into knowledge domains that focus on incremental design and innovation and then to frontier innovation is ridden with lack of success. Several countries on a supposedly sound catch-up path often do not move as predicted or regress along this path mainly due to the inability of these countries to manage the coordination efforts required in setting up a sound basis to move to the next knowledge domain. This is not surprising since the efforts required are significant and need to be designed to combat both market failure and government failure simultaneously. Merely focussing on industrial policy that does not take into account the scale effects, thresholds of scientists or engineers and minimal standards of domestic knowledge infrastructure as well as conducive policy environment for domestic innovation are common flaws in latecomer countries.

Comparative Performance: Nigeria and Vietnam

Vietnam is a Socialist Republic, located in Southeast Asia. The coastline of Vietnam covers more than 3,000 km long and the mainland area stretches to 331,690 square km. The country is administratively divided into 63 provinces and 5 municipalities. The terrain of Vietnam includes mountain, hills, delta and rivers. The country is rich in natural resources such as coal, bauxite, petroleum and gas, hydropower, wood and so on, out of which the main mineral exports are coal and petroleum. The oil industry is state-owned by PetroVietnam, which operates under the Ministry of Industry and Trade. Initially, the trade of Vietnam was based on crude oil exports. However, crude oil exports peaked in 2004, then gradually declined.

Subsequently, Vietnam gradually achieved structural transformation from trade in natural resources to manufacturing and services sectors. This diversification resulted in a substantial increase in the contribution to GDP of both sectors. However, the contribution to GDP by the services sector has been much higher than the manufacturing sector; the services sector increased its share while the manufacturing sector has witnessed a declining trend. The CAGR of the services and manufacturing sectors during this period was 0.41 and −0.42 per cent, respectively.

While many countries are endowed with natural resources and became dependent on such assets, Vietnam is one of the countries that made successful use of natural wealth in building dynamic and competitive economies. It has done so by drawing on a strong macroeconomic performance, good governance, building quality institutions, reduction in corruption and due attention to human resource development.

The country has experienced dynamic industrialization due to activist industrial policies leading to strong growth and socio-economic development initiatives of its successive five-year plans. The major change in socio-economic development came after 1985 as the industrial weaknesses were recognized and greater openness was introduced in the system to enhance efficiency, which resulted in a market-oriented economy and called 'Doi-Moi'. Prior to this move, the economy was a highly centralized command economy. After liberalization, the strategy adopted a shift towards small-scale industries support and growth and exports rather than heavy industries.

More than 499 industrial parks were established by 2018: housing several foreign- invested enterprises (7,745) and domestically invested (6,992) enterprises were established (Oh et al., 2020). Vietnam derives over 60 per cent of its GDP from industrial parks. The country's economic policies focused on diversification that enabled Vietnam to grow uninterruptedly for the last three decades. Despite its abundant natural resources, the country, unlike oil-dependent African countries, successfully diversified resulting in high sustained growth. Consequently, Vietnam has become major exporters of phones, textiles, electronic goods, computers and footwear.

Comparative Performance of Nigeria and Indonesia

The comparison of performances of Nigeria and Indonesia offers dramatic evidence of developmental reversal driven mainly by contrasting policy choices at critical junctures in the nations' histories. We used the case of oil palm in the two countries to illustrate the divergences in approach and concomitant performance. Over the span of five decades, the oil palm sector that was Nigeria's main export commodity declined as with other commodities replaced by crude oil export. In contrast, Indonesia recorded great sectoral success in its oil palm industry, as well as in industrialization and economic development. In the past, more than 70 per cent of the Indonesian economy was dependent on agriculture; this has been reduced to only 40 per cent due to economic diversification.[13] Nigeria also needs to reduce its dependence on the oil sector and pay more attention to the non-oil sectors. Nigeria can learn from Indonesia's determination to improve its agricultural sector, especially in palm oil seedling.

The loss of competitiveness in commodity export was compounded by the lack of evolution into processing and value addition and in acquiring capabilities for economic diversification. Sectoral and structural transformation translated to a higher standard of living for Indonesians arising from a GDP double that of Nigeria. Indonesia equally achieved a relatively more equal society through equitable growth.

There were seven distinct areas of policy divergence: First, Indonesia was deliberate in targeting agriculture as a means for poverty reduction. Second, it gave higher priority to a commodity in which it had significant comparative advantage using its vast landmass to outpace Nigeria which does not have a shortage of land itself. Third, Nigeria relied on natural forces to grow the oil palm, while Indonesia applied science to increase yield per unit of land. Fourth, Indonesia made explicit effort and moved away from import-substituting industrialization, while Nigeria remained stuck in import substitution. Fifth, while both have considerable natural resources, Nigeria lags far behind in manufactured exports. Sixth, Indonesia has been better at managing public finance and corruption, relatively. Seventh and more central to this book, Nigeria has lost the opportunity to develop industrial capacity over the last five decades due to its pathology of resource dependence and short-term easy income policy. We have shown the outcome of these policy stances using several metrics of economic performance of the two countries; it is clear why and when they began to diverge.

What do we recommend? Clearly, the Nigerian government should make greater effort and implement policies for the diversification of the economy. For over 25 years, successive Nigerian governments' effort to industrialize the economy has been a failure. This lack of success in industrializing the agriculture sector has in the main led to the country's desired economic growth. In turn, these policies will help contribute to sustaining economic growth of the country. Additionally, the country and its policymakers need to focus on policies which foster more rapid and targeted infrastructural investment towards industrial development and sustained economic growth.

At the sectoral level, Nigeria needs more explicit investment in growth and transformation strategy for agribusiness. The key objectives are: first, to raise productivity of on-farm activities (primary agriculture) to generate competitiveness in the downstream (off-farm) areas. Second, facilitation of more effective coordinative structures across the agricultural value chains. This will include, for example, assisting smallholders to cluster for oil palm and eliminate atomistic spot markets and replacing them with organization fostering effective vertical integrations. Third, creating incentives to expand manufacturing processing of higher-value farm products from crude palm oil. This recommendation applies to other crops discussed in other chapters. Processing generates automatic backward and forward linkages in ways that feed productive value chain development approaches that establish strong links with primary agriculture.

Fourth, strengthen organizations and institutional structures that upgrade and foster access to knowledge, skills and quality certification. Agribusinesses in Nigeria's oil palm sector have been short on skills due to a lack of continuous learning and the lack of public investment in R&D and manufacturing processing infrastructure. While some private sector organizations have thrived, including on-farm and off-farm processing, much of the skills remain locked in these organizations. The growth of off-farm agribusiness, especially small and medium private enterprises, depends on public sector support, as the cases of Indonesia and Malaysia's oil palm industry demonstrate. This is largely absent in Nigeria.

Comparative Performance: Nigeria and Malaysia's Oil Palm and Oil Palm Products

Malaysia and Nigeria were at the same oil palm production level in 1950. Nigeria was a major exporter at the time, but Malaysia caught up and surpassed it both in production and export. We consider the main success and failure factors that might have contributed to this divergence in outcomes. The factors that came out prominently in explaining the divergence in the sector are role of government in providing policies and institutions, investment in scientific research and the nature of the markets in production and orientation towards export.

The sector in Malaysia enjoyed systematic investment including R&D spending, aggressive breeding and tissue culture developments[14] investment in science and technology. Malaysia's average spending per scientist grew enormously over time. However, while Nigeria has the largest number of FTE researchers in Africa (11 per cent of the region's total), its spending is only 7 per cent of the region. Malaysia targets research areas under the scheme called Intensification of Research in Priority Area while Nigeria conducts significant public agricultural research, but there is little research capacity in the private sector.

In Nigeria, there was no significant institutional support for R&D and innovation in the sector. The country established the Nigerian Institute for Oil Palm Research (NIFOR) where almost half of the research force (47 per cent) had PhD degrees for the most part. However, this did not translate to any significant effect on the sector compared to its counterpart – Malaysia Palm Oil Board which had generated more than 300 technologies and products.

Funding for R&D and innovation has been limited in Nigeria. For a period of 10 years, NIFOR only received 4 per cent of the approved budget of the institute. Even then, the money released was only a fraction of the ideal funding requirement. For the period 1992 to 2002, no fund was released for R&D in the institute. Lack of finances not only put a ceiling on the capabilities required to conduct higher stages of research in a systematic way within the various PRIs and universities but sometimes also hindered the capabilities of organizations to install the required facilities even to perform screening satisfactorily. The only exceptions were researchers who had succeeded in receiving individual grants to perform parts of their research in laboratories abroad, where the requisite technological capacities were available. Another group was those that secured institutional support to equip local laboratories. Second, efforts to enhance organizational capabilities through a competitive process have been unsuccessful due to a lack of governmental funds and support (since most respondents complained about the inadequacy and difficulties in obtaining governmental grants). Partly due to the problems in providing up-to-date facilities and research funds, the most talented university graduates either do not show interest in pursuing research careers within Nigeria, or those who do and are very good choose to do so in developed countries. The problem of basic infrastructure exacerbates that of poor funding in the context of up-to-date facilities, as discussed in the earlier sub-sections.

State Capacity and Industrialization

We show in this chapter that the Nigerian state has weak and declined capacity which explains its industrial backwardness relative to Asian comparators. The country, despite its abundant human and natural resources, lacks fundamentals of state capacity or has weak state capacity to foster such change. We demonstrate that state capacity has been a critical component of sustainable development for successful countries. Again, we conceptualize development in the broadest term to mean a shift away from agriculture to engagement in high-value manufacturing production and export, and such changes are driven largely by skilled manpower (technicians, engineers and scientists).

This chapter sought in large part to juxtapose state capacity and development in Nigeria's quest for structural transformation. At a broader level, we contextualized the Nigerian state's laggard and failing status. Its resource profile and the abundance of human capital would suggest a country deserving of the epithet, 'Giant of Africa'. On the contrary, Nigeria qualifies to be called the 'The Crippled Giant'. We show with empirical data that Nigeria is increasingly a fragile and failing state.

Nigeria qualifies to be referred to as a weak or fragile state based on governance arrest in such areas as social services, legitimacy, poor economic growth characterized by rising debts, oil-dependence pathology, widespread insecurity and failure to overcome a protracted multifaceted insurgency. In broad conceptual terms, there are two aspects of state fragility that tend to define Nigeria's reversal, namely, the failure to provide public and social goods, including security; and secondly, a legitimacy gap to the extent that important actors in society differ on the extent to which state power is exercised on behalf of the entire nation.

Nigeria's increasing state of fragility has to a large extent been a result of monumental corruption which has robbed Nigeria of its development potential, setting it in a tragic race to the bottom. As we show systematically with several metrics, in Chapter 2, the country for decades has performed sub-optimally and in comparative perspective with other African and Asian countries. Any programme for reinvention of the Nigerian state must deal with ways and strategies of overcoming the capability deficits which have in turn led to developmental and governance stagnation. The Nigerian state must be able to balance its religious and ethnic diversity through effective and inclusive leadership to prevent the wild play of centrifugal forces from devouring the country's fortunes. Undoubtedly, not much progress can be made until Nigeria overcomes the corruption in public life, the ineffectiveness of institutions, the cronyism in politics resulting in state capture as well as the neo-patrimonial ways of the elite class.

Importantly too, the sense of entitlement which treats public resources as a bonanza to be shared by competing elites must be replaced with transformational leadership that will reform the state, not just in precepts but by example.

Leadership and Industrialization

This chapter focusses on the role of leadership, a subject that is not frequently associated with economic growth in the large body of research explaining development. We set a significant store on leadership for many reasons. In poor and low-income countries, leaders determine in large measure the effectiveness of public sector funding. Also, the pivotal role of leaders' network, leadership propensities and the elite in national development can have a significant effect on economic outcomes. In the previous chapters, we analysed a few of the several factors and variables that determine the rate and direction of economic growth. This chapter shows that due to the idiosyncratic conditions of developing countries, the nature of leadership can impact negatively on other factors.

Leaders and 'elites', especially in developing countries where governments and their leaders hold and control the levers of power, tend to trump all other factors. Their interests and predilections in a weak institutional regime which characterize post-colonial nations could push their nation into a trajectory of a positive or negative economic development pathway. In post-colonial states with weakened or absent institutions and poor coordination across the economic system, the evolution of a capable state is critical to the long-term emergence of nations. In other words, leadership in some form needs to be in place to prevent chaos and to manage the process of nation-building. Nation-building necessitates that a 'builder' or a collection of builders is devoting explicit and deliberate effort to the process of nation-building. For most African countries, the end of colonialism was abrupt, chaotic and disorderly. The nation-building process requires a complex and difficult long-term investment in diverse capabilities to create an equitable society and engineer fast economic growth. Leadership is essential to providing purpose and direction during the process of nation-building. A new nation may falter without capable, legitimate and visionary leaders.

The chapter examined the key roles that leadership and social capabilities play in managing industrialization, as well as the investment necessary for human and physical capital formation. We conclude that leadership and capabilities are critical to efficient institutions, especially in navigating complex industrial systems, in terms of defining structures and functions, ensuring necessary financing and creating a coherent management system. Additionally, good leadership gives direction in promoting good institutions to administer transparent sanctions, incentives and authority, while bad leadership corrupts their institutions. More crucially, leadership influences the role of individual actors be they politicians, bureaucrats or scientists, as these actors run organizations and therefore transmit the effectiveness of institutions. The behaviour of governments plays an important role in stimulating or discouraging economic activity, as does the behaviour of entrepreneurs, parents, scientists or priests.

Notes

1 Okereke (2017), "Causes of Failure and Abandonment of Projects and Project Deliverables in Africa." December 9, 2021.
2 Hanachor (2012), "Community Development Projects Abandonment in Nigeria."
3 Andawei (2015), "Causes of Public Sector Project Abandonment in Nigeria." 2 December 10, 2021
4 Bunu (2011), "Presidential Project Assessment Committee Report." www.ccsenet.org /ibr. *International Business Research*, 66(11): 2013159.
5 African Development Bank (2015); International Monetary Fund (2012).
6 Easterly et al., (1993); Pritchett (2000).
7 Easterly, William, Michael Kremer, Lant Pritchett, and Lawrence H. Summers (1993), "Good Policy or Good Luck? Country Growth Performance and Temporary Shocks." *Journal of Monetary Economics*, XXXII: 459–83.
8 Mikesell (1997), Kronenberg (2004).
9 Innis (1930, 2017) and Mackintosh (1923,).
10 Viner (1953), Lewis (1955), Spengler (1960).
11 Oyelaran-Oyeyinka and Gehl-Sampath (2010), *Latecomer Development*.
12 World Bank (2008).
13 Othman and Bello, "Indonesia-Nigeria Foreign Economic Relations."
14 https://www.researchgate.net/publication/342245806_OIL_PALM_ECONOMIC _PERFORMANCE_IN_MALAYSIA_AND_RD_PROGRESS_IN_2019, accessed May 1, 2021.

BIBLIOGRAPHY

Acemoglu, D. and J. A. Robinson (2006). "De Facto Political Power and Institutional Persistence." *American Economic Review*, 96(2): 325–30.

Acemoglu, D., S. Johnson, J. Robinson, and Y. Thaicharoen (2003). "Institutional Causes, Macroeconomic Symptoms: Volatility, Crises and Growth." *Journal of Monetary Economics*, 50(1): 49–123.

Adesina, A. (5 June 2013). *The Opportunity in Nigeria's Cocoa Sector.* Washington, DC: Special Address to the World Cocoa Foundation.

Adeyeye, M. (2017). "Governing for Development: Whither State/Local Relations in Nigeria?" *Being a Paper Delivered at the International Conference Organized by the Faculty of Administration, Obafemi Awolowo University,* Ile-Ife, Nigeria on 27–28 November 2017.

African Development Bank (2015). "African Economic Outlook 2015: Regional Development and Spatial Inclusion." African Development Bank, Organisation for Economic Co-operation and Development, United Nations Development Programme. https://www.afdb.org/en/documents/document/african-economic -outlook-2015-51613

African Development Bank and United Nations Economic Commission for Africa (2013). *African Economic Outlook 2013 Structural Transformation and Natural Resources: Structural Transformation and Natural Resources.* OECD publishing.

African Economic Outlook (2018),. "African Development Bank." https://www.afdb.org /fileadmin/uploads/afdb/Documents/Publications/

Afriyanti et al. (2023). "The Role of the Agricultural Sector on Economic Growth in Indonesia." *Indonesian Journal of Multidisciplinary Sciences (IJoMS),* 2: 167–79. https:// doi.org/10.59066/ijoms.v2i1.325

Ahmed N. (2009). "Sustaining Ready-Made Garment Exports from Bangladesh." *Journal of Contemporary Asia,* 39(4): 597–618. https://doi.org/10.1080/00472330903076891

Ake, Claude. (2001). *Democracy and development in Africa.* Brookings Institution Press.

Akter, P. (2020). "An Overview of the Ready-Made Garment (RMG) Sector of Bangladesh: From Origin to the Current State of Pinnacle." *Kyushu University Graduate School of Economics.* https://doi.org/10.15017/4067129

Aljarallah, R. A. (10 Jul 2020). "Natural Resource Dependency, Institutional Quality and Human Capital Development in Gulf Countries." *Heliyon,* 6(7): e04290. https:// doi.org/10.1016/j.heliyon.2020.e04290. PMID: 32685711; PMCID: PMC7355996.

Alliance for a Green Revolution in Africa (AGRA) (2014). *Africa Agriculture Status Report: Climate Change and Smallholder Agriculture in Sub-Saharan.* Nairobi, Kenya.

Almond, G. and J. Coleman (eds.) (1960). *The Politics of Developing Areas.* Princeton: Princeton University Press.

Aman Tex (nd). "Red-Herring Prospectus of Aman Tex Limited." https://www.icml.com .bd/ISSUE/Draft%20Red%20Herring%20Prospectus%20of%20Aman%20Tex %20Limited.pdf. Accessed 30 June 2024

Americas Business Dialogue (2018). "Action for Growth: Policy Recommendations and Plan of Action 2018-2021 for Growth in the Americas." https://americasbd.org/en/2018-report/

Amsden, A. H. (1989). *Asia's Next Giant: South Korea and Late Industrialization*. New York and Oxford: Oxford University Press.

Amsden, A. H. (1992). *Asia's Next Giant: South Korea and Late Industrialization*. Oxford: Oxford University Press.

Amsden, A. H. and W. W. Chu (2003). *Beyond Late Development Taiwan's Upgrading Policies*. Cambridge: The MIT Press.

Amuge, O. (21 August 2021). *Nigeria Losing Out in $39bn Rubber Industry*. Retrieved March 9, 2022, from Business A.M.:https://www.businessamlive.com/nigeria-losing-out-in-39bn-rubber-industry/

Andersen, A. D. (2012). "Towards a New Approach to Natural Resources and Development: The Role of Learning, Innovation and Linkage Dynamics." *International Journal of Technological Learning, Innovation and Development*, 5(3): 291–324.

Anochirionye, Onyekachi (2016). "Government Policy, Oil & Gas, Technology; the Impact of Local Content Policy in the Nigeria Oil & Gas Sector on the Economy." Accessed on 18 July from https://teneceblog.wordpress.com/2016/05/24/the-impact-of-local-content-policy-in-the-nigeria-oil-gas-sector-on-the-economy/

Anyanechi, O. (2020). "Nigeria: Legal Framework for the Operation of Marginal Fields in Nigeria." Accessed on 17 July 2021. https://www.mondaq.com/nigeria/oil-gas-electricity/964746/legal-framework-for-the-operation-of-marginal-fields-in-nigeria

Arndt, H. W. (1983). "OIL AND THE INDONESIAN ECONOMY." ISEAS - YusofIshak Institute, 136–50. Accessed on 18 July from https://www.jstor.org/stable/pdf/27908478.pdf?refreqid=excelsior%3A7734942db390d4d3036e3a572a13a4b8

Aryeetey,Court, Nissanke, and Weber (1998). *Africa and Asia in the Global Economy*. Tokyo: United Nations University Press.

Asaolu, T. O., O. Oyesanmi, P. O. Oladele, and A. M. Oladoyin (2005). "Privatisation and Commercialisation in Nigeria: Implications and Prospects for Good Governance." *South African Journal of Business Management*, 36(3): 65–74.

Aunty, R. M. (1993). *Sustaining Development in Mineral Economies: The Resource Curse Thesis*. London: Routledge.

Auty, R. M. (1994). "Industrial Policy Reform in Six Large Newly Industrializing Countries: The Resource Curse Thesis." *World Development*, 22(1): 11–26.

Auty, R. M. and D. Evans (1994). *Trade and Industrial Policy for Sustainable Resource-Based Development: Policy Issues, Achievements and Prospects*.Geneva: UNCTAD.

Balandrán-Quintana,R. R. and A. M.-C.-O. Mendoza-Wilson (2019). "Chapter 4 - Plant-Based Proteins." In C. M. Galanakis (ed.), *Proteins: Sustainable Source, Processing and Applications*, 97–130. Cambridge: Academic Press.

Baldwin, R. E. (1966). "Economic Growth and Structure." *The Journal of Economic History*,26: 125–7. https://doi.org/10.1017/S0022050700061970

Bamberg, J. (2000). *British Petroleum and Global Oil 1950-1975: The Challenge of Nationalism*. Cambridge University Press.

Bashiru, U. K. and M. A. Salisu (2015). "Growth Without Development in Nigeria's Economic Mallaise." *Journal of Economic and Sustainable Development*, 6(22): 148–50.

Baudoin, A., P. M. Bosc, C. Bessou, and P. Levang (2017). "Review of the Diversity of Palm Oil Production Systems in Indonesia." *Center for International Forestry Research*, 1–6.

Bayart, J.-F. (1999). "The Social Capital of the Felonious State." In J.-F. Bayart et al. (eds.), *The Criminalisation of the State in Africa*, 32–44. Oxford: James Currey.

Bersch, K., S. Praça, and M.M. Taylor (2017). "State Capacity, Bureaucratic Politicization, and Corruption in the Brazilian State." *Governance*, 30(1):105–124. https://doi.org/10.1111/gove.12196

Bertrand, Marianne, and Antoinette Schoar. (2003). "Managing with Style: The Effect of Managers on Firm Policies." *The Quarterly Journal of Economics*, 118.4: 1169–1208.

Besley, T. and T. Persson (2011). *Pillars of Prosperity: The Political Economics of Development Clusters*. Princeton: Princeton University Press.

BGMEA (2021). "A Success Story: The Bangladeshi Garment Sector has Made Remarkable Progress in Recent Years." Accessed on 30 June 2024 from https://www.bgmea.com.bd/index.php/page/A_success_story:_The_Bangladeshi_garment_sector_has_made_remarkable_progress_in_recent_years

Blomström, M. and A. Kokko (2007). "From Natural Resources to High-Tech Production: The Evolution of Industrial Competitiveness in Sweden and Finland." *Natural Resources:Neither Curse Nor Destiny*, 213–56.

Borrus, M., D. Ernst, and S. Haggard (2000). "Cross-Border Production Networks and the Industrial Integration of the Asia-Pacific Region." In M. Borrus, D. Ernst, and S. Haggard (eds.), *International Production Networks in Asia. Rivalry or Riches?* London: Routledge.

Bragg, J. B. (2016). *The Spark that Ignited the Industrial Revolution: An Examination of the Institutions Surrounding the Development of the Steam Engine in England and France* (Master's thesis, Norwegian University of Life Sciences, Ås).

Brandi, C., T. Cabani, C. Hosang, S. Schirmbeck, L. Westermann,and H. Wiese (2013). *Sustainability Certification in the Indonesian Palm Oil Sector: Benefits and Challenges for Smallholders*(No. 74). Studies.

Bratton, M. and Van De Walle (1994). "Neo-patrimonial Regimes and Political Transition in Africa." *World Politics*, 46 (July) : 453–489.

Brennenraedts, R. M. F., R. Bekkers, and B. Verspagen (2006). "The Different Channels of University-Industry Knowledge Transfer, Empirical Evidence from Biomedical Engineering." *ECIS WP06-04*.

Busse, M., C. Erdogan, and H. Mühlen (2019). "Structural transformation and its relevance for economic growth in sub-saharan Africa.." *Review of Development Economics*, 23(1):33–53. https://doi:10.1111/rode.12543

Cadoni, P. (2013). *Analysis of Incentives and Disincentives for Cocoa in Nigeria*. FAO, Rome.

Castells, M. (1992). "Four Asian Tigers with a Dragon Head: A Comparative Analysis of the State, Economy and Society in the Asian Pacific Rim." In R.Henderson and J. Applebaum (eds.), *State and Development in the Asian Pacific Rim*. London: Sage Publications.

Centeno, M. A., A. Kohli, and D. J. Yashar (2017). *States in the Developing World*.Cambridge: Cambridge University Press.

Centeno, M. A., A. Kohli, and D. J. Yashar (2017). "Unpacking States in the Developing World: Capacity, Performance, and Politics." *States in the Developing World*, 1–32.

Central Bank of Nigeria (2020). "2020 Statistical Bulletin: External Sector Statistics." Retrieved 22 June 2024 from https://www.cbn.gov.ng/documents/statbulletin.asp

CGIAR (15 April 2019). "Plant Breeding for the Future - The Time is Now." Retrieved 6 July 2024 from https://ccafs.cgiar.org/news/plant-breeding-future-time-now

Chabal, P. and J.-P. Daloz (1999). *Disorder as Political Instrument*. Oxford: James Currey.

Chang, H.-J. (1994). *The Political Economy of Industrial Policy*. New York: St. Martin's Press.

Chang, H. J. (1999). "The Economic Theory of the Developmental State." In Woo-Cumings (ed.), *The Developmental State*, 182–99. Ithaca: Cornell University Press.

Chang, H.-J. (ed.) (2001). *The Rebel Within: Joseph Stiglitz and the World Bank*. London: Anthem Press.

Chang, H.-J. and R. Rowthorn, (Eds.) (1995). *The Role of the State in Economic Change*. Oxford: Oxford University Press.

Chattopadhyay, Raghabendra, and Esther Duflo. (2004). "Women as Policy Makers: Evidence from a Randomized Policy Experiment in India." *Econometrica*, 72.5: 1409–1443.

Cingolani, L. (2013). The State of State Capacity: A Review of Concepts, Evidence and Measures.

CIRAD. (2022). *Oil Palm*. Retrieved from CIRAD:https://www.cirad.fr/en/our-activities -our-impact/tropical-value-chains/oil-palm/plant-and-uses

Collier, P. (2007). *The Bottom Billion: Why the Poorest Countries are Failing and What Can Be Done About It*. Oxford: Oxford University Press.

Commission on Growth (2008). *The Growth Report: Strategies for Sustained Growth and Inclusive Development*. Washington, D.C.: World Bank Publications.

Corden, W. M. (1982). "Exchange Rate Policy and The Resources Boom." *Economic Record*, 58(1): 18–31.

Corden, W. M. (1984). "Booming Sector and Dutch Disease Economics: Survey and Consolidation." *Oxford Economic Papers*, 36(3): 359–80.

Corden, W. M. and J. P. Neary (1982). "Booming Sector and De-Industrialisation in a Small Open Economy." *The Economic Journal*, 92(368): 825–48.

Craig, K. (2015). "Understanding General and Technical Competencies." *HRSG*, 6 November. Available at: https://resources.hrsg.ca/blog/understanding-general-and-technical-competencies.

D'Arcy, M. and M. Nistotskaya (2017). "State Capacity, Development, and the Politics of Incremental Reform." *Governance*, 30(1): 35–52.

Dahl, R. A. (1957). "The Concept of Power." *Behavioral Science*, 2(3): 201–15.

De Palma, A. and A. Guimard (2015). "Urbanization: An Overview." *Quality of Life in Cities*, 1–43.

Development Finance International/Oxfam (2018). "CRI Index on Commitment to Social Spending."

Drackley, J. K. (2010). "Applications of Palm Oil in Animal Nutrition." *Journal of Oil Palm Research*, 835–45.

Echavarria, R., C. E. Vázquez Moreno, and K. Sherdek (2016). "The Resource Curse Mirage: The Blessing of Resources and Curse of Empire?" *Real-World Economics Review, Issue*, 75.

Elias, S. and C. None (2011). "The Growth and Development of the Indonesian Economy." Accessed on 27 July 2021 from https://www.rba.gov.au/publications/bulletin/2011/dec/pdf/bu-1211-4.pdf

Energy Information Administration (2012). *Country Analysis Briefs: Vietnam*. Washington: US Energy Information Administration.

Engerman, S. L. (2000). "Institutions, Factor Endowments and Paths of Development in the New World." *Journal of Economic Perspective*, 3: 217–32.

Engerman, S. L. and K. L. Sokoloff (1997). "Factor Endowments, Institutions and Differential Paths of Growth among New World Economies." In S. H. Haber, *How Latin America Fell Behind*, 260–304. Stanford: Stanford University Press.

Ernah, Parvathi, P. and H. Waibel (2016). "Adoption of Sustainable Palm Oil Practices by Indonesian Smallholder Farmers." *Journal of Southeast Asian Economies*, 291–316.

Evans, P. (1995). *Embedded Autonomy. States and Industrial Transformation*. Princeton: Princeton University Press.

Evans, P. and D. Rueschemeyer (1985). "The State and Economic Transformation: Toward and Analysis of the Conditions Underlying Effective Intervention." In P. Evans, D. Rueschemeyer, and T. Sckocpol. *Bringing the State Back In*. Cambridge University Press.

Export Genius (21 December 2022). "Bangaldesh Regains its Position as Second-Biggest Textile Exporter in 2021." Accessed on 30 June 2024 from https://www.exportgenius.in/blog/bangladesh-regains-its-position-as-second-biggest-textile-exporter-in-2021-676.php

Falola, T. and J. Ihonvere (1985). *Rise and Fall of Nigeria's Second Republic*. London: Zed Publishers.

Fawehinmi (5 March 2015). "Did Dahiru Managal Kill the Nigerian Textile Industry?" Accessed on 1 July 2024 from https://aguntasolo.co/did-dahiru-mangal-kill-the-nigerian-textile-industry-cf7708af083d

Ferguson, J. (1990). *The Anti-politics Machine*. New York: Cambridge University Press.

Foa, R. S. and A. Nemirovskaya (2016). "How State Capacity Varies: A Multivariate Analysis of Twenty-First Century State Performance." *Governance*, 29(3): 283–98. https://doi.org/10.1111/gove.12165

Forrest, J. B. (1998). "State Inversion and Non-State Politics." In L. A. Villalon and P. A. Huxtable (eds.), *The African State at a Critical Juncture: Between Disintegration and Reconfiguration*, 45–56. Boulder: Lynne Rienner.

Fortune Business Insights (2022). *Plastics Polymers & Resins / Rubber Market*. Retrieved March 8, 2022, from Fortune Business Insights:https://www.fortunebusinessinsights.com/industry-reports/rubber-market-101612

Fukuyama, F. (2001). "Social Capital, Civil Society and Development." *Third World Quarterly*, 22(1): 7–20.

Fukuyama, F. (2002). "Social Capital and Development: The Coming Agenda." *SAIS Review*, 22(1): 23–37.

Freeman, C. (1987). *Technology Policy and Economic Performance: Lessons from Japan*. London: Frances Printer.

Fuady, A. H. (2015). "Aid and Policy Preferences in Oil-Rich Countries: Comparing Indonesia and Nigeria." Accessed from https://doi.org/10.1080/01436597.2015.1041490

Gayi, S. and K. Tsowou (2016). *Cocoa Industry: Integrating Small Farmers into the Global Value Chain*. New York and Geneva: United Nations.

Geddes, B. (1994). *Politician's Dilemma: Building State Capacity in Latin America*. California: University of California Press.

Genova, A. W. (2007). *Oil and Nationalism in Nigeria, 1970-1980*. Ann Arbor: UMI.

Gerschenkron, A. (1962). *Economic Backwardness in Historical Perspective*. Cambridge: Harvard University Press.

Giddens, A. (1979). *Central Problems in Social Theory* [Preprint]. doi:10.1007/978-1-349-16161-4.

Giddens Anthony. (1999). "Elements of the Theory of Structuration." In *The Blackwell Reader. Contemporary Social Theory*, 119–130.

Giesecke, S. (2000). "The Contrasting Roles of Government in the Development of Biotechnology Industry in the US and Germany." *Research Policy*, 29(2): 205–23. https://doi.org/10.1016/S0048-7333(99)00068-8

Global Business Guide: Indonesia. Accessed on 18 July 2021 from http://www.gbgindonesia.com/en/energy/article/2011/overview_of_the_oil_gas_sector

_in_indonesia.php#:~:text=The%20main%20players%20in%20the,Total%2C%2
0Conoco%20Phillips%20and%20Medco

Gomide, A. (2018). "The Concept of State Capacity and its Operationalisation in Empirical Research." *Being a Paper Delivered at the International Public Policy Association Conference held at the University of Pittsburgh on 26-28 June, 2018.*

Gopal, J. (2002). *The Development of Malaysia's Palm Oil Refining Industry: Obstacles, Policy and Performance* (Doctoral dissertation, University of London).

Gray, B. S. (1969). *A Study of the Influence of Generic, Agronomic and Environmental Factors in the Growth, Flowering and Bunch Production on the West Coast of West Malaysia.*

Grimm, S. et al. (2014). "Fragile States: Introducing a Political Concept." *Third World Quarterly*, 35(2): 197–209.

Gylfason, T. (1999). "Natural Resources and Economic Growth: A Nordic Perspective on the Dutch Disease."

Haack, R. C., P. Sundararaman, J. O. Diedjomahor, H. Xiao, N. J. Gant, E. D. May, and K. Kelsch (2000). "Chapter 16: Niger Delta Petroleum Systems, Nigeria." In M. R. Mello and B. J. Katz (eds.), *Petroleum Systems of South Atlantic Margins: AAPG Memoir 73*, 213–31. American Association of Petroleum Geologists (AAPG).

Hamilton, D. I. (2011). "Oil and Gas Companies and Community Crises in the Niger Delta." *American Review of Political Economy*, 3. Accessed on 18 July 2021 from https:// sites.bemidjistate.edu/arpejournal/wp-content/uploads/sites/2/2015/11/v9n1 -hamilton.pdf

Harbers, I. (2015). *Political Topographies of the African State: Territorial Authority and Institutional Choice.* Cambridge: Cambridge University Press.

Harbers, I. and B. J. Steele (2020). "The Impact of State Infrastructural Power on Security Outcomes: A Comparative Analysis." *Journal of Strategic Studies*, 43(6–7): 896–915. https://doi.org/10.1080/13523260.2020.1764581

Hasan, I., M. N. Islam, and S. R. Khan (2020). "Ready-made Garment Industry Attractiveness: The Case of Bangladesh Garments' Blue-Collar Employees." *International Journal of Emerging Markets.* https://doi.org/10.1108/IJOEM-03-2019-0232.

Hausmann, R. and C. A. Hidalgo (2011). "The Network Structure of Economic Output." *Journal of Economic Growth*, 16: 309–42.

Hedley, D. D. (1987). "Diversification: Concepts and Directions in Indonesian Agricultural Policy." *Soybean Research and Development in Indonesia*, 10: 17.

Henley, D. (2012). "The Agrarian Roots of Industrial Growth: Rural Development in South-East Asia and Sub-Saharan Africa." *Development Policy Review*, 30: s25–s47.

Henley, D. (2015). *Asia-Africa Development Divergence: A Question of Intent.* Zed books.

Herrendorf, B., R. Rogerson, and A. Valentinyi (2013). *Growth and Structural Transformation.* Working paper. Cambridge, Massachusetts: National Bureau of Economic Research.

Hidalgo, C. A., B. Klinger, A. L. Barabási, and R. Hausmann (2007). "The Product Space Conditions the Development of Nations." *Science*, 317(5837): 482–7.

Hirschman, A. (1958). *The Strategy of Economic Development.* New Haven: Yale University Press.

Holmén, H. (2005). "The State and Agricultural Intensification in Sub-Saharan Africa." In *The African Food Crisis: Lessons from the Asian Green Revolution*, 87–112. Wallingford UK: Cabi Publishing.

Hossain, M. S. and Latifee E. H. (7 August 2017). "Readymade Garment Industries Going Green." *Financial Express.* Accessed on 30 June 2024 from https://today .thefinancialexpress.com.bd/public/stock-corporate/readymade-garment-industries -going-green

Hossian, M. S., R. Kabir, and E. H. Latifee (2019). "Export Competitiveness of Bangladesh Readymade Garments Sector: Challenges and Prospects." *International Journal of Research in Business and Social Science,* 8(3): 45–63. https://doi.org/10.20525/ijrbs.v8i3.205

Hunter, J. (1966). "The Indonesian Oil Industry." *Australian Economic Papers.*

Hyden, G. (1983). *No Shortcuts to Progress: African Development Management in Perspective.* London: Heinemann.

Hyden, G. and M. Bratton, (Eds.) (1992). *Governance and Politics in Africa.* Boulder, Colorado: Lynne Rienner Publishers.

Ibirogba, F. (8 October 2018). "84,000 Lose Jobs as 16 Cocoa Companies Go Under." *The Guardian.*

ICMM, I. (2014). *Enhancing Mining's Contribution to the Zambian Economy and Society.* Lusaka: Chambers of Mines of Zambia.

Ijeomah, S. "National College of Ireland. Challenges of Supply Chain Management in the Oil & Gas Production in Nigeria (Shell Petroleum Development Company of Nigeria)." Accessed from http://norma.ncirl.ie/4724/1/stephanieijeomah.pdf

Iloani, F. A. (15 August 2019). "Nigeria Spent N40trn on Food Imports in 21yrs – Data." Accessed on 27 July 2021 from https://web.archive.org/web/20200730220925/https://www.dailytrust.com.ng/nigeria-spent-n40trn-on-food-imports-in-21yrs-data.html

IMF (2024). IMF Data Mapper - GDP, Current Prices. Retrieved 16 June 2024 from https://www.imf.org/external/datamapper/NGDPD@WEO/AFQ/DZA/ZAF/MAR/NGA/EGY?year=2019

IMF Staff Discussion Note (May 2016). "Corruption: Costs and Mitigating Strategies." Accessed on 27 July 2021 from https://www.imf.org/external/pubs/ft/sdn/2016/sdn1605.pdf

Industrial Rubber Goods (2022). *Rubber Industry Global Overview.* Retrieved March 8, 2022, from Industrial Rubber Goods: The Buyer's Guide: http://www.industrialrubbergoods.com/global-overview.html

Innis, H. A. (1930). "The Hudson Bay Railway." *Geographical Review,* 20(1): 1–30.

Innis, H. A. (1940). "The Cod Fisheries: The History of an International Economy." *Geographical Review,* 30(2): 351.

Innis, H. A. (2017). *Essays in Canadian Economic History.* Toronto: University of Toronto Press.

Intarakumnerd, P., Pun-arj Chairatana, and T. Tangchitpiboon (2002). "National Innovation Systems in Less Successful Developing Countries: The Case Study of Thailand." *Research Policy,* 31(8–9): 1445–57.

International Monetary Fund (2012). "Regional Economic Outlook: Sub-Saharan Africa." October 2012. International Monetary Fund. https://www.imf.org/en/Publications/REO/SSA/Issues/2016/12/31/Regional-Economic-Outlook-October-2012-Sub-Saharan-Africa-Taking-Stock-A-Decade-After-the-Global-26167

Irikefe, P. (2013). *Why Nigeria is not Working: The Predicament and the Promise.* Ibadan: Kraft Books Limited.

Islam, M. S. (2021). "Ready-made Garments Exports Earning and its Contribution to Economic Growth in Bangladesh." *GeoJournal,* 86(3):1301–09. https://doi.org/10.1007/s10708-019-10131-0

Jacquemard, J. C. (2012). *Le Palmier à Huile.* Gemboux, Belgium: Quae, CTA, Presse Agronomique de Gembloux. http://www.cairn.info/la-ville-durable-du-politique-au-scientifique--9782738012029-page-1.htm

James, A. (2019). "Fata Morganas in Oil-Rich, Institution-Poor Economies." *Resources Policy,* 60: 234–42.

John, D. A. and G. R. Babu (2021). "Lessons from the Aftermaths of Green Revolution on Food System and Health." *Frontiers in Sustainable Food Systems*, 5: 644559.

Johnson, B. and B.-A. Lundvall. "National Systems of Innovation and Development." In M. Muchie, P. Gammeltoft, and B.-A. Lundvall (eds.), *Putting Africa First: The Making of African Innovation Systems*. . Aalborg Universitetsforlag: Aalborg University Press. (Compendium).

Johnson, W. B., Magee, R. P., Nagarajan, N. J., & Newman, H. A. (1985). "An Analysis of the Stock Price Reaction to Sudden Executive Deaths: Implications for the Managerial Labor Market." *Journal of Accounting and Economics*, 7(1–3), 151–174.

Joseph, R. (1987). *Democracy and Prebendal Politics in Nigeria: The Rise and Fall of the Second Republic*. Cambridge: Cambridge University Press.

Joseph, R. (1998). "Africa (1990-1997): From Abetura to Closure." *Journal of Democracy*, 9(2): 3–17.

Joseph, R. (2016). "State, Governance and Democratic Development: The Nigerian Challenge." *Being a Keynote Address Delivered at the Inaugural Workshop of the Ibadan School of Government and Public Policy (ISGPP) on 1st February, 2016 at the International Conference Centre*, University of Ibadan, Ibadan, Nigeria.

Kadandale, S., R. Marten, and and R. Smith (2019). "The Palm Oil Industry and Noncommunicable Diseases." *Bull World Health Organ*, 118–28.

Kaldor, N. (1967). *Strategic Factors in Economic Development*. New York State School of Industrial and Labor Relations, Cornell University.

Kaufmann, D., A. Kraay, and M. Mastruzzi (2010). The Worldwide Governance Indicators: Methodology and Analytical Issues. *World Bank policy research working paper*, (5430).

Kawabata, M. (2006). "An Overview of the Debate on the African State. African Centre for Peace and Development Studies, Ryukoku University." Working Paper Series.

Kawano, M. (2017). "Upgrading Malaysia's Rubber Manufacturing: Trajectories and Challenges." *Southeast Asia beyond Crises and Traps: Economic Growth and Upgrading*, 193–223.

Kawano, M. (2018). "Changing Resource-Based Manufacturing Industry: The Case of the Rubber Industry in Malaysia and Thailand." In K. Tsunekawa and Y. Todo (eds.), *Emerging States at Crossroads. Emerging-Economy State and International Policy Studies*, 145–162. Singapore: Springer.

Kehati (2006). *Indonesian Path Toward Sustainable Energy: A Case Study of Developing Palm Oil as Biomass in Indonesia*. Bogor, Indonesia: The Indonesian Biodiversity-KEHATI; Sawit Watch Social Economic Research Institute–INRISE; Bogor Agricultural Institute Media Indonesia Group/Daily Research & Development. http://www.bothends.org/strategic/061211_Biomass%20 case%20study%20Indonesia.pdf

Kenneth E., M. Sunday, O. Anulika, O. Chimsunum, and M. Chuks (2019). "Producers'make or Buy Decision and Business Shutdown: An Evaluation of Choice in Textile Industry. *Cogent Business & Management*, 6: 1.

Kim, Anthony B. (2020). "Indonesia: An Asian Powerhouse Growing Fast." Accessed on 27 July 2021 from https://www.dailysignal.com/2020/07/09/indonesia-an-asian-powerhouse-growing-fast/

Konanykhin, A. (2018). "How Transparency can Help the Global Economy to Grow." Accessed on 27 July 2021 from https://www.weforum.org/agenda/2018/10/how-transparency-can-help-grow-the-global-economy/

Kronenberg, T. (2004). "The Curse of Natural Resources in the Transition Economies." *Economics of Transition*, 12(3): 399–426.

Kuznets, S. S. (1966). *Modern Economic Growth*. New Haven: Yale University Press.

Lall, S. and A. Pietrobelli (2002). *Failing to Compete: Technology Development and Technology Systems in Africa*. Cheltenham: Edward Elgar.

Latifee, E. H. (2 February 2016). "RMG Sector Towards a Thriving Future." Accessed on 30 June 2024 from https://www.thedailystar.net/supplements/25th-anniversary -special-part-2/rmg-sector-towards-thriving-future-210886

Lavassani, K. M. and B. Movahedi (2021). "Firm-level Analysis of Global Supply Chain Network: Role of Centrality on Firm's Performance." *International Journal of Global Business and Competitiveness*, 16: 86–103. https://doi.org/10.1007/s42943-021-00026-8

Lederman, D. and W. F. Maloney (2007). "Neither Curse Nor Destiny: Introduction to Natural Resources and Development." *Natural Resources: Neither Curse Nor Destiny*, 1–14.

Lee, C. K. and Y. Zhang (2017). "The Power of Instability: Unraveling the Microfoundations of Bargained Authoritarianism in China." *American Journal of Sociology*, 122(6)" 1620–56.

Levang P. (1997). *La terre d'en face. La transmigration en Indonésie*. Paris: ORSTOM Editions.

Levi, M. (1988). *Of Rule and Revenue*. California: University of California Press.

Lewis, A. (1955). *The Theory of Economic Growth*. London: Allen & Unwin.

Lewis, P. (2007). *Growing Apart: Oil, Politics, and Economic Change in Indonesia and Nigeria*. Michigan: The University of Michigan Press. https://doi.org/10.1080 /00220380802160127

Lewis, W. A. (1954). "Economic Development with Unlimited Supplies of Labor." *The Manchester School*, 22: 139–91.

Lewis, W. A. (2013). *Theory of Economic Growth*. Routledge.

Lindvall, J. and J. Teorell (2016). State Capacity as Power: A Conceptual Framework.

Lorch, Klaus (1991). "Privatization Through Private Sale: The Bangladeshi Textile Industry". In Ravi Ramarmurti and Raymond Vernon (eds.), *Privatization and Control of State-owned Enterprises*, 93–128. Washington, D. C.: World Bank. ISBN 978-0-8213-1863-8.

Lundvall, B.-Å. (1988). "Innovations as in Interactive Process: From User-Producer Interaction to the National System of Innovation." In G. Dosi, *Technical Change and Economic Theory*, 349,369 . London: Printer.

Lundvall, B.-Å., B. Johnson, E. S. Andersen, and B. Dalum (2002). "National Systems of Production, Innovation and Competence Building." *Research Policy*, 31(2): 213–31.

Mabogunje, A. and R. Kates (2004). "Sustainable Development in Ijebu-ode, Nigeria: The Role of Social Capital, Participation and Science and Technology." CID Working Papers No. 102. Centre for International Development, Harvard University.

Mackintosh, W. A. (1923). "Economic Factors in Canadian History." *Canadian Historical Review*, 4(1): 12–25.

Mackintosh, W. A. (1935). "The Progress of Canada's Recovery." *International Affairs (Royal Institute of International Affairs 1931-1939)*, 14(3): 389–401.

Maiwada and Renne (2013). The Kaduna Textile Industry and the Decline of Textile Manufacturing in Northern Nigeria, 1955–2010.

Manley, G. (2017). "Scaling and Transforming Olam Cocoa to Spur Growth." *Olam Insights*, 1: 1–3.

Mann, M. (1984). "The Autonomous Power of the State: Its Origins, Mechanisms and Results." *European Journal of Sociology/Archives européennes de sociologie*, 25(2): 185–213.

Martone, D. (2003). "A Guide to Developing a Competency-Based Performance- Management System." *Employment Relations Today*, 30(3): 23.

Mathews, J. A. and D. S. Cho (2000). *Tiger Technology: The Creation of a Semiconductor Industry in East Asia*. Cambridge: Cambridge University Press.

McKinnon, R. I. (1976). "International Transfers and Non-Traded Commodities: The Adjustment Problem." *The International Monetary System and the Developing Nations*, 157–67.

Mehlum, H., K. Moene, and R. Torvik (2006). "Cursed by Resources or Institutions?" *World Economy*, 29(8): 1117–31.

Mehlum, H., K. Moene, and R. Torvik (2006). "Institutions and the Resource Curse." *The Economic Journal*, 116(508): 1–20.

Menzel, A. and C. Woodruff (2021). "Gender Wage Gaps and Worker Mobility: Evidence from the Garment Sector in Bangladesh." *Labour Economics*, 71: 102000.

Mikesell, R. F. (1997). "Explaining the Resource Curse, with Special Reference to Mineral-Exporting Countries." *Resources Policy*, 23(4): 191–9.

Mills C. W. (1956). *The Power Elite*. New York, NY: Oxford University Press.

Mojeed, A. (19 January 2022). *Anchor Borrowers'Programme: Over 4.8 Million Farmers Financed - Buhari*. Retrieved March 9, 2022, from Premium Times:https://www .premiumtimesng.com/news/506666-anchor-borrowers-programme-over-4-8 -million-farmers-financed-buhari.html

Møller, J. and S. Skaaning (2011). *Democracy and Democratization in Comparative Perspective: Conceptions, Conjunctures, Causes, and Consequences*. Routledge.

Mohammed, U. (2013). "Corruption in Nigeria: A Challenge to Sustainable Development in the Fourth Republic." *European Scientific Journal*, 9(4): 118–37.

Mokyr, J. (2002). *The Gift of Athena: Historical Origins of the Knowledge Economy*. Princeton: Princeton University Press.

Momodu, I. K. "The Impact on Economic Growth of Nigeria's Oil Dependency." *International Institute of Social Studies* , 1.

Momokhere, J. (2018). "Understanding the Phenomenon of State Capture and its Manifestation in South Africa." Accessed 15 March 2022 https://journals.co.za/doi /epdf/10.25159/2663-6549/6314

Mottaleb, K. A. and T. Sonobe (October 2011). "An Inquiry into the Rapid Growth of the Garment Industry in Bangladesh." *Economic Development and Cultural Change*, 60(1): 67–89. https://doi.org/10.1086/661218

Muchie, M., P. Gammeltoft, and B.-Å. Lundvall (2003). *Putting Africa First: The Making of African Innovation Systems*. Aalborg: Aaalborg University Press.

Muhammed, M., M. Mukhtar, and G. Lola (2017). "The Impact of Chinese Textile Imperialism on Nigeria's Textile Industry and Trade: 1960–2015." *Review of African Political Economy*, 44(154): 673–82.

Murphy, D. J., K. Goggin, and R. R. Paterson (11 October 2021). "Oil Palm in the 2020s and Beyond: Challenges and Solutions." *CABI Agriculture and Bioscience*.

Murtala M., B. Rahmatu, Y. Agboola, and L. Kafilah (2018). "Nigeria Textile Industry: Evidence of Policy Neglect." *Sarjana*, 33(1): 40–56.

Myrdal, G. (1968). *Asian Drama: An Inquiry into the Poverty of Nations*. New York: Twentieth Century Fund.

Nagar, K. T., G. Umar, and F. A. Addull (2013). "Corruption and Economic Development: Evidence from Nigeria." *Kuwait Chapter of Arabian Journal of Business and Management Review*, 3(2): 40–56.

National Bureau of Statistic (2019). "Nigerian Gross Domestic Product Report." https:// www.nigerianstat.gov.ng/

NEPC (2020). *Promising Markets Cocoa Beans*. Abuja: Nigerian Export Promotion Council.

Lundvall Bengt-Ake (1992). *National Innovation Systems: Towards a Theory of Innovation and Interactive Learning*. London: Frances Printers .

Nelson, R. (1993). *National Innovation Systems a Comparative Analysis*. New York and Oxford: Oxford University Press.

Nelson, R. and S. Winter (1982). *An Evolutionary Theory of Economic Change*. Cambridge: Belknap Press.

Nelson, R. R. (1987). *Understanding Technical Change as an Evolutionary Process*. Amsterdam: North Holland.

Nelson, R. R. and B. Sampat (2001). "Making Sense of Institutions as a Factor Shaping Economic Performance." *Journal of Economic Behavior and Organization*, 44: 31–54.

van Neuss, L. (2019). "The Drivers of Structural Change." *Journal of Economic Surveys*, 33(1): 309–49. doi:10.1111/joes.12266.

Newfarmer, R., J. Page, and F. Tarp (2019). *Industries Without Smokestacks: Industrialization in Africa Reconsidered* (p. 480). Oxford: Oxford University Press.

Newman, C., J. Page, J. Rand, A. Shimeles, M. Söderbom, and F. Tarp (2016). *Made in Africa: Learning to Compete in Industry*. Washington D.C: Brookings Institute Press. Retrieved from https://muse.jhu.edu/pub/11/oa_monograph/book/44208/pdf on 17 June 2024

Nigerian Country Commercial Guide. Accessed on 18 July 2021 from https://www.trade .gov/country-commercial-guides/nigeria-oil-gas-and-mining-sectors

Njoku, R. C. (2001). "Deconstructing Abacha: Demilitarization and Democratic Consolidation in Nigeria after the Abacha era." *Government and Opposition*, 36(1): 71–96.

NNPC GROUP (2020). https://www.nnpcgroup.com/Investor-Relations/Pages/ Upstream-Opportunities.aspx

North, D. C. (1989). "Final Remarks-Institutional Change and Economic History." *Journal of Institutional and Theoretical Economics (JITE)/Zeitschrift für die gesamte Staatswissenschaft*, 238–245.

North, D. C., ed. (1996). *Economic Perfomance through Time*. Cambridge: Cambridge University Press.

North, D. C. (2005). "Institutions and the Performance of Economies Over Time." In *Handbook of New Institutional Economics*, 21–30. Berlin, Heidelberg: Springer Berlin Heidelberg.

North, D. P. (1990). *Institutions, Institutional Change, and Economic Performance*. Cambridge: Cambridge University Press.

Nurul (2007). "Implementation of Privatization Policy: Lessons from Bangladesh." *The Innovation Journal: The Public Sector Innovation Journal*, 12(2).

Obaje, N. G. (2009). *Geology and Mineral Resources of Nigeria*. Berlin, London: Springer.

OECD/FAO (2016). *OECD-FAO Agricultural Outlook 2016-2025*. Paris: OECD Publishing. https://doi.org/10.1787/agr_outlook-2016-en

OECD/FAO (2020). *OECD-FAO Agricultural Outlook 2020-2029*, Paris/FAO, Rome: OECD Publishing. https://doi.org/10.1787/1112c23b-en

Ofobruku, S. A., C. P. Sidi, and P. Nkiru (2020). "Impact of Corruption on the Oil Industry in Nigeria: Implication for Economy Growth." Accessed on 19 July from https://www.researchgate.net/publication/341621872

Oh, Jung Eun "Jen", P. M. Đuc, C. Kunaka, and R. C. Skorzus (2020). *Vietnam Development Report 2019: Connecting Vietnam for Growth and Shared Prosperity*. Washington: International Bank for Reconstruction and Development/World Bank.

Oil Palm India Limited (2017). *History of Palm Oil*. Retrieved July 13, 2022, from Palm Oil History: http://oilpalmindia.com/palm-oil-history/

Oil World (2011). *Hamburg.* Germany: Oilworld. Accessed on 13 December 2016 from http://www.oilworld.biz/home

Ojoye, T. (2019). "NNPC Loses N228.1bn Revenue as Refineries Remain Dormant." *The Punch News.* Accessed on 18 July 2021 from https://punchng.com/nnpc-loses-n228 -1bn-revenue-as-refineries-remain-dormant/

Okpan, S. O. and N. Precious (2019). "Evaluation of Corruption and Conflict in Nigerian Oil Industry: Imperative for Sustainable Development." *International Journal of Sociology and Anthropology Research,* 5(4): 14–26. Accessed from https://www.eajournals .org/wp-content/uploads/Evaluation-of-Corruption-and-Conflict-in-Nigerian-Oil -Industry.pdf

Okwu, U. N., O. Eguavoen, and I. K. Okore (2015). "Three Decades of Natural Rubber Production in Nigeria: Policies, Problems and Prospects." 21–29.

Olowu, D. (2009). *Rethinking African Governance. Paper delivered at the.*

Olukotun, A. (2013a). "State Failure and The Contradictions of The Public Sphere, 1995-2005." In O. Okome (ed.), *Contesting the Nigerian State: Civil Society and the Contradictions of Self-Organization,* 57–78. New York: Palgrave Macmillan.

Orngu, T. D. (2012). "Nigeria Democracy: A Panacea to Poverty Alleviation?" *Nnamdi Azikiwe Journal of Political Science,* 3(2): 201–12.

Osaghae, E. (1998). *Nigeria Since Independence, the Crippled Giant.* London: Hurst and Company.

Othman, M. F. and I. Bello (September 2019). "Indonesia-Nigeria Foreign Economic Relations: A Partnership for Economic Development." *Journal of Economic Cooperation and Development.* Accessed from https://www.researchgate.net/publication/33614091

Oyelaran-Oyeyinka, B. (2006). *Learning to Compete in African Industry: Institutions and Technology for Development.* London: Ashgate Publishers.

Oyelaran-Oyeyinka, B. (2014). *Rich Country Poor People: Nigeria's Story of Poverty in The Midst of Plenty.* Lagos: Technopol.

Oyelaran-Oyeyinka, B. (2020). *Resurgent Africa: Structural Transformation in Sustainable Development.* Anthem Press, Routledge.

Oyelaran-Oyeyinka, B. and L. A. Barclay (2003). "Human Capital and Systems of Innovation in African Development." In M. Muche, P. Gammeltoft, and B.-Å. Lundvall, *Puting Africa First: The Making of African Innovation System,* 93–108. Aalborg: Aalborg University Press.

Oyelaran-Oyeyinka, B. and P. Gehl-Sampath (2010). *Latecomer Development: Innovation and Knowledge for Economic Growth.* Routledge.

Oyelaran-Oyeyinka, B. and K. Lal (2005). "Internet Diffusion in Sub-Saharan Africa: A Cross-Country Analysis." *Telecommunications Policy ,* 29(7): 507–27.

Oyelaran-Oyeyinka, B. and K. Lal (2016). *Structural Transformation and Economic Development: Cross Regional Analysis of Industrialization and Urbanization.*

Oyelaran-Oyeyinka, B. and P. G. Sampath (2009). *Latecomer Development: Innovation and Knowledge for Economic Growth.* Routledge.

Oyelaran-Oyeyinka, B., L. Adeloye, B. Adebowale, and A. Esubiyi (1998). *Ailing Public Enterprises: Technological Project Failures and Prospects for Industrial Renewal in Nigeria.* Obafemi Awolowo: Obafemi Awolowo University Press.

Oyelaran-Oyeyinka, O. (2017). *From Consumption to Production.* Ibadan: Dominion Publishers.

Oyelaran-Oyeyinka, O. and O. Ola-David (2017). "Structural Transformation in Nigeria: Steering Foreign Direct Investment Towards Inclusive Growth." *Africa*

Development Perspectives Yearbook-Africa's Progress in Regional and Global Economic, Lit Verlag, Germany, 207–250.

Ozor, C. "An Overview: Foreign Participation in Business in Nigeria." Accessed on 18 July 2021 from https://businessday.ng/opinion/article/an-overview-foreign -participation-in-business-in-nigeria/

Patel, P. and K. Pavitt (1997). The Technological Competencies of the World's Largest Firms: Complex and Path-Dependent, but not much Variety." *Research Policy,* 26(2): 141–56.

Paul, R. and S. Quadir (4 May 2013). "Bangladesh Urges No Harsh EU Measures Over Factory Deaths." *Reuters.* Accessed on 30 June 2024 from https://www.reuters.com/ article/us-bangladesh-factory-idUSBRE94304420130504/

Pearson, S. R. (1970). *Petroleum, and the Nigerian Economy.* Stanford: Stanford University Press.

Perkins, Dwight H. and Vu Thanh Tu Anh (2010). "Vietnam's Industrial Policy: Designing Policies for Sustainable Development." *UNDP Policy Dialogue Paper Number 3,* 1–61.

Poindexter, P. M., S. Meraz, and A. S. Weiss (2008). *Women, Men, and News: Divided and Disconnected in the News Media.* Landscape: Taylor & Francis Group.

Pointer (1999). "A Daily Newspaper Published in Nigeria by Pointer Newspaper." Asaba Nigeria.

Poku, K. (2002). "Small-Scale Palm Oil Processing in Africa." *FAO Agricultural Services Bulletin 148.* Retrieved June 6, 2022,from Small-Scale Pal: https://www.fao.org/3/ y4355e/y4355e00.htm#Contents

Punch (1999). "A Daily Newspaper Published in Nigeria by Punch Newspapers." Lagos.

Pye, L. (1971). *Crises and Sequences in Political Development.* Princeton: Princeton University Press.

Qiu, Larry D. (2005). *China's Textile and Clothing Industry.* Mimeo, Hong Kong University of Science and Technology.

Rabbinge, R. (2015). "MS Swaminathan: His Contributions to Science and Public Policy." *Current Science,* 439–46.

Rahman, S. (2021). *The Bangladesh Garment Industry and the Global Supply Chain: Choices and Constraints of Management.* Routledge. https://doi.org/10.4324/9781003153238.

Rasel, M., D. Das, and M. Khan (2019). "Current Scenario of Textile Sector in Bangladesh: A Comprehensive Review." *International Journal of Innovative Studies in Sciences and Engineering Technology (IJISSET)* 2020, 6(1): 52–55

Rauch, J. E. and P. B. Evans (2000). "Bureaucratic Structure and Bureaucratic Performance in Less Developed Countries." *Journal of Public Economics,* 75(1): 49–71. https://doi.org/10.1016/S0047-2727(99)00044-4

Renne, E. (2015). "The Changing Contexts of Chinese-Nigerian Textile Production and Trade 1900–2015." *Textile,* 13(3): 212–33.

Rodrik, D. (1998). "Trade Policy and Economic Performance in Sub-Saharan Africa."National Bureau of Economic Research. Working Paper 6562. Accessed at https://www.nber.org/papers/w6562, 8 July 2024.

Rodrik (2014). An African Growth Miracle. Richard H. Sabot Lecture, delivered at the Center for Global Development, Washington, DC on April 24, 2014. https://drodrik .scholar.harvard.edu/files/dani-rodrik/files/an_african_growth_miracle.pdf

Rosenberg, N. (1982). *Inside the Black Box: Technology and Economics.* Cambridge: Cambridge University Press.

Rosenberg, N. and L. E. Birdzen (1986). *How the West Grew Rich. The Economic Transformation of the Industrial World.* London: L.B. Tauris & CO. Ltd. Publishers.

Rosenstein-Rodan, P. N. (1943). "Problems of Industrialisation of Eastern and South-Eastern Europe." *The Economic Journal,* 53(210–211): 202–11.

Rostow, W. W. (1960). *The Five Stages of Growth--A Summary* (pp. 4–16).

Rotberg (2003a). *State Failure and State Weakness in a Time of Terror.* Cambridge: World Peace Foundation and Washington DC: The Brookings Institution.

Rothchild, D. (1987). "Hegemony and State Softness: Some Variations in Elite Responses." In Z. Ergas (ed.), *The African State in Transtion,* 117–48. London: Macmillan.

Sachs, Jeffrey and Warner, Andrew. (1995). "Natural Resource Abundance and Economic Growth." *Development Discussion Paper* 517.

Sala-i-Martin, X. and A. Subramanian (2013). "Addressing the Natural Resource Curse: An Illustration from Nigeria." *Journal of African Economies,* 22(4): 570–615.

Salisu, O. U. (2011a). "The Capacity and Conduct of Corruption in the Nigeria Oil Sector Beyond the Rhetoric of the Anti-corruption Crusade." *Journal of Sustainable Development in Africa,* 13(2): 298–9.

Sampath, P. G. (2019). "Pharmaceutical Manufacturing in Bangladesh–A Success Story: What Can We Learn." *FEAPM Advocacy Series,* 1.

Sampath, P. G. and B. Oyelaran-Oyeyinka (2010). "Rough Road to the Market: Constrained Biotechnology Innovation and Entrepreneurship in Nigeria and Ghana." *Journal of International Development,* 22(7): 962–77.

Scott, J. C. (1998). *Seeing Like a State: How Certain Schemes to Improve the Human Condition Have Failed.* Yale: Yale University Press.

Sevin, O. and P. Levang (1989). "80 ans de Transmigration en Indonésie (1905–1985)." *Annales de Géographie,* 98(549): 538–66. https://doi.org/10.3406/geo.1989.20927

Shirley, M. M. (2003). "What Does Institutional Economis Tell Us About Development." *Budapest, Hungary: Paper Presented at ISNIE.* Accessed on December 2004. www.coase.org

Singer, H. W. (1950). "The Distribution of Gains between Investing and Borrowing Countries." *American Economic Review,* 40: 473–85.

Slav, I. (2020). "Nigeria Oil Industry Overview." Accessed on 18 July 2021 from https://drillers.com/nigeria-oil-industry-overview/

Soifer, H. (2008). "State Infrastructural Power: Approaches to Conceptualization and Measurement." *Studies in Comparative International Development,* 43: 231–51.

Soifer, H. D. (2008). "State Infrastructural Power: Approaches to Conceptualization and Measurement." *Studies in Comparative International Development,* 43(3–4): 231–51. https://doi.org/10.1007/s12116-008-9024-0

Spengler, J. J. (1960). "Economic Development: Political Preconditions and Political Consequences." *The Journal of Politics,* 22(3): 387–416.

Statisa (2020). *Production of Major Vegetable Oils Worldwide from 2019/2020.* Retrieved from Statista:https://www.statista.com/statistics/263933/production-of-vegetable-oils-worldwide-since-2000/.

Stijns, J. P. (2006). "Natural Resource Abundance and Human Capital Accumulation." *World Development,* 34(6): 1060–83.

Szeftel, M. (1998). "Misunderstanding African Politics: Corruption and the Governance Agenda." *Review of African Political Economy,* 76: 221–40.

Teoh, C. H. (2002). *The Palm Oil Industry in Malaysia: From Seed to Frying Pan.* Selangor: WWF Malaysia.

Terazono, E. (18 December 2014). "Welcome to the World of Big Chocolate: Three Companies Will Dominate Processing Sector." *Financial Times.*

The Star (17 February 2014). *Oil Palm Leftovers, Alternative Food for Livestock.* Retrieved from All About Feed:https://www.allaboutfeed.net/animal-feed/feed-additives/oil-palm -leftovers-alternative-food-for-livestock/

The World Bank (1989). *Sub-Saharan Africa: From Crisis to Sustainable Growth.* Washington, D.C.: World Bank.

Thorbecke, W. (July 1998). "The Impact of the Indonesian Economic Crisis on Income Distribution: A Social Accounting Matrix Application." In *The Asian Crisis: The Economics Front-An International Seminar.*

Tlemcani, R. (2005). "Reflections on the Questions of Political Transition in Africa: The Police State." In Tukumbi Lumumba-Kasongo (ed.), *Liberal Democracy and its Critics in Africa* , 26–45. Dakar: CODESRIA.

Transparency International. "Corruption Perception Index." Accessed on 27 July 2021 from https://www.transparency.org/en/countries/indonesia

Trung, Le V., T. Q. Viet, and P. Van Chat (2016). "An Overview of Vietnam's Oil and Gas Industry." *Petroleum Economics & Management,* 10: 64–71.

Umejei, E. (2015). "China's Engagement with Nigeria: Opportunity or Opportunist?" African East Asian Affairs: The China Monitor Issue 3 and Issue 4 December.

UNCTAD (2015). Technology and Innovation Report 2015 - Fostering Innovation Policies for Industrial Development. UNCTAD, Geneva. https://unctad.org/system /files/official-document/tir2015_en.pdf

UNCTAD and UNIDO (2011). Economic Development in Africa Report: Fostering Industrial Development in Africa in the New Global Environment. United Nations, Geneva.   https://unctad.org/system/files/official-document/aldcafrica2011_en .pdf

UNFPA (2024). World Population Dashboard - Nigeria. Retrieved from https://www .unfpa.org/data/world-population/NG on 16 June 2024.

UNIDO (2013). Industrial Development Report: Sustaining Employment Growth:The Role of Manufacturing and Structural Change. UNIDO, Vienna. Retrieved from https://www.unido.org/sites/default/files/2013-12/UNIDO_IDR_2013_main _report_0.pdf

UNIDO (2016). Industrialization in Africa and Least Developed Countries - Boosting Growth, Creating Jobs, Promoting Inclusiveness and Sustainability. A Report to the G20 Development Working Group by UNIDO. UNIDO, Vienna. https://www .unido.org/sites/default/files/2016-09/G20_new_UNIDO_report_industrialization _in_Africa_and_LDCs_0.pdf

Van der Ploeg, F. (2010). "Natural Resources: Curse or Blessings?" *Journal of Economic Literature,* 49(2):366–420.

Van Neuss, L. (2019). "The Drivers of Structural Change." *Journal of Economic Surveys,* 33(1), 309–349.

Vanguard (2 December 2019). "Nigeria Spends $4 billion to Import Textiles Yearly." *Vanguard.* Accessed on 1 July 2024 from https://www.vanguardngr.com/2019/12/ nigeria-spends-4-billion-to-import-textiles-yearly/

Vartiainen, J. (1999). "The Economics of Successful State Intervention in Industrial Transformation." *The Developmental State,* 200–34.

Vassiliou, S. (2009). *The A to Z of the Petroleum Industry.* Scarecrow Press.

Viner, J. (1952). *International Trade and Economic Development.* Glencoe, IL: Free Press.

Viner, J. (1953). *International Trade and Economic Development* (p. 39). Oxford: Clarendon Press.

Vogel, Ezra F. (2013). *Deng Xiaoping and the Transformation of China*. Cambridge, MA: Belknap Press / Harvard University Press.

Vollrath, D. (2009). "How Important are Dual Economy Effects for Aggregate Productivity?" *Journal of Development Economics*, 88(2): 325–34.

Wahid, M. B., S. N. Akmar Abdullah, and I. E. Henson (2004). *Oil Palm: Achievements and Potential*. Kuala Lumpur, Malaysia: 4th International Crop Science Congress. http://www.cropscience.org.au/icsc2004/symposia/2/4/187_wahidmb.htm

Walsh, S. T. and J. D. Linton (2001). "The Competence Pyramid: A Framework for Identifying and Analyzing Firm and Industry Competence." *Technology Analysis & Strategic Management*, 13(2): 165–77.

Wangwe, S., D. Mmari, J. Aikaeli, N. Rutatina, T. Mboghoina, and A. Kinyondo (2014). "The Performance of the Manufacturing Sector in Tanzania." *Challenges and the Way Forward*.

Wen, Y. (2016). "China's Rapid Rise." *Federal Reserve Bank of St. Louis The Regional Economist*, 24(2): 8–14.

Wen, Y. (2021). "China's Industrial Revolution: A New Perspective." *China Economic Review*, 69: 101671.

Wijnbergen, S. V. (1984). "The Dutch Disease': A Disease After All?" *The Economic Journal*, 94(373): 41–55.

World Bank (2005). *End of MFA Quotas: Key Issues and Strategic Options for Bangladesh Readymade Garment Industry*. rep. Washington, DC: The World Bank.

World Bank (2018). Nigerian Biannual Economic Update - Connecting to Compete. Retrievedfromhttps://documents1.worldbank.org/curated/en/769551524576691390/pdf/WP-NigeriaBiannualEconomicUpdateAprilFinalVersion-PUBLIC.pdf on 17 June 2024.

World Bank (30 April 2018). "Strengthening Economic Diversification in Nigeria through Connectivity." Retrieved from https://www.worldbank.org/en/country/nigeria/publication/strengthening-economic-diversification-in-nigeria-through-connectivity on 17 June 2024

World Bank (2019). *World Bank Biannual Economic Update on Nigeria*. Washington DC.

World Bank (2022). *World Development Report 2022: Finance for an Equitable Recovery*. Washington D.C: World Bank.

World Economic Situation and Prospects (2019). "United Nations." https://www.un.org/development/desa/dpad/wp-content/uploads/sites/45/WESP2019BOOKweb

Wright, G. and J. Czelusta (2007). "Resource-Based Growth Past and Present." *Natural Resources: Neither Curse Nor Destiny*, 185.

Yeats, A. (2002). "What Can Africa Expect From Ito Traditional Exporto?" *World Bank Africa Region Working Paper Series*, 26.

Yusuf (2018). "Colonialism and Dilemmas of Transitional Justice in Nigeria." *International Journal of Transitional Justice*, 12(2): 257–76.

Zaman, S. (2021). "Researching the Garment Sector in Bangladesh: Feldwork Challenges and Responses." *Field Guide for Research in Community Settings*. Edward Elgar Publishing. https://doi.org/10.4337/9781800376328.00013

APPENDIX

Agriculture shares and manufacturing shares in GDP.

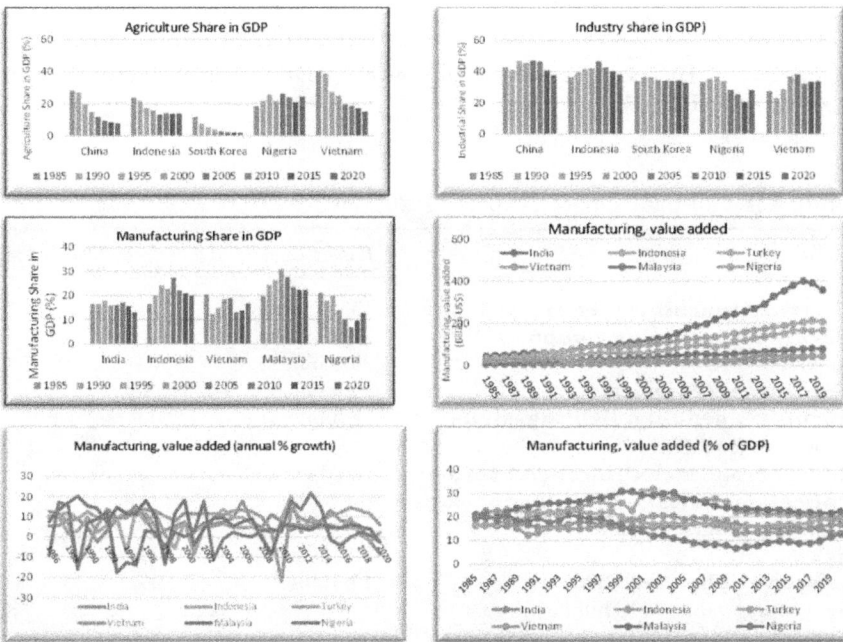

Figure A.1. Sectorial share in GDP. Source: World Development Indicators (WDI) 2021.

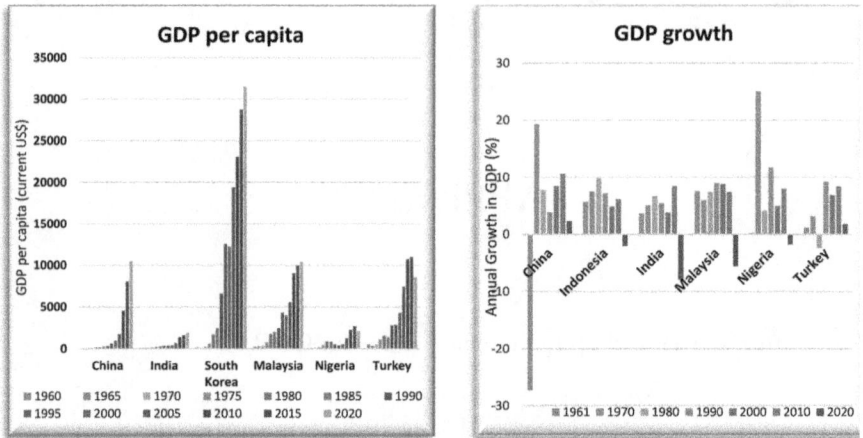

Figure A.2. GDP per capita and annual growth in GDP. Source: World Development Indicators (WDI), 2021.

Table A.1. Vietnam's highest exports (2020).

Product	Export Value (USD)	% of Total Exports
Electrical machinery, equipment	153.5 billion	44.1
Machinery including computers	23.9 billion	6.9
Footwear	23.8 billion	6.8
Clothing, accessories	15.5 billion	4.5
Furniture, bedding, lighting, signs, prefab building	15.5 billion	4.4
Knit or crochet clothing, accessories	15.2 billion	4.4
Optical, technical, medical apparatus	5.7 billion	1.6
Plastics, plastic articles	5.5 billion	1.6
Fish	5.1 billion	1.5
Rubber, rubber articles	4.6 billion	1.3
Total export value: $348 billion		
Export per capita: $3600		

Source: Per Capita calculated using World Bank population data in the same year.

INDEX

Note: Page locators in **bold** indicates figures

Delta Steel Company (DSC) 189–91, 219
democracy dividends 28
democratic leadership style 200
de-nationalization 164
Deng Xiaoping 181; and transformation
 of China 192–94
destructive inequality 43
development reversal 230, 240;
 understanding of 231–32
developmental embeddedness 222
Direct Reduction/Electric Arc Furnace
 (DR/EAF) 189
divergent development paths 80–82
diversification 22, 75, 80–82, 90, 173; of
 economy 241; types of 169–71
diversification policy 86, 140
'Doi-Moi' 67, 82, 88, 90, 240
domestic shocks 96
DR/EAF: *see* Direct Reduction/Electric
 Arc Furnace
DSC: *see* Delta Steel Company
Duisberg, Carl 14
Dunlop 129
DuPont Corporation 195
Dutch disease 18, 24, 33n7, 40, 233;
 phenomenon of 237
dynamism 132

economic diversification 19, 59, 75–76,
 241; Malaysia 120; technological
 capability drives 25–27
economic growth 15, 18, 233; of United
 States 16
economic liberalization 163; Indonesia
 8
economic order 182
economic policies, in Indonesia and
 Nigeria 94
economic reversal 36–37, 236
economic stabilization programs 116n12
economies/economic: development of
 24, 36; disparities 52–54, **53**; elite 182;
 history 48; inequality 42–43; literature
 203n4
ECOWAS region 38
Eichengrün, Arthur 14
electronics sector, development of 23
Enterprise Law 2005 89
entrepreneurial private sector 132
EPZs: *see* export processing zones
Ershad, Hussain Muhammad 164
Esanov, A. 25
European Union (EU) 75, 143–44

Evans, D. 15
Evans, P. 222, 224n16
evolutionary economics 209
explicit industrialization 33
export diversification 145, 152, 175; in
 Bangladesh 161; in Malaysia 122
export processing zones (EPZs) 164–65,
 172
export-led-growth strategy 82
export-oriented industrialization strategy
 105, 144
export-oriented refineries 145
exports: of agriculture 6, **6**; of
 agriculture raw materials 98; agro-
 food 69; of crude oil 83, 94, 119, 217;
 diversification 6, 9n4; of fossil fuels
 and minerals 237; GDP and 234; of
 high-value products 82; price of cashew
 kernels 75; of ready-made garments
 industry 159, **160**
external shocks 96–97
extractive economic regimes 28

Failed States Index 215
FAO: *see* Food and Agricultural
 Organization
FCTA: *see* Federal Capital Territory
FDI: *see* foreign direct investment
Federal Capital Territory (FCTA) 207
Federal Fertilizer Company 192
Federal Land Development Authority
 (FELDA) 140, 144; land resettlement
 programme 131
Federal Superphosphate Fertilizer
 Company (FSFC) Limited 2, 46, 206,
 219
FELDA: *see* Federal Land Development
 Authority
Ferrostaal AG 47
firm-level competencies 20–21
fishing 73
Food and Agricultural Organization
 (FAO) 76, 195, 197
food-crop agriculture 105
food-crop farming, artificial fertilizer in
 105
foreign direct investment (FDI) 81, 87, 89,
 122, 174
foreign exchange 161
forestry 73
Fragile States Index 215
FSFC: *see* Federal Superphosphate
 Fertilizer Company

www.ingramcontent.com/pod-product-compliance
Lightning Source LLC
Chambersburg PA
CBHW030644270326
41929CB00007B/196